ZOLA'S DREAM

Émile Zola was the nineteenth century's pre-eminent naturalist writer and theoretician, spearheading a cultural movement that was rooted in positivist thought and an ethic of sober observation. As a journalist, Zola drove home his vision of a type of literature that described rather than prescribed, that anatomised rather than embellished – one that worked, in short, against idealism. Yet in the pages of his fiction, a complex picture emerges in which Zola appears drawn to the ideal – to the speculative, the implausible, the visionary – more than he liked to admit. Spanning the period from Zola's epic *Germinal* to his fateful intervention in the Dreyfus Affair, *Zola's Dream* is the first book to explore how the 'quarrel' between idealists and naturalists shaped the ambitions of the novel at the end of the nineteenth century, when differences over literary aesthetics invariably spoke of far-reaching cultural and political struggles.

CLAIRE WHITE is Associate Professor of French at the University of Cambridge and a Fellow of Girton College. She is the author of *Work and Leisure in Late Nineteenth-Century French Literature and Visual Culture* (2014) and co-editor of *The Labour of Literature in Britain and France* (2018).

ZOLA'S DREAM

Idealism on Trial

CLAIRE WHITE

University of Cambridge

CAMBRIDGE
UNIVERSITY PRESS

Shaftesbury Road, Cambridge CB2 8EA, United Kingdom

One Liberty Plaza, 20th Floor, New York, NY 10006, USA

477 Williamstown Road, Port Melbourne, VIC 3207, Australia

314–321, 3rd Floor, Plot 3, Splendor Forum, Jasola District Centre, New Delhi – 110025, India

103 Penang Road, #05-06/07, Visioncrest Commercial, Singapore 238467

Cambridge University Press is part of Cambridge University Press & Assessment, a department of the University of Cambridge.

We share the University's mission to contribute to society through the pursuit of education, learning and research at the highest international levels of excellence.

www.cambridge.org
Information on this title: www.cambridge.org/9781009576680

DOI: 10.1017/9781009576659

When citing this work, please include a reference to the DOI 10.1017/9781009576659

First published 2025

A catalogue record for this publication is available from the British Library

A Cataloging-in-Publication data record for this book is available from the Library of Congress

ISBN 978-1-009-57668-0 Hardback

Contents

Figures

Acknowledgements

'Do you know a dream I have?', Zola reportedly asked Edmond de Goncourt. 'It would be to throw myself into a book that I would never finish.' On several occasions, during the decade it has taken me to bring this book to completion, I have paused to contemplate such a prospect, albeit with far less relish. I am deeply indebted to the many friends and colleagues who have made the University of Cambridge – both the Faculty of Modern and Medieval Languages and Linguistics and Girton College – such supportive, lively, and intellectually stimulating communities in which to teach, research, and, especially, work on the nineteenth century. I am grateful to both Faculty and College institutions, moreover, for their material and financial support of this project. I have been fortunate to work with an excellent team at Cambridge University Press, in particular, Bethany Thomas, George Laver, and Aiswarya Narayanan. My sincere thanks, also, to Michelle Brumby for her expert work on the index.

A section of Chapter 1 appeared, in French, in *Les Cahiers naturalistes*; and in Chapters 3 and 4, I draw on articles that first appeared in *Romance Studies* and *French History*, respectively. I am grateful for the kind permission of the editors of those journals to re-use that material here.

For their precious intellectual companionship and invaluable encouragement with this project along the way, I should like to express my appreciation to Victoria Baena, Edmund Birch, Sam Bootle, Andrew Counter, Elizabeth Emery, Alison Finch, Emma Gilby, Marion Glaumaud-Carbonnier, Susan Harrow, Olivier Lumbroso, Alain Pagès, Rebecca Sugden, and Marcus Waithe. I have had the privilege of working with three brilliant PhD students in recent years – Eleanor Stefiuk, Ellamae Lepper, and Isabel Maloney – and I have benefited enormously from our many conversations, about their work and mine. The seeds of this project were sown while I myself was a graduate student; and I owe a special debt of gratitude to Nick White, my former PhD supervisor, friend, colleague, and fellow *zoliste*, for inspiring and supporting this research from the very beginning.

Finally, I should like to thank my dearest friend Freya; my family – my Mum, my Dad, my brother Jon; as well as my family-in-law – Alison, Mike, Caz, and Steph. I am eternally grateful for the love, patience, and unbending support, of my husband, Tom, and for our two boys – Joshua and Sam – who have come into our lives since the writing of this book began.

Notes on the Text

References to Henri Mitterand's five-volume edition of *Les Rougon-Macquart* (Paris: Gallimard, Bibliothèque de la Pléiade, 1960–67) are given in the abbreviated form *R-M*, followed by the volume and page numbers. References to the twenty-one-volume edition of Émile Zola, *Œuvres complètes*, ed. Henri Mitterand et al. (Paris: Nouveau Monde, 2002–09) are given as *OC*, followed by volume and page numbers. Where possible, I have drawn on the most current – though as yet, unfinished – edition of Zola's *Œuvres complètes*, by Classiques Garnier. References to the eleven-volume edition of Émile Zola, *Correspondance*, ed. Bard H. Bakker (Montreal; Paris: Presses de l'Université de Montréal and CNRS, 1978–2010) are given as *Corr*, followed by volume and page numbers.

Translations in this book are my own, except where stated otherwise. For extracts from *Germinal* and *Le Rêve*, I have used translated editions by Oxford World's Classics: the first, by Peter Collier (1993); and the second, by Paul Gibbard (2018). References are given to the translation first, followed by the French source. References to Zola's Dreyfus journalism are made to Alain Pagès's edition, translated by Eleanor Levieux. I have chosen not to translate the titles of works, except where directly relevant to the argument.

Introduction
Zola and the Return of Idealism

In 1897, British aesthete and influential literary critic Arthur Symons penned 'A Note on Zola's Method'. Admiring enough of Zola's writing to have produced his own translation of *L'Assommoir* three years earlier, Symons's summary assessment of the French author's style was at best ambivalent, at worst sneering. In a concluding flourish, the critic declared Zola's art of observation clouded by preconceived ideas, formulas, and theories: 'His realism is a distorted idealism, and the man who considers himself the first to paint humanity as it really is will be remembered in the future as the most idealistic writer of his time.'[1] Posterity, of course, has hardly borne out Symons's prediction. To this day, Zola is considered the nineteenth century's pre-eminent European naturalist writer, and naturalism's foremost theoretician. And yet, Symons was hardly alone in venturing such a provocation. By the 1890s, it had even become something of a routine critical gesture to attribute to Zola those very aesthetic tendencies – if in 'distorted' form – against which he pitched his own naturalist credo. For Zola's detractors, claiming that the author had fallen prey to idealism offered a way of subverting, or (mis)reading, of calling out the malfunctioning of the naturalist method. More straightforwardly, such polemical characterisations of Zola's writing invited readers to grapple with what seemed to be an intriguing, if latent, contradiction. What pull could the ideal – the 'dream' as Zola so often put it – hold for the author whose theory of naturalist literature systematically demanded its exclusion? Is there such a thing as an idealist Zola?

In keeping with the thrust, if not the spirit, of Symons's critique, this book argues that Zola was drawn to the idealist imagination more than we tend to assume, and indeed more than he himself would admit. That naturalism proudly constructed itself in theory as an 'anti-idealism', rooted in positivist thought and sober observation, is uncontroversial. Across his literary criticism and journalism, Zola drove home his vision of a literary form, whose primary impulse was to 'tell it how it really is', to describe rather than prescribe, to anatomise rather than embellish, speculate, or console. But far less well understood is the more complex, and more compromised, fate of this aesthetic philosophy in Zola's fiction. My aim, then, is to restore to naturalism, as Zola best embodied it, precisely a sense of its dependence on idealism – not just as a convenient or caricatural foil for its own claims, but as fundamental to its own self-conception.[2] This book is the first to explore in full the ways in which the sustained 'quarrel' between idealists and naturalists shaped the literary field from the early 1880s onwards, especially the ambitions and parameters of the novel. In doing so, it yields new insights into the pressures and contradictions that cut across Zola's fiction, bound as it was to negotiate with those resurgent forms of idealism, which became the rallying point of a 'reaction' against naturalism's cultural dominance. Against the kind of binary thinking Zola himself did so much to entrench, the book tracks in his literary project a shifting and far more dynamic, even obsessive, engagement with its rival form. Filled with utopian radicals, visionaries, and dreamers of all kinds, Zola's novels insistently took up the very impulses and strains of imagination that the writer had made it his rhetorical mission to stigmatise.[3] Whether the naturalist novel could tolerate, even harness, those impulses will be a guiding concern of this study. What will emerge from it is a compelling, even surprising, account of the writer as an important thinker of the ideal, and one who was increasingly willing to revise his own aesthetic principles.

On the face of it, these might seem to be relatively introverted concerns of literary history. But the burden of this book will be to show how competing differences over literary aesthetics – especially as they crystallised around the terms of naturalism and idealism – can be understood as signs of far-reaching cultural anxieties, and indeed how these differences matter to our understanding of the political and intellectual history of the early Third Republic. I argue for the vital importance of these aesthetic debates to what historians tend to call the 'culture wars' of the late nineteenth century when the nation was split, in the famous words of Republican politician Jules Ferry, into 'two enemy Frances', secular and Catholic.[4] In France, conflicts over the role of religion embraced virtually every area of social life, from education to debates over popular sovereignty, and culminated in the Dreyfus Affair. Accordingly, the book focuses on Zola's treatment of those issues that divided the nation the most: in Chapter 2, the rise of mass politics and socialist idealism, which he depicts most famously in his novel of the strike, *Germinal* (1885); in Chapters 3 and 4, the religious 'revival' that suffuses Zola's *Le Rêve* (1888) and is the prime target of his novel of the Catholic shrine, *Lourdes* (1894);

and, in Chapter 5, the ideological polarisation that the Dreyfus Affair produced, and which Zola recast in his last finished novel, *Vérité* (1902). In this last instance, fiction trailed history most closely, as Zola took it upon himself to speak truth to power and defend the wrongly-accused Jewish captain against treason, as well as against the wider anti-Semitism at play in his conviction. With Zola's secular consecration in the Pantheon, five years after his death (and following Dreyfus's exoneration), this *grand homme* was – and indeed still is – rolled into the French Republic's self-mythologizing identity, as a beacon of civic duty, of intellectual freedom and responsibility. In its Conclusion, the book interrogates this legacy, by broaching the long history of Zola's importance to the French Republic's self-image, which is to say to a particular brand of Republican idealism.

It will be immediately clear, then, that this book by no means claims to establish a full genealogy of Zola's engagement with idealism, and far less to provide an exhaustive survey of the very many permutations of idealism, or anti-idealism, across his writing.[5] The works I read closely are deliberately drawn from Zola's mid-to-late career: after, that is, the so-called triumph of naturalism feted by *chroniqueurs* at the turn of the 1880s, and the phase of combative journalism during which Zola sought to impose his naturalist credo. Though, throughout the book, I draw frequently on Zola's campaign writing from precisely this period, as well as on a wider range of his fiction, my focus is on a set of novels that either coincide with or follow a supposed changing of the guard. Naturalism, as we shall see, was to meet with many *fausses fins*, as Zola's detractors declared his brand of the novel exhausted, even defunct – but we might take the first watershed moment to be the publication of Joris-Karl Huysmans's Decadent novel *À rebours* (1884). In a preface written twenty years later, Huysmans recalled walking with Zola in his grounds at Médan shortly after the novel had appeared: Zola accused him of dealing naturalism 'a terrible blow', of burning his bridges, unable to understand the need Huysmans had felt to 'open the windows, to escape from an environment that was suffocating me, [. . .] to break the limits of the novel'.[6] If there are no doubt other origin stories for the purported 'crisis' of the naturalist novel in the mid-1880s, this exchange between former *maître* and disciple – apocryphal or otherwise – certainly conjures up, most poetically, the sense of broken loyalty on which Zola's more virulent critics would seize.[7]

With the publication of *Germinal* the following year, Zola came to command, even among his sceptics, a new (if sometimes grudging) respect. In fact, as we shall see in Chapter 1, the novel was accompanied by a marked shift in tone among certain critics, for whom *Germinal* betrayed a lyrical, even epic, imagination that appeared to run counter to Zola's theory of naturalist art. More broadly, however, the novel's success galvanised those adversaries seeking to challenge the naturalist status quo. Two months after *Germinal* appeared in book form, the arch antinaturalist critic Ferdinand Brunetière published a statement article-cum-manifesto, 'L'Idéalisme dans le roman'. In what was ostensibly a tribute to the idealist novelist Octave Feuillet, Brunetière rehearsed his case against naturalist fiction, turning to *Germinal* in particular, and its systematic refusal of that which, Brunetière insisted, all art ought to cultivate: pleasure, sympathy, consolation, finer feelings – in short, an ideal.[8] Later that year, Maurice Barrès augured 'the aesthetic of tomorrow' that was set to replace Zola's positivist paradigm: 'it is clear just how keen newcomers are [. . .] to move beyond the straightforward recording of facts; they are moving, to put it plainly, towards metaphysics'.[9] Our focus, then, is on a period dominated by a backlash against naturalism – one driven, as these examples alone suggest, by a variety of aesthetic, philosophical, ideological, and professional agendas, but which we might broadly conceive, in the spirit of my title, as a feted 'return' of idealism. For those advocating an antinaturalist or postnaturalist turn increasingly bankrolled what became known as an 'idealist reaction', in which different wranglings over the shape of the literary field found themselves condensed, if not resolved.

In taking up works from all three of Zola's fictional series – *Les Rougon-Macquart* (1871–93), *Les Trois Villes* (1894–98), and the ultimately unfinished *Les Quatre Évangiles* (1899–1902) – my aim is to better understand the evolution of the naturalist novel, its ambitions and compromises, especially in the light of its embattled status on the cusp of a new century. How, I ask, was Zola in some sense obliged to negotiate, even experiment, with the resurgent idealist aesthetic he had systematically repudiated, downgraded, scorned? Further still, how were these episodes and dynamics of literary evolution and 'crisis' almost invariably bound up with wider struggles over the future of the Republic? This book shows how wrestling with, and attempting to resolve, the ideological rifts of the age so often meant thinking through literary form – that is, through questions of plausibility, truthfulness, verisimilitude, ethical purpose, and the rights and dangers of the imagination. If reconstructing the terms of these debates matters, then, it is, I am suggesting, because idealism and naturalism were frequently understood not just as rival aesthetics, but as rival *styles* of thought, and indeed, *styles* of politics. Crucially, in fact, as we shall see in Chapter 1, Zola himself provides the most polemical, and overdetermined, vision of that equivalence.

Take, for now, as emblematic the clarion call he delivered to readers of *Le Figaro* on 20 April 1879: 'the Republic will be naturalist, or it will not be'.[10] The novelist was echoing and adulterating, his readers knew, the terms of the existential dilemma delivered by the first President of the Third Republic, Adolphe Thiers, some seven years earlier. Before the nation's foundling parliament, still reeling from France's defeat at the hands of the Prussians and the explosion of socialist radicalism that was the Paris Commune, Thiers had declared: 'the Republic will be conservative, or it will not be'.[11] Order and calm were vital, he urged, if the Republic was to withstand the pressures of the Left and the resurgence of monarchists. Zola's version of this national ultimatum was delivered at the very moment the future of the Republic seemed secured after a decade of equivocation: President MacMahon's government of 'Moral Order', and its royalist and conservative majority, had been defeated in the elections of October 1878. 'The incubation period is over, the Republic exists as a matter of fact', Zola wrote, before placing the cultural movement of which he was the figurehead at the heart of the Third Republic's future.[12] For naturalism, he repeated, was a properly Republican literature: scientific, secular, democratic. And the Republic, in turn, was a form of democratic governance rooted in the same 'experimental method' that guided naturalist fiction.

Hyperbolic, mystifying, even fantastically narcissistic, Zola's call for a naturalist Republic could not but invite polemic as well as satire.[13] Albert Robida famously pictured Zola as Napoleon, teetering on top of the Vendôme column, his oversized quill inscribed with an imperial version of his Republican crusade: 'The world will be naturalist, or it will not be!' (Figure 0.1). Certainly, the privileged relationship between literature and the state Zola had set out was continually reasserted and contested by early Third Republic writers, intellectuals, and politicians alike. Across the articles Zola went on to write for *Le Figaro* in 1880–81 as part of *Une campagne*, he lambasted the factional conflicts and cynical ambition that he saw governing national affairs, instead supplying the regime with the salutary censure he felt it required. Zola duly established the figure of the naturalist writer as not only its best judge but also a model of the independent, analytical or experimental thinking that Republican politicians ought to adopt in turn. In fact, in 'La République et la littérature', Zola lauded the 'naturalist' politician – 'the genuine labourer of present times' – as part of his otherwise satirical, and alarmist, taxonomy of Republican figures, which included the doctrinaire, the fanatic, and the romantic.[14] In effect, what Zola claimed to determine were different aesthetics of politics, linked to different kinds of rhetoric, and, in the case

Figure 0.1   Albert Robida, 'The Triumph of Naturalism'.
Illustration from *La Caricature*, 7 February 1880. Lithograph. Bibliothèque des arts décoratifs, Paris, France. © Archives Charmet / Bridgeman Images.

of naturalist and romantic republicanism, to different types of literature. Naturalism in politics, Zola insisted, would, by definition, be anti-romantic, 'stripped [. . .] of the idealism of poets', based on analysis and observation; and, as such, it offered the only sure means of guaranteeing the Republic in perpetuity.[15] If naturalism staked its claims to body forth the best interests of the nation, these depended on cultivating a suspicion of idealism, in all its iterations, as a fundamental impediment to the project of securing the Republic's future. And yet, what we will find across our close readings of Zola's fiction – *Germinal* and *Vérité* in particular – is a rather more complex, even self-problematising, engagement with idealism in politics than such polemical discourse would allow. For all its admonishments, naturalist literature returned insistently, I argue, to the terms of the lyrical and, indeed, the idealist imagination as so many remedies to the social and political ills it diagnosed.

For Idealism

Now, to our guiding term, idealism, which is locked into Zola's discourse on aesthetics as naturalism's inverted mirror image, although it is often, as we shall see, loosely associated in his writing with a host of other concepts: poetry, lyricism, sentimentalism, spiritualism, utopianism, symbolism, and, chiefly, romanticism. In its workaday sense, I am taking idealism as an aesthetic to connote that which is prescriptive, consoling, imaginative, implausible, embellished, uplifting, or speculative. Tied to this is the assumption that the idealist operates with some degree of independence from the mimetic labour of the realist and naturalist artist, whose principal task it was, Zola insisted, to observe and anatomise, to 'feel nature and [. . .] render it as it is'.[16] In his own attempt to define the terms of 'naturalism' and 'idealism', Brunetière articulated a similar principle – albeit with a different ascription of value:

> we shall call *Naturalists* all those who deem the imitation of nature to be the last word in art, and, conversely, we shall give the name *Idealists* to all those who use the resources of nature to express their idea of how it could be or how it should be.[17]

For the literary critic, naturalism, and its investment in mimesis as an end in itself, is to be understood as ethically inferior to those types of idealist art that assign to themselves a higher purpose: to imagine the world differently. It will be clear from what follows that this book is not invested in rehearsing the complex history of idealist aesthetics and thought on its own terms in this period.[18] Rather it takes as its chief concern Zola's particular, and deliberately polemical, conception of idealism, however much of a misprision this may have been. In other words, I want to explore idealism, first and foremost, as a function of naturalist fiction and theory, and, in turn, reconstruct a prevailing dynamic that seemed to many almost inescapable.

Such, in fact, was the apparent inextricability of these aesthetic antitheses that all talk of idealism at the end of the century seemed to lead back to the naturalist novel. The principal theorist of idealism in this period, Remy de Gourmont, lamented the fate of a term that had not only become (over) determined by its relationship to naturalism but whose intellectual heft had been diminished by overuse: 'It is a catch-all word. For those with a superficial, slightly blinkered outlook, idealism is the opposite of naturalism – and that is that.'[19] For Gourmont, idealism was, first, a moral or religious notion, close to spiritualism; and second, a philosophical conception of the world (one, he said, it might have been better to call 'ideaism' [idéisme]), and which was the opposite of materialism.[20] Here and in Chapter 1, we shall explore some of the valences of idealism in art, thought, and politics. But what Gourmont's complaint makes clear is just how loosely the idea could be worn, how contested its uses could be, and, indeed, how stubbornly it remained yoked to the discourse of its chief critic – Zola.[21]

For all its slipperiness, then, this book privileges the concept of idealism for a number of reasons. First, idealism is a chief preoccupation of naturalist meta-discourse, and, as we shall see, the master concept in the extended battle over the movement, in which a demand for the ideal was brandished, as Pascaline Hamon has argued, as an 'antinaturalist banner'.[22] Second, unlike its associated terms, idealism allows us, even obliges us, to cross between disciplines and discourses – namely, philosophy, politics, aesthetics, ethics, and psychology– and in ways which, I hope to show, Zola himself exploited. Third, an inclination among critics to focus on Zola's relationship to romanticism has tended to obscure the wider resonance of idealism as, in Zola's vocabulary, not only a cognate of romantic writing, but also a vital term linking such disparate forms as classicism, symbolism, and sentimental fiction. To absorb idealism under the rubric of romanticism is to frame Zola's engagement with the former as, above all, a matter of (dis)inheritance, and idealism itself as another kind of literary anachronism.[23] More broadly, as Toril Moi argues, recuperating the concept of idealism for literary criticism can afford us a better understanding of how literature and philosophy intersected in a period (1870–1914) that was marked by various 'highly self-conscious aesthetic attempts to *negate* idealism':

if we take idealism to be just another word for romanticism, we deprive ourselves of the resources we need to understand European art and litera-ture after the demise of romanticism as an active artistic movement. We will also fail to understand why the advent of naturalism and modernism provoked the most intense culture wars in European literary history.[24]

Significantly for us, Moi pins her narrative of aesthetic crisis in European culture to the French context: the nation's defeat at the hands of the Prussians and the fate of the Paris Commune in spring 1871 are held to have 'confirmed the bankruptcy of idealism'.[25] This was, at any rate, Zola's interpretation of these twin historical episodes; and it was one that became embedded in the Third Republic's narrative of its origins. Take the reflections of the influential philosopher Alfred Fouillée, some twenty-six years later, when idealism's star was on the rise once more:

> The war of 1870 seemed to have brought about, once and for all, the victory of force over right, of fact over idea. In literature, positivist realism was winning out with the likes of Zola and the Goncourts; even painting was taking a realist turn with Courbet and Manet. Historians were doing away with sweeping syntheses, and instead immersing themselves, like novelists, in the 'document'. Lastly, the politics of ideas had given way to the positivist politics of facts, or better still, 'of affairs'.[26]

Fouillée's broad-brush vision of France's military defeat as inaugurating the new reign of positivism – contaminating culture, history, and politics alike – is, of course, as remarkable for its imprecision as for its ideological bias. But if we can take it to be somehow emblematic, it is because Fouillée conjures up, first and foremost, a mood, a disposition, a tendency, or – to borrow Richard Thomson's definition of naturalism – 'a state of mind'.[27] When, in February 1896, Brunetière gave an important public lecture entitled *La Renaissance de l'idéalisme*, the reaction against naturalism by then fully-fledged, he eschewed strict definitions ('it is good [. . .] to avoid pinning these terms down too much'), describing it as a 'conviction', an 'innermost persuasion', which coloured all parts of life.[28] Beyond the specific implications of these ostensibly polar concepts in aesthetics and philosophy, it was precisely their availability, their resonance for matters as diverse as fictional plots, private beliefs, and national politics that made them the hooks for so many cultural struggles.

In making the case for retrieving idealism as a key to our understanding of nineteenth-century European culture, Moi acknowledges her debts to Naomi Schor's magisterial and pioneering book *George Sand and Idealism* (1993). My own approach too, it will be clear, is indelibly shaped by Schor's recuperation of idealism as realism's forgotten 'binary opposite', as well as by her wider call to reinstate Sand's idealism as '*a politics at least as much as an aesthetics*'.[29] The former claim, though now part of the critical doxa, bears rehearsing here:

> Realism in the nineteenth century signified overwhelmingly in relation to idealism, so much so that to consider one term in isolation from the other is to deplete, even distort its significance. Realism, cut off from idealism, is a radically decontextualized representational mode, a perennial trend rather than a historically specific literary, aesthetic, and political movement. Uncoupled from its binary other, realism is caught up in an endless semantic drift. [...] And yet, so massive, so crushing has been the triumph of realism that at least in the field of literature [...] idealism has all but vanished from our critical consciousness, taking with it the literary reputation of its most eminent French representative, George Sand.[30]

Any explanation of Sand's decanonisation must deal with the wholesale devalorisation of the idealist aesthetic with which she was most closely aligned. In other words, Schor tells the story of how, in the culture wars of nineteenth-century French fiction, realism wins out over idealism; and it is a victory that, she argues, has continued to shape our critical discourse, assumptions, and predilections. For even if realism, and its mimetic claims, have had something of a rough ride in structuralist and poststructuralist theory, idealism has languished, at least from the early twentieth century onwards, in relative obscurity. In recuperating the rubric of the idealist novel, Schor explains how realism was tethered to idealism from its inception, and, as my own book will argue, through their respective changing fortunes beyond Sand's death.

The present study thus responds, in part, to the imperative Schor sets out: to restore to realism – or naturalism, as Zola best embodied it – precisely a sense of its dependence on idealism. For cut loose from it, naturalism risks being subject, I am suggesting, to precisely the same sort of 'semantic drift'. Of course, where Sand is the most distinguished practitioner of idealism in nineteenth-century France, Zola was – and, in some sense, continues to be – the beneficiary of the 'crushing [...] triumph of realism' that Schor describes, just as he was also one of its chief architects. Zola repeatedly drove home, as we shall see, his combative vision of nineteenth-century literary history as a dramatic (if foregone) struggle between idealists and naturalists: 'here are two worlds', he averred, 'and one must kill the other'.[31] As much, then, as my return to idealism via Zola is inspired by the scholarship of Schor and of Margaret Cohen, whose own recuperation of the early nineteenth-century female-authored sentimental novel has reshaped our understanding of realism 'as a displacement of sentimental codes', I can hardly claim to be furthering the same political, or feminist, agendas.[32] What we will find in Zola's writing on idealism, and on Sand specifically, is, if anything, a paradigmatic example of the gendering of aesthetic categories that Schor and Cohen take up, and which, they demonstrate, have excluded not only Sand but a whole subset of women's writing from the canon. Indeed, in a very straightforward sense, Zola's objective is to consign idealism – as he too, I shall argue, thought Sand best embodied it – to a cul-de-sac of literary history.

As these comments would suggest, Zola's own relationship to Sand lies at the heart of this book's endeavour to think through the draw and the perils of idealism for the naturalist writer. Sand will be a focal point of Chapter 3, but she will also return as a guiding, if often invisible, thread through my readings of Zola's engagement with socialism (in *Germinal*) and his vision of a future Republic (in *Vérité*), where Sand's 'politics of idealism', as Schor puts it, are both critiqued and rescued. In fact, what I hope to demonstrate by reconstructing aesthetic debates at the end of the nineteenth century is just how much the idealist Sand that Schor retrieves for us is, in some respects, a Third Republic invention. For it was, as Schor briefly acknowledges, Sand's 'posthumous promoters' – some of whom, in fact, were Zola's arch-critics – who announced the woman writer's return to favour by extolling her idealism.[33] And as Martine Reid points out, the gendered opposition between realism and idealism that Schor makes axiomatic only became firmly established after 1870, largely on account of Zola's own interventions.[34] What were, then, the political and ideological interests driving this revalorisation of Sand's idealist aesthetic? How was Sand established, in the wake of her death, as a rival to Zola's brand of naturalism? These are questions that will hover over this account of Zola's own engagement with the 'rise', or return(s), of idealism in its many fin-de-siècle forms. But, more broadly, my own return to Schor's *George Sand and Idealism* has a lot to do with the fate of that scholarship. Put bluntly, for all that Schor's book has been absolutely pivotal to Sand's recanonisation, its powerful arguments for idealism as a major aesthetic and political, not to mention psychoanalytical, category seem to have gained less traction.[35] Has idealism really taken root, we might wonder, in the vocabulary of nineteenth-century literary critics? Moi's version of the field, some sixteen years after Schor's book appeared, suggests not: 'at the beginning of the twenty-first century', she claims, 'we appear to have forgotten how important idealism was as a way of understanding art and literature'.[36] Certainly, we might venture that where idealism can be found, it is more often than not incorporated into, or subsumed by, a focus on its kin: utopianism, religion, romanticism, sentimental literature.[37]

In the French context, no doubt the most important corrective to this occlusion of idealism in our literary histories is Jean-Marie Seillan's *Le Roman idéaliste dans le second XIXᵉ siècle* (2011). Seillan exhumes a whole body of largely forgotten idealist fiction of the Second Empire and the early Third Republic by Octave Feuillet, Victor Cherbuliez, Albert Depit, *entre autres*, whose immensely popular novels represent the other side of the literary field Zola sought to dominate. 'How can we understand the existence of a naturalist battle', asks Seillan, 'if those against whom it was fought are kept in the shadows?'[38] In reconstructing the fiction of these writers on their own terms, Seillan not only makes a compelling argument for the idealist novel as a coherent aesthetic, 'a "formula" just as strong as Zola's' (13), he also calls for us to reframe the rivalry between Zola and his idealist adversaries as a relationship of complementarity or 'mutual dependence' (35). In these respects, we might simply note, Seillan's engagement with idealism shares many of the same imperatives as Schor's, though it surely tells us something about the limited reach of anglophone literary criticism in France that her book goes unmentioned.

The present study, it will be clear, speaks directly to Seillan's and, in foregrounding Zola's own vision of idealism, teases out some of the implications of his arguments for our understanding of the naturalist polemic itself. In other words, I too am interested in naturalism and idealism as inextricable binaries that, to some degree, ordered the later nineteenth-century literary field, not least because, in most dominant critical narratives of the trajectory from realism to modernism, idealism has almost invariably been construed as a byway or a shared foil. To take up Rita Felski's own gloss on Schor's study, 'the male intelligentsia' may have disagreed about the relative merits of 'naturalist or modernist techniques' as the means of representing modern life, but 'they were largely united in their disdain for an idealist aesthetic associated with an outmoded and cloying feminine sentimentality'.[39] Restoring the largely occluded role of idealism in this period requires us not only to grapple with that derision, precisely as a cornerstone of the naturalist (and modernist) self-image, but also to track the complex pull of the idealist imagination in the distorting mirrors of Zola's own literary writing.

Zola malgré lui

So far, I have given an impression of some of the ways in which Zola theorised the relationship between naturalism and idealism; and the wider debates he stoked on this aesthetic rivalry will be the focus of Chapter 1.

But the book is primarily concerned with reading the convictions and anxieties Zola expressed in his journalism and polemical writing through, even against, his handling of idealism in fiction. It probes the gap, in other words, between naturalism's confident self-theorisation and the complex, even contradictory, poetics of Zola's literary writing in the detail. Broadly speaking, this gesture – interrogating, that is, the fit of naturalist theory and fiction – lies at the heart of Susan Harrow's path-breaking monograph, *Zola, The Body Modern* (2010). Taking up Henri Mitterand's call to '[prise] Zola out of the nineteenth century', Harrow makes a resounding case for imagining Zola as a 'proto-modernist', far more interested, and implicated, in probing the limits of the referential project than reductive critical frameworks would allow.[40] Harrow's account of 'Zola's prospective modernism' demands that we interrogate those 'categorical, conservative' (3) and overdetermined assumptions about the parameters of naturalism and of 'aesthetic modernity', which would position Zola's fiction 'almost as an anti-modernism (in terms of its assumed transparency, hypertrophy, and extreme *lisibilité*)' (6). Instead, Harrow invites us, through superlative close readings, to scrutinise those precisely 'non-Naturalist' dimensions of Zola's prose writing (7), opening up a plethora of forward connections with twentieth-century experimentalism. To similar ends, Émilie Piton-Foucault has analysed exhaustively the crises of visibility in Zola's *Rougon-Macquart*, revealing its kinship with what would become known as the non-figurative arts, as well as recalibrating our understanding of naturalism as 'an aesthetic that would appear [. . .] far less confident in its ability to depict the real than it is often assumed'.[41] Both critics effectively heed Mitterand's caution against immersing ourselves in narrative (*histoire*), or what Harrow calls the 'thematic modernity' of Zola's fiction, at the expense of style and discourse: 'It is a case of [. . .] moving the target, of reading his writing not only for the wealth of information it provides about daily life, and about the way people lived and thought in a bygone era, but also as an oblique, intensifying mode of perception.'[42] Indeed, Mitterand ventures, can we not see Zola as – to co-opt André Breton's epithet – 'the "definitive" dreamer', whose creative intelligence and experimental imagination bring his writing 'to the brink of a certain surrealism'?[43]

To put all this otherwise, the kind of modernist- and postmodernist-inflected readings that Mitterand, Harrow, and Piton-Foucault provide involve scrutinising those moments, episodes, and places where the identity – or to be precise, self-identity – of Zola's fiction-writing comes under strain. Where, they invite us to ask, does Zola look least like 'Zola'? This book seeks to offer another angle on that question. Rather than map Zola forwards, it fosters a synchronic understanding of the ways in which Zola's writing was shaped by his struggle with that contemporary, and most conspicuously 'non-Naturalist', aesthetic: idealism. This does not mean abandoning Harrow's portrait of Zola as 'more vanguard than rearguard' (4), but instead restoring to Zola's own understanding of naturalism's *avant-gardisme* – not least as it was spelt out in the early 1880s, at the high-water mark of the movement's self-theorisation – those vital negotiations with an aesthetic that he repeatedly invoked as the rearguard. One of the claims this book makes, then, is that the anti-idealism Zola places at the core of his naturalist vision is invariably complicated in, and by, the fiction he produces. In this respect, it heeds Mitterand's call to 'un-read' Zola – to break 'the doctrinaire shell of naturalist discourse (that of *Le Roman expérimental*)' and to restore to Zola 'his truth as a novelist: as a *man of narrative*, as a *man of fiction* – even, we might say, a *man of reverie*'.[44] For, in tracking Zola's relationship to idealism, we shall inevitably encounter precisely the disjunction between theory and fiction that Mitterand has described: 'naturalist discourse theorises a novel that hasn't been written, or that has been written differently'.[45] And yet, such is the spirit of suspicion that has prevailed in approaches to Zola, in the past twenty years at least, that relativising his discourse on naturalism has become a quasi-ubiquitous if still undeniably vital, critical gesture. Armed with reservations about Zola's own dogmatism, we are invited to show how the Zolian novel is not doing the work it is supposed to, or, indeed, to demonstrate that the writer fails to remain true to the word of naturalist doxa – and this so as to give free rein to the nuanced play, inconsistency, and instabilities at work in his fiction. In this respect, the critic's task is, as Chantal Pierre-Gnassounou puts it, to 'defend Zola against himself, against his theories, [...], against the overt scientism of his method and his aesthetic principles'.[46] A sceptical mode of reading allows us to observe the many ways in which Zola's fiction is less transparent, less mimetic, less predictable, less coherent, indeed less 'naturalist' than Zola might have us imagine.

Such an impulse to read Zola against himself – or in the language of his day, *à rebours* – is one this book inevitably shares, just as it also subjects it to scrutiny. As we shall see in Chapter 1, Zola's own contemporaries were well aware of the discrepancies between his theory and poetics; in fact, several claimed to identify a lyrical, even idealist, tendency in his fiction that could be construed precisely as a betrayal of his own aesthetic principles. In other words, Zola's direct adversaries were arguably the masters of the deconstructive gesture. Take, as one salient example, the judgement of Anatole France at the height of his antinaturalist campaign:

> M. Zola is less faithful to his doctrines than he proclaims, and than he believes. He has not managed to stifle his powerful imagination. [...] Though he sets out to copy, the graceless oaf is soon making things up! His conception of the *Rougon-Macquart*, which involves presenting all the physiological states and all the social conditions in a single family, has something vast and symmetrical about it that speaks of the most ardent idealism in its author.[47]

For those with points to score, the best way to undermine Zola's naturalist vision was to determine latent contradictions, or inconsistencies, between idea and practice, which could be taken as proof that the naturalist novel is, ultimately, *not what it thinks it is*. Such ways of reading the writer against his word, whether admiring or denunciatory, have tended to form part of what Aurélie Barjonet has called 'the thesis of the two Zolas'.[48] This posits the uneasy, if not downright contradictory, coexistence of scientific ambition with a lyrical, romantic, symbolist, or epic imagination – the latter captured in Zola's own metaphor of 'the leap into the stars', which Colette Becker makes a signature style in her anthology and study of Zola's aesthetics.[49]

In his 1883 portrait of Zola, Guy de Maupassant offered one of the most eloquent, and appreciative, accounts of the author's apparently split dispositions, his poetic temperament giving rise, Maupassant claimed, to a relentless internal struggle:

> son of the romantics, romantic himself in all his methods, he carries within him an inclination towards the poetic, a need to enlarge, to exaggerate, to create symbols out of creatures and things. He is, moreover, well aware of this tendency; he fights it constantly, only to give into it every time. His teachings and his works are forever at odds.[50]

Zola had, as Maupassant knew, already reached a similar self-diagnosis, one he extended, in fact, to an entire generation of likeminded writers whom he described as 'riddled with romanticism to their very core', despite their 'passion for precise truth'.[51] However heroic their attempts at self-mastery, the lyrical penchant was insurmountable – even, Zola dared to imagine, the very thing that made their writing palatable: 'it makes me sad to admit, given how fiercely I have fought against romanticism, but our successes, those of every one of us, owe something to the lyricism that *nonetheless seeps into our works*.'[52] Elsewhere, Zola conceded in a similar spirit that, for all their attempts to disinherit their romantic cultural baggage, naturalist writers '*unwittingly* retain some of the finery of 1830 around their shoulders'.[53] The idea that naturalist fiction was incapable of shaking off the imaginative residue of romantic writing thus seemed something of an open secret.

Certainly, the Bloomian psychodrama of the writer's perennial struggle with his forebears is appealing, and it is one that has, to an extent, been taken over by critics as the dominant model for conceptualising Zola's relationship to non-naturalist aesthetics. Sophie Guermès evokes the pull of romanticism for Zola as 'this dissonance between his determination to free himself and his inevitable contamination'; François-Marie Mourad describes the novelist's attempt to exorcise such influences as a 'battle with himself'; Mitterand, meanwhile, determines in Zola 'a curious splitting', whereby there remains in the naturalist author 'a fervour, a writing style that bears all the rapture, sentimentality, idealism, and reverie of 1830'.[54] In Chapter 3, we too shall broach these issues of (dis)inheritance, conflict, and self-censorship when we explore Zola's relationship to Sand. But in tracking Zola's wider engagement with a set of contemporary aesthetic and political debates about idealism, this book also argues for the need to find different ways of conceptualising the draw of idealism for the writer – other, that is, than as a *susceptibility*, an id-like mode to which he is 'prone', or into which he lapses, often in spite of his better judgement. Indeed, we first need to recall that such a mode of interpreting Zola's fiction – that is, as independently from, even against, his declared intentions – was, as Andrew J. Counter makes clear, a tactic, cultivated predominantly by hostile detractors. From Louis Ulbach to Max Nordau, antinaturalist (or at least, anti-Zola) critics have tended to posit 'a *hermeneutics of the "malgré-lui"*', whereby the author's works are held to be subordinate to the pressures of physiological, libidinal, and automatic impulsions, drives or manias.[55]

However rooted in ideological convictions we would wish to disown, this 'symptomal' strain of critical discourse survives in altered forms; and it is, as Counter notes, most clearly operative where the trajectory of Zola's later career is concerned.[56] For the prevailing narrative of Zola's aesthetic development – namely, the utopian bent of his final series, which is effectively announced far earlier – is one of circularity, in which the writer can be understood to *return* to an original disposition. Guermès's account is, in this sense, emblematic: Zola's last two cycles signal 'an enhanced return to early experiences, after thirty years of self-repression'.[57] For Jacques Noiray too, the shift he determines at the close of *Les Rougon-Macquart* is to be grasped as 'the resurgence of an inherent romanticism, which is also for the writer a happy return to his true nature – sentimental and lyrical'.[58] In fact, Noiray takes over the precise vocabulary of Zola's admiring contemporary critic, Georges Pellissier, for whom the naturalist writer's 'inherent romanticism' took full flight in his final novels, together with a latent idealism that dared, at last, to speak its name: 'his innate idealism gradually freed itself from those artistic theories that had long constrained it'.[59] There is, of course, much that can be, and has been, said about the connections between Zola's writing 'before the *Rougon-Macquart*', to echo John C. Lapp's study, and his later works.[60] In fact, Zola himself fostered this kind of diachronic criticism when, in September 1889, he offered up a new edition of one of his earliest novels, *Le Vœu d'une morte* (1866), 'for the interesting comparison that literary enthusiasts might be tempted to make one day, between these first pages of mine and those I wrote later'.[61] It is no doubt the job of the literary critic to make, and make sense of, connections across Zola's career, and indeed to challenge, as those recent accounts do, a fallacy of artistic development that would have Zola straightforwardly surpass, or outgrow, his earliest (immature) inclinations. Still, what might strike us most about those explanations of the 'turn' Zola takes after *Les Rougon-Macquart* – variously utopian, sentimental, religious, lyrical, and, I am arguing, idealist – is just how they draw on a loosely psychoanalytical model, whereby the writer's late fiction betrays a (happy) regression, the heeding of an impulse otherwise carefully sublimated, if not repressed.

While it is not my objective in this book to encompass the full span of Zola's writing – we shall be dealing only, in Chapter 5, with the closing bookend of his career – the least I think we can say about this critical narrative is that it risks *deintellectualising* idealism in general, and specifically, as Zola practised it. In describing Zola's late 'return' to a former state of authenticity, or the resurfacing of what Victor Brombert calls 'a natural and, at one time, predominant tendency' of his character, the idealist mode emerges as the subterranean, emotional, or instinctual, counterpoint to the cerebral project of the 'middle' Zola.[62] Take Guermès's account of the novelist's trajectory: 'Zola constructs *Les Rougon-Macquart* by *thinking* a form'; and this requires him to abandon, she adds, 'an essential part of himself, made up of dreamy ramblings and spiritual concerns', which he will later retrieve.[63] In part, such distinctions between Zola's 'high' naturalism and idealism are an inevitable response to the writer's own account of his creative drives. They reinscribe, in other words, a vision of aesthetic difference in which Zola himself colluded: between polemic, strategy, thought, on the one hand; feeling, disposition, need, on the other.

Indicatively, where the novelist portrayed himself as a romantic *malgré lui*, he more often than not consigned that influence to the lower regions, to below the belt.[64] 'If the upper body is intact', comments Noiray, 'the lower part remains forever tainted by the dubious romantic concoction in which it has been immersed'.[65] For all that critics, Noiray included, have questioned the legitimacy of Zola's self-portraiture – mostly by arguing that his romantic inheritance runs still deeper than he would allow – the fundamental terms in which aesthetic differences are captured have not shifted: idealism remains bound to the unconscious.

What I am arguing, then, is that this prevailing narrative of Zola's relapse in his later works has tended to occlude a broader understanding of the novelist's engagement with idealism as a deliberate, intellectual strategy, as self-conscious experimentation, as integral to the evolution and adaptation of his fiction as the writer navigated wider cultural politics, and – perhaps most importantly – as a political gesture, even a political solution. In short, my contention is that Zola finds idealism *good to think with*, and that, in fact, he has something serious to say about it. All of which is not to suggest that the character of his idealism is entirely cerebral rather than emotional; on the contrary, as Counter has shown, affect and sentiment are as pivotal to the politics of Zola's utopian communities as they are to the style of his final works of fiction.[66] Rather, I am suggesting, Zola is increasingly drawn to *the idea of idealism*, and to idealism as an expression of ideas as much as ideals. Indeed, *Les Quatre Évangiles*, the late novels of the so-called fourth Zola, can be aligned with the genre of the *roman à idées*, practised to most acclaim at the end of the nineteenth century by Paul Bourget – that is, when they do not fall, less flatteringly, into the territory of the latter's second-rate counterpart, the *roman à thèse*.[67] Certainly, the titles of Zola's gospels (*Fécondité*, *Travail*, *Vérité*, *Justice*) signpost an investment in the abstract or conceptual, and in ways that undoubtedly resonated with the rhetoric of the Dreyfusard campaign unfolding directly contemporaneously. 'It is significant', writes Ruth Harris, 'that in their letters to each other – and increasingly in printed material – [Dreyfusards] capitalized these words [Truth and Justice] to stress that they were fighting for *absolute* values'.[68] Zola may long have been, according to Gustave Flaubert's derisory epithet, a 'devourer of capital letters', his pivotal engagement in the Dreyfus Affair emboldened his faith in the universal idea as a solution to political conflict.[69]

This was, in any case, the view of many of Zola's contemporaries, for whom the novelist's idealist turn in his final cycle was to be rationalised as an extension of his political engagement. Consider Octave Mirbeau's admiring review of Zola's *Fécondité* (1899), the first of *Les Quatre Évangiles*, penned from the writer's self-imposed exile in Norwood, London, following the repercussions of his incendiary open letter to President Félix Faure. This 'epic painter of the truth' has, Mirbeau declares, succeeded in turning bitterness and suffering into a creative and generous vision of hope for the future, his exile an impetus to remake his *patrie* in a different image:

> He still had to escape from the world, to recreate it – better, peaceful, and bigger still – to step into the future so as to show us new hope springing up from the ground. . .
> Hence the *Quatre Évangiles*.
> And in this new series, the first work, *Fécondité*, contrasts the realities of where we are with the ideal reality to which we aspire, the painful present with the happy future, the mediocrity of today with the Beauty of tomorrow.
> It is more than a novel, and something other than a poem: it is the work of a prophet, or visionary, albeit one who can see with singular precision and ambition when he beholds the darkness of the earth, or explores the splendid magnificence of the future dream. . .[70]

Surely sensing the keen generosity that coloured Mirbeau's eulogy, Zola was bashful in reply, supplying the aesthetic critique that his Dreyfusard ally had left unspoken: 'I am well aware of the flaws in my book: the parts that are far-fetched, the overdetermined symmetries, the banal truths of morality in action.'[71] Such flaws, as Zola put it – those we tend to associate, in fact, with the characteristically 'antimodern' *roman à thèse* – were the aesthetic compromises he was ready to make in the name of political expediency. Indeed, it remains an acute irony for critics, as Counter has argued, that 'it is the very novels in which Zola is at his most self-consciously forward-looking [. . .] that prove least amenable to aesthetically prospective readings'.[72]

As Zola's reply to Mirbeau makes clear, he was at the very least self-conscious about his aesthetic evolution, even if there was something undeniably disingenuous about his own explanation for it. 'It's all very utopian', he admitted. 'But what can you do? I've been dissecting for forty years now; I must be permitted to dream a little in my old age.'[73] Elsewhere, in a direct contradiction of the remarks he had made in the *Ébauche* for his final cycle of novels, Zola asserted more confidently a sense of coherence with his earlier body of writing: 'I have been accused from all quarters of changing my way of writing', he wrote to Dreyfusard and writer Marcel Drouin; in fact, 'my current works are simply the development of, and something of a conclusion to, my previous ones'.[74] Whether or not Zola accepted his style had changed, he remained adamant that his utopian fiction represented a natural evolution: 'after a lengthy examination of reality, an extension into tomorrow's world, [. . .] my need for truth and justice bursting forth at last'.[75] According to the logic Zola provides, his idealist fiction is but an expression, or amplification, of what was there all along. Though we might also wonder what is being obscured by Zola's insistence on the capacity of the naturalist novel to reinvent itself, to make space for difference. Or to recall Mirbeau's musings on Zola's *Fécondité*: was this a novel, let alone a naturalist novel?

No doubt it is possible to trace the positive thinking that defines Zola's final works to a host of anterior figures and aesthetic choices: the irrepressible optimist of *L'Argent* (1891) Caroline Hédouin, perhaps, or more broadly, the 'complete shift of philosophy' that Zola ascribes to *Au Bonheur des dames* (1883) – a novel offering that rarest commodity in Zola's corpus, the happy ending. Certainly, his preparatory notes offer a striking anticipation of both the tone and the metaphorics of his last series: 'no more pessimism, first of all; no concluding with the stupidity and sadness of life. Instead, conclude with its continual labour, with the power and delight of making life'.[76] In other words, we might wish to think of the writer's 'philosophical' inclinations to optimism as a thread that passes over and under his works, in and out of view, and indeed, we might to wish to make a case, as Julia Pryzbos has done, for 'the early and middle idealist' Zola.[77] Though there also remains something to be said, as I shall suggest in Chapter 1, about the precise relationship between optimism and idealism as functions of one another in Zola's fiction. In any case, what we find, more often than not, in Zola's own conceptualisations of his evolving philosophy and aesthetic is a desire to smooth over changes ('handle carefully the leap into utopia' was a characteristic note to self), to resist breaking, that is, with his theory of the naturalist novel.[78] Under pressure from rival literary avant-gardes in the early 1890s, Zola augured a kind of 'soft' naturalism, less dogmatic, more open, that could better contend with the prevailing religious revival and a waning faith in the promises of science. In a spirit of compromise, Zola sought to conjure up, across his final cycle, 'the dream that science permits', the ideal 'stripped', in Malcolm Scott's words, of its 'supernatural associations, grounded in the human and biologically possible'.[79] Of course, Zola had already broached the prospect of reclaiming, or repurposing, the power of the idealist imagination in the *Rougon-Macquart*'s closing, metafictional novel, *Le Docteur Pascal* (1893), when the deceased scientist-hero is tentatively recast, at least in Clotilde's consciousness, as 'a dreamer': 'for he had had the most beautiful of dreams, this ultimate belief in a better world, when science will have invested man with an incalculable power'.[80] Zola's most transparent avatar, Pascal, articulates a secular optimism, and a curative drive, that will pulsate through subsequent novels, as the writer reflects on the kind of accommodations with idealism he was willing to make.

Such moments of transition crystallise the strategy of experimentation and reinvention that, as Olivier Lumbroso has argued, characterises Zola's creative process – his ongoing imperative, that is, to balance continuity and versatility, to 'stay true to himself while taking the greatest possible distance from himself'.[81] In tracking the various turns and returns that mark Zola's mid-to-late career, this book offers its own reflections on the writer's negotiations with aesthetic difference and self-identity, including, in Elizabeth Emery's words, on 'what scholars have often considered the sudden and disturbing shift to idealism' that accompanies Zola's exit from *Les Rougon-Macquart*.[82] Certainly, this aesthetic trajectory can tell us much about the writer's creative consciousness, as well as the pressures of a shifting literary field. But more broadly still, I want to suggest, Zola's accommodations with idealism register the historical and political limitations of realistic representation and prevailing narrative paradigms that Fredric Jameson describes in his classic study, *The Political Unconscious* (1981), and to which we shall return in Chapter 2. By the later nineteenth century, 'high realism', Jameson contends, finds itself weighed down by 'a massively homogeneous narrative apparatus', incapable of imagining 'alternate histories' or transformed futures; and 'the result is the Utopian or science-fiction novel, of which Chernyskevsky's *What's to Be Done?* is the monument'.[83] If Zola offers us an ideal case-study for thinking about the evolution of literary fiction in this period, then, it is in no small part because the pathways of his own career give us a map of just such a split: the forking between the *roman de mœurs* and the utopian novel, between description and prescription, or amelioration. Over the course of this book, we shall see how Zola undertakes his own (failed and successful) experiments with idealism in order to determine what else the naturalist novel could be.

Return to Zola

The main purpose of this Introduction has been to argue that a close attention to idealism can tell us much about Zola's aesthetic, political, and intellectual ambitions, as well as the wider landscape of literary fiction at the end of the nineteenth century. But at the close, I would also like to make an altogether more fundamental case: for returning to Zola. As one of the most widely taught and read French authors in the anglophone world, the task of justification might, in one sense, be readily dispatched. Zola is – and always has been – a genuinely popular novelist. As the last

great nineteenth-century realist (or naturalist) writer before the explosion
of modernism, his works are singularly poised between mass culture and
high art. In fact, as Jameson remarks, 'Zola may be taken as the marker for
the last coexistence of the art novel and the best-seller within a single
text'.[84] While his immense readability may have made him a maligned
figure of academic study for the first half of the twentieth century, Zola has
since become a touchstone for understanding not only the aesthetic
evolution of the novel, but also the fraught history of the early Third
Republic – of which he remains one of the most important chroniclers,
critics, and icons. No doubt the rise of cultural history has played its part,
exerting as it has such a definitive influence over the discipline of literary
criticism in recent decades. For, as Nicholas White argues, cultural history's role in renegotiating the relationship between literature and history,
the aesthetic and the ideological, makes 'particular sense in the context of a
writer such as Zola', who already prizes 'the everyday, the subliterary', and
who 'is himself such a fine cultural historian'.[85] More than most, we might
venture, Zola's works lend themselves to prevailing ways of reading texts
that are rooted in ethnographical concerns, ideology critique, and the
weighty issues of cultural politics.

  And yet, for all that a cultural-historical sensibility has served to confirm
Zola's centrality to our understanding of both the period and the practice
of the novel, it remains the case that the burden of the literary historian
working on Zola is so often one of defence. 'Stereotypes die hard',
remarked Mitterand. 'In saying "this is straight from Zola", you really
mean "this is miserabilism, naive scientism, rubbish, kitsch."'[86] Some of
the most important counters to sniffiness of this kind have involved, as we
have already noted, renegotiating Zola's relationship to the nineteenth-
century mimetic tradition, dispelling clichés of the writer as an 'unrecon-
structed Realist', and thereby carving out a place for him on the path
to modernism, between the towering figures of Flaubert and Proust.[87]
Such endeavours have rightly insisted on Zola's writing as precisely
an experimental art – less dogmatic, more subtle, and indeed more
self-problematising than it might seem (and than Zola's own discourse
on naturalism would have us believe). This book sets out, in a similar spirit,
to take Zola seriously on both aesthetic and intellectual grounds. But it
also seeks to grapple with a vital dimension of Zola's writing – especially his
later fiction – that, arguably, is not so easily married with arguments
contesting his *lisibilité*: the author's social and political commitment.
In other words, what has often been construed as Zola's referential naivety
can be dispelled, to be sure, under the scrutiny of close reading. Yet it is

also true that Zola's sheer conscientiousness demands an ethics of style, an attachment to legibility, in order not to shirk its main responsibility: to speak truth to power.

The task of reconciling Zola's art to the ethical and political duties he ascribes to it is anything but straightforward. Perhaps especially so given that one of the most influential conceptions of the 'politics of literature' in recent years – that elaborated by the philosopher Jacques Rancière – has involved discarding precisely those versions of it that we might readily associate with a writer like Zola: 'The politics of literature is not the politics of its writers', nor does it deal with a writer's 'personal commitment', nor with 'the modes of representation of political events [and] [. . .] social struggles in their books'.[88] Instead, Rancière makes way for a fundamentally different understanding of the kind of politics literature *does*, one concerned with how a text might allow us to innovatively reconceive, or experience anew, the framing of a common world of sensory perception, to challenge the boundaries of what he calls 'the partition of the sensible, of the visible, and the sayable'. No doubt Rancière's thought can be brought to bear on Zola's fiction in all kinds of productive ways.[89] What's more, Rancière's provocative periodisation of the arts into three loose regimes (the ethical regime of images, the representative regime of the arts, and the aesthetic regime of art) can be understood to offer an important escape route from the eternal polemic over where modernism begins and ends, and who therefore it includes and excludes.

It is nevertheless remarkable that, even where the parameters are shifted, Zola continues to stand for a type of art that is less readily amenable to the kind of thinking that would make politics a matter of aesthetic experience – that is, in Rancièrian terms, of forms of disruption that reveal how our perceptual order might be contingent. Better, for Rancière, the formal and temporal experimentation of modernist prose than the 'social epic' and its purposeful representation of the politically oppressed: 'for thinking and writing democratic history', he declares, 'it is necessary to look toward Virginia Woolf more so than toward Émile Zola'.[90] What ultimately emerges from the philosopher's distinctly counterintuitive renegotiation of the relationship between literature and politics is a conspicuous privileging of (canonical) modernism over naturalism – and indeed of Flaubert, the ostensibly indifferent, 'apolitical writer', as a paradigmatic expression of that modernism. Put differently, the agendas of the naturalist novel – its representational choices and strategies, its author's intentions – would appear as a *fausse piste* for the critic in search of literature's properly political potential. For all, then, that Rancière surely wishes to put clear water between himself and a Marxist tradition of literary criticism and ideology critique that, as we shall see in Chapter 2 (on *Germinal*), has had its own reasons for determining the limitations of naturalism as a political project, what persists is a tendency to capture Zola's writing, however obliquely, as a weak experiment. Zola's fiction is made to stand for a type of literature whose political insufficiencies would reside, faintly paradoxically, in the strength of its convictions.

In what follows, I wish to wrestle with the contradiction that such positions (knowingly) entail: the political, ideological, and ethical ambitions that underpin Zola's naturalist fiction, and which we may well wish to abstract or deconstruct, also chime with the very extra-literary commitment for which the writer remains a national hero – his defence of Dreyfus. Inevitably, Zola's biographical destiny casts a retrospective light on his literary career, just as it continues to offer readers an important way into, and out of, his works of fiction. If there is – to recall the guiding terms of my book – an idealism, or dream, inherent in Zola's naturalism, it is surely this: here is a type of literature that, simply by bearing witness, is capable of acting on the world around it. Whether or not we wish to determine in this conviction yet another expression of the writer's naivety, the fact remains that Zola's vision bears an irresistible pull. There could scarcely be a better writer with whom to think through the aspirations, and the delusions, of literature.

Notes

1 Arthur Symons, 'A Note on Zola's Method', in *The Symbolist Movement in Literature*, ed. Matthew Creasy (Manchester: Carcanet Press, 2014), pp. 116–22 (p. 121). The essay was first published in *Studies in Two Literatures* (1897); it was added to the expanded 1919 edition of the influential *The Symbolist Movement in Literature*. Symons rehearses here the conclusion of his (unsigned) 1893 review of *Le Docteur Pascal*, in which he used the term 'imaginative' rather than 'idealistic'. See 'Literature. *Le Docteur Pascal*. Par Émile Zola', *The Athenæum*, 5 August 1893, no. 3432, pp. 181–82 (p. 182).

2 Henri Mitterand establishes this principle whereby 'naturalism is defined as much by what it claims for itself as it is by what it refuses': mystical idealism, classical idealism, romanticism, theological dogmatism, even naïve mimetic realism. *Zola et le naturalisme* (Paris: Presses Universitaires de France, 2002), p. 25.

3 An inexhaustive list might include: Silvère Mouret, Florent Quenu, Étienne Lantier, Claude Lantier, Angélique Rougon, Sigismond Busch, Princesse d'Orviedo, Clotilde Rougon.

4 *Discours et opinions de Jules Ferry publiés avec commentaires et notes par Paul Robiquet*, 7 vols (Paris: Armand Colin et Cie, 1893–98), vol. 2 (1894), 236.

5 Florence Beillacou's (unpublished) PhD thesis has tackled the broad question of naturalism's anti-idealism, 'Tuer l'idéal: L'anti-romantisme de Zola et les naturalistes' (Université Sorbonne Paris Cité, 2018).

6 Joris-Karl Huysmans, *À rebours*, ed. Marc Fumaroli (Paris: Gallimard, 1977), p. 71.

7 On this crisis, see Michel Raimond, *La Crise du roman: des lendemains du Naturalisme aux années vingt* (Paris: José Corti, 1966), and René-Pierre Colin, *Zola, renégats et alliés: la Répubique naturaliste* (Lyon: Presses Universitaires de Lyon, 1988), pp. 227–60.

8 Ferdinand Brunetière, 'L'Idéalisme dans le roman', *Revue des Deux Mondes*, 1 May 1885, 215–25.

9 Maurice Barrès, 'L'Esthétique de demain: l'art suggestif', *De Nieuwe Gids*, 1 December 1885, 140–49 (p. 143).

10 Émile Zola, 'La République et la littérature', subsequently included in *Le Roman expérimental*. *OC*, vol. 9, 488–507 (p. 489).

11 *Journal officiel de la République française*, 14 November 1872, p. 6981.

12 'La République et la littérature', 489.

13 See, for instance, Adrian Huart, 'La République-Zola', *Le Charivari*, 2 May 1879, pp. 1–2.

14 *OC*, vol. 9, 494.

15 'La République et la littérature', 495.

16 Zola, 'Le sens du réel', in *OC*, vol. 9, 415–18 (p. 416).

17 Brunetière, 'Une définition de mots', *Revue des Deux Mondes*, 92 (1889), 215–26 (p. 218; original emphasis).

18 For a wide-ranging account of idealist philosophy and aesthetics in the later nineteenth century, see Sandrine Schiano-Bennis, *La Renaissance de l'idéalisme à la fin du XIXᵉ siècle* (Paris: Champion, 1999).

19 Remy de Gourmont, *L'Idéalisme* (Paris: Mercure de France, 1893), p. 11.

20 See Gourmont, 'Les racines de l'idéalisme', *Mercure de France*, October 1904, 5–24 (p. 6).

21 For a discussion of the semantics of the term 'idealism' in this period, see Pascaline Hamon, 'Constructions de la notion d'idéalisme dans la critique de la fin du XIXᵉᵐᵉ siècle chez F. Brunetière et R. de Gourmont' (2013), available online: www.crp19.org/filebank/568d3d82-43e7-1031-8016-8b7ac158774a/SJCPascalineHamon.pdf

22 Pascaline Hamon, 'L'idéal dans la critique littéraire fin de siècle: un étendard antinaturaliste?' (2018), available online: https://serd.hypotheses.org/files/2018/08/IdealismePascalineHamon.pdf

23 For a recent reflection on Zola's relationship to romanticism, which is read and understood almost exclusively in terms of Zola's ongoing negotiation with Hugo, see Jacques Noiray, '"J'en suis et j'en enrage": Zola romantique?' *Revue d'histoire littéraire de la France*, 116 (2016), 137–50.

24 Toril Moi, 'Idealism', *The Oxford Handbook of Philosophy and Literature*, ed. Richard Eldridge (Oxford: Oxford University Press, 2009), pp. 271–97 (p. 272, original emphasis).

25 Moi, 'Idealism', p. 272.
26 Alfred Fouillée, 'Le Mouvement idéaliste en France', *Revue des Deux Mondes*, 134 (1896), 276–304 (p. 284).
27 Richard Thomson, *Art of the Actual: Naturalism and Style in Early Third Republic France, 1880–1900* (New Haven, CT: Yale University Press, 2013), p. 3.
28 Brunetière, *La Renaissance de l'idéalisme* (Paris: Firmin-Didot et Cie, 1896), pp. 18–19.
29 Naomi Schor, *George Sand and Idealism* (New York: Columbia University Press, 1993), pp. 29, 14 (original emphasis).
30 *George Sand and Idealism*, p. 29.
31 'Victor Hugo', in *Les Documents littéraires*, *OC*, vol. 10, 655–77 (p. 661).
32 Margaret Cohen, *The Sentimental Education of the Novel* (Princeton, NJ: Princeton University Press, 1999), p. 19.
33 *George Sand and Idealism*, p. 29.
34 Martine Reid, 'Post-scriptum: Naomi Schor trente ans après', in *George Sand et l'idéal: une recherche en écriture*, ed. Damien Zanone (Paris: Honoré Champion, 2017), pp. 449–57 (p. 456).
35 For an assessment of Schor's influence on Sand studies, see Reid, 'Post-scriptum'.
36 Moi, 'Idealism', p. 271.
37 Sophie Guermès invokes idealism at numerous junctures in her wide-ranging study of religion in Zola's complete works, *La Religion de Zola: naturalisme et déchristianisation* (Paris: Honoré Champion, 2006). Recent studies of uto-pianism and Zola include Fabian Scharf, *Émile Zola: de l'utopisme à l'utopie* (Paris: Champion, 2011); Julia Pryzbos, 'Zola's Utopias', in *The Cambridge Companion to Zola*, ed. Brian Nelson (Cambridge: Cambridge University Press, 2007), pp. 169–87; Béatrice Laville, 'L'Écriture de l'utopie', in *Zola à l'œuvre: hommage à Auguste Dezalay*, ed. Gisèle Séginger (Strasbourg: Presses universitaires de Strasbourg, 2003), pp. 233–44; and Laville, *Une poétique des fictions autoritaires: les voies de Zola, Barrès, Bourget* (Bordeaux: Presses Universitaires de Bordeaux, 2020).
38 Jean-Marie Seillan, *Le Roman idéaliste dans le second XIXe siècle: Littérature ou 'bouillon de veau'?* (Paris: Classiques Garnier, 2011), p. 10.
39 Rita Felski, *The Gender of Modernity* (Harvard, MA: Harvard University Press, 1995), p. 79.
40 Susan Harrow, *Zola, The Body Modern: Pressures and Prospects of Representation* (Oxford: Legenda, 2010), p. 1.
41 Émilie Piton-Foucault, *Zola ou la fenêtre condamnée: la crise de la représentation dans 'Les Rougon Macquart'* (Rennes: Presses Universitaires de Rennes, 2015), p. 15.
42 Mitterand, *Zola, tel qu'en lui-même* (Paris: Presses Universitaires de France, 2009), p. 113.
43 Mitterand, *Zola, tel qu'en lui-même*, pp. 107–24 (p. 109).
44 Mitterand, *Zola, tel qu'en lui-même*, p. vi (original emphasis).
45 Mitterand, *Zola et le naturalisme*, 4th edition (Paris: Presses Universitaires de France, 2002), p. 18.

46 Chantal Pierre-Gnassounou, 'Fictions, imaginaires, imaginations dans "Les Rougon-Macquart" d'Émile Zola' (PhD thesis, Université de la Sorbonne Nouvelle, 1996), p. 4. See also the book version of this thesis, *Zola: les fortunes de la fiction* (Paris: Nathan, 1999).

47 Anatole France, 'La Vie littéraire: un roman et un ordre du jour. – Le *Cavalier Miserey*', *Le Temps*, 6 March 1887, p. 2.

48 Aurélie Barjonet, *Zola d'Ouest en Est: le naturalisme en France et dans les deux Allemagnes* (Rennes: Presses Universitaires de Rennes, 2010), p. 26. Barjonet is expanding on the notion, established by J. H. Matthews's study, of a split between the scientific and imaginative facets of Zola's writing: *Les Deux Zola: science et personnalité dans l'expression* (Geneva: Librairie E. Droz, 1957).

49 See Colette Becker, *Zola: le saut dans les étoiles* (Paris: Presses de la Sorbonne Nouvelle, 2002).

50 Guy de Maupassant's study was first printed in *Revue bleue*, 10 March 1883, before appearing as a volume in the 'Célébrités contemporaines' series, *M. Émile Zola* (Paris: Quantin, 1883), p. 18.

51 'Les Romanciers contemporains', in *OC*, vol. 10, 598–624 (p. 601).

52 'Les Romanciers contemporains', 602 (my emphasis).

53 'Victor Hugo', in *Les Documents littéraires*, 661 (my emphasis).

54 Guermès, *La Religion de Zola*, p. 95; François-Marie Mourad, *Zola critique littéraire* (Paris: Honoré Champion, 2003), p. 232; Mitterand's preface to Zola, *Face aux romantiques* (Brussels: Éditions complexes, 1989), p. 11.

55 Andrew J. Counter, 'Le Symptôme de Zola: fragment d'autoanalyse critique', *Les Cahiers naturalistes*, 2017 (91), 61–71 (p. 65; original emphasis).

56 'Le Symptôme de Zola', 64.

57 Guermès, *La Religion de Zola*, p. 20. Éléonore Reverzy makes a similar point about Zola's circling back to Sand in his last works of fiction: Zola was 'lapsing back into the dream that, in his youth, he had so admired in George Sand'. 'Sand et Zola: littérature et valeurs', in *George Sand: écritures et représentations*, ed. Eric Bordas (Paris: Eurédit, 2004), pp. 103–19 (p. 116).

58 Noiray, 'Zola lecteur de Musset', in *Le Simple et l'Intense: vingt études sur Émile Zola* (Paris: Classiques Garnier, 2015), pp. 39–55 (p. 54). Elsewhere, Noiray posits, in relation to Zola's final cycle: 'The renewal of his style will entail this complete sense of abandon, this delightful liberation from naturalist censorship after so many years.' '*Fécondité*, conte, légende, féerie', in *Le Simple et l'Intense*, pp. 131–46 (p. 132).

59 Georges Pellissier, '*Vérité*, par Émile Zola', *La Revue*, 15 February 1903, 479–83 (p. 483).

60 John C. Lapp, *Zola Before the 'Rougon-Macquart'* (Toronto: Toronto University Press, 1964).

61 See Zola's preface, dated 1 September 1889, to Zola's new and corrected edition of *Le Vœu d'une morte* (Paris: G. Charpentier et Cie, 1889).

62 Victor Brombert, *The Intellectual Hero: Studies in the French Novel, 1880–1955* (Chicago, IL: Chicago University Press, 1964), p. 72.

63 Guermès, *La Religion de Zola*, p. 20 (original emphasis).

64 'I am a man of my time; I am steeped up to my waist in romanticism', Zola confided to the Italian writer, Giuseppe Giacosa, on 28 December 1882. *Corr*, vol. 6, 357.

65 Noiray, '"J'en suis et j'en enrage"', 146.

66 Counter considers 'the sentimentalization of the political' in Zola's late novel, *Vérité*, as well as Dreyfus journalism, in 'A Sentimental Affair: *Vérité*', *Romanic Review*, 102 (2011), 391–409 (p. 392).

67 Mitterand, 'Le Quatrième Zola', *Œuvres et critiques*, 16 (1991), 85–98.

68 Ruth Harris, *Dreyfus: Politics, Emotion and the Scandal of the Century* (New York: Picador, 2011), p. 384 (original emphasis).

69 See Armand Lanoux, 'Zola vivant', in *Œuvres completes*, ed. Henri Mitterand, vol. 1 (Paris: Hachette, Cercle du livre précieux, 1962), 9–346 (p. 143).

70 Octave Mirbeau, '*Fécondité*', *L'Aurore*, 2 July 1899, p. 1.

71 Letter to Mirbeau of 29 November 1899, *Corr*, vol. 10, 100–1 (p. 100).

72 Counter, 'A Sentimental Affair', 407.

73 *Corr*, vol. 10, 101.

74 Letter of 7 June 1901, *Corr*, vol. 10, 288–89.

75 Zola, *Ébauche* for *Travail*: Paris, Bibliothèque nationale, NAF 10333, fol. 350.

76 BN, NAF 10277, fol. 2.

77 Pryzbos, 'Zola's Utopias', p. 171.

78 See, for instance, Zola's *Ébauche* for *Travail*: BN, NAF 10333, fol. 441.

79 Malcolm Scott, *The Struggle for the Soul of the French Novel: French Catholic and Realist Novelists, 1850–1970* (London: Macmillan, 1989), p. 113.

80 Zola, *Doctor Pascal*, trans. Julie Rose (Oxford: Oxford University Press, 2020), p. 289. Original reference: *R-M*, vol. 5, 1212.

81 Olivier Lumbroso, *Zola Autodidacte: genèse des œuvres et apprentissages de l'écrivain en régime naturaliste* (Geneva: Droz, 2013), p. 352.

82 Elizabeth Emery, *Romancing the Cathedral: Gothic Architecture in Fin-de-Siècle French Culture* (Albany, NY: State University of New York Press, 2001), p. 39.

83 Fredric Jameson, *The Political Unconscious: Narrative as a Socially Symbolic Act* (London: Routledge, 1981), p. 180.

84 Jameson, *Postmodernism, or, The Cultural Logic of Late Capitalism* (Durham, NC: Duke University Press, 1992), p. 63.

85 Nicholas White, 'Introduction: Zola, Cultural Historian *avant la lettre?*', *Romanic Review*, 102:3–4 (2011), 295–303 (pp. 300–1, 303).

86 Mitterand, *Lire/Dé-lire Zola*, ed. Jean-Pierre Leduc-Adine and Henri Mitterand (Paris: Nouveau Monde, 2004), p. 15.

87 Harrow, *Zola, The Body Modern*, p. 3.

88 Jacques Rancière, 'The Politics of Literature', *SubStance*, 33:1 (2004), 10–24 (p. 10).

89 See, for example, Patrick M. Bray, *The Novel Map: Space and Subjectivity in Nineteenth-Century Fiction* (Evanston, IL: Northwestern University Press, 2013), pp. 151–68.

90 Rancière, *The Politics of Aesthetics: The Distribution of the Sensible*, ed. and trans. Gabriel Rockhill (London: Bloomsbury, 2004), p. 61.

CHAPTER I

The Quarrel of the Idealists and the Naturalists

To describe the history of naturalism as a series of campaigns, struggles, feuds, defections, and retaliations is to adopt the martial history that Zola wrote, even mythologised, in collaboration with his adversaries. For naturalism, Zola knew, had always derived much of its energy from its embattled status: 'I am still being attacked, therefore I still exist' ran his own Cartesian motto.[1] When Zola returned to journalism in December 1895 with his 'Nouvelle Campagne', after a fifteen-year hiatus, it was in part to respond to the many 'crapauds' – Zola's epithet for insulting articles – that he had been obliged to swallow and which, he claimed, filled his attic to the brim. Though Zola never did, as he thought he might, collect the best (or worst?) of those together under the title *Their Insults*, much critical ink has since been spilled over the ire and tactics of his detractors, not least during the novelist's Dreyfusard campaign that soon followed.[2] Antinaturalism took many forms, its major actors driven by a diverse set of ideological, aesthetic, and philosophical convictions. But it remains the case that Zola and his antagonists were locked into a battle – one built on their mutual dependence.[3] What has emerged, in fact, from Jean-Marie Seillan's masterful recuperation of the idealist novel as a vital, if largely occluded, category in the later nineteenth century is a sense of how so much antinaturalist discourse converged around the terms and claims of idealism and, indeed, of how naturalism came to define its own agendas and poetics in opposition to this mostly forgotten form of fiction.[4]

This chapter takes up Seillan's corrective account of the dynamics that shaped the literary field of this period by tracking the long history of what Zola dubbed 'the quarrel of the idealists and the naturalists' – the formulation no doubt intended to recast the grandiose quarrel of the '*Anciens*' and '*Modernes*'.[5] Zola was referring specifically to a group of contemporary writers whom he had lumped together, in his 1878 survey of the novel, as the 'idealist school'. Octave Feuillet, Victor Cherbuliez, Jules Claretie, André Theuriet: these were the idealist writers Zola described as the 'complete progeny of George Sand', though none had the talent, he claimed, to fill her shoes.[6] As a result, Zola delighted in proclaiming that the future of idealist fiction was in peril: 'the idealist novel is crumbling [. . .]. The day is nearly upon us when it will die a beautiful death, for want of novelists'.[7] In a patronising tone of conciliation, he called for compassion for this diminished arrière-garde, fatefully out of step with the century's aesthetic forward march: 'it is a fading trend, and we must be gentle with those novelists at the tail-end of romanticism. They will soon be punished enough by the desertion of their readers'[8]. The likes of Feuillet's mondain fiction, so favoured by Empress Eugénie, had no place in the new Republic: readers accustomed to a diet of realist prose had, Zola insisted, lost their appetite for such romanesque offerings. The unlikely survival of writers peddling this retrograde and bland by-product of romanticism was assured only, he claimed, by the patronage of the Revue des Deux Mondes, which had been an influential bastion of conservative taste from its inception in 1829.[9] Like Sand before them, most of these writers pre-published their novels in its pages, benefiting from the Revue's loyalty and generosity, as well as from its close ties with the Académie française – Feuillet, Cherbuliez, Claretie, and Theuriet all becoming Immortels. . . .[10] Such apparent complicity only deepened Zola's aversion to an anachronistic literary institution that, in recent years, had done little but trade on its associations with Sand and Feuillet: 'In literary terms, [. . .] [the Revue] no longer exists [. . .] [I]t can still help a mediocre man into the Académie. As far as the shaping of minds is concerned, it holds no sway.'[11] Ever hostile to naturalism, Zola's arch-critic Ferdinand Brunetière became the Revue's editor shortly after his own election to the Académie française on 7 June 1893.

In the strictest terms, then, the quarrel was closely aligned with Zola's efforts to delegitimise the publishing success of those writers protected by the Revue des Deux Mondes. Zola retold a convenient fiction of the idealist school's demise as a loss of public appeal, even though it remained the case, as Seillan points out, that he himself never equalled the sales of a Feuillet or a Paul Bourget.[12] Of course, Zola was not alone in expressing his distaste for a type of fiction he found distinctly second-rate. In À vau-l'eau (1882), Joris-Karl Huysmans had his downtrodden hero Jean Folantin ventriloquise his own contempt for 'the veal broth cooked up by the likes of Cherbuliez and Feuillet'; Guy de Maupassant, meanwhile, mocked the 'gentle literary cliché' that was Cherbuliez's attempt at the pastoral.[13] But it was Zola who dramatised most schematically the confrontation of idealist and naturalist fiction as a quarrel – even, taking over the combative spirit captured in the 1879 manifesto of La Revue réaliste, as a war: 'Lined up in close ranks, we enter the battlefield to the cry: War on Idealism!'[14] Certainly, this was how Anatole France viewed Zola's ruthless campaign for naturalist hegemony another decade on. The campaign against idealism was, he claimed, one Zola had started, even if the novelist was prone to those same inclinations he so forcefully repudiated:

> There is always confusion in the human fray, and one never knows exactly why and with whom one is in combat. M. Zola, who was the very first to declare such a ruthless war on idealism, is at times a great idealist himself; he verges on the symbolic; he is a poet.[15]

As we shall see in this chapter, France was not the first – nor indeed the last – to blur the battle lines in this literary conflict, either by asserting that Zola harboured a covert idealist sensibility or by calling into question Zola's portrait of his adversary. 'Is it not possible that he is often taking aim at imaginary enemies?' mused Brunetière in his riposte to Zola's aesthetic manifesto, *Le Roman expérimental*.[16] Zola's various definitions of idealism were, the critic objected, not only nonsensical, they failed to map onto the idealist novels he censured. No doubt caricature prevailed, as Zola erected a 'straw' idealism to suit his own agendas.[17]

The aim of this chapter is not to test the legitimacy (or otherwise) of Zola's vision of idealism, but rather to make a case for understanding the quarrel between naturalism and its rival aesthetic as fundamental to the evolution of the novel at the end of the nineteenth century. For where much critical energy has been spent dislodging the idea of naturalism (and realism, more broadly) as modernism's opposite, what has often been overlooked is just how idealism instead tended to function in that role – and by the 1880s, in ways that were made fully explicit. This, we saw in the Introduction, is the thrust of Toril Moi's positing of idealism as the hegemonic aesthetic mode against which naturalism, especially, determines its agendas. In fact, as Simon Joyce suggests, glossing Moi, 'it might be seen that naturalism and modernism converge, at least on the philosophical ground of a shared anti-idealism'.[18] What, then, I want to ask here, can a close attention to this form of binary thinking, which dominated critical discourse of the last decades of the century, tell us about the constitutive importance of idealism to the naturalist self-image? How did this relationship of mutual animosity and dependence belie Zola's strategic repudiations of his idealist counterparts? And how, and to what end, was Zola's anti-idealist campaign always already being deconstructed?

Accordingly, the chapter begins by setting out some of the key charges against idealism that Zola formulated, for the most part across a series of polemical articles penned around 1880. In placing idealism 'on trial' – to recall the subtitle of this book – Zola sought to justify, by distinction, naturalism's ethical, political, and aesthetic superiority. The second half of the chapter de-centres Zola's own vision of this quarrel, by surveying the wider, shifting literary field towards the end of the nineteenth century. First, I explore a previously unexamined thread of literary criticism from the 1880s and 1890s that sought to trouble the antagonisms Zola established, precisely by claiming to determine in the naturalist author's writing a reverse idealist tendency, 'un idéalisme à rebours'. I then describe the so-called idealist reaction that took hold in the late 1880s and which claimed to seek a way out of the perceived impasse of naturalist dominance. Here, the struggle Zola had staged at the beginning of the decade was further recast by his adversaries to encompass, under the aegis of idealism, a host of rising aesthetic trends, from Symbolism to the psychological novel. Zola found himself bound, as we shall see, to negotiate with other imposing visions of the future of literary fiction and to at least contemplate ways of adapting to the demands of a younger generation. At the close, we will gesture towards the shifting ideological grounds of antinaturalist critique, when Zola's intervention in the Dreyfus Affair reignited longstanding hostilities.

Philosophical Differences

However diffuse, or implicit, an individual writer's own intellectual convictions, 'at the heart of literary quarrels', Zola opined, 'there is always a philosophical question'.[19] Across the combative essays that made up *Le Roman expérimental*, Zola sketched out just what those base philosophical ideas at stake in literary differences might be; and his arguments hinged on a schematic, often caricaturally overdetermined, vision of romanticism and naturalism as divergent intellectual traditions. Both movements, Zola claimed, are born of 'the great philosophical movement' of the Enlightenment: its return to nature, its war on conventions, its mistrust of intellectual abstractions.[20] But in the grand, intellectual family tree Zola conjures up, they descend from different ancestors: the pantheist Rousseau is 'father of the romantics', his first daughter Sand, and his first son Chateaubriand, who in turn 'gave birth to Hugo'; the materialist Diderot is 'the real forefather of the naturalists', whose firstborn Stendhal cultivated an analytical style that Balzac would take over in turn.[21] Of course, Zola proudly asserted the superiority of the latter philosophical lineage – 'Diderot, especially, remains the great figure of the century' – and, in turn, the crushing dominance of its naturalist progeniture, whose writing is held to be the very expression of 'a century of science that believes in facts alone'.[22]

Indeed, Zola tied the naturalist project to contemporary iterations of what he termed retrospectively, or anachronistically, Diderot's 'positivist' spirit, after the philosophy of Auguste Comte. Zola did not engage with Comte's thought directly, but instead, as Roger Ripoll explains, drew his working definitions from Émile Littré, who had popularised Comte's writing and whom the novelist casts as 'a new type of intellectual hero'.[23] In his article 'Hugo et Littré', Zola raised the lexicographer and philosopher above the totemic Victor Hugo as 'the man of the century', insofar as 'he embodied its need for scientific certainty and worked with all his might to supplant old theological and romantic methods with a positivist one'.[24] The particularities of Comtean thought aside, what mattered most to Zola was its refusal of metaphysical speculation as well as the spirit of rigorous scepticism it inspired; and he used the term 'positivism' loosely – sometimes interchangeably with 'materialism' – to describe his unwavering intellectual commitment to rationality and scrupulous observation as the only legitimate means of understanding the world.[25]

Arguably, what distinguished romantic and naturalist philosophies of literature, above all, in Zola's account, was their respective relationships to the ideal. For naturalists, Zola was emphatic: bound to record observable and experiential phenomena, 'the ideal is, if not eliminated, at least set aside'.[26] Romantics, meanwhile, had taken over Rousseau's deism and remained wedded to metaphysics: 'they retain an absolute and an ideal. The rigid dogmas of Catholicism are no more. Instead, there is a hazy kind of heresy, the lyrical heresy of Hugo and Renan, who put God at once everywhere and nowhere'.[27] In this instance, the ideal appears as a byword for a new kind of religion. But across his theoretical writing, Zola fully exploits the indeterminacy, and sheer capaciousness, of a term that – drained of philosophical specificity – is made to represent the unknown, the obscure, the irrational, the supernatural, the mysterious, the occult, the speculative, the hypothetical, the indeterminate, the suprasensible, the dangerous lure of the abstract, the dogmatic, the ill-defined. In short, the ideal becomes, in Zola's hands, precisely de-idealised, cut adrift from its predominant associations with the aspirational and recoded as a kind of simulacrum. From here, the elimination, or sidelining, of the ideal can be cast as the very founding gesture of the naturalist writer; and Zola can establish his 'experimental' method of knowledge production, famously inspired by the physiologist Claude Bernard, as an aggressive counter-idealism:

> All that we do not know, all that still escapes us, that is the ideal; and the point of our human endeavour is to reduce the ideal, day by day, and to capture truth from the unknown. We are all idealists, if we take this to

> mean that we are all busying ourselves with the ideal. Only I call 'idealists' those who take refuge in the unknown for the sheer pleasure of it – those with a taste for only the most dubious hypotheses.[28]

To the extent that naturalism was to engage with the ideal, it was either as a problem to which the experimental novelist would seek a solution or – in Zola's favoured geopolitical language – as terrain to be conquered: 'As science advances, the ideal must retreat.'[29] Idealists, on Zola's terms, wilfully embrace those 'mysterious forces outside of the determinism of phenomena', precisely on the grounds that the unknown is more beautiful or more noble.[30] Naturalists remain soberly preoccupied with 'what is', taking the ideal as an object of investigation, an unknown to be explained, rather than as an accepted principle: 'Our quarrel with the idealists', Zola reflected, 'lies solely in the fact that we start out from observation and experience, whereas they start out from an absolute'.[31] As such, the laws of nature – or what Zola calls 'the unknown of the *how*' – are the experimental novelist's exclusive domain, while the idealist remains tied up in irresolvable, and ultimately futile, conjectures about 'this unknown of the *why*'.[32]

In effect, Zola was adapting the version of positivism that Hippolyte Taine, his former *maître à penser*, had put forth in *Les Philosophes français du XIXᵉ siècle* (1857):

> Positivists [...] declare to know nothing about how life or the universe came about. They simply record the amount and the direction of chemical reactions and physical actions that constitute our existence, and gather together the experimental laws that encapsulate all the observed facts in our universe.[33]

What Zola finds in Bernard's *Introduction à l'étude de la médecine expérimentale* (1865) is an authoritative case for this kind of investigative, or anti-hypothetical, method – and one which asserted its own independence from all medical and philosophical doctrines in a way that appealed to Zola's vision of naturalism as a practice, rather than a school. Indeed, Bernard's declared suspicion of philosophical systems – even of philosophy altogether, and its 'intellectual gymnastics' – clearly spoke to Zola's own desire to extricate the novel from its ties to the metaphysical and theological a priori. 'Never before have philosophers been told so eloquently that their hypotheses are pure poetry.'[34] Scientific experimentation, of the kind Zola claims to adapt to the naturalist novel, promises to recapture the domain of speculation. Put differently, Zola casts philosophy as, by definition, a form of idealism, and the scientific method itself as a kind of anti-philosophy.

Emerging from the writer's polemic is, then, the assertion of naturalism as a distinctive style of thought and intellectual praxis – one wedded, above all, to a strict sense of pragmatism, application, and purpose. In turn, we shall now find, these claims could be extrapolated to the realm of politics, whereby differences of philosophical and aesthetic disposition would be held to explain the state of the nation.

Zola's Republic

On 20 April 1879, Zola delivered to the readers of *Le Figaro* – we saw in the Introduction – a national ultimatum: 'the Republic will be naturalist, or it will not be'.[35] In his 'Lettre à la jeunesse', published a month later, Zola further schematised the survey of contemporary politics with which he propped up his appeal, by spelling out in full the dangers of idealism for the Republic. The letter was conceived as a response to two recent events: the revival of Hugo's *Ruy Blas* at the Comédie-Française, performed to much acclaim on 4 April 1879; and Ernest Renan's admission to the Académie the day before, where he took up the vacant seat of Zola's much-admired Claude Bernard. The coincidence of those two events had been described by one journalist as 'poetry's revenge on the scientific spirit', auguring the imminent defeat of those who had boldly, if naively, declared 'war on the ideal'.[36] No such thing, retorted Zola, for whom these twin episodes were less a victory than a spur to consider the future of a nation at the crossroads: France's youth must choose carefully between 'the way of idealism' and 'the way of naturalism' (366). These paths are signposted by intellectual role models: Hugo and Renan, one way; 'the lofty, stern figure of Claude Bernard' (358) the other. For although, as Robert D. Priest explains, the left-wing press had declared Renan's election to the Académie 'a victory over the clergy', a new generation – to which Zola spoke – was 'dubious about Renan's status as a scientific icon'.[37] Zola himself was at pains to distinguish between 'the Renan of legend' and the 'Renan of reality'. The former's sceptical, even sacrilegious, best-selling history *Vie de Jésus* (1863) turned him into a controversial critical thinker, a symbol of 'science killing faith'.[38] The latter, Zola insisted, had never really left his faith behind, despite abandoning the priesthood as a young adult. For all that Renan extolled the life and work of Bernard in his reception speech, then, his own lyrical account of modern science revealed an entirely different thinker: 'he accepts scientific discoveries in the fashion of a versatile idealist, who uses everything he can to pursue and expand his dreams'.[39] For Zola, Renan's 'repressed' beliefs and contemplative temperament had simply found another outlet: poetry.

What Zola determined in these opposing role models were two types of patriotism: one idealist, nostalgic, lyrical, effeminate; the other naturalist, virile, prospective. The former is pure declamation, or 'lyrical madness' (351), tied to the romantic strain of bombast, posturing, and outlandish invention that he derides in *Ruy Blas*: 'it involves nothing but [. . .] a rhetorical form of virtue and honour. [. . .] Theirs are puffed up words, bursting underneath the elaborate excesses of the idea' (352). Such flights of rhetoric inspired the (misplaced) nationalist pride with which Renan had schmoozed the Académie, exalting the refined Gallic spirit – in Renan's own words, 'our old French society, so brilliant, so polished, so eager to please' – over the dreary temperament and 'unintelligent materialism' of their Prussian victors.[40] To believe in France's all-conquering charm is, Zola warned, no road back to former imperial glories: 'these are but beautiful, nervous emotions [. . .]. Today we need the virility of the true in order to be glorious in the future, just as we have been in the past' (350). France must acknowledge, with sobriety, that it had been outmanoeuvred precisely by the very pedantic science and muted military generals Renan caricatured – in short, by what he called the 'scientific formula' (363) with which the Prussians had transformed their own 'art' of war. Anti-rhetorical, dispassionate, calculated, analytical, logical: Zola extolled, in Brian Nelson's words, a 'technocratic form of government', and in turn a vision of France as a leading light in modern Europe (even as 'a beacon illuminating the world'), its politics rooted, Zola put it elsewhere, 'in reason and a precise knowledge of the nation's needs'.[41] Indeed, it was on this, he concluded, that the *revanchiste* dream of taking back Alsace-Lorraine would depend.

The ultimatum Zola issued over the direction of the nation's future was clearly framed by his understanding of political history – namely, the mistakes that had been made with France's two previous attempts at becoming a Republic. The truth about the Second Empire, Zola declared, was that it owed its existence to a Republican regime that had imploded, propped up as it had been on rhetoric and good intentions, rather than actions:

> Never did it have a clear idea of the France it wished to govern. It sought to experiment on her as upon a dead body. Certainly, the words were splendid: liberty, equality, fraternity, virtue, honor, patriotism. But they were just words, and in order to govern, acts were needed.[42]

The likes of Hugo, Alphonse de Lamartine, and Sand provided the Republic with its lyrical imagination and its blind optimism, extolling those worthy ideas that Zola insistently qualifies as 'romantic', and which frequently find themselves condensed in the figure of the 'humanitarian dream'.[43] Of course, Zola's derisive association of idealism and romanticism with 1848 was less idiosyncratic obsession than conventional wisdom by the time of writing. But Zola nevertheless did more than most to theorise the failure of the Republic as a specifically philosophical problem – one which rested on what we might call the 'apriorism' at work in idealist thought altogether, whereby principles precede experience and analysis. In those heady days of revolutionary ferment, politicians applied a formula for republicanism to an entirely theoretical version of the nation, to 'pure abstractions tailored to an ideal'.[44] For to deal in abstract dogma, absolutes or ideals (all synonyms in Zola's discourse on politics) is to posit, even to demand, a people that does not exist: 'you cannot turn a people into an equation'.[45] If the endeavour was ill-fated, as the First Republic had been, it was, Zola made clear, because of a failure to take into account 'that terrible human element' – the customs, environment, and caprices of a population, that is, which disrupt any given formula or doctrine. Indeed, the Terror figures in Zola's theory of political history as the logical end-point of the particular strain he calls Republican fanaticism, and whose advocates are invariably desperate 'to enjoy the ideal state they dream about', prepared to purge man of his past, his blood, crush his obstinate dispositions, in the vain hope of seeing a nation transformed overnight.[46] For the fanatical Republican shares with the romantic Republican, in Zola's typology, a belief in the quasi-divine right of the Republican state, its figurehead 'God the Father wearing a Phrygian cap, bathed in sunlight' (499). This is what Zola invites us to think of, with a deliberate sense of paradox, as an absolute Republic.

According to Zola's political philosophy, the opposite of ideals are facts; and it is precisely as 'the man of facts' that the naturalist Republican engages in what the novelist calls 'experimental politics'. This Zola defines as an inductive model of observation, whereby laws are extracted from experience, 'without forcing them to bend to some ideal or other'.[47] The naturalist Republican is patient, pragmatic, reasonable: he accepts that the nation has a life of its own and that the Republic will depend on the gradual evolution of mentalities. Zola derides in the romantic Republican, then, precisely his counterfactual imagination – the longing, that is, to abstract from the nation *as it is* a speculative version of what it might be (or indeed, might have been); to behave *as though* ('*comme si*', Zola repeats) the facts were different.[48] We shall see in Chapter 2 how Zola establishes an important kinship between the romantic Republican and the radical socialist, both of whom, he implies, not only stoke the imagination of their public with dreams of an implausible, even impossible, future but are also prone to base their politics on an idea of a people that does not exist.

Such suspicions had already been integral to the defence Zola mounted against critics of *L'Assommoir*, who claimed that the writer's brutal representation of the working classes was incompatible with his Republican sympathies. On the contrary, Zola claimed – setting out in miniature his campaign to follow – the novel was meant to counter precisely the strain of romantic, or idealist, political thinking that would wish away the facts and, in turn, threaten the Republic: 'Idealist politicians play the role of the doctor who would rather gloss over his patients' suffering. I have chosen to display that suffering.'[49] This concept of an idealist politics will run through our discussion of Zola's second novel of the people, *Germinal*, and its pastiche of utopian socialism. But what we might simply note here is how versatile the category appears across Zola's political commentary, applied as it is to a motley band of figures on the Left: from 'romantic' Republicans to Communards. (The latter Zola described in his reporting on the 1871 uprising as 'idealist revolutionaries, moralists with a nebulous set of beliefs').[50] Two decades later, Zola claimed to find in a burgeoning anarchist movement an expression of the same political imagination: 'The dark dream of the destroyers will always exist alongside the blue dream of the idealists. Both are born of one and the same need.'[51] The disparate content of those respective dreams aside (the apocalyptic and the fairytale), what mattered was their shared idealism; and this represented, first and foremost, for Zola, a *form* of political thought – impatient, impulsive, poetic. For, as we shall see throughout this book, Zola's interventions on politics necessarily lead back to questions of style and (literary) vision. What we are calling the 'aesthetics of politics' that Zola sets out is to be understood not simply as a rhetorical flourish or an adornment of the political, but as a systematic appeal to a host of existing (legitimate or illegitimate) aesthetic tastes and practices that determine the public's engagement with political ideas and possibilities. Indeed, political problems, of the kind we broach in Chapter 5 on the Dreyfus Affair, are shown to be rooted in an aesthetic imagination; and their solution demands nothing other than a refashioning of our expectations, as readers, about plausibility and plot, character types and endings – in short, of our own literary pleasures.

The Case Against

So far, we have broached the ways in which Zola establishes naturalism as a broadly anti-idealist intellectual and political project. At this point, I want to distil some of the charges Zola levelled at the idealist aesthetic specifically, often, though not always, in a spirit of counter-attack against anti-naturalist critique. First, *idealist literature is not morally uplifting*. Zola delighted in turning those admonishments of naturalism's purported immorality back onto his idealist adversaries, whose fictions of chastity, duty, decency, and *pudeur* were not only, he claimed, the means with which a middling writer could push open the doors of the Académie, they inspired in their reader little more than the ritual performance of virtue. Likened to the non-practicing Catholic, the idealist writer is charged with hypocrisy; his worthy idealism in fact veiled – this was one of Zola's favourite metaphors – the most sordid licentiousness:

> For these people, the ideal is a veil behind which anything is permitted. When the curtains of the ideal are drawn, when the candle of truth is blown out, [...] they light up the darkness with their filthy revelries.[52]

Here we have the master image of Zola's anti-idealist diatribe, whereby suspicions about aesthetics are rehearsed, almost exclusively, in terms of sexual ethics. In contrast to the exhibitionist imperative of naturalist fiction, the idealist novel 'polices' its subjects in the name of propriety, only the better to charm or seduce its impressionable (female) reader. Like Flaubert, and Maupassant after him, Zola determines in idealist fiction a precisely inverse correlation between the lofty virtues it declares and the latent desires or covert fantasies it excites: 'The ideal is the root of all dangerous reveries. It is the ideal that throws young women into the arms of a stranger; it is the ideal that creates the adulteress.'[53] In this respect, Zola was no doubt conjuring up that archetypal victim of romantic literature, Flaubert's Emma Bovary, whose taste for Lamartine, Sand, and Walter Scott arouses her own ill-fated, 'mimetic desires'.[54] We shall see in Chapter 3 how Zola imputed to the woman writer Sand, in particular, the responsibility for having created 'a generation of insufferable dreamers [*rêveuses*]', her idealist fiction, I argue, the unacknowledged model for Angélique's dream of the sublime.[55] But what we might note here is that, in seeking to denounce, even proscribe, this kind of perilously seductive day-dreaming, the naturalist novel clearly assigned to itself a superior moral purpose; anti-idealism, on Zola's terms, was nothing if not salutary.

In fact, Zola's attacks on the duplicity of the idealist novel are invariably the prelude to his claims about naturalism's own high-mindedness. The naturalist writer may refuse to censor or embellish the world, his uncompromising truth-telling is, in fact, the very condition of the novel's moral rectitude:

> If the spectacle of debauchery for debauchery's sake is an abominable thing, the precise examination of passionate desire – even taken to bloody extremes – assumes a high moral character when it provides the certain facts of an experiment, and when it becomes a document that criminalists and legislators must take into account.[56]

Zola takes over the realist, and specifically Flaubertian, rhetoric of impartial description all the better to assert naturalism's ultimate ethical utility or practical value. Far from falling foul of the law, their sincere records of the world, however obscene, should command the attention of the legislator, whose own job it is to promote the good and 'wrestle with evil, in order to eradicate and destroy it'.[57] We shall return to Zola's handling of the relationship between the truth and the law in Chapter 5, as part of our analysis of *Vérité*. For there, in the crucible of the Dreyfus Affair, Zola forges an ethical vision of truth-telling that goes beyond the courtroom, and which is tied to his later fiction's prescriptive purpose. For now, we might simply note that Zola couches naturalist fiction's claims to the moral high ground, at this point in his critical writing, in precisely the kind of prospective, even utopian, terms that would become the bread and butter of his final series. For it is as experimental moralists, he claimed, that naturalist novelists participate in the grand mission of turning observations into the known constants that will guide the beneficent master of the future: 'we shall enter a century in which man, all-powerful, will dominate nature and make use of its laws to bring about the greatest possible amount of justice and freedom on this earth'.[58]

Here, then, we find the roots of what we will come to call, with a full sense of contradiction, the *anti-idealist idealism* at work in Zola's later fiction – a superior species of idealism, and indeed the only kind he could allow. Certainly, Zola's foundational claims for an ethics of the naturalist novel are contained in these retaliations against the pseudo-moralising objections of his adversaries – those, like Louis Ulbach, who determined in Zola's lascivious portrait of Nana the symptoms of a pathological imagination that had much in common with the Marquis de Sade.[59] In 'De la moralité dans la littérature', Zola deflected this charge of naturalism's pornographic bent by redescribing Sade – in perhaps one of the worst epithets he could muster – precisely as an 'idealist' (!).[60] If Sade's legacy was anywhere to be seen, Zola ventured, it was in the extravagant imagination of his adversaries (Sade's 'direct descendents'), and most conspicuously, Zola's long-time antagonist, Barbey d'Aurevilly, whose romanticised version of satanic eroticism amounted to a kind of 'Marquis de Sade for polite society' (823). In painting Sade as both an 'inverted Catholic' and 'an exasperated romantic', Zola drew a direct line to Barbey, whose own perverted Catholicism offered fertile ground for libertine pleasures – the kind of purposeless obscenity, that is, of which Zola stood accused. In an audacious inversion, Sade's diabolical vision emerges in Zola's account as a kind of idealism *in extremis*: the spectacle of filth, shorn of an alibi, is said to be the idealist novel's original, unacknowledged fantasy.

Such connections, we must admit, are at the very least counterintuitive. And yet, they epitomise most plainly Zola's diagnostic reading of idealist literature as saturated by latent impulses. In reaching for a sublimated form of sexual desire – its fetishisation of virginity was emblematic – idealism fed the most transgressive kinds of eroticism. Of course, Zola's account of the novel's seductive duplicity stood as a straightforward moral reproach. But it also entailed another important concern about the relationship between desire and aesthetics, since *idealism was*, Zola maintained, *an art of sterility*. Most obviously, this related to the sexual ethics at stake in the literature Zola targeted. For what idealism tended neither to capture nor to promote were the virtues of reproductive sexuality, which fell between its twin poles of abstinence and degradation. Zola rehearsed this perverse vision of eroticism again and again in his fiction, where it was tied, most prominently in *La Faute de l'Abbé Mouret* (1875), to his indictment of Catholicism as a kind of death cult: a dramatic struggle between the pulsating drive of 'life' (nature, vegetation, impulse) and the mortifying draw of the religious ideal (celibacy). Elsewhere, in *Le Ventre de Paris* (1873), Zola imagined his utopian dreamer Florent emasculated by his political flights of fancy, or ideas: 'too much of his virility was expended in dreams'.[61] But the charge of infertility was also aimed at the idealist conception of art itself as, in Sophie Guermès's terms, 'a substitute religion'.[62] Rarely is this more conspicuously captured than in Zola's art novel, *L'Œuvre* (1886) – for which, in fact, 'L'Idéal' was one of the sixty-five titles the author considered – when the artist Claude Lantier produces *L'Enfant mort*, a grisly portrait of his own deceased child, who has suffered from parental neglect. Lantier's obsession with capturing the ideal or absolute has entailed, Zola makes clear, an unethical disregard for the real; and the child, as a rival figure of (pro)creation, is the paradigmatic victim.

In his address 'À la jeunesse', published in *Le Figaro* on 7 February 1895, these twin concerns about sex and aesthetics acquired a proper political edge. For while France's declining birth rate was, Zola claimed, no doubt the result of a rise in non-reproductive sexual practices – what he euphemistically calls 'the love which produces no children' (whether hetero- or homosexual) – these tendencies were themselves owing to the deleterious influence of intellectual and literary tastes on contemporary French morals.[63] A few weeks later, in an article on 'Dépopulation' (*Le Figaro*, 23 May 1896), Zola singled out Schopenhauer and Wagner for their nefarious sway over young minds. While the philosopher inspired 'lovers of the void' [*les amoureux du néant*] with his anti-life pessimism, the composer exalted a cult of virginity, which turned sex into a purely sublimated thought experiment: 'The only intercourse is of the cerebral kind; giving birth is but the result of communing souls.' Whether Zola inveighed against Decadence, Symbolism, or the mondain psychological novel, it became clear, as Andrew J. Counter has argued, that he understood 'depopulation as an *aesthetic* problem, [...] as a phenomenon rooted in the domain of art and, especially literature, and consequently demanding an artistic solution'.[64] Indeed, we might add, anti-natalism was cast specifically as a problem rooted in, and exacerbated by, idealism in its diverse philosophical and aesthetic forms – 'this idealism that lapses so easily into the worst perversions, the most pernicious social dangers'.[65]

In his paean to family values *Fécondité* (1899) – his most direct attempt to imagine a 'solution' to the nation's population problem – Zola took aim at precisely the kind of idealist novel that was bound, in Seillan's words, to 'eliminate the child'.[66] Zola's Catholic novelist Charles Santerre – a figure seemingly inspired by Bourget – stands as a foil to the naturalist writer and a pastiche of the kind of idealist sensibility Zola identified in his Decadent and Symbolist counterparts. Having specialised in novels of adultery ('infertile love that never produced offspring'), Santerre's latest work, *L'Impérissable Beauté*, offered up a melding of romance and *roman d'artiste*, which instead privileged a sublimated form of fruitless passion:

> He told the fine story of a certain countess, Anne-Marie, who, in order to escape a brutish husband – a virile, child-producing male – took refuge in Brittany with a young artist, Norbert. Graced with divine inspiration, he had undertaken to decorate a convent chapel with paintings of his visions. For thirty years, he pursued this project, his poignant artistry like a colloquy with the angels. The story told of nothing but those thirty years spent in Anne-Marie's arms, of a communion of sterile caresses. Her feminine beauty remained untouched by a single wrinkle: she was as young and fresh after those thirty years of infertility as she had been the very first day they fell in love.[67]

Santerre's heroine Anne-Marie – the onomastic mirror-image of Zola's exceptionally prolific child bearer, Marianne – is precisely the antithesis to

Zola's thesis: a mondain version of the fetishised Virgin Mary who represents, for the fictional novelist, 'the ideal of womanhood, the ideal of motherhood itself' (45), the mother, that is, who doesn't have to fall. As the novel spirals *en abyme*, the sexual politics of the idealist aesthetic become ineluctably clear: the anti-mimetic project, encapsulated in the decorative fresco of Zola's would-be Michaelangelo, is strictly tied to the non-reproductive, or purposeless, sexuality of the artist. Without children, Anne-Marie becomes a still life in a romance that is, as Zola's parodic summary implies, ultimately plotless.

That Zola chose a painter to capture, in miniature, the aesthetic he pastiches in the novel is unsurprising given how often his indictments of the 'beau idéal' applied to the visual arts – and specifically, to academic painting. In fact, as Florence Beillacou suggests, Zola's censures of idealist literature and art tend to work by analogy with one another: 'he criticises [...] idealist writers by comparing them to bad painters, whereas idealist painters are described as bad writers'.[68] In *Mon Salon* (1866), Zola took aim at those literary-idealist painters, '[who] have thrown themselves into the dream, into a tawdry heaven, all glitter and silk', adding that '[o]ur artists are poets. [...] Look at the Salon: it is nothing but verses and madrigals.'[69] Academic painters, Zola lamented, had come to privilege stories and ideas, odes and fables, over colours and forms; and the very literariness of their canvases was symptomatic of their slavish reproduction of a classical ideal:

> The great artists of the Renaissance started out by learning how to crush pigments. Nowadays, things happen differently: painters first learn the ideal; then, when they have been thoroughly taught the classical ideal, they begin to daub colour onto a canvas, tending to the subject, careful only to make sure that the execution is immaculate.[70]

Putting subject before form, and abstract type, or 'absolute', before material incarnation, academic painting (albeit with some exceptions) emblematised precisely the idealist model Zola derided elsewhere. The quest for aesthetic perfection, according to certain physical or metaphysical conventions, not only involved a grotesque denial of human touch and experience, it was another form of religious devotion – art as idol: 'absolute perfection [...] is but the material expression of a divinity dreamed of and worshipped by men'.[71]

And yet, the recurring irony in Zola's reflections on academic idealism is that the pursuit of an absolute almost invariably collapses into kitsch, feeding the public's appetite for 'a trumpery heaven, with celestial paintings and superhuman abstractions'.[72] For all its elitist pretensions, in other words: *idealism is tasteless, fake, phony, inauthentic*; its fantasy of ideal beauty is always prone to fall into mere embellishment. Zola conjured with this critique via his painter Luigi Pozzo in *Son Excellence Eugène Rougon* (1876), whose portrait of Clorinde posing as the mythical Diana appeals to the philistine tastes of his audience: 'her face beamed with a pretty, doll-like smile, with curved lips, arched eyebrows, and glowing soft-red cheeks. It was a Diana, fit to adorn a tin of pastilles'.[73] If the ideal, precisely by definition, cannot be realised, the art of idealisation, Zola implies, risks becoming an art of infinite copy, its shadowy double the object of mechanical reproduction. This inclination to cliché was one Zola persistently identified in the idealist novel, whose angelic heroines and habitual plot arcs (notably, demanding the ultimate triumph of virtue) appeared endlessly replicable. In objecting to the ubiquitous strategy of idealisation, Zola was not alone. 'For God's sake, show us a heroine who is not splendidly beautiful and fabulously intelligent!', complained Jules Lemaître, in his portrait of Feuillet.[74] In 'Le Naturalisme au théâtre', Zola defended the right of naturalist writers to eschew this kind of characterisation *sur mesure*, 'likable characters, ideal conceptions of man and woman', in favour of an impartial vision of human nature.[75] Of course, to cast the delicate vessels of idealist literature as types and tropes was to offer a riposte to that most well-rehearsed of antinaturalist critiques: namely, that the naturalist novelist was exclusively preoccupied with matters of physiology and environment, and therefore incapable of producing characters of moral or psychological depth. As we shall see in Chapter 3, Zola's detractors lamented what they saw as the lack of dualism in the naturalist novel, its refusal to undertake, in Zola's own words, 'the study of the soul, as a separate entity'.[76]

Take, as a salient example of this attitude, Brunetière's 1885 statement article for the *Revue des Deux Mondes*, 'L'Idéalisme dans le roman'. Against the noise generated by the publication in book form of *Germinal* just two months earlier, Brunetière celebrated two new editions of Feuillet's best-selling novels; and he did so by reiterating the superior psychological interest the idealist writer's (well-born) protagonists represented, over and above those of his (more lowly) realist and naturalist counterparts. 'Charles Bovary, but especially Catherine Maheu', Brunetière opined, 'are unworthy subjects for observation; they are all too quickly and easily laid bare; their actions are too simple, and the motives dictating them simpler still'.[77] Zola and Flaubert's democratisation of literary fiction could only offer a superficial exploration of the human character, let alone afford the kind of readerly pleasure and escape from banality that the likes of

Brunetière ascribed to art in general – art that was, he claimed, 'aristocratic in essence'.[78] In effect, the antinaturalist critic was openly assuming the charge against writers like Feuillet that Zola had broached in different forms: *idealism is classist, even anti-democratic*. For Zola had long targeted what he dubbed 'the school of beauty' (to which he no doubt saw Feuillet belonging), and which was destined to appeal to ladies of high society who treat their books like fashionable ornaments or saccharine treats: 'ladies sip the sugary water offered up by a refined novelist, into which he has poured with gloved hand, and in an act of daring excess, three drops of orange blossom water'.[79] In Brunetière's hands, this vision of aristocratic leisure is recoded as the condition of the idealist novel's psychological and ethical complexity, its characters at least sufficiently educated and exempt from material hardship to cultivate feelings of conscience, virtue, and honour. For Zola, of course, such elitism was not only risible, it would simply not survive the shift to an enduring age of Republic, the best literature of which would body forth a mass politics of cultural representation befitting its democratic aspirations. If anything, though, the claims of critics like Brunetière set out openly the terms of a quarrel that would continue to hinge, over the following decade, on issues of distinction, legitimacy, taste, pleasure, and freedom that had as much to do with class as aesthetics.

Zola à rebours

While by no means exhaustive, the key principles of Zola's anti-idealism that we have adumbrated here give a sense of just how the author sought to assert the superiority of naturalism on stylistic, ethical, and political grounds. What we shall trace in the next part of this chapter is an attempt, on the part of Zola's critics, to trouble the very foundations of the writer's quarrel with idealism, by refocusing naturalism in turn as a form and practice that was not simply at war, but also, whether it knew it or not, itself somehow conflicted – as constituting, that is, precisely an idealism *à rebours*.[80]

The emergence of this particular thread of literary metadiscourse coincided with a broader shift in appreciations of naturalism in the mid-1880s, when, especially in the wake of the publication of *Germinal*, numerous commentaries on the novel betrayed, as Alain Pagès has noted, 'a critical motif revolving around the idea of Zola as a poet', and an idealist one at that.[81] If it was by no means the first time that critics had discerned in the writer a certain lyricism – and one that appeared to exceed naturalism's declared objectives – this reading of Zola was constituted in the wake of *Germinal* as a common thesis. Gustave Geoffroy captured the spirit of such critiques when he determined in the hallucinatory quality, the cadences, the rhythms of Zola's mining novel 'the poet that people generally refuse to see, the pantheist poet who lavishly enhances and idealises things'.[82] But it was Jules Lemaître's substantial review of *Germinal* for the *Revue politique et littéraire*, published on 14 March 1885, that had set the tone. There, the critic insisted on the disjunction between Zola's understanding of his naturalist principles and the aesthetic strategies he deployed in practice; indeed, he established the image of the writer as at odds with himself – even in some sense opaque to himself:

> M. Zola is not [...] a 'naturalist' novelist in the sense he understands it. Rather M. Zola is an epic poet and a pessimistic poet. [...] By poet I mean a writer who, in accordance with an idea or in pursuit of an ideal, substantially transforms reality and brings it, newly modified, to life. By this definition, many novelists and playwrights are, then, poets. But *what's interesting is that M. Zola denies this, and yet he is more of a poet than anyone else.* [...] M. Zola invents much more than he observes; he is truly a poet, if we take the word in its etymological sense, which is somewhat crude – and *an idealist poet, if we take the word in the opposite sense to its usual meaning [au rebours de son sens habituel].*[83]

Lemaître's vision of Zola as a reverse idealist is thus tied to a wider interrogation of the naturalist novelist's mimetic claims. In the service of a single idea – namely, that of man's ugliness and animality – the writer transforms reality through selection, simplification, exaggeration, and subtraction: 'it is [the animal] that he likes to put on show, and the rest he eliminates, in the opposite way [*au rebours*] to actual idealist novelists' (255). Privileging invention over observation, Zola thus produces a curious idealism of the coarse, lowly, or 'grossier'.

With these claims, Lemaître effectively extended the account Remy de Gourmont had given of naturalism, three years prior, as a reverse form of aestheticism: 'M. Zola likes ugliness for ugliness's sake.' Naturalist novelists may aspire to the status of the photographer – to record, that is, 'without prejudice or omissions, disinterestedly and with ruthless impartiality' – they ultimately produce, Gourmont argued, inversions of the real, or to extend his pictorial metaphor, negatives: these are 'photographers who, unlike [*au rebours de*] their counterparts in the darkroom, make objects uglier'.[84] Crystallised in Gourmont and Lemaître's respective visions of naturalist fiction, then, is the following paradox: Zola takes up an art of idealisation that is, crucially, devoid of an ideal. Their diagnoses resonated throughout critical discourse of the 1880s and early 1890s, with several commentators deploying the same vocabulary, often barely modified, of – in the philosopher Jean-Marie Guyau's words – an 'inverted idealism' [*idéalisme retourné*].[85] In fact, in his *L'Art au point de vue socio-logique* (1889), Guyau described, in precisely Lemaîtrian terms, the natur-alist writer's (mis)appropriation of idealist aesthetic strategies:

> Now, it is not difficult to show that every false realist practices a reverse idealism [fait de l'idéalisme à rebours]. The process of simplification, abstraction, and absolute generalisation, which characterises classical *ideals*, [...] is the very process of contemporary naturalism. Only, instead of eliminating visible *ugliness*, in the manner of classical idealists, they elimin-ate visible beauty, or simply all that is intellectual and *psychological*, so that only the bestial and material is left.[86]

In his *Mouvement littéraire au XIXᵉ siècle*, published the same year, the critic Georges Pellissier identified in Zola specifically just such 'an unstop-pable drive toward idealisation and synthesis', his imagination prone to enlarge, exaggerate, or disfigure both people and things to the point at which they acquire 'a mysterious existence'.[87]

These assertions of naturalism's unavowed idealist impulse were no doubt rooted in Taine's influential aesthetic thought, in particular, those lectures at the École des Beaux-Arts he published as *Philosophie de l'art* (1865) and *De l'Idéal dans l'art* (1867). According to Taine's definition of the work of art, every aesthetic representation involves the transformation of its object, insofar as 'its aim is to make manifest some essential or prominent characteristic, and this more completely and more clearly than is the case for real objects'.[88] This was, in fact, a definition that appealed to Zola, who offered the following commentary in his 1866 article on Taine (and which he subsequently included in *Mes Haines*):

> What the professor calls an 'essential character' is nothing other than what dogmatists term 'the ideal'; only, the essential character is an ideal of beauty or ugliness, the prominent feature of any magnified object as it is inter-preted by the artist's temperament.[89]

Zola thus found in Taine's language of the 'essential' a useful way of sidestepping the overdetermined distinction between the beautiful and the ugly. What matters, above all, is rendering the 'character' of a given object, 'exaggerating one of its prominent features', according to the idea – Zola's favoured term is temperament – of the artist. Effectively, Zola isolates here the first element of what Naomi Schor calls 'Taine's double definition of aesthetic idealism': '*the heightening of the essential* and *the promotion of the higher good*'.[90] In other words, idealisation as an aesthetic practice need not, on Zola's terms, be conjoined with the imperative of instilling in readers an aspiration to moral improvement.

Notably, Taine found in Sand just such a twinning of essentialisation, or hyperbolisation, and ethical purpose, singling her out in *De l'Idéal dans l'art* for her admirable portrayal of 'fine feelings and superior souls'.[91] In fact, as Schor suggests, it is Taine's distinct theory of the ideal in art that allows us to make sense of the celebrated conversation reported to have taken place between Sand and Balzac, the idealist writer and the realist writer, about their own differences. In the account of this that Sand gave in her autobiography, *Histoire de ma vie* (1854–55), Balzac supposedly admitted to the arch-idealist that he too engaged in a kind of idealisation – if only *à rebours*:

> I too like exceptional people; I *am* one. Besides, I need them – in order to set off my vulgar people – and I never sacrifice them if I can help it. But these vulgar people interest me more than they do you. I magnify them; *I idealism them in reverse*, in their ugliness or stupidity. I give their deformities frightening or grotesque proportions.[92]

If the opposition between realist and idealist holds true in their choice of subject, it does not prevail, Balzac states, at the level of method. Beyond their respective inclinations to the ugly and the vulgar, on the hand, and to the beautiful and the pretty, on the other, Balzac claims to share with Sand the same aesthetic imperative: to produce larger-than-life characters, or in Taine's terms, to essentialise. The distinction between (Sand's) positive idealisation and (Balzac's) negative idealisation is thus, in Schor's words, 'one of quality not quantity; it is of a thematic rather than rhetorical order'.[93] According to Balzac, both he and Sand undertake a form of idealisation that stretches, albeit in different directions, the limits of plausibility.

This fragment of Balzacian self-analysis contains in miniature the kind of rhetoric that can be observed in critical discourse on naturalism of the mid-1880s. Consider, for instance, Lemaître's reproach of the style Zola deploys in *Pot-Bouille* (1883): 'Not a single figure free from *hyperbole*, either in its baseness or its banality; [. . .] the smallest details have clearly been *selected* on account of a single, entrenched idea, which is to degrade humankind.'[94] Two months later, in May 1885, Brunetière adopted a similar discourse, reprising this notion of Zola's idealism 'à l'envers', albeit with a certain reluctance:

> I shall not say that, if they [naturalist writers] write, it is so as to teach us that real life is far flatter, more vulgar and pitiful than we have ever known it [. . .]. For if that were the case, it would still be idealism – *reverse idealism* [*de l'idéalisme à rebours*], but idealism all the same, and even the only way they have of understanding idealism: as uglier or more beautiful than nature.[95]

If Brunetière takes up the terms of Lemaître's account, he refuses to collapse the distinction between *idealism* and *idealisation*, the latter (mis)understood by naturalists as nothing more than hyperbolisation, whether positive or negative. For the idealist novel, he insists, always exceeds idealisation; it is distinguished by its charm – what he calls its 'power to please' – as well as by the ideas that underpin it: 'idealism – in the novel as elsewhere – may well amount to having ideas, and naturalism – conversely – in not having any' (224). Irredeemably empty-headed, naturalism does not think; and this explains, for Brunetière, the sheer unreadability of the Zolian text, which takes an absurdly idiotic pleasure in 'the insignificance of the detail': 'You show me a rug in a bedroom, a bed on a rug, a counterpane on the bed, an eiderdown on the counterpane ... whatever next?'[96] If Zola also appears to Brunetière as a poet, then, it is strictly in the crude ('grossier') etymological sense of the word that Lemaître invokes in his own account: that is, as a manual 'maker' (rooted in the Greek *poiein*, to make), or even from the related Sanskrit word, *cinōti*, to arrange or 'pile up'. For Lemaître too, what distinguishes Zola, more than anything, from other writers are precisely his Herculean attempts to describe the world in its minutiae: 'Yes, this artist has a magnificent ability to heap detail upon detail [...] He constructs a book like a mason builds a wall, by piling stones on top of each other.'[97] Zola's descriptive poetics is cast by both critics as a form of alienated, and alienating, labour.

Famously, Zola broached the question of his purported inclination to excessive detail in his letter to Henry Céard of 22 March 1885. Written shortly after the publication of Lemaître's article, Zola's letter appeared to provide a response to the critic, while speaking directly to Céard's own critique of *Germinal*. Zola took up two issues: the first, his supposed abstraction of characters; the second – cited here – that of his poetic temperament:

> The second point concerns my [...] magnification of the truth. You have long known this to be the case. You're not astonished, as others are, to find a poet in me [...]. I exaggerate, that much is certain, *but I do not exaggerate like Balzac, any more than Balzac exaggerates like Hugo*. This is key, the work is in the conditions of the operation. We all lie more or less, but what are the mechanics and the mentality of our lie? Yet – and perhaps I am deceiving myself here – I still believe that my lies serve to advance the truth [*je mens pour mon compte dans le sens de la vérité*]. I am afflicted with an over-developed sense of true-to-life details, leaping towards the stars on the springboard of precise observation. With a beat of its wings, truth rises up to the symbol.[98]

Freely acknowledging his tendency to lyricism, to exaggeration, hyperbolisation, and the magnification of the truth, Zola reformulates here, in all but name, those critiques of his purported '*idéalisme à rebours*'. If every representation is in some sense a lie, Zola remains convinced that his own way of lying is legitimate. His vision of the world may involve hyperbole and distortion, it nevertheless points to the truth. At stake in this avowal, it seems, is an implicit distinction: Zola lies *à rebours de l'idéalisme*, that is, in the opposite direction to an idealist aesthetic that indulges in pure fantasy.

The hallmark of the naturalist aesthetic – its precision in observation – is thus rendered as a 'springboard' [tremplin], in a metaphor that Zola happily borrows from Céard's review of *Germinal*: 'For Zola, facts only exist as springboards [des tremplins] allowing his imagination to reach infinite heights.'[99] It is a figurative analogy that has many possible inter-texts, though none more apt than the (surely incidental) echo of Flaubert's private critique of Zola in his letter to Ivan Turgenev on 8 December 1877. There, Flaubert harnessed precisely the same metaphor to lament Zola's dull, and exasperating, materialism:

> Reality, to my mind, is but a *springboard* [*un tremplin*]. Our friends are persuaded that it alone constitutes all Art! This materialism makes me indignant. – And nearly every Monday, I have a fit of irritation when I read the *feuilletons* of this Zola chap.[100]

Zola's own embellishment of Céard's image thus provides an unwitting riposte to Flaubert's objections. What the naturalist writer diagnoses as his 'hypertrophy of real detail' – that is, a meticulous, almost pathological, attention to the material world – is not an end in itself, but rather the very condition of the elevated figuration, the 'leap towards the stars', to which the artist aspires. Put differently, Zola shares with Flaubert – contrary to the latter's indications – an understanding of the writer's documentary obsession as a necessary springboard. In a letter to Léon Hennique, Flaubert had confided of his mania for documents, information, research: 'Well, I see all that as quite secondary and less important. Material truth (or what counts as such) is only a springboard [*un tremplin*] that helps you to rise higher.'[101] The circulation of this metaphor between Zola and Flaubert – via the reader-critic, Céard – might tell us much about the mutual, and specifically vertical, ambitions of two contemporary writers who were prone to misinterpret one another.

What Flaubert rightly recognised in Zola, perhaps as a matter of projection, was an inclination to magnification, even to symbolism, which remained nonetheless rooted in referential concerns. 'Nana becomes a Myth, without ceasing to be real', Flaubert famously wrote of Zola's heroine prostitute.[102] His objections, as stated in the letter to Turgenev, tended to dwell instead on the dogmatic theory Zola hammered home in his *feuilletons*. In this respect, Flaubert pointed towards that prevalent mode of reading Zola against himself – that is, against his aesthetic doxa – that, we have seen, would characterise so many contemporary attitudes. It has also, as we set out in the Introduction, become the signal gesture of recent critiques seeking to extricate Zola's writing from charges of excessive representationalism, scientism, naivety, and which tend to rely, Susan Harrow writes, on 'literalist approaches to [his] theoretical texts'.[103] Harrow's compelling call for a 'categorical pliancy' in our understanding of 'where modernism starts and ends' – one that could properly take into account the aesthetic innovation of Zola's writing in the detail – involves, in fact, cultivating just such a scepticism about the author's thesis of naturalist art: 'We need to test Zola's theoretical pronouncements against his fiction, for narrative reveals more oscillation and less resolve than critics have tended to see.'[104] The point is to react against an enduring alignment of Zola's naturalist fiction with the 'classic/*lisible*/masterly' (24), whereby it is posited all too often as a foil to the twentieth-century experimental novel.

In a broad sense, we have been tracking here one fork in what we might consider the genealogy of this style of criticism – though, crucially, one in which 'idealism', and more broadly 'poetry', operate as the master terms for all that cuts against the letter of Zola's theory. Take, by way of an emblematic example, Marcel Fouquier's deconstructive take on Zola, as part of his commentary on *Germinal*:

> As a result of this juxtaposition in M. Zola's writing between the theorist of scientific experimentation and the romantic poet, his critical works represent, at least in part, a condemnation of his methods as a novelist, just as his novels represent a decisive objection to his aesthetic theories. [...] In *Germinal*, M. É. Zola is much more a poet and a painter than he is an observer. The book has a sort of sad and tragic greatness. But even on the hard, black earth of the mining village, M. Zola has picked the little 'blue flower' of the *Ideal* that shoots up everywhere.[105]

Arguably, what has been largely occluded by the (rightful) insistence, among late twentieth- and early twenty-first-century Zola critics, on the writer's modernist, or proto-modernist, credentials is just how that slippage between naturalism's aesthetic philosophy and its prose (also) engaged questions of idealism. For strikingly, where Zola's contemporaries sought out such inconsistencies, they tended to determine a betrayal of the mimetic project that was less a deliberately playful experiment with representational principles than an irresistible concession to a hitherto hegemonic idealist tradition.

At the very least, then, we can wonder how a closer attention to the dynamic between naturalism and idealism, as it was construed, might inflect a strain of critical discourse concerned with contesting naturalism's status as a foil to modernism. What we have tracked here are some of the ways in which, in the hands of his adversaries, Zola's naturalism appears mired in internal contradictions, always already prey to the very aesthetic regime it claimed to defeat. By the middle of the 1880s, to reveal in Zola an idealist *malgré lui*, lacking in self-knowledge, had become a familiar conceit. Frequently, as we shall find in Chapter 3, this went hand-in-hand with a wider pathologisation of the naturalist writer's vision. Reflecting on what he saw to be the hypersexual bestiality of Zola's peasant novel *La Terre* (1887), Anatole France added a further nuance to the trope of distorted idealism: '[this novel] is not so much the work of an exacting realist as that of a perverted idealist'.[106] To read Zola *à rebours* and to write *à rebours de* Zola were, as judgements like this suggest, a twin enterprise. No doubt the resonance of this rhetoric of a 'reverse idealism' (if not a perverse one), as it was harnessed by critics like Brunetière in the mid-1880s, invited echoes of Huysmans's watershed Decadent novel *À rebours* (1884). Whether or not Zola and his disciple did in fact come to (meta-phorical) blows at Médan shortly after the novel's publication, a sense of betrayal hung in the air.[107] What Huysmans retrospectively described as a pressing desire to escape the tyranny of the naturalist novel loomed large in the wake of *À rebours*, when increasingly, as we shall see now, the word 'reaction' was on everybody's lips.

Naturalist Terror

On 30 December 1890, Anatole France penned an article on Octave Feuillet to mark the appearance of his latest – and, as it turned out, last – novel, *Honneur d'artiste*. Unbeknownst to France, Feuillet had passed away just the day before, and this lent a poignant, if rather ironic, tone to a piece, which, under the guise of a book review, set out to declare Feuillet's ultimate triumph over his literary adversaries. What, retrospectively, should have been an obituary of Feuillet instead read as a different *nécrologie* altogether – that of Zola:

> During the naturalist Terror, M. Octave Feuillet did not just survive, like Sieyès; he contined to write. [. . .] It seemed that there would be no end to the regime of literary demagogy, that the Committee of Public Safety, led by M. Émile Zola, and the Revolutionary Court, presided over by M. Paul Alexis, would be in charge forever. On all artistic monuments, we read:

'Naturalism or death!' And we thought that this maxim would be everlasting. Suddenly, out of the blue, came the Thermidorian Reaction. [...] And M. Zola fell, brought down by those who had, only yesterday, followed him with blind obedience. [...] Anyway, the naturalist Terror is defeated. We are free to write in whatever way we see fit.[108]

Feuillet could at last breathe a sigh of relief. Zola-Robespierre's reign of Terror had been brought to an end by that unexpected Thermidorian Reaction: the revolt in Zola's ranks that had become known as *Le Manifeste des cinq*. On 18 August 1887, five young writers, who claimed to have been loyal to Zola, signed an open letter protesting the vulgar bestiality and obscene bent of his *La Terre*.[109] Declaring their repulsion, they had claimed, was a matter of integrity, of conscience. Zola's fiction had, of course, long been derided for its excavation of the underbelly of society, of the base and sordid impulses of human nature. But this angry diatribe from those posturing as former disciples was widely understood as a tipping point, triggering what Brunetière hastily dubbed 'the bankruptcy of naturalism'.[110] In Michel Raimond's classic account, this was an act of rebellion that represented 'the most spectacular demonstration of the crisis of the novel'.[111]

The fall of the naturalist regime that Anatole France had described became an obsessive point of debate in the months that followed; indeed, 1891 proved to be a watershed year for naturalism, and the novel form in general. By September, the critic Jules Case could declare, with tongue-in-cheek hyperbole, that 'all we hear about now is the crash of the book, the crisis of the novel, the collapse of literature. It's a catastrophe, the end of a world'.[112] Economic pressures in the publishing industry saw books left unsold and prices tumble, as the market appeared to reach saturation. But it was more precisely the 'liquidation of realism' that this former ally of Zola's proclaimed across a series of venomous articles in *L'Événement*.[113] The public was tired, Case insisted, of 'this base literature, without ideals or ideas', which has reigned 'like a despot' for the past fifteen years. Its sterile, materialist art, 'a peculiar combination of faits divers and snippets of science', no longer appealed to readers, who were duly voting with their feet.[114] From his self-imposed exile in Copenhagen, Léon Bloy rehearsed similar claims. Zola's latest novel, *L'Argent* (1891), was not selling, despite what the newspapers might suggest; and this, he opined, was a sure sign that the French public was beginning to lose its taste for 'a form of literature that can only acclaim the never-ending triumph of the human brute'.[115] Across a series of public lectures, Bloy duly performed, with ferocious delight, the 'funeral of naturalism', adding his voice – and his distinctively spiteful tone – to a chorus of critics reading Zola his last rites.

Whatever the economic realities, the 'crisis' of the naturalist novel had become a self-confirming narrative in the wake of Jules Huret's phenomenally successful *Enquête sur l'évolution littéraire*. Between late March and early June 1891, the journalist undertook a provocative series of interviews with sixty-four leading writers, published day by day in the newspaper *L'Écho de Paris*, and a couple of months later in book form. One of the first investigations of its scale into the state of French literature, it sought to capture those rapid changes to the literary field augured by the likes of Brunetière. Like the numerous *enquêtes* that followed, Huret's investigation made Zola the symbolic lynchpin, its strategy, as Marie-Ève Thérenty has argued, to 'orchestrate, more or less skilfully, a battle over the opposition between naturalism and idealism'.[116] To each writer, Huret posed variations on the same (leading!) questions: 'Is naturalism ill? Is it dead?'; 'Can it be saved?'; 'What will it be replaced by?' The answers provided Huret, by and large, with the sense of combat he was trying to curate. Rivals for the vanguard stated their claims in what was, according to Pierre Bourdieu, 'a sort of symbolique coup d'État', as many writers, including those with naturalist roots, worked out 'their right to inherit'.[117] Zola still had his allies, of course. Paul Alexis's famous telegram in reply to Huret's investigation – 'Naturalism not dead: letter follows' – captured succinctly the prevailing struggle over naturalism's, and Zola's, vital signs.[118] And in his own interview, Zola greeted the journalist with a jocular reference to his excellent health (189). But most writers agreed that the tables had turned: with naturalism's dominance waning, idealism's star was on the ascent. 'There is no doubt', declared Gourmont, 'that the inclinations of new literary generations are strictly antinaturalist' (163). For novelist and critic Édouard Rod, what had been 'the literary expression of an entire positivist and materialist movement no longer meets our present needs' (64). In prioritising the material conditions of human behaviour, naturalism – it was repeatedly claimed – had provided only a blunt tool with which to unpick the complex mechanics of individual consciousness. Instead, the psychological novel, Symbolism, mysticism returned again and again under Huret's pen as the dominant modes of reaction – and with them a new vocabulary: 'the dream', 'the unknown', 'the ideal', 'the beyond', 'mystery'. . .

However wary many writers may have been about the schematic allegiances Huret's taxonomical approach sought to establish – he grouped interviewees as 'Psychologists', 'Magi', 'Symbolists and Decadents', 'Naturalists', 'Neo-Realists', 'Parnassians', 'Independents', and 'Theorists and Philosophers' – the format succeeded in dramatising the literary field for avid readers. Indeed, it was a measure of contemporary appetites for this kind of metadiscursive sparring that, mid-way through Huret's interviews, the journalist Fly launched yet another survey, this time on the 'romanesque novel', which appeared in the pages of *Le Gaulois* between 14 and 25 May.[119] The ostensible pretext for this *enquête* was the literary manifesto penned by the young writer Marcel Prévost for *Le Figaro* two days prior, and with which he launched his forthcoming novel, *La Confession d'un amant*. The future of literary fiction, Prévost declared, lay with neither of those *chefs d'école*, Zola or Bourget, whose respective blueprints for the novel had run their course; all routes instead led back to the 'romanesque'. This he cast, in necessarily broad terms, as an expression of 'this religion of the soul' – the life of sentiment, dream, hope, passion, which had been captured most successfully by none other than George Sand (181). What Prévost called the 'antiromanesque' novel, 'born of positivist philosophy', may have been represented by the most talented of novelists, it never really managed to extinguish those idealist impulses: 'At the height of naturalism's arrogance and dominance, lovers were still gazing dreamily at the stars, leaning on Indiana's balcony.'[120] Sand conjured up a rebellious state of mind, a dream state, that had survived the past decade underground, indifferent to the tyranny of naturalist doctrine.

The following month, Brunetière, whose campaign against Zola's naturalism had provided the likes of Fly and Huret with all the impetus they needed, declared himself scathing of this mania for the *enquête*, as well as of Prévost's publicity strategy. Pursuing his own reflections on what 'the novel of tomorrow' would look like, however, Brunetière was emphatic: 'without doubt, [it] will be idealist', bound by observation, and yet subordinate to more high-minded ends than 'the reproduction of ever-changing appearances'.[121] In fact, Brunetière suggested, 'this return to idealism' was already underway, and it would itself become the object of widespread speculation. Critics like Auguste Sautour conjured up the oscillatory, and unstoppable, momentum of literary taste, swinging, pendulum-like, from one extreme to the other: 'Would people flock once more down the sunlit paths of dreams and ideals?', he mused. 'Yes, it will! This reaction has been much anticipated. The exaggeration of the ugly and the filthy was bound to bring about the victory of the complete opposite.'[122] A year later, 'The Idealist Reaction' was precisely the topic of Benjamin Guinaudeau's *enquête*, which appeared in *La Justice* between March and June 1892. The final interview in Guinaudeau's series, with the philosopher Pierre Laffitte, concluded by exculpating positivism from the charges made against it.[123] But idealism continued to dominate the rhetoric of antinaturalist criticism. When, in January 1895, Albert Fleury launched the periodical *La Renaissance idéaliste*, he positioned its chief claim – 'The only Art possible is idealist' – in relation to Zola's realism and its apparent disregard for the depths of the human soul.[124]

With Brunetière's 1896 public lecture, entitled 'La Renaissance de l'Idéalisme', this discourse of regime change reached its climax. Before a full theatre at Besançon, Brunetière described the different forms that idealism's reemergence had taken over the past decade, across the arts, literature, and politics. Wagnerism, symbolism, Catholic socialism, and mysticism were so many symptoms, he declared, of a contemporary malaise: 'an intimate protest of the modern soul against the brutal tyranny of facts'.[125] A late convert to Catholicism, emboldened by his recent visit to the Vatican, Brunetière reiterated the insufficiencies of positivism and naturalism in grounding a social morality, just as he rehearsed the limitations of mimetic art, blind as it was to the suprasensible, the mystical and metaphysical – in short, to the idea.[126] Zola figured largely by allusion in Brunetière's lecture, though it was nevertheless on the naturalist movement's own physiological, or sanguineous, terms, that he set out his grand narrative of cultural shifts:

> It could be argued [. . .] that idealism and naturalism are two tendencies – one of which should sometimes be encouraged and the other sometimes restrained, or vice versa. [. . .] What can be said, Messieurs, other than that there are times to be an idealist, and times to be a naturalist? [. . .] So as to counteract [naturalism's] negative effect, I hasten to add that now is the time to be an idealist and, in every way, and in every sense, to react against the naturalism that we all, so to speak, have in our blood.[127]

Brunetière's metaphor of tainted blood makes manifest the very porosity between discourse and metadiscourse at this point in the century: naturalism no longer simply described the hereditary transmission of traits and flaws – in Zola's case, through a family's bloodline – the aesthetic strain itself was held to determine a collective disposition in the reading public. As, in Christopher Prendergast's words, 'the person who in France first appropriated Darwinism for literary study', Brunetière had done a great deal to further an evolutionary paradigm of aesthetic history.[128] Here, the critic casts that fateful evolution as internal struggle, prescribing idealism to his audience as the antidote to an insidious vein of naturalist writing whose time is up. Elsewhere, he would be more sanguine about this perpetual transfer of dominance as the sign of a wider, and immutable, constitutional difference in mankind: 'One does not become an *idealist* or a *naturalist*; one either is one or isn't one; volition can do no more about this than it can the shape of one's face or the colour of one's hair.'[129]

It was just such a congenital account of authorial identity that Anatole France had put forward in his ode to Feuillet. Before Zola's purportedly unquashed dream of dominating the literary field, France called for the tolerance of other aesthetic inclinations, which he too understood as an innate form of difference: 'how can he not see that one is born a naturalist or an idealist as one is born brunette or blond, that there is after all something charming about this diversity, and that all that matters is to remain true to oneself?'[130] In Chapter 3, we shall see how, in both *Le Rêve* and *Le Docteur Pascal*, the idealism of his heroines, Angélique and Clotilde, is framed as a hereditary disposition that it is almost impossible to 'correct'. And in turn, this biological determinism becomes bound up with wider questions about whether the naturalist novel could itself adapt, even escape, its own laws of mimetic reproduction. In his public reflections on the evolution of the novel, meanwhile, Zola shifted between, on the one hand, a vision of generational strife – a Darwinian 'struggle for life' – and, on the other, a relatively philosophical acceptance that the pendulum would always swing between opposite poles: 'Do you not know that [. . .] too much truth leads to too much dream, and that too much dream brings us back to too much truth? Observation can no more be buried than the imagination.'[131] In effect, Zola agreed with Prévost that there would always be readers with 'romanesque' appetites – at least, he clarified, among those unable to stomach reality, '[those] who want lies, [. . .] in order to live in thought alone, in an ideal world'.[132] But to embrace the 'so-called romanesque novel' would be nothing short of a step backwards; and the future of the novel inevitably lay elsewhere, bound inextricably to the forward-march of scientific endeavour.

Zola had already conceded to Huret that literary fiction needed new blood, though he refused to accept that his potential usurpers ('those who claim to kill us off so quickly') could provide it. Instead, he had declared himself up to the job, prepared to carry out precisely the *dépassement* of the naturalist project with which his adversaries were attempting to outmanoeuvre him: 'Besides, if I have the time, I'll have a go myself at what they're asking for!'[133] What Zola tentatively gestured towards, as part of his exchange with Huret, was a way of enlarging, and renewing, the naturalist novel, without betraying its principles:

> The future will belong to the person, or to the people, who can capture the soul of modern society, who – freed from overly rigid theories – adopt a more logical, more tender acceptance of life. I believe in a broader, more complex, depiction of truth, in a more open outlook on humanity, in a sort of classicism of naturalism. (192)

The question of whether or not we can see such a project realised in Zola's post-*Rougon-Macquart* fiction lay, as we shall see in Chapter 4, at the heart of critical responses to the novel Zola wrote shortly afterwards, *Lourdes*, and above all to the writer's declared open-mindedness in dealing with the supernatural. For many, the jury was out. But Zola's declared willingness – here and elsewhere – to assimilate, or adapt to, changing demands allows us to register at least the importance of the idealist 'reaction' to his own understanding of naturalism's continued *avant-gardisme*.

Émile, or Optimism

In his 1903 preface to *À rebours*, Huysmans looked back on the exchange he purportedly had with his former *maître* in the wake of the novel's publication, recalling how Zola had objected to his own apparent change of manner, and change of heart, 'sending up in smoke what was once adored'. And yet, Huysmans reflected with the benefit (or irony) of hindsight, was that not precisely what Zola went on to do? 'After the dark pessimism of his first books, have we not had, under the guise of socialism, the blissful optimism of his last?'[134] The question of Zola's aesthetic 'turn' or compromises in the latter stages of his career is integral, as I set out in the Introduction, to the wider trajectory this book tracks, especially in Chapters 4 and 5. What I wish to note here is just how the 'blissful optimism' to which Huysmans alludes came to capture something of Zola's apparently paradoxical relationship to idealism. For just as optimism was synonymous with what many perceived to be the ideological and stylistic idealism of Zola's later fiction, it was also construed – by Zola himself – as a point of (irreconcilable) difference with a younger generation of so-called neoidealists, intent on pursuing their 'ruthless fight' against naturalism.[135] In his adversarial opinion-piece, 'À la jeunesse', Zola framed his optimistic disposition as a direct rebuke: 'Optimist, yes! – to my very core, against idiotic pessimism, the shameful inability [*impuissance*] to desire and love.' Targeting especially those young writers who had declared their reverence for the recently-deceased poet Paul Verlaine as a paragon of originality unappreciated by his peers, Zola sought once again to conflate literary health with reproductive sexuality – Verlaine's affair with Arthur Rimbaud the implicit subtext for explaining the former's 'irreparable decline'.[136] Futurity, a belief in truth, an affection for progress, a positivist outlook, hard work, and 'faith in life': these were the inflexions of Zolian optimism on which he could envisage no compromise.[137]

Under pressure from antinaturalist rivals in the early 1890s, Zola's quarrel was, then, increasingly with a strain of pessimism that he attached to the Decadent as well as the broadly idealist imagination, and which he wished to dissociate from naturalism. In effect, this meant debunking the kind of (mis)characterisation of naturalist fiction that the likes of Brunetière had fostered in his 1885 'Le Pessimisme dans le roman' – a follow-up to his acclamation of the idealist novel two months prior. There, the critic had asserted the idealist conception of art as fundamentally anti-pessimist: 'men did not invent [art] so as to add yet another reason to all those they might already have to complain about life'.[138] Meanwhile, naturalist writers, Brunetière clarified – taking Maupassant's *Bel-Ami* (1885) as his prime example – were guilty of fostering a gloomy sense of despair at the flat mediocrity of existence: 'the horrifying prospect of impending nothingness spoils their pleasure of being in the world'.[139] Such alignments of naturalism with an almost obsessive morbidity, and, by contrast, of idealism with an art of pleasure and consolation, find themselves reconfigured in Zola's own philosophical reflections. Pitched against a version of Catholicism that he describes as a kind of death cult, Zola elaborates – as we shall see in Chapter 5 of this book – a naturalist mission to emancipate mankind from its 'darkest pessimism', and in turn, to elaborate an alternative religion 'that would not be an appetite for death'.[140] This alternative, in fact, is what France conjured up in his ambivalent review of Zola's *L'Argent*, when he determined 'a sort of religious naturalism' in the novel's conception, or in Zola's own words, 'a tranquil belief in the energies of life'.[141] Such a philosophical bent was, France noted, crystallised in the outlook of Zola's indulgent, and unfailingly optimistic, heroine Mme Caroline, a figure France connects to the eponymous hero's love interest in Voltaire's *Candide, ou l'optimisme* (1759). For Mme Caroline's misadventures with the womaniser Saccard are, he explains, rolled into a serene acceptance of life's vicissitudes: 'being widely read, she has undoubtedly learned from Cunégonde that a woman of honour may be vulnerable to such accidents, but that her virtue is the stronger for them'. As an emblem of what France calls 'physiological optimism' – glossed as an instinctual, even animalistic, acquiescence to the universal laws of creation – Mme Caroline is given the last word in the novel. Her ultimate appeal to hope and her faith in an unknowable purpose of existence acquires a Panglossian edge that is apparently untempered by irony.

With *Le Docteur Pascal*, the closing novel of the *Rougon-Macquart* series, Zola supplied in full those symbols of vitalism with which he intended to condense the cycle's wider philosophy: 'love of life; eternal renewal; fresh sap breathing new life into old, withered tree trunks'.[142] Certainly, such faith in the promise of the future – of generational renewal – provides the dominant note of Zola's final two series. And yet, the logical evolution, even hyperbolisation, of this idealist-optimistic vision in Zola's fiction also came to be inflected by his wider intellectual commitments – namely, his intervention in the Dreyfus Affair. We shall explore in our reading of *Vérité* the precise terms on which Zola sought to recast idealism as a necessary form of optimism in the wake of Dreyfus's trial. But by way of a coda to this chapter, I wish to gesture towards the evolution of the wider quarrel that we have been tracking, reframed as it was, to some degree, by the eruption of the Affair. For predictably, the naturalist writer's involvement in the Dreyfus case galvanised longstanding intellectual resentments, just as it polarised the chief agents of antinaturalism: Mirbeau and France rallied to Zola, while the likes of Brunetière, Bourget, and Lemaître joined the anti-Dreyfusard camp.

In Brunetière's case, the Affair triggered a new episode in the critic's struggle with the naturalist figurehead, having remained silent on Zola's fiction over the previous decade.[143] With the publication of *Paris* (1898), the final novel of Zola's *Les Trois Villes* trilogy, Brunetière returned to past animosities – this time, fuelled by his conviction in the illegitimacy of Zola's campaign. Though written before Zola had become involved in the Dreyfus Affair, *Paris* was only halfway through its serialisation when the writer penned his explosive 'J'accuse..!', on 13 January 1898; and the novel was published in book form on 25 February, just two days after Zola was convicted of libel.[144] Brunetière's review of *Paris* appeared in the *Revue des Deux Mondes* that April; and though he made no direct reference to the Dreyfus Affair, both his slight on Zola's 'intellectual' hero, Pierre Froment, and his disdain for Zola's wider hymn to 'justice' in the novel (the watchword of Zola's Dreyfusard journalism) are clearly coloured by contemporary events. In his tirade against what he deemed *Paris*'s tiresome, exaggerated, even nonsensical, style, Brunetière seized on the following (tortuously) extended metaphor:

> Justice is the sun, a sun of beauty, harmony, and strength, because the sun is the only justice, blazing in the sky for everybody, bestowing upon poor and rich alike its magnificence, its light, and its warmth, which are the source of all life.[145]

As indulgent as we might feel towards Zola's wider social vision, we would hardly wish to quibble with Brunetière's aesthetic judgement... But for the critic, what such moments really revealed was a latent confusion, or contradiction, in Zola's writing, which he delighted in making known: 'But what is "naturalist" or even just "natural" about this fanatical – or, if you like, visionary – style? [. . .] M. Zola should reread those pages he once devoted to the bankruptcy of romanticism.' Here, we encounter another iteration of a critical gesture we have tracked through this chapter: the claim that Zola had betrayed (consciously or not) his declared aesthetic principles. In this instance, of course, that admonishment comes to serve, albeit indirectly, a specific ideological purpose: that of discrediting the writer's humanitarian appeal to 'justice' (for Dreyfus) as an expression of flamboyance, even fanaticism, rather than 'naturalist' sobriety.

Zola, Brunetière made clear, had taken liberties in *Paris*, not the least of which were stylistic. Still more irritating was that he had chosen to rehearse the struggle with his literary rivals in the novel, and this precisely by projecting onto the young, Decadent aristocrat Hyacinthe Duvillard 'downright despicable vices' – an array, that is, of intellectual, aesthetic, political, and sexual inclinations that Zola's narrator enumerates thus: '[he was] by turns collectivist, individualist, anarchist, pessimist, symbolist, even sodomist, all the while remaining Catholic, as the ultimate in fashion'.[146] Understood as an attempt to take revenge on a younger generation that no longer looked to Zola as a model, this pastiche was, Brunetière declared, not only underhand and in poor taste, but – in the language governing the novel itself – unjust ('that is what he understands by "justice"!', 933). In a review of *Paris* published that same month, Rachilde pursued a similar line of reproach. Combining latent anti-Dreyfusard and anti-Semitic sentiments, she decried Zola's scorn for his rivals: 'He reserves special contempt for those seeking the impossible, far more so than gold diggers – those *aesthetes* he deems *sodomites*, the lot of them.'[147] No doubt, as Counter argues, Zola's portrait of Hyacinthe as a follower of fads (homosexuality apparently among them) allowed him to recast those claims he had made, two years earlier, in his address 'À la jeunesse', whereby 'movements such as Decadence and Symbolism [. . .] paved the way for "the worst intellectual and moral perversions"'.[148] That the original blanket term in that address, 'idéalisme', does not figure in the list of Hyacinthe's superficial passions might tell us something about the later Zola's interest in extricating idealism from a mesh of intellectual trends, pessimism included, and redeeming it as political necessity. But certainly, Zola intended to pathologise, via Hyacinthe, a broad set of tastes or proclivities that required exorcising, not least insofar as they appeared – as we shall also find in *Vérité* – inimical to the pursuit of justice.

At base, the critiques of *Paris* proffered by both Rachilde and Brunetière involved rehearsing that most familiar objection on the antinaturalist side of the quarrel: that Zola's vision of naturalism was absolutist, if not tyrannical in its handling of literary differences. For the problem was, Rachilde determined – wittily reformulating Zola's own famous mantra – that 'the century was to be naturalist, or it would not be'.[149] In the months following Zola's decisive intervention in the Affair, the writer's dogmatism in matters of aesthetics could readily be recast as the sign of another kind of ideological imperiousness: his cast-iron conviction in Dreyfus's innocence. Those looking to call into question Zola's capacity for fair judgement in the case need look no further, the likes of Rachilde implied, than to the writer's dogged refusal to doubt his own naturalist and positivist principles, and indeed to the unwillingness of 'this persecutor' to tolerate dissent. In the end, it seemed, the long and arduous quarrel Zola had wrought with idealism could be called upon, by his anti-Dreyfusard counterparts, in a different public trial: to prove the illegitimacy of his divisive arbitration in what was the great political rift of the age.

Notes

1 Émile Zola, 'Le Crapaud', *Le Figaro*, 28 February 1896, p. 1.
2 This scholarship includes Alain Pagès, *La Bataille littéraire: essai sur la réception du naturalisme à l'époque de 'Germinal'* (Paris: Librairie Séguier, 1989); David Baguley, *Naturalist Fiction: The Entropic Vision* (Cambridge: Cambridge University Press, 1990), esp. ch. 7; René-Pierre Colin, *Zola, renégats et alliés: la République naturaliste* (Lyon: Presses Universitaires de Lyon, 1988); Catherine Dousteyssier-Khoze, *Zola et la littérature naturaliste en parodies* (Paris: Eurédit, 2004).
3 See Pascaline Hamon, 'Les Antinaturalismes fin-de-siècle de Barbey à Barrès (1877–1908): exploration d'un labyrinthe critique, sociologique, philosophique, esthétique et moral' (unpublished PhD thesis, Paris, Université Sorbonne Paris Cité, 2018), esp. p. 4. On the role of idealism in antinaturalist thought, see pp. 69–108.
4 Jean-Marie Seillan, *Le Roman idéaliste dans le second XIXe siècle: littérature ou 'bouillon de veau'?* (Paris: Classiques Garnier, 2011).
5 See Zola, 'Les Romanciers contemporains' (1880), in *Les Romanciers naturalistes*; *OC*, vol. 10, 598–624 (p. 607).
6 Zola, 'George Sand', in *Documents littéraires*, in *OC*, vol. 10, 727–48 (p. 747).
7 Zola, 'Les Romanciers contemporains', 607.
8 Zola, 'Les Romanciers contemporains', 605.
9 As Seillan points out, the *Revue* never published a line of Flaubert, Goncourt, Daudet, Zola, or their disciples. *Le Roman idéaliste*, p. 38.

10 Seillan, *Le Roman idéaliste*, p. 21. As Seillan explains, Sand published nearly fifty novels in the *Revue des Deux Mondes*, and the entirety of her novelistic production from 1858 to her death (p. 41). The *Revue* disposed of ten votes in the Académie française (p. 22, fn 1).

11 Zola, 'La Critique contemporaine', in *Documents littéraires*; *OC*, vol. 10, 789–809 (p. 808).

12 Seillan, *Le Roman idéaliste*, p. 15.

13 Joris-Karl Huysmans, *À vau-l'eau*, in *Nouvelles*, ed. Daniel Grojnowski (Paris: GF Flammarion, 2007), p. 104; Guy de Maupassant, 'M. Victor Cherbuliez', *Gil Blas*, 1 May 1883, p. 1.

14 Raoul Vast and Georges Ricouard, 'Notre programme', *La Revue réaliste*, no. 1, 5 April 1879, 1–2 (p. 1).

15 Anatole France, 'Octave Feuillet', in *La Vie littéraire* (Paris: Calmann-Lévy, 1891), troisième série, pp. 368–78 (p. 371).

16 Ferdinand Brunetière, 'Le Roman expérimental', *Revue des Deux Mondes*, 37 (1880), 935–47 (p. 938).

17 For similar reflections on antiromantic tactics, see Sarah Al-Matary and Stéphane Zékian, 'Antiromantismes', *Romantisme*, 182 (2018), 5–14 (p. 6).

18 Simon Joyce, *Modernism and Naturalism in British and Irish Fiction, 1880–1930* (Cambridge: Cambridge University Press, 2015), p. 14.

19 Zola, 'La République et la littérature', in *Le Roman expérimental*; *OC*, vol. 9, 488–507 (p. 501).

20 Zola, 'Le Naturalisme au théâtre', in *Le Roman expérimental*; *OC*, vol. 9, 371–93 (p. 373).

21 'Le Naturalisme', first published on 17 January 1881 in *Le Figaro*, then in *Une campagne*; *OC*, vol. 11, 755–59 (p. 756).

22 'Le Naturalisme au théâtre', 373; 'La République et la littérature', 501.

23 Roger Ripoll, 'Zola et le modèle positiviste', *Romantisme*, 21–22 (1978), 125–35 (pp. 125–26).

24 Zola, 'Hugo et Littré', first published on 13 June 1881 in *Le Figaro*; subsequently included in *Une campagne*; *OC*, vol. 11, 832–36 (p. 836).

25 'Whether they call us positivists, materialists, atheists, this is a philosophical quarrel, and we welcome it', Zola declared in 'De la moralité dans la littérature'; *OC*, vol. 10, 809–29 (p. 824).

26 'La République et la littérature', 501.

27 'Le Naturalisme', 757.

28 'Le Roman expérimental', in *Le Roman expérimental*; *OC*, vol. 9, 324–48 (p. 339).

29 Zola, 'Lettre à la jeunesse', first published in *Le Voltaire*, 17 May 1879, then in *Le Roman expérimental*; *OC*, vol. 9, 349–70 (p. 363).

30 'Le Roman expérimental', 335.

31 Zola, 'Lettre à la jeunesse', 363.

32 'Le Roman expérimental', 341 (Zola's emphasis).

33 Hippolyte Taine, *Les Philosophes français du XIXe siècle*, 2nd edition (Paris: Librairie de L. Hachette et Cie, 1860), p. v.

34 'Le Roman expérimental', 344–45.

35 'La République et la littérature', subsequently included in *Le Roman expérimental*; *OC*, vol. 9, 488–507 (p. 489).

36 'Lettre à la jeunesse', 349.

37 Robert D. Priest, *The Gospel According to Renan: Reading, Writing, and Religion in Nineteenth-Century France* (Oxford: Oxford University Press, 2015), p. 191.

38 'Lettre à la jeunesse', 355.

39 'Lettre à la jeunesse', 357. On Renan's election, see also Zola's 'Pluie de couronnes' (first published in *Le Figaro* on 15 August 1881), *Une campagne*; *OC*, vol. 11, 835–37.

40 Ernest Renan, *Discours de réception à l'Académie française prononcé le 3 avril 1879*, Bibliothèque nationale, Paris, NAF 16384.

41 Brian Nelson, *Zola and the Bourgeoisie: A Study of Themes and Techniques in 'Les Rougon-Macquart'* (London: The Macmillan Press, 1983), p. 24. Zola, 'De la moralité dans la littérature', 828.

42 'La République et la littérature', 500.

43 Take, for instance, Zola's caricature in 'La République et la littérature': 'The romantics set off on horseback in pursuit of humanitarian dreams, the universal brotherhood of nations' (493).

44 'La République et la littérature', 494.

45 'La République et la littérature', 490.

46 'La République et la littérature', 491.

47 'La "Politique expérimentale"'.

48 See Zola's 'Victor Hugo', in *Documents littéraires*; *OC*, vol. 10, 655–77: 'He decrees the universal Republic, as though [comme si] the elements were to follow his orders and bring about a new world and a new people' (p. 658).

49 Zola, '*L'Assommoir*. À monsieur le Directeur du *Bien public*', *Le Bien public*, 13 February 1877, p. 2.

50 'Lettres de Paris', *Le Sémaphore de Marseille*, 4 May 1871, pp. 1–2 (p. 2).

51 Jean Carrère, 'Entretiens sur l'anarchie: Chez M. Émile Zola', *Le Figaro*, 25 April 1892, p. 2.

52 'Lettre à la jeunesse', 368.

53 'Lettre à la jeunesse', 369. Compare Gustave Flaubert to Mlle Leroyer de Chantepie: 'I am convinced that the fiercest material appetites are produced *unknowingly* by bursts of idealism, just as the most appalling carnal excesses are brought about by a pure desire for the impossible, an ethereal longing for supreme joy.' Letter of 18 February 1859; *Correspondance*, ed. Jean Bruneau and Yvan Leclerc, 5 vols (Paris: Gallimard, Bibliothèque de la Pléiade, 1973–2007), vol. 3 (1991), 15–17 (p. 16; original emphasis). Maupassant made a similar point, if more hesitantly, in his article, 'M. Victor Cherbuliez': 'Besides, I have this idea, which is probably false, that altogether the most dangerous and immoral books are those reputed to be the most moral, the most poetic.'

54 I borrow this term from René Girard; see *Mensonge romantique et vérité romanesque* (Paris: Grasset, 1961). Zola himself speaks to Flaubert's archetype

in *Une page d'amour* (1879), when he imagines Hélène Grandjean's absorption in Scott's *Ivanhoe*: 'She felt she was in a beautiful falsehood, walking around in it as though in an ideal garden, filled with golden fruit, and where she was drinking in all kinds of illusions.' *R-M*, vol. 2, 848.

55 'De la moralité dans la littérature', in *Documents littéraires*; *OC*, vol. 10, 809–29 (p. 828).

56 'De la moralité dans la littérature', 822.

57 'Lettre à la jeunesse', 369.

58 'Le Roman expérimental', 334.

59 Louis Ulbach, 'À propos de *Nana*', *Gil Blas*, 24 February 1880, p. 1.

60 'De la moralité dans la littérature', 824.

61 *RM*, vol. 1, 738.

62 Sophie Guermès, *La Religion de Zola: naturalisme et déchristianisation* (Paris: Honoré Champion, 2003), p. 295.

63 'À la jeunesse', repr. in *Nouvelle Campagne*; *OC*, vol. 17, 388–91 (p. 390).

64 Andrew J. Counter, 'Zola's Fin-de-Siècle Reproductive Politics', *French Studies*, 68 (2014), 193–208 (p. 195; original emphasis).

65 'À la jeunesse', 390.

66 Seillan, *Le Roman idéaliste*, pp. 70–71; and note that Seillan points to Zola's rebuke of Bourget's psychological novel *Cosmopolis* (1893) for its effacement of the child (p. 71, fn 3).

67 Zola, *Fécondité*; *OC*, vol. 18, 43, 44.

68 Florence Beillacou, 'Tuer l'idéal: l'anti-romantisme de Zola et les naturalistes' (unpublished doctoral thesis; Paris, Université Sorbonne Paris Cité, 2018), p. 178.

69 'Le Moment artistique', first published in *L'Événement*, 3 May 1866; repr. in *Mon Salon. Œuvres complètes. Critique littéraire et artistique*, vol. 1, *Écrits sur l'art*, ed. Robert Lethbridge (Paris: Classiques Garnier, 2021), pp. 145–49 (p. 148).

70 'L'Ouverture', first published in *L'Événement illustré*, 2 May 1868; repr. in *Le Salon de 1868. Œuvres complètes. Critique littéraire et artistique*, vol. 1, 171–76 (pp. 174–75).

71 'La République et la littérature', 502.

72 'La République et la littérature', 501–2.

73 *R-M*, vol. 2, 80.

74 Jules Lemaître, 'Octave Feuillet', *Les Contemporains: études et portraits littéraires*, 3ᵉ série (Paris: H. Lecène et H. Oudin, 1887), pp. 5–35 (p. 25).

75 'Le Naturalisme au théâtre', 379. For a discussion of the formulaic and stereotypical with which Feuillet was associated, see Jean-Marie Seillan, 'Stéréotypie et roman mondain: l'œuvre d'Octave Feuillet', *Loxias*, 17 (2007), available online: http://revel.unice.fr/loxias/index.html?id=1684

76 See Zola's letter to Jules Lemaître, 14 March 1885; *Corr*, vol. 5, 244–46 (p. 245).

77 Brunetière, 'L'Idéalisme dans le roman', *Revue des Deux Mondes*, 69 (May 1885), 215–25 (p. 218). The new editions were of Feuillet's *Monsieur*

de Camors (1867) and *Julia de Trécœur* (1872). The class dimension of the quarrel over idealism and naturalism was apparent in the frustrations of critics like Lemaître, who objected: 'there are men and women on earth far livelier and worthier of attention than those who spend their mornings riding in the woods and their evenings in their box at the Opera'. 'Octave Feuillet', p. 26.

78 'L'Idéalisme dans le roman', 218.

79 Zola, 'Causerie du Dimanche', *Le Corsaire*, 3 December 1872; *OC*, vol. 5, 944–48 (p. 946).

80 This section draws on my article 'Zola à rebours', *Les Cahiers naturalistes*, 91 (2017), 123–34, with the kind permission of the editor.

81 Pagès, *La Bataille littéraire*, p. 238.

82 Gustave Geoffroy, 'Revue littéraire', *La Justice*, 14 July 1885, p. 2.

83 Subsequently reproduced in Lemaître, 'Émile Zola', *Les Contemporains*, 1ère série (Paris: H. Lecène et H. Oudin, 1886), pp. 249–84 (pp. 253–54; my emphasis).

84 Remy de Gourmont, 'Le Naturalisme', *Le Contemporain*, April 1882.

85 See Jean-Marie Guyau, *L'Art au point de vue sociologique* (Paris: Félix Alcan, 1889), p. 148.

86 *L'Art au point de vue sociologique*, p. 152 (original emphasis).

87 Georges Pellissier, *Le Mouvement littéraire au XIXᵉ siècle*, 6th edition (Paris: Librairie Hachette et Cⁱᵉ, 1900), p. 344.

88 Taine, *Philosophie de l'art* (Paris: Fayard, 1985), p. 373.

89 Zola, 'M. H. Taine artiste', *OC*, vol. 1, 820–36 (p. 834).

90 Naomi Schor, *George Sand and Idealism* (New York: Columbia University Press, 1993), p. 40 (original emphasis).

91 Taine, *De l'Idéal dans l'art: Leçons professées à l'École des Beaux-Arts* (Paris: Germer Baillière, 1867), p. 104.

92 George Sand, *Œuvres autobiographiques*, ed. Georges Lubin (Paris: Gallimard, Bibliothèque de la Pléiade, 1971), vol. 2, 161–62. My emphasis.

93 *George Sand and Idealism*, p. 41.

94 Lemaître, 'Émile Zola', pp. 259–60; original emphasis.

95 Brunetière, 'L'Idéalisme dans le roman', 217; emphasis added.

96 Brunetière, *Le Roman naturaliste* (Paris: Calmann Lévy, 1883), p. 119.

97 Lemaître, 'Émile Zola', p. 268.

98 Zola, *Corr*, vol. 5, 248–51 (p. 249); emphasis added.

99 Henry Céard, 'M. Émile Zola et *Germinal*', translated from Spanish by Albert J. Salvan, in *Zola: mémoire de la critique*, ed. Sylvie Thorel-Cailleteau (Paris: Presses de l'Université Paris-Sorbonne, 1998), pp. 179–91 (p. 182).

100 Flaubert, *Correspondance*, vol. 5 (2007), 337. Flaubert's emphasis.

101 Cited in Zola, *Corr*, vol. 5, 68, n. 3.

102 Flaubert, *Correspondance*, vol. 5, 834.

103 Susan Harrow, *Zola, The Body Modern: Pressures and Prospects of Representation* (Oxford: Legenda, 2010), p. 24.

104 Harrow, *Zola, The Body Modern*, pp. 26, 35, n. 4.

105 Marcel Fouquier, '*Germinal* de M. Émile Zola', *La France*, 23 March 1885, pp. 2–3 (original emphasis).

106 See France's interview with Jules Huret, *Enquête sur l'évolution littéraire*. Preface by Daniel Grojnowski (Paris: José Corti, 1999), pp. 54–59 (p. 54).

107 On the relationship between the two authors in this period, see Jacques Noiray, 'Huysmans critique de Zola et du naturalisme (1884–1907)', in *Champ littéraire fin de siècle autour de Zola*, ed. Béatrice Laville (Pessac: Presses Universitaires de Bordeaux, 2004), pp. 121–39.

108 France, 'Octave Feuillet', pp. 368–69.

109 The open letter was signed by Paul Bonnetain, J.-H. Rosny, Lucien Descaves, Paul Margueritte, and Gustave Guiches, and appeared on the front page of *Le Figaro*.

110 Brunetière, 'La Banqueroute du naturalisme', *Revue des Deux Mondes*, 83 (1887), 213–24. In his own article on Feuillet, written the following year, Brunetière too augured the rightful return to prominence of Feuillet's fiction. This, he said, would be tied to the imminent resurgence of idealism: 'Feuillet's novels will perhaps be undervalued [. . .] for a while yet. But they will find their place once more – when idealism, and even the romanesque, have regained their rights.' 'Octave Feuillet', *Revue des Deux Mondes*, 103 (1891), 664–94 (p. 694).

111 Michel Raimond, *La Crise du roman: Des lendemains du Naturalisme aux années vingt* (Paris: José Corti, 1966), p. 25.

112 Jules Case, 'La Débâcle du réalisme', *L'Événement*, 21 September 1891, p. 1.

113 See 'La Réaction idéaliste, Émile Zola', *La Justice*, 30 April 1892, pp. 1–2 (p. 2).

114 Case, 'La Débâcle du réalisme'.

115 Léon Bloy, *Les Funérailles du naturalisme*, ed. Pierre Glaudes (Grenoble: Publications de l'Université Stendhal-Grenoble, 1990), pp. 19–45 (p. 29).

116 Marie-Ève Thérenty, 'Sacre de l'événement/sacrifice de l'écrivain. Les enquêtes littéraires dans le quotidien avant l'affaire Dreyfus', in *L'Interview d'écrivain: figures bibliques d'autorité*, ed. Sylvie Traire, Marie Blaise, and Marie-Ève Thérenty (Montpellier: Presses Universitaires de la Méditerranée, 2004), [para. 20], available online: http://books.openedition.org/pulm/320

117 Pierre Bourdieu, *Les Règles de l'art. Genèse et structure du champ littéraire* (Paris: Seuil, 1992), p. 181.

118 Huret, *Enquête sur l'évolution littéraire*, p. 205.

119 The author interviewed thirty-seven writers. Seillan suggests that Fly was probably the pseudonym of Charles-Armand Dieudé-Defly. *Enquête sur le roman romanesque ('Le Gaulois', 1891)*. Introduced by Jean-Marie Seillan (Amiens: Centre d'Études du Roman et du Romanesque de l'Université de Picardie, 2005), p. 141, fn 5.

120 *Enquête sur le roman romanesque*, pp. 181, 182. See Seillan's thorough analysis, 'Ce qu'on appelait romanesque en 1891', in Fly, *Enquête sur le roman romanesque*, pp. 139–77. Prévost attributed both the psychological novel and the naturalist novel to the lamentable influence of Hippolyte Taine's philosophy (p. 182).

121 Brunetière, 'Le Roman de l'avenir', *Revue des Deux Mondes*, 105 (June 1891), 685–98 (pp. 693, 692).

122 Auguste Sautour, *Idéal et naturalisme, à propos du roman 'L'Amour de Jacques' de Charles Fuster* (Paris: Fischbacher, 1891); cited and discussed by Pascaline Hamon, 'L'Idéal dans la critique littéraire fin de siècle: Un étendard anti-naturaliste?', p. 2, available online: https://serd.hypotheses.org/files/2018/08/IdealismePascalineHamon.pdf

123 See 'La Réaction idéaliste', *La Justice*, 3 June 1892, pp. 1–2 (p. 2).

124 Albert Fleury, 'Prothême', *La Renaissance idéaliste*, no. 1, January 1895, pp. 1–8 (p. 4).

125 Brunetière, *La Renaissance de l'idéalisme* (Paris: Firmin-Didot et Cie, 1896), p. 62.

126 Brunetière was received by the Pope in November 1894; see 'Après une visite au Vatican', *Revue des Deux Mondes*, 127 (January 1895), 97–118.

127 *La Renaissance de l'idéalisme*, pp. 109–10.

128 Christopher Prendergast, 'Evolution and Literary History: A Response to Franco Moretti', *New Left Review*, 34 (July – August 2005), 40–62 (p. 47). Brunetière's 1890 treatise, *L'Évolution des genres dans l'histoire de la littérature*, had sought to establish an analogical relationship between literary history and natural history.

129 Brunetière, 'Une définition de mots', *Revue des Deux Mondes*, 92 (1899), 215–26 (p. 219; original emphasis).

130 France, 'Octave Feuillet', p. 373.

131 'À la jeunesse', 390.

132 Fly, *Enquête sur le roman romanesque*, p. 193.

133 Huret, *Enquête sur l'évolution littéraire*, p. 193. Similarly, in his conversation with Guinaudeau, Zola calmly reiterated his intention of handling the question of idealism's claims: 'As for what is legitimate and serious about the idealist or mystical reaction, I am giving it thought [. . .]. I will do something on the subject.' 'La Réaction idéaliste, Émile Zola', *La Justice*, 30 April 1892, p. 2.

134 Huysmans, 'Préface écrite vingt ans après le roman', in *À rebours*, ed. Marc Fumaroli (Paris: Gallimard, 1977), pp. 55–76 (p. 71).

135 'À la jeunesse', 389.

136 See Zola's article 'Le Solitaire', first published on 18 January 1896 in *Le Figaro*, and later reproduced in *Nouvelle campagne*; *OC*, vol. 17, 383–87 (p. 384).

137 'À la jeunesse', 390.

138 'L'Idéalisme dans le roman', p. 216.

139 Brunetière, 'Le Pessimisme dans le roman', *Revue des Deux Mondes*, 70 (July 1885), 214–26 (p. 218).

140 Zola, *Lourdes. Œuvres complètes. Les Trois Villes – I*, ed. Bertrand Marquer (Paris: Classiques Garnier, 2015), pp. 376, 494.

141 France, 'La Vie littéraire: L'Argent, par M. Émile Zola', *Le Temps*, 22 March 1891, p. 2.

142 See Zola's letter to Philippe Gille, 12 June 1893; *Corr*, vol. 11, 250.

143 See Antoine Compagnon, *Connaissez-vous Brunetière? Enquête sur un anti-dreyfusard et ses amis* (Paris: Seuil, 1997), p. 125.

144 *Paris* was serialised in *Le Journal* between 23 October 1897 and 9 February 1898.

145 Citation from *Paris* in Brunetière, 'Le *Paris* de E. Zola', *Revue des Deux Mondes*, 146 (April 1898), 922–34 (p. 932).

146 Brunetière, 'Le *Paris* de E. Zola', 933; and Zola, *Paris*, *OC*, vol. 17, 41.

147 See Rachilde's review of *Paris* in *Mercure de France*, 26 (April – June 1898), 236–40 (p. 239; original emphasis).

148 Andrew J. Counter, 'One of Them: Homosexuality and Anarchism in Wilde and Zola', *Comparative Literature*, 63:4 (2011), 345–65 (p. 351).

149 Rachilde, *Mercure de France*, 237.

CHAPTER 2

The Politics of Impossibilism: Germinal

Generally speaking, Zola has had a rough ride at the hands of Marxist intellectuals and literary critics. Friedrich Engels famously judged Balzac to be 'a far greater master of realism than all the Zolas *passés, présents et à venir*'.[1] And Georg Lukács duly turned this distinction into something of a paradigm. In spite of, or even because of, his reactionary politics, Balzac produces – so Lukács's story goes – a biting and deeply imaginative vision of history as a dynamic struggle of 'vital contradictions' and opposing forces; he participates in, and narrates, a social world in flux, replete with possibilities for transformation.[2] Writing on the other side of the failed 1848 revolution, Zola figures, by contrast, as a detached observer in an increasingly reified world, his descriptive naturalism draining from history a sense of direction. With its rationalised specialisation of society into discrete categories, naturalist fiction passively accepts the social order as a natural fact, having already capitulated to the dehumanising capitalist system it describes. And so, Zola's 'sincere and courageous criticism of society is', Lukács laments, 'locked into the circle of progressive *bourgeois* narrow-mindedness'.[3] When all is said and done, the endemic fatalism of naturalist fiction appears irreconcilable with a Marxist vision of dialectical history.

Predictably, the Marxist critic's principal charges against the naturalist novel have aroused numerous impassioned, even indignant, defences; and it is not my intention here to add another file to the case Lukács v. Zola.[4] Rather what I should like to revisit in this chapter is the seemingly intractable problem that Marxist criticism, especially that inspired by Lukács, sets out: that for all its sincere admonishments of capitalism, the naturalist novel cannot write a way out of it. Put differently, what does (or what must) naturalist literature *do* to the radical or revolutionary impulses it describes? I wish to begin by evoking what we might take to be one of the most persuasive (Marxist) answers to this question: that is, the vision of naturalism set out by Fredric Jameson, a deep, though not uncritical, admirer of Lukács. In *The Political Unconscious* (1981), Jameson describes naturalism as a 'homogeneous narrative apparatus', in which 'alternate histories', 'alternative social worlds', and alternative narrative modes give way to 'a kind of obligatory "indicative" register'.[5] The naturalist novelist is bound, by his 'own narrative and aesthetic vested interests' (193), to reproduce the status quo, to evoke the solidity of the social world – even when, or especially when, that solidity is under threat. Intriguingly, it is the strike that emerges, just briefly, in Jameson's account as a kind of limit case for the naturalist novel's conservative project:

> a curious subform of realism, the proletarian novel, demonstrates what happens when the representational apparatus is confronted by that supreme event, the strike as the figure for social revolution, which calls social 'being' and the social totality itself into question, thereby undermining the totality's basic preconditions: whence the scandal of this form, which fails when it succeeds and succeeds when it fails [...]. Meanwhile, the realists themselves are necessarily engaged in a host of containment strategies, which seek to fold everything which is not-being, desire, hope, and transformational praxis, back into the status of nature; these impulses toward the future and toward radical change must be systematically reified. (181)

Jameson develops this account of the proletarian novel in a chapter on the English novelist George Gissing – 'the most "French"', Jameson remarks, 'of British naturalists' (173). Zola thus floats in the background as an occasionally evoked, but largely implied, cross-Channel reference. And yet, the wider story Jameson tells about Gissing's novels of the people – and precisely, of popular, radical militancy – bears, even draws, on Zola, and in ways which, I believe, have largely escaped the attention of Zola scholars.

Over the course of this chapter, I should like to reflect on Jameson's reference to the strike as a 'figure for social revolution', one that leads to an explosion of radical energies, which the naturalist novel would necessarily seek to 'contain'. The strike, that is, as a 'supreme event' – an event, Jameson might say, in the subjunctive register – which, in order for the naturalist form to succeed, must fail. My focus, of course, will be on Zola's 1885 novel of a miners' strike, *Germinal* – the work brandished most often by Lukács's critics as counter-evidence of Zola's sound grasp of class conflict. Set in Northern France under the late Second Empire, the novel tracks the ambitions and disappointments of its hero Étienne Lantier, who arrives in the mining community of Montsou, boards with the Maheu family, and ends up galvanising an ill-fated strike, which culminates in a confrontation with troops that leaves the *père de famille* Maheu (and others) dead. In tracking the miners' political awakening, the novel exploits precisely the symbolism Jameson mentions: Zola's strike blends, that is, with other episodes of social uprising and revolution (the Terror, June 1848, 1871), and in a way that was, as Michael Hardt and Antonio Negri claim, typical of 'popular understandings [of strikes] after the Paris Commune'.[6]

Part of my concern, then, will be to think about the strike along those emblematic lines Jameson draws, as a figure for, or agent of, future-oriented idealism – an idealism that Zola widely stigmatised and discredited. But before going any further, I want to make a simple observation: that among those 'impulses toward the future and radical change' that Jameson mentions, 'idealism' or the 'ideal' do not figure. Instead, he prefers 'not-being, desire, hope', etc. Naomi Schor has already noted this perennial suspicion of the ideal among Marxist critics (Jameson included), 'so obsessed with rooting out idealism wherever it springs up'.[7] Indeed, Schor's book on Sand is all about what, as she herself notes, Jameson calls the 'common-or-garden variety [of idealism]': this 'everyday mode', in Schor's terms, 'whose familiarity and omnipresence has rendered it self-evident' (84), and in which the dominant tradition of Marxist literary criticism has shown little interest. Notably, in *The Antinomies of Realism* (2013), Jameson does include 'idealism' in a list of what he calls the (many) opposites of realism, and he duly references Schor's book. But he remains sceptical, it seems, about the usefulness of dealing in these kinds of binary pairs, insofar as they 'arouse a passionate taking of sides, in which realism is either denounced or elevated to the status of an ideal (aesthetic or otherwise)'.[8] Here is an example of exactly that suspicion of the 'ideal' in action, as a byword for mystification.

Now, I have already set out a number of arguments in favour of reinstating the term 'idealism' in our accounts of the naturalist novel, thereby risking, we must assume, the overdetermination of difference Jameson cautions us against. In the case of Zola's 'socialist novel' *Germinal*, the most obvious, or at least the most literal, reason for harnessing the term lies in the fact that Zola rendered socialism so systematically as an idealism – and this precisely in the bad, Jamesonian sense, as a form of illusion.[9] Zola found abundant confirmation of this view of socialist politics in those contemporary works of economics he read in preparing the novel. Take as emblematic the orthodox economist Paul Leroy-Beaulieu, who warned of the endemic idealism that feeds socialism ('this dangerous scourge') by tapping into deep-rooted impulses: 'There is in man an indomitable instinct that drives him to form an ideal of perfect justice and complete happiness.'[10] Socialism, according to such diagnoses, at once expressed a kind of timeless collective psychology, and it displaced, or rerouted, religious fervour as part of its own irresistible conception of a this-worldly paradise. The socialist dream, as a new form of faith, had become the opium of the people. 'No more religious belief, no afterlife, and so the need to possess and enjoy in this life', ran Zola's notes on his reading.[11]

Of course, to point out that Zola perpetuates this sweeping conflation of the socialist and idealist imagination is hardly to say anything new. As Jacques Noiray argues, Zola has his strike leader cultivate 'a mystical conception of the people and of political engagement' that is, for the writer, 'inevitably common to all forms of socialism'.[12] To be sure, at the moment of the novel's publication in book form, Zola reflected on the problem of grasping the many currents of socialist politics: 'I ran into a difficulty. There are so many sects, so many different schools!' Instead, as critics have rightly determined, Zola – like many of the political economists he read – tended to condense these doctrines into a set of shared instincts or impulses, 'a kind of general aspiration'.[13] After all, as 'a reader of digests', Christophe Reffait reminds us, Zola encountered much socialist thought second-hand.[14] What I will argue here, though, is that a set of distinctions and divisions on the Left did, in fact, colour Zola's conception of politics in the novel, however broadly conceived: crucially, the splintering of the nascent socialist party into rival camps of 'Possibilists' and 'Impossibilists' – the latter representing the earliest manifestation of French Marxism. By returning to this episode, my aim in this chapter is to reframe the prevailing conflation of socialism and idealism as a matter of debate that was internal to socialist politics in the early 1880s, as disagreements flared up about the legitimate routes to working-class emancipation.

In the first part, I will track Zola's transposition of this socialist rupture in *Germinal,* and think about how and why it captured his imagination. My hunch is that the rhetoric of 'Possibilism' and 'Impossibilism' appealed to Zola's existing vision of what 'good' and 'bad' politics looked like. For what Zola describes in his strike novel is the dangerous lure of a certain type of political thinking, which is cast as idealist, or more precisely, I shall suggest, as 'impossibilist'. Beyond the immediate context in which they emerged, these epithets provide, I venture, an important way of thinking about the naturalist novel's own political vision. In the second part, we shall focus on the strike itself as a divisive object of political debate, both within socialist circles and in the press more widely, as commentators wondered what role the strike could play in bringing about a revolution. I shall read Zola's novel as a negotiation with those contemporary debates about the legitimacy – both ethical and political – of this weapon of working-class struggle. More than a catalyst for drama, the strike, I argue, offered a way for Zola to reflect on a speculative form of politics that he had long derided.

In the third and fourth parts of the chapter, we shall return to Jameson, and his take on Gissing's proletarian novel, as we examine the fate Zola has in store for his strike leader Étienne, whose function it is to enjoin a desperate community to fight for 'the enchanted society of the future'.[15] If, as Jameson suggests, the naturalist novel 'reifies' radical impulses, determined as it is by a certain structural conservatism, I explore how this depends on the systematic delegitimisation of its working-class militant hero. For Zola effectively rehearses via his scrutiny of Étienne a set of suspicions about an idealist, and idealising, imagination, which he believes incompatible with socialist ambitions. In the final part, we shall look at how Zola's novel drives home its anti-idealist 'thesis', notably by conceptualising idealism (or, as I am arguing, impossibilism) as a vehicle for catastrophe. Throughout this chapter, then, my concern will be to show exactly how Zola's critical account of political idealism functions, and in turn, how this entails a set of anxious reflections on the politics and ethics of the naturalist novel's own modes of representation. In doing so, I return to an important tradition of Marxist literary criticism that has, understandably, proven unpalatable to many Zola scholars, insisting as it has on the insufficiencies of naturalist fiction – its structural determinism, its asphyxiation of radical impulses. Rather than defend *Germinal* against accusations of conservatism, I want to show how working through such critiques might help us to think more clearly about the naturalist novel's decidedly equivocal sense of political purpose.

Impossibilism

On 7 March 1884 – just five days after Zola set down the first page of *Germinal* – fellow novelist Paul Alexis took Zola to a lively political meeting organised by the Parisian branch of the Parti ouvrier français at the Salle de la Redoute. On the podium were Jules Guesde, leader of the Marxist faction of the socialist party; two of Karl Marx's sons-in-law, Paul Lafargue and Charles Longuet; and *citoyen* Lefebvre, a delegate from the syndicate of Northern miners. The latter regaled those present with the brave defiance of the Anzin strikers, whose stand Zola had witnessed firsthand just a few days earlier.[16] But what seemingly drew Zola to the spectacle of the political meeting was a distinct curiosity about the personalities driving contemporary socialism. Alexis was writing pseudonymously for the socialist newspaper *Le Cri du peuple* at the time, alongside Guesde; and two days after the meeting, Alexis noted down some more information about the socialist leader that Zola had requested. Even the name of this great agitator, Alexis enthusiastically opined, 'seems straight out of Balzac or Stendhal'. Since returning from exile in 1877, having been prosecuted for his outspoken support of the Commune, Guesde had been breathing new life into socialist politics: '[he] is said to be the strongest of them all, very well known, a hundred times better than [Paul] *Brousse*'.[17] No doubt impressed by Guesde's powers of oration, Alexis invited Zola to hear him speak again at a meeting the following week – an offer Zola politely declined.

The rivalry to which Alexis alludes had no doubt been on Zola's mind. In his plans for *Germinal*, Zola noted his intention of conjuring with the doctrinal differences that were polarising the Left.[18] Chief among these was the rupture of the nascent socialist party into two main rival camps: the Marxist minority, led by Guesde, which founded the Parti ouvrier français; and the remaining Fédération des travailleurs socialistes de France, with Brousse at the helm.[19] It was at the socialists' Congrès de Saint-Étienne in September 1882 that Guesde (and his supporters) formally defected, following disagreements over what became known as the party's 'minimum programme', a set of radical political, economic, and social demands that had been co-written by Guesde and endorsed by Marx. Guesde's initiative provoked a backlash among those who insisted on the need to push more readily realisable ambitions, and who were suspicious of any kind of Marxist authoritarianism. The rupture, then, had been long in the making, with both factions using their respective newspapers (principally, *L'Égalité* in Guesde's case; *Le Prolétaire* in Brousse's) to set out their differing visions of the doctrinal and organisational direction the party should take.[20]

In the wake of his defection, Guesde claimed the party had split into two elements – one parliamentary, the other revolutionary.[21] Dismissing Brousse's brand of political pragmatism as 'Possibilism', Guesde called on all like-minded revolutionaries to join his cause, 'those who think, as we do, that [. . .] everything has to be destroyed'.[22] Clearly intended as a grave insult, the characterisation was subsequently appropriated by Broussists, who returned the epithet of 'Impossibilists' to designate their Guesdist rivals.[23] Jules Joffrin, Brousse's ally, glossed the term as a politics of futility, pastiching the Guesdists' revolutionary convictions as follows: 'To declare oneself an Impossibilist is to say: "We are aimless agitators; we utter the word 'revolution' at every turn, though only for show; we aren't interested in achieving anything."'[24] In an article of 19 November 1881, Brousse had already painted his Marxist counterparts as utopian dreamers, whose uncompromising vision of momentous social change yielded no tangible political gains:

> I prefer to dispense with the 'all-at-once' approach taken so far, which tends to lead to 'nothing-at-all', and instead break down the ideal goal into several important steps. It is a way of making some of our demands immediately achievable, possible at last, rather than spending all my energy treading water.[25]

Guesde was incredulous, lambasting his rivals' retreat from what they deemed 'impossible', whether through myopia or indecision, as political opportunism.[26]

These epithets were, clearly, caricatures – and probably for that reason were all the more appealing to Zola's schematic political imagination.[27] They certainly stuck as ways of capturing the dominant schism in socialist doctrine. On the one hand, the Guesdists' apparently intransigent Marxism and their condemnation of all complicity with the capitalist system and Third Republic institutions, '[believing] government', as Julia Nicholls explains, 'to be a distraction'.[28] On the other, the Broussists' gradualism, or 'politics of possibilities', which fostered workers' unions and made economic and institutional reforms a condition of social revolution.[29] On 3 January 1885 – during, that is, the serialisation of *Germinal* – Brousse set out the prevailing dissensions on the Left in an article for *Le Prolétariat*, 'Possibilistes, Impossibilistes, et Anarchistes'. The latter he summarily dismissed as fanatics, by virtue of their boundless faith in social revolt as the only legitimate revolutionary tactic. Though anarchist absolutism, he clarified, was surely preferable to the hypocrisy of 'Impossibilists', whose 'revolutionary phrasemongering' belied their perpetual ineffectiveness. Only Possibilists were capable of improving the conditions of workers' lives, and of drawing those workers into the political struggle, by employing all available (legal and revolutionary) means to make realisable claims. Brousse stuck fast, in effect, to the vision of politics with which he had first countered Guesde's – that of a daily struggle played out 'on the grounds of possibility, *thereby achieving its ideal piece by piece*, [. . .] leaving contemplation behind in order to begin its real march toward the future'.[30] The socialist schism, in Brousse's account, is articulated as the confrontation of two strains of idealism: one measured, methodical, realisable; the other uncompromising, absolute, prophetic.

It was, of course, with some critical distance that Zola transposed this politics of personality in his novel, where the factionalism on the Left is loosely drawn around his three main political 'figures'. First, the anarchist, his Russian miner Souvarine; then Zola's chief rivals: the miner and strike leader, Étienne Lantier, who falls prey to the distant influence of the Guesde-like Pluchart, a travelling militant of the First International; and the former militant-turned-innkeeper Rasseneur, whose political colours Zola had nailed to the mast.[31] '[A] possibilist', Zola noted, 'who sees only the war on injustice, the reforms that are needed, but who stops short of a political uprising.'[32] With his calm temperament, Rasseneur is, so unmistakeably, a *raisonneur*; and in this too, Zola replicated the terms of Possibilist self-portraiture. For Brousse's allies distinguished themselves from Guesde – 'in favour of immediate revolution' – by claiming to take the path of reason: 'We Possibilists want to achieve the same outcome by thinking rationally [le raisonnement].'[33] It was, as such statements made clear, not so much the ends of political activity that divided these camps as the means. At least in the early 1880s, Broussists held to their belief in the inevitability of revolution; and Brousse himself retained from his anarchist origins a faith in the dynamics of working-class action.[34] What might strike us, then, about Zola's transposition of these socialist doctrines in the novel is the extent to which he exaggerated their differences, deradicalising the Possibilist position as a cautious reformism. In Zola's hands, Rasseneur retreats from his own former militancy into moderation in direct proportion to Étienne's emerging radicalism. When, in Part Four of the novel, the would-be leaders' disagreements are brought to a head over Pluchart's intervention in their affairs, Zola explains the polarisation of Étienne and Rasseneur's political stances as, first and foremost, a matter of mutual suspicion and personal enmity:

> The two men had stopped shouting; they had turned bitter and spiteful, feeling cold and hostile as their rivalry was revealed. That was the fundamental reason behind the exaggerated difference between the systems they expounded, throwing one into revolutionary excess and forcing the other into an affectation of prudence, so that they both tended to get transported in spite of themselves to extremes, which did not represent their true convictions. (240; 325)

Provoked by escalating rhetoric rather than deeply held convictions, Zola's version of the socialist rupture effectively taps into a wider scepticism about the meaningfulness of the positions it generated.[35]

Of course, Zola does not take up these precise epithets of Possibilism/ Impossibilism in his novel, most obviously because they post-date the Second Empire history he was telling. But he does reproduce the rhetoric in which such dissensus was couched. Most obviously, the novel expresses Étienne's idealism as a kind of Impossibilism: the *tabula rasa* he prophesies, and the 'mirage' of a new world he brandishes, are described as 'the dream [growing] continually vaster and finer, all the more seductive for riding higher and higher into the realms of impossible fantasy' (169; 261). And when Étienne's vision spirals out of control, taking root in Zola's hitherto level-headed matriarch La Maheude, the narrator insists, in the same terms, on its deleterious consequences: 'the impossible ideal was turning to poison, in the depths of her mind crazed with suffering' (396; 467). In casting Lantier's collectivist dream as utopianism, Zola effectively takes over Brousse's caricature of his rivals as 'the invalids of utopia', and of their desire to make *immediate* change as a childlike frustration: 'They were impatient to discover the promised land, and hungered to taste their share of happiness' (183; 276). At the point of Rasseneur's rupture with Étienne, Zola has the innkeeper ventriloquise a 'Possibilist' suspicion of all such promises of sudden and radical transformation. Here, the language of Broussism is transposed into the worker's idiom, via *style indirect libre*, in a way that feels distinctly contrived:

> Wasn't it foolish to believe that you could *change the world at a stroke*, put the workers in charge of the bosses, and share out the money like an apple? You would need thousands and thousands of years even if it ever did come to pass. So you could stop pestering him with your miracles! The most sensible thing to do, if you didn't want to come a cropper, was to behave yourself, make *realistic claims*, in fact improve the workers' conditions at every possible opportunity. (237–38, emphasis added; 323)

Zola thus casts the would-be leaders' political dispute as a matter of both ethics and aesthetics. First, as a straight-talker, and a straight-walker, Rasseneur sees 'realistic claims' as the only morally legitimate grounds for mass action, opposed as he is to Étienne's high-risk model of revolt. Second, Rasseneur's circumscribed narrative of social change is concerned, above all, with plausibility; its aesthetic foil is the enchanting 'fairytale' with which Étienne seeks to galvanise his fellow miners. When Étienne harangues the Maheu family, his sunny new social order appears as if by miracle: 'in a dazzling, magical vision, justice descended from heaven' (168; 261). Those evenings of political discussion in the Maheu household are a forum for wishful thinking, the seductive dangers of which Zola has his miners intuit: 'Don't you listen, my dear!', La Maheude implores her husband Maheu. 'Can't you see he's telling us fairy-tales?' (169; 261). Here, the worker anticipates her own fate as, in David Baguley's words, 'the victim of rhetoric', charmed by what he calls, after Gérard Genette, Étienne's 'predictive narratives'.[36] And yet, so too is the narrative Rasseneur peddles one of prediction, or counter-prophesy: 'you're not going to get anywhere with all this performance [*vos histoires*]', he tells

Étienne, 'you're going to make the condition of the workers even more wretched...' (237; 323). Zola thus sets up his Possibilist as a voice of caution, and in this, Rasseneur levels the same charge Zola had at a certain type of extravagant storytelling: that it was, ultimately, unethical.

I shall return to this question of storytelling and ethics below. For now, I want to insist – at the risk of stating the obvious – on the fact that the political imagination that Zola's novel describes is so clearly coded as a *literary* imagination. Put differently, the stakes of political *credibility* are conflated with those of aesthetic *plausibility*. In one sense, this was hardly surprising: Zola was replicating a conflation exploited by contemporary politicians. Brousse himself, we should note, gave a positivist, even natur-alist, inflexion to his brand of socialism as 'a new politics based on science'.[37] The modern politician, he clarified, 'no longer attempts flying leaps toward the ideal; he uses his specialist knowledge to bring into the realm of reality not the idea he nurtures, [...] but the idea that can be achieved. He leaves the impossible behind in favour of the possible'.[38] Later, the Broussist Henri Galiment declared his party's programme to augur 'the victory of realist politics over the sentimental tactics that are prized by veterans of romantic politics'.[39] As we saw in Chapter 1, such aesthetic stylisations of politics had long been the mainstay of Zola's own journalistic writing. In fact, one of the most paradigmatic examples of this concerned Zola's first 'novel of the people' *L'Assommoir*.

On 13 February 1877, Zola had published an open letter to Yves Guyot – editor in chief of *Le Bien public*, and a left-wing political figure to whom we shall have cause to return – in which he responded to resounding critiques of the novel, the first part of which had been serialised in Guyot's republican newspaper, before being dropped.[40] The reason for this, Zola explained, was that he was deemed to have betrayed his Republican principles by painting the *peuple* 'in such odious colours'. To these reproaches the novelist replied with his own version of the politics of aesthetics:

> In politics, as in literature, as in all contemporary human thought, there are nowadays *two quite distinct currents: the idealist current and the naturalist current*. I call 'idealist politics' the kind that indulges in grand expressions, that *speculates about men* as though they were pure abstractions, that dreams of utopia without first studying reality. I call 'naturalist politics' the kind that intends to proceed first by experience, that is based on facts, that, in short, attends to a nation according to its needs.[41]

Here, in miniature, Zola sets out the fundamentals of a political vision that he will, we have seen, hammer home over the next four years. Setting the Republic on firm foundations required what he later called an 'experimental politics', rooted in facts and observation, and, crucially, shorn of an idealism that he associates with empty grandiloquence, speculation, and utopian dreaming.[42]

If France had twice failed to turn itself from a monarchy into a Republic without slipping back into the 'dictatorship' of Empire, this was, Zola continued, the logical conclusion of it having been raised on nebulous and impractical political theories:

> Think back to that period of the 1848 Republic. All of its attempts failed, because [...] it was consumed by mawkish humanitarianism, by a *purely speculative kind of socialism*, by romantic rhetoric and the religiosity of deist poets. It never had a clear idea of the France it wanted to govern.[43]

Socialism; romanticism; humanitarianism; poetry; spiritual feeling... These were the disparate terms that Zola happily strung together, each interchangeable with its master-concept, idealism – and in turn metonymically associated in his imagination with two *quarante-huitard* writers in particular, George Sand and Victor Hugo. In a lengthy article for *Le Figaro* of 2 November 1880, Zola ridiculed Hugo's prophetic humanitarianism as a kind of senility and warned his young readers against worshipping this false idol.[44] No doubt, Zola admitted, 'Victor Hugo is a gentle soul when he dreams of the universal embrace of peoples, the end of war, mankind arriving in a city of light.' Such utopian imaginings remained, however, a political and intellectual cul-de-sac:

> It is not enough to preach an ideal of goodness and harmony, and there is a danger in waiting for a poetic future that will never come to pass. True courage lies in setting to work in order to *achieve what is possible* [*conquérir le possible*] in the real world, and this is the task of our century.[45]

At last, then, we can venture the formulation: that naturalism, in politics as in aesthetics – or indeed as an aesthetics of politics – takes itself to be a kind of 'possibilism' (small 'p').

In one sense, we might say that the rivalry Zola sets up over the dominant 'aesthetic' of Republicanism finds itself replayed in *Germinal* via the political differences of his competing leaders. Étienne's prophetic vision, 'his religious dreams of a compassionate society where justice would triumph and all men would be brothers' (238–39; 324), is caricaturally Hugolian, a pastiche, if you like, of the writer's socialist-romantico-lyrico-religiosity. Rasseneur's political pragmatism, meanwhile, borders on the language of naturalist metadiscourse: 'he only wanted the bosses to be reasonable [*il demandait seulement le possible aux patrons*], unlike so many other people, he didn't want to demand the impossible (68; 165–66). What I want to turn to now is the strike itself, not simply as a catalyst for this political dissensus in the novel, but as a figure for that 'speculative' form of socialism Zola derided – 'speculative' insofar as strike action demands, of course, deprivation in the present for the promise of future reward. How exactly, I want to ask, does Zola harness the strike as a vehicle for thinking about a 'politics of the possible'?

The Strike and 'Mass Idealism'

Workers acquired the legal right to strike on 25 May 1864, when the Loi Ollivier lifted the prohibitions that had been in place, by and large, since 1791. Though restrictions remained – namely, around strikers' use of violence and threats, and punishments for impinging on others' 'right to work'– the law stimulated a wave of strike action.[46] Zola learned about the 1866 coal strike at Anzin and Denain when he visited in 1884; and he no doubt intended to condense in *Germinal* features of the 1869 series of strikes that culminated in bloody stand-offs between striking labourers and the military at Aubin and La Ricamerie.[47] But Zola was, of course, also attuned to more contemporary debates about this militant tactic, which remained nothing if not controversial through the early Third Republic. Both Broussist and Guesdist factions encouraged strikes in the early 1880s, but they differed in their ideas about what these should aim to achieve. For Brousse, the strike, allied to a 'trade union' attitude, represented an important channel of the working-class organisation that could ultimately lead to the implosion of the capitalist system.[48] Guesdists, meanwhile, remained cautious about the efficacy of the strike, which they viewed as the opportunity to pursue wider political objectives.[49] In the wake of the great Anzin strike of 1884, these debates reached a crescendo. Guesde wrote a lengthy article, 'Le Résultat', for *Le Cri du peuple* in which he expressed his unbound admiration for the miners' heroic resistance while casting doubt on their means. Zola read Guesde's article and duly noted down: 'The strike is not salvation, but it paves the way.'[50]

In essence, Guesde was rehearsing the line that he had set out in his 1878 pamphlet *La République et les Grèves*, and which he had repeated across his journalism since. As a tactic or weapon, the strike might force some material concessions, which either protect or materially improve the conditions of salaried workers. But it remains powerless to alter the exploitative relationship between capital and labour, '[leaving] proletarians as proletarian as they were before'.[51] It was not, Guesde repeated, on economic grounds – rebelling as employees – that the workers' struggle would be won. For even the most successful strike would not bring the proletariat closer to the horizon of their emancipation: that is, collective ownership of the means of production. But what the strike could achieve, even where it failed, or especially where it failed, was the feat of opening workers' eyes to political chicanery, of fostering class consciousness, of demonstrating the insufficiencies of the law as a means of contesting capitalist power – in short, of pointing the way towards the serious master-task of expropriating the capitalist class. In the Guesdist scenario, writes Robert Stuart, 'disillusioned trade unionists would supposedly emerge from defeats as militant socialists'.[52] Or as *Le Socialiste* put it, in the wake of the infamous Decazeville strike of 1886: 'End of strike, beginning of the Revolution.'[53] If the immense suffering produced by a failed strike could be understood by Guesdists as a necessary ill, it was insofar as it proved to workers that they could expect nothing of their employers until they took power for themselves.

In his *Ébauche*, Zola took over this conception of the strike as a vital catalyst.[54] And yet, the novel itself remains sceptical about the politicisation of the strike that Guesdists, in particular, sought to promote. Zola casts his (Guesdist) revolutionary intellectual Pluchart as an opportunist, seeing in the strike 'an excellent opportunity to persuade our men to join his great enterprise…' (176; 269). The militant's support for the strike is a means of drawing the miners into a vast network of international solidarity, a 'plan for world-wide victory' (281; 365), that will ultimately fail to deliver on its promise when the strikers' provident fund runs dry. Predictably, Rasseneur is Pluchart's (as well as Étienne's) chief critic: the innkeeper wants a strike that pursues 'sensible claims' (175; 269), or no strike at all. At such moments, he acts as the novel's voice of reason: 'all of his patience and good sense [toute sa nature d'homme raisonnable] poured forth in an untroubled flow of effortlessly clear declarations' (237; 323) – his role to act as a check on the political free-wheeling Étienne sets in motion.

In this respect, Rasseneur is also something of a literary type. Yves Guyot's 1882 strike novel, *La Famille Pichot: scènes de l'enfer social* – with which Zola would almost certainly have been familiar – had staged a similar battle for miners' hearts and minds.[55] There, it was the miner and syndicalist Pierre Ringard, the very embodiment of moderation and self-control, who provided an antidote to the fiery tirades of the novel's chief agitator, or '*gréviculteur*', one Lèchepique. The latter attempts to seduce the strikers with a radical, collectivist vision that Zola will have Étienne articulate, albeit in a different spirit. Ringard's task is to persuade his fellow miners to eschew violence and adhere to his vision of the strike as a peaceful, rational means of pursuing 'specific reforms'.[56] With his pleas for caution, Ringard represents the twin risks that the miners' unchecked fervour might bring: failure and bloody repression. He is also concerned with preserving the legitimacy of the strike as a weapon, by calling upon his fellow miners to be unimpeachable – to avoid providing, that is, grist to the mill of conservative critique (154). In this, Ringard echoes the rhetorical imperative of Guyot's own journalism, namely his reports on the Anzin strike that appeared in *Le Voltaire* between 20 and 28 July 1878. Zola was himself writing for the newspaper at the time and returned to Guyot's articles in the course of preparing *Germinal*.[57] In his reports from the frontline, Guyot set a sombre tone. Confronted by the ominous presence of troops at Valenciennes station, he described the resurgence of painful memories of the 1870 war with Prussia and the ensuing Paris Commune. But rather than public gatherings and streets filled with desperation, what he found at Anzin instead was quiet and patient resignation, as most miners waited out the strike indoors. Across his dispatches, he described straightforwardly 'the extreme poverty' that had made the miners' positions untenable.[58]

In short, Guyot was clearly concerned with undercutting those well-rehearsed clichés of anti-strike discourse: that strikers sought out confrontation; that they became scroungers through their self-imposed deprivation; and, above all, that their protests were baseless. The claim that miners had simply failed to understand the relative privileges of their own condition was a familiar conceit rehearsed by the conservative press, including those articles Zola cut out for his preparatory *dossier*. Reporting on the 1884 Anzin strike for *Le Figaro*, the journalist Georges Grison urged his readers to curb their sympathy, since they are, in fact, sorely mistaken in believing the miners' existence to be one of desperate poverty.[59] Having visited Anzin himself, Grison could declare that, in comparison with the Parisian labourer, 'the miner lives in incredible economic conditions'. *Le Sémaphore de Marseille* drove home a similar point: 'in Anzin, workers enjoy a host of advantages that in fact raise, exceptionally, the price of their labour'.[60] Where the grounds for striking were not dismissed altogether, commentators often called on strikers to exercise restraint. In a climate of economic difficulty, exacerbated by foreign competition, the miners should rein in their demands. According to *L'Écho du Nord*, 'calls to act with moderation and good sense were needed in abundance', for this strike was 'perhaps even more unreasonable than the others'.[61] Such reports are remarkable for their lack of compassion and were clearly designed to antagonise a conservative readership. But even for moderate commentators, the nagging question remained: where should the line be drawn in the strike's ambitions? Or at what point did a strike risk losing its legitimacy?

For the Republican government, which was to formally legalise trade unions in March 1884, the strike had to be understood as a permissible strategy, albeit one that could be used more or less wisely.[62] Parliamentary debates that March centred on the need for government intervention in the Anzin strike, with the socialist deputy for Valenciennes, Alfred Giard, warning of growing unrest and antagonisms on the ground. (Giard had taken Zola, in February, to visit the Anzin miners, at the very moment the strike was breaking out.) Giard pleaded for the Republican government to ward off violent confrontation by making changes to legislation on mines. The Ministre des Travaux Publics, one M. Raynal, responded dismissively by vaunting the miners' admirable pacifism and 'sagesse', capable as they were of managing their own affairs:

> Workers have had the good sense to understand that the strike is a weapon that needs to be wielded with a certain skill, wielded in a way that is, let me tell you [. . .], rational and almost scientific. [. . .] [T]heir attention must be drawn to [. . .] the fact that it is in their interests not to push their demands and claims too far.[63]

In this case, the ubiquitous rhetoric of rationality and self-control is applied to strikers on whom the government's hopes of a conciliatory resolution would depend. And it is, of course, a double discourse of descriptive praise and ideological prescription, whereby the sensible qualities of the miners' temperament are readily extolled by those in whose interests it lies to curb their anger.

Now, Zola redeploys such rhetoric in his novel rather liberally: the narrator insists on La Maheude's 'moderation and good sense' (184; 277), while Maheu is 'the [miner] whose good sense was quoted as an example' (215; 301). And Zola does so all the more, it would seem, to heighten the novel's regret at the gradual erosion of the workers' level-headedness through the strike. As passions rise, Étienne recoils before La Maheude's transformed demeanour: 'He found her so changed that he hardly recognized her, from being such a good woman formerly [de tant de sagesse autrefois], [. . .] and now at this moment refusing to listen to reason, speaking of killing people all around her' (395; 466). Diagnosing a kind of *morbus democraticus*, Zola taps into that truistic identification of revolutionary impulses with madness, or loss of reason, tracked by the historian Laure Murat.[64] (Moreover, Zola no doubt makes La Maheude Étienne's most ardent proselyte in order to conjure up a particular sense of panic about women's susceptibility to socialist politics, and their role in inciting men to sacrifice.)[65] Certainly, the naturalist novel casts the utopian imagination, through its own metacommentary, as a form of *égarement*. At the height of Étienne's prophetic speech at the Plan-des-Dames, the narrator – a self-styled voice of rationality – redescribes the miner's discourse as the manifestation of both loss of reason and monomania: 'At this peak of mental tension his rational arguments faltered and gave way to the obsession of the prophet' (284; 367). In this respect, then, Rasseneur is to Étienne what Jean will be to Maurice in *La Débâcle* (1892), a novel in which differences in temperament come to crystallise prevailing divisions over the Republic's future: the 'folie' of the intellectual Communard Maurice, on the one hand; the 'good sense' of the soldier Jean, on the other ('the healthy part of France, the reasonable, solid, peasant part').[66]

It is with a similarly transparent ideological bias that *Germinal* mercilessly pathologises the miner *as radical*. And yet, the novel also reflects critically, I want to suggest, on the relationships of power that determine, or arbitrate, what (and who) is and isn't reasonable. Although Rasseneur's words of caution about the risks of Étienne's designs will ultimately be vindicated, the narrator also hints at the relative comfort that has softened the radical convictions the miner-turned-barkeeper once held: 'behind his plump, jovial, beery exterior he fostered a secret jealousy' (175; 269). Rasseneur's animosity towards Étienne periodically tempts him into a quietist complicity with his former employer, 'forgetting his grudge for having been sacked from his job at the mine'. The problem is, Zola implies, that the language of reason and moderation his Possibilist employs tends to be the preserve of those operating at one remove from the coalface. Worse still, such scepticism about militant action – 'Really, this strike was a damn silly idea!', Rasseneur declares (176; 270) – risks lapsing into the censorious, and paternalist, rhetoric of conservative critique. This Zola rehearses most directly in the pronouncements of his middle-class stakeholders. When M. Hennebeau finds Maheu standing awkwardly in his drawing room, about to voice the claims of his fellow malcontents, the manager's disappointment is directed towards 'a sensible man and a good workman' (217; 303). And when Hennebeau entreats his employees to accept their new conditions, return to the mine, and drop their threat to strike, it is with a typically paternalistic flourish: 'You'll die of hunger before the week's out: how will you manage?... But I'm sure that I can count on your good sense [*votre sagesse*]' (222–23; 309). In the mouth of Zola's employer, the miner's '*sagesse*', his sagacity, is given its other, infantilised sense of good behaviour.

Hennebeau's appeal to the miners is what we might call a 'reality check': a reminder of the odds stacked against them, and thus the futility of strike action as a remedy to their ills. The caution he offers is obviously a stroke of managerial self-interest, but this call to 'realism' also belonged to a wider anti-strike discourse. Take the entry for 'Strike' in Pierre Larousse's *Grand Dictionnaire universel,* which Zola consulted: 'in this fight between the capitalist's coffers and the worker's stomach, the odds of winning strongly favour the former'.[67] All capitalists have to do is wait patiently for the workers' resources to be exhausted and bring in foreign labourers with more modest demands. Zola duly noted: 'no fight possible between the capitalist's coffers and the worker's stomach (therein lies my drama)'.[68] It was the improbability of the strike's success – note that Zola rephrases it as an impossibility – that would furnish the narrative with its own form of (economic) fatalism. On these terms, the strike certainly held an aesthetic appeal; it emerged, as Zola later put it, as 'the only dramatic backdrop, the only one that could bring the facts to the fore as needed'.[69] But Larousse's pessimism also chimed with Zola's longstanding political convictions. When he reported for *Le Sémaphore de Marseille* on the first French Congrès ouvrier, held in Paris in October 1876, Zola expressed his hopes that this forum might prevent violent conflict between labourers and employers, the strike being, he noted, a 'last resort, always disastrous, for those who use it'.[70]

Such bleak characterisations of industrial action were part of a familiar rhetorical manoeuvre, whereby a matter-of-fact appeal to mathematical probability (namely, the strike's rigged odds) passed itself off as salutary – a way of protecting workers' interests. 'But we would like [workers] to reflect and to recognise, once and for all, just how little they gain from strikes', implored one journalist, reporting on the Anzin strike.[71] Yet in reality, as Michelle Perrot demonstrates, successful strikes outweighed failures overall, in the fifty years that followed the legalisation of the right to strike in 1864.[72] What's more, Perrot asserts, the effectiveness of the strike would need to be measured by more than immediate results: workers envision their local fight as 'a tableau of a play in several acts', an act of solidarity, a call on the government's attention, and a way of forcing its hand (65). To object to the enormity of the costs, then, in relation to the benefits – to cast the strike, that is, as a bad calculation – is not only to obscure the real gains bought by militant tactics but to express a humanitarian concern that risked becoming a liberal ruse.

Zola's strike is, of course, cast as an impossible proposition from the get-go: the miners' paltry reserves make it a reckless kind of risk-taking. Off to war, as Guesde put it, with 'empty rifles', theirs is an act of self-harm, which Zola's narrator renders in Guesdian terms as 'the heroic suicide of labour'.[73] But the point is, in Zola's telling, that it doesn't matter to the strikers how plausible their claims are, their sense of hope is undimmed, even perversely emboldened, by the dawning impossibility of success:

> Since they had been shown the promised land of justice, they were ready to suffer on the road to universal happiness. [...] When their eyes became blurred with fatigue, they could see the ideal city of their dreams beyond the horizon, but now somehow close and real; there all men were brothers, in a golden age where meals and labour were shared between equals. Nothing could shake their conviction that they were already on the threshold. The fund was empty, the Company would never yield, every day could only make the situation worse, and yet they kept faith in their hope, showing a blithe contempt for reality. (226; 313)

Here, Zola gives voice to that Jamesonian evocation of the strike as a 'supreme event', as a set of particular demands that turns into a call for 'universal' revolution – albeit one that can only be conceived by the novel as a set of clichés (a golden age, a communal meal). The strikers' avidly counterfactual imagination propels them into a struggle that inevitably exceeds its original purpose, just as it escapes the control of its leader.

In fact, what Zola describes is the phenomenon that, some twenty years later, the Marxist radical Rosa Luxemburg would call 'mass idealism', in the wake of the revolutionary turmoil and mass strikes that swept across swathes of the Russian Empire. In her 1906 pamphlet, *The Mass Strike, the Political Party and the Trade Union*, Luxemburg declared a new epoch in the development of class struggle, which had at last put to rest the defeatist attitude, and reformist ideology, of social democracy. What this great historical experiment had shown is that revolution cannot be effectively staged and countermanded around questions of provisioning and regulation. Instead, it must arise spontaneously – and this spontaneity is its great force:

> At the moment that a real, earnest period of mass strikes begins, all these *'calculations' of 'cost'* become merely projects for exhausting the ocean with a tumbler. And it is a veritable ocean of frightful privations and sufferings that is brought by every revolution to the proletarian masses. And the solution that a revolutionary period makes of this apparently invincible difficulty consists, under the circumstances, of *such an immense volume of mass idealism* being simultaneously released that the masses are insensible to the bitterest sufferings.[74]

In the heat of the struggle, collective ideals diminish the 'costs' that a general strike entails, turning, Luxemburg says, 'the most provident paterfamilias' into a 'revolutionary romanticist', for whom material well-being – nay, life itself – are readily compromised. In this game of endurance, strikers, borne along by the revolutionary 'storm', have an astonishing ability to survive on fresh air and fury.

Luxemburg's elegiac vision of mass insurrection speaks, of course, to an ideological and political context that Zola's novel can only loosely 'predict' on its horizon. In the aftermath of the strike's defeat, Zola's spurned leader dares to imagine a new syndicalist dawn, the revolution 'accompanied by a general strike and agreements between all the workers with relief funds' (522; 581). Still, Zola's own version of the strike is undoubtedly driven by the same impulses: its self-sustaining momentum, its draw to self-sacrifice, its casting-off of any rational calculations of means and ends. It hardly needs saying, of course, that the similarities between Zola and Luxemburg stop there. What, for the Marxist radical, is proof of the working class's readiness to emancipate themselves remains for Zola an ethical problem, his miners' suffering never sublimated or anaesthetised in the way Luxemburg suggests. Moreover, however powerfully Zola conjures up the workers' 'mass idealism', it inevitably remains the product of 'mediation', to borrow the guiding term of Naomi Schor's seminal study of Zola's crowds. It is set in motion, if not contained, by a leader for whom the strike becomes a grave matter of conscience.[75] Indeed, Zola charges his militant leader with eroding the collective 'good sense' of a working community for whom moderation is a prerequisite of survival – however much this moderation might militate against their own emancipation.

In what follows, we shall return to Jameson's reading of Gissing and his populist novels in *The Political Unconscious* in order to think through the ideological interests at stake in Zola's representation of his own strike leader. Zola's narrator casts, of course, an obvious suspicion on the fragile power that the miner-cum-demagogue wields over 'those 3,000 chests whose hearts he caused to beat in tune with his every word' (285; 368). In focalising the working-class uprising through the experience and imagination of the popular leader, Zola taps into a set of prevailing concerns about a figure whose legitimacy was always in doubt, just as he probes the limits of the people's capacity for self-determination. What (or whose) fantasy, we might ask, is played out via Étienne Lantier's rise and fall?

Demagogues and *ressentiment*

Few images conjured up more powerfully, or more pointedly, a sense of middle-class fascination with socialist politics in this period than Jean

Figure 2.1   Jean Béraud, *À la Salle Graffard* (1884). Oil on canvas.
Private collection. Photo by Fine Art Images/Heritage Images/Getty Images.

Béraud's oil painting *À la Salle Graffard* (Figure 2.1). It was first exhibited at the 1884 Salon, just two months after Zola saw Guesde hold forth in a similar meeting at the Salle de la Redoute. Poised between gravity and caricature, Béraud's spectacle of passionate oration – the imposing red *tribune*, the acclamations, the outstretched hands of an impassioned crowd – seemed to condense a prevailing set of clichés about the politicised working classes and the dangerous allure of leftist demagoguery. Salon reviewers fixed on the central speaker, imagining his thundering indictments of 'vile capital' and the 'terrible bourgeois': 'his hand is clenched over his heart as though he wanted to rip it out of his chest and toss it to the Left [*la Sociale*]'.[76] Just that April, a month before the official Salon, the Salle Graffard (a popular institution in the working-class neighbourhood of Ménilmontant) had hosted meetings in solidarity with the Anzin strikers, not unlike the event Zola witnessed across town.[77]

Béraud's scene of populist politics seemed to capture something of the tone that ended up dominating press reports on the Anzin strike in February and March of that year, especially where journalists had the strike leaders in their sights. In *Le Figaro*, Grison warned of loquacious interlopers whipping up miners into a frenzy and undermining the strategic purpose of the strike by urging them to stake impossible claims: 'they listen to those great speech-makers, risking everything'.[78] Commentators were well aware that the strike leader derived his authority, first and foremost, from being a skilled speaker; and, in their own version of events, his pernicious rhetoric served to stoke the passions of those who could be easily manipulated. 'Unfortunately', declared *Le Voltaire*, 'the suffering and deprivation [strikers] endure leave them all too willing to listen to ring-leaders' propositions', and so they are turned once again into an 'unwitting instrument of those political passions stoked by anarchists and hardliners, who see in the strike nothing but a weapon against the government'.[79] Such accounts tended to operate, then, on two broad assumptions: first, that strike-leaders were unscrupulous politicos capitalising on the miners' desperation, exploiting the exploited, in order to pursue their own larger (often anti-Republican) objectives; second, that workers would not have possessed the energy to drive strike action otherwise.

Of course, to cast the strikers as suggestible victims is a gambit designed to deprive them of political initiative; and it is a gambit that Zola has his manager Hennebeau try out in reaction to the miners' demands: 'I can see that you've been changed, you were so peaceful before. It's true, isn't it? You've been promised milk and honey instead of bread and butter' (219; 306). Hennebeau's rhetoric reads here as a pastiche of the kind of pseudo-paternalist concern for the strikers' plight that Zola encountered in abundant conservative commentaries. *Le Figaro*'s take on the Anzin strike was emblematic: it exploited 'the misery of all for the benefit of the few – *ambitious individuals dreaming of electoral success*, [. . .] foolish men who are intoxicated by words and who [. . .] can find no better way to alleviate misery than by adding unemployment to the mix'.[80] The author duly calls upon 'all sensible people' to speak with those labourers who risk becoming 'the victims of some Basly', duped by the promise of progress that no strike can realise. The allusion was to one Émile Basly, general secretary of the Syndicat des ouvriers mineurs du Nord, and emergent leader of the Anzin strike. Zola had met Basly during his visit to Anzin and noted the former miner's growing popularity, as well as his aspirational demeanour: 'found himself drawn to politics, took lessons in secret, read about miners' hygiene, acquired some gentlemanly manners [*est devenu un demi-monsieur*]. Boots, a coat over his pullover, an intelligent face with prominent cheekbones'.[81] Zola recognised a type – indeed, one constructed as such by the conservative press – and planned to cast him as Pluchart: 'My member of the International is a Basli' [sic].[82] In the final version, Basly's traits are instead divided, as Henri Marel suggests, between Pluchart, Rasseneur (Basly was an innkeeper), and Étienne, whose new boots are the emblem of his growing self-regard.[83]

What Basly emblematised for the conservative imagination was the upward trajectory of the ambitious labour leader – those the economist Leroy-Beaulieu described as 'social climbers' [ouvriers parvenus].[84] Such intelligent, eloquent, charismatic specimens were, he explained, 'the peculiar products of a time when ambition takes root in every class' (38). These workers' 'superficial' learning gave them just enough leverage to charm the crowd, whose aspirations they flattered, albeit not insincerely: 'they too are believers; they have faith in their *creed*' (84; original emphasis). In tracking Étienne's rise, Zola rehearses precisely these anxieties about the impassioned, proletarian autodidact, whose half-baked knowledge feeds his messianic zeal. (*Germinal* was to be, let us recall, 'the study of ambition').[85] In Zola's hands, the 'demi savant' strike leader is periodically prone to crises of conscience, to fears 'that he was not the right man for the situation' (227; 314), only to lapse into the resurgent fantasy of pursuing his own political, even parliamentary, career:

> And he started to dream again of becoming a popular leader: once Montsou was at his feet, Paris would beckon from the misty distance, and, who knows, election to Parliament, speaking to a packed audience from the hallowed benches, and he saw himself slaying the bourgeoisie in the first speech every made to Parliament by a working man.

As the narrative slips in and out of *style indirect libre* – the speculative 'who knows' the rhetorical sign of the worker's limitless ambition – Zola assists Étienne in the exposition of his own, half-articulated bad faith: the worker who claims to speak in the name of his fellow labourers is no longer one of them, always already *déclassé*.

In effect, Étienne has already committed what Jameson calls, in relation to Gissing's proletarian novels, 'that form of class treason which is fascination with or aspiration to the status of those on the other side of the class line'.[86] Indeed, Jameson's seminal reading of Gissing has, I want now to suggest, a number of implications for our understanding of Zola's own treatment of his radical leader.[87] Of particular importance to us is Jameson's analysis of Gissing's contemporary novel *Demos* (1886), which tells the story of the young mechanic and working-class militant Richard Mutimer, who inherits an unexpected fortune, invests the money in a factory founded on socialist principles, and moves up in the world through his marriage to an upper-middle-class woman. When his inheritance is proven to be a mistake, Mutimer falls back into poverty and attempts to revive his populist political career, only to die at the hands of those workers who had once followed him. In one sense, then, Gissing gives free rein – for a time – to the hubristic, class-bound ambitions that Zola too has his hero express; he 'experiments' (in Jameson's terms) with the narrative of social transformation, only to rehearse its impossibility. In proving, at every turn, the unsuitability of the worker who enters (or aspires to enter) a new social station, Gissing's novel provides, Jameson argues, 'a virtual object lesson in snobbery' (185). If Zola, by contrast, leaves the prospect of his own worker's class ascension a private fantasy, we might nevertheless wish to apply to *Germinal* a similar verdict. For Zola describes and generates a mistrust of the militant worker type, which hinges on such commonplace anxieties about class confusion: the influence of what Leroy-Beaulieu called 'this little working-class aristocracy', or those destined to be a contradiction in terms.[88]

In this respect, Zola and Gissing's militants both belong, to adopt Chantal Jacquet's neologism, to the category of 'the transclasses'.[89] Jacquet's reformulation of the phenomenon of social mobility in horizontal, rather than vertical, terms is intended to offer an alternative to those pejorative metaphors that have been, and remain, tied to the idea of flight or betrayal – metaphors which, of course, both Zola and Gissing's populist fictions exploit. In Zola's case, it is the ladder – that ubiquitous instrument of the miners' labour – that acquires a metaphorical double in the form of Lantier's social climbing: 'he had moved up a rung, he had entered the despised world of the bourgeoisie' (227; 313). The fact that Zola worried about the plausibility of Étienne's character, wondering whether 'perhaps a bourgeois was needed' rather than a precocious miner, was no doubt symptomatic of these concerns.[90] But if Zola ultimately entrusts the revolutionary project to his mechanic, he nevertheless polices in the narrative the dynamic he represents. Put differently, Zola effectively repeats the injunction Jameson identifies across a range of nineteenth-century novels of the people: 'stay in your place!' Or rather, 'do not attempt to become another kind of character from the one you already are!'[91] In its most schematic form, this is the warning delivered by the ending of Gissing's *Demos*. The rise and fall of Gissing's hero concludes with the latter's gratuitous punishment at the hands of 'Demos', the blood-thirsty crowd who turn on their would-be leader with stones in an act of collective murder. Though the striking structural similarity with *Germinal* and its own climactic lapidation scene goes unmentioned in

Jameson's account, it surely forms part of what he would call the 'narrative apparatus' of high realism, which demands that the energies of 'the conscious political revolutionary' be contained (181).

In Zola's hands, punishment comes, of course, the day after the strike's bloody conclusion, when Étienne is forced to confront the 'inevitable reaction to his previous popularity' (443; 509). Faced with the unbound anger of the other miners, the former leader suffers the same fate – the same martyrdom – as his namesake, (Saint) Étienne:

> A wild clamour arose, everyone took up bricks, broke them, and threw the pieces, trying to tear him apart as they would have liked to tear the soldiers apart. He was so dazed that he gave up trying to escape, and turned to face them, trying to calm them down by reasoning with them. His former speeches, which had been so warmly welcomed in the past, sprang to his lips. He repeated words that he had used to intoxicate them in earlier days, when he held them in the palm of his hand like an obedient flock; but the spell failed to work, and the only response he elicited was a hail of stones. (445; 510)

Just as, in Gissing's scenario, brutality wins out when the crowd grows 'tired of listening to mere articulate speech', Étienne experiences the diminished returns of his rhetoric as a broken spell.[92] Or, to reprise the terms of Claude Duchet, we witness in the scene of popular violence 'a veritable catastrophe of speech', whereby eloquence and power have become dislocated.[93] These fantasies of vengeance, perpetrated against the militant individual who claims to speak in the name of the people, thus do far more than rehearse the middle-class terror of the baying mob. Rather they draw on the same narrative, or mythological, paradigm that Schor determines in Zola's strike novel, whereby the leader becomes 'the surrogate victim, the single object of an entire community's rage and frustration'. His fate recalls, she adds, an ancient Greek ritual: 'the ostracism of the *isotheos*, that is, the God-like member of the community'.[94]

Ultimately, then, a similar, though not identical, structural logic prevails in Zola and Gissing's populist novels: their leaders must expiate the crime of their inauthenticity by enduring the same ordeal. Mutimer and Lantier's punishment is, first and foremost, one of ritual humiliation, in the proper sense of abasement (making humble) – or more precisely still, we might venture, one of *reclassement*. Lantier, like Mutimer, rouses the people with good intentions. And yet, the idealist leader cannot be strictly separated from his ostensible opposite number, the cynical or unscrupulous rabble-rouser. In fact, such distinctions between 'good' and 'bad' militants are, Schor argues, 'rendered inoperative' if we assess the figure solely in terms of his effects on the crowd, rather than the nature of his motives.[95] We can be in no doubt that Étienne is, in spirit, quite unlike what Schor calls 'the sinister provocateur, a figure already fully realised in the pre-Commune *Les Mystères de Marseille*', and whose 'persistent function is to lead his followers into a death trap'.[96] Here, Schor has in mind Mathéus, the malevolent double agent who disguises himself as a revolutionary during the Marseilles workers' uprising of 1848, and manipulates the marchers to his own ends. The revolutionary imposter draws the unarmed labourers into a deadly confrontation with the National Guard in order to produce a corpse around which to rally the crowd's anger ('Now that the people are mad, I will shepherd them in whichever way I want. . .').[97]

That Zola was reviewing the text of *Les Mystères* for a second edition with Charpentier while writing *Germinal* (he composed the preface in July 1884) no doubt explains some of the resonances in the latter. And perhaps the most conspicuous of these is the culminating scene of the strike: the labourers' catastrophic provocation of those armed soldiers guarding the mine, resulting in the death of one soldier and several miners, Maheu included.[98] Unlike Mathéus's plot, however, this tragic confrontation is not choreographed by Zola's strike leader, but rather operates precisely beyond his control. For the miners Étienne has incited to revolt – 'those brutes that he had unleashed' (335; 431) – perform the fantasy of a heroic death that he himself repeatedly articulates but does not ultimately fulfil: 'Oh, if one of those bloody soldiers could strike me down with a bullet to the heart, what a fine way to go that would be!' (400; 471). Retained by the feverish hope of a possible victory, Étienne's dream of dying for the cause is endlessly postponed. In *Germinal*, the function of the cynical provocateur or malevolent imposter has been subsumed by the fervent idealist, whose betrayal of the people operates not by conscious scheming, but through his own gradual, ineluctable alienation from those he would save.

Zola thus clearly operates at one remove from the most embedded stereotypes of anti-strike discourse: his leader acts with sincerity – he believes, that is, in the idealism he expounds – even as he remains caught up in an ambition that precludes his self-sacrifice. For all his complexity, Étienne remains the object of what Jameson calls, in his account of Gissing, '*ressentiment*', a complex concept he takes over and adapts from Friedrich Nietzsche, and which bears reflecting on here. *Ressentiment* is defined by Jameson as a 'psychological mechanism': one rooted in a 'slave morality', which vilifies masters, resents what they have, and allows the enslaved (in Nietzsche's own words) to 'preserve themselves from harm through the exercise of imaginary vengeance'.[99] This revenge does not require slaves to assert their strength; instead, it involves 'infecting' masters with their own slave mentality, which then expresses itself as Judaeo-Christian ethics, namely, the virtues of charity and pity (189). Nietzsche sets forth this master narrative, Jameson clarifies, as part of 'a critique of Victorian moralism and hypocrisy', but the concept also, and more importantly for us, has a wider 'political function' in later nineteenth-century thought – one Jameson traces to the philosopher and historian Hippolyte Taine's *Les Origines de la France contemporaine* (1876–94).[100] For Taine uses the motif, Jameson suggests, to '"explain" the phenomenon of revolution [...] in a twofold way': first, to account 'for the destructive envy the have-nots feel for the haves'; second, in a more 'overdetermined' sense, to 'explain the conduct of those who incited an otherwise essentially satisfied popular mass to such "unnatural" disorders' as an expression of their 'private dissatisfactions'. Individuals inclined to the vocation of political militancy had, according to this conservative logic, a personal axe to grind: they were 'unsuccessful writers and poets, bad philosophers, bilious journalists, and failures of all kinds' (189) – in short, alienated intellectuals.

Now, Taine's impassioned account of the Revolution was nothing if not controversial; and Zola openly complained about the historical vision his former *maître à penser* had put forth. Taine had reduced revolutionary action to episodes of pillaging, murders of landowners, the seizing of property, or to reprise Jameson's terms, 'destructive envy' towards the 'haves': 'The words he uses to define the Revolution reveal the concerns of a businessman', Zola objected.[101] In turn, the novelist took issue with Taine's caricature of the people as a menacing, modern Hydra, susceptible to 'the contagion of the democratic dream that disturbs the best minds'.[102] If Taine's judgement on the Revolution and Terror was severe, it was, Zola surmised, because it had been shaped by more recent history: the shock of the Commune, whose uproar Zola imagines intruding on the philosopher's splendid, scholarly isolation (33). In other words, Zola diagnoses in Taine's historical account the symptoms of the intellectual's own *ressentiment*.[103] And yet, for all Zola takes up a critical distance from Taine's brand of counter-revolutionary ideology, he rehearses, as we have seen, comparable anxieties in his fiction – not least about the radical agitator, whose paradigm, on Taine's reading, is Robespierre.[104]

To co-opt the terms in which Jameson describes the 'high realist' proletarian novel in general, we might venture that Zola likewise subjects his 'conscious revolutionary' to 'a very special kind of naturalizing operation'. At base, it is one that transforms his 'impulses toward the future and toward radical change' into '"feelings" and psychological attributes': in Étienne's case, those private, barely-acknowledged drives of ambition, vanity, and pride.[105] Indeed, Zola's portraits of the militant leader in *Germinal* (Pluchart, Étienne, and Rasseneur) appear connected to the string of ambitious Republican politicians the writer had repeatedly derided in his journalism a few years earlier. There, he cast the politician, in the precise manner of Jameson's reading, as a failed writer:

> In times of trouble, politics is, then, *the refuge of all those frustrated in their ambitions*, the battleground where the useless, the powerless, the defeated gather to launch their bid for success. [. . .] Nearly all of them carry in their pockets the manuscripts of plays and novels that have been rejected twenty times over by theatre directors and publishers; or else there lurks inside them an embittered journalist, a failed historian, or a misunderstood poet.[106]

Zola's mediocre politician thus appears to be the archetypal figure of *ressentiment*: his exclusion from the world of letters, his disappointed ambition, is held to explain, in Zola's account, his own obsession with policing the literature of others. For such opportunists, politics is not simply the domain of careerism, it is a substitute for bad writing.

What implications might Zola's curious attempt to delegitimise the politician as a fourth-rate writer have for his portrait of Étienne as a would-be politician? To adapt the exact terms of Jameson's verdict on *Demos*'s Richard Mutimer, we might say: Zola resents Étienne, and what he resents most is the latter's *ressentiment*.[107] But where the theory of *ressentiment*, for Taine and Gissing, amounts, Jameson claims, to 'an expression of annoyance at seemingly gratuitous lower-class agitation' (189), for Zola it manifests itself primarily, I shall suggest later, as an ethical problem – and one in which the writer is implicated. In fact, what clearly distinguishes Zola's story of populism from Gissing's is the (problematic) identification that the author cultivates with his militant hero. It is a form of identification that Robert Lethbridge has evocatively set out, describing Étienne's role as a 'surrogate novelist', via whom Zola can project, in the 'embedded mirrors of *Germinal*', his own anxieties and fantasies about the process of fiction-writing.[108] As Lethbridge has shown, Zola slips in and out of third- and first-person pronouns where he imagines the strike-leader's experience in his preparatory notes, notably rendering Étienne's tentative and often poorly-digested education in socialist thought as his own: 'it's my whole development'.[109] More broadly still, Lethbridge argues, Étienne's rivalries with other would-be leaders, along with his aspirations to popularity, to impose his vision of the future, to lead a militant group, all transpose elements of the novelist's own career trajectory.[110] On this reckoning, Zola self-reflexively attributes to Étienne a set of aspirations, the most compelling – and contradictory – of which, we might then venture, is that of *being* a politician.

Despite Zola's consistent derision of professional politicians, the possibility of a political career was one he admitted to entertaining. In an interview with Jules Huret in 1893, Zola responded to speculation about whether he would consider standing for Parliament by restating his conviction that he possessed many of the requisite qualities: 'But yes! [...] And why not?', he replied. 'I believe [...] that I can *act* effectively on a gathering of men. I have lucid, precise ideas; I have great clarity of mind; and that's important for anybody who wants to get involved in public affairs.'[111] Zola felt well-placed to lead, and yet his entry into politics was precluded by the fact that he lacked, by his own admission, the talents of a public speaker. Four years later, Zola again dismissed new rumours that a turn to politics was afoot, all while confessing that this had once been his ambition:

> I had a dream, a beautiful dream: of becoming an orator who, through the power of his arguments and the strength of his eloquence, succeeded, if not in impressing some of his ideas on the Chamber, then at least in spreading them throughout the country, just as the sower spreads his seeds in the furrow of a fertile field.[112]

In one sense, the writer's dream of parliamentary success – couched as it is in terms that reprise the verdant master-metaphor of *Germinal* – belied his own longstanding suspicions of a political class that he claimed was driven by self-interest. As Guillaume McNeil Arteau observes, 'Zola has always thought about his relationship to the parliamentarian in terms of rivalry.'[113] Or to reprise Zola's earlier caricature of the Republican politician, the successful novelist covets the oratory skills of the writer *manqué* – the kind of rhetorical power that would allow him to impose his own *ideas*, to convert the crowd.

Arguably, what we find in these later admissions, then, is not just a curious contradiction with Zola's outspoken criticism of professional politicians, but the slippery ground of his submerged identification with Étienne. For both, of course, share an ambition to influence a crowd on which they depend, but to which they cannot, or do not wish to, belong. Zola made this relationship to the crowd clear, in fact, in a letter to his childhood friend Antony Valabrègue following the publication of *Les Mystères de Marseille*. Unlike those writers who could afford to remain holed up in their ivory tower, Zola remarked, he was forced to obey more pressing imperatives: 'I need the crowd; I go to them as best I can; I try all available means to tame them. Right now, there are two things I most need: publicity and money.'[114] As Schor has so persuasively demonstrated, this reliance on the crowd, which is also a will to mastery, would remain a fundamental structuring property of Zola's fiction. But it also conveys a very particular class anxiety, one that Jameson has placed at the heart of the naturalist project. For what distinguishes the naturalist *roman du peuple* from sentimental accounts of the poor in Dickens or Hugo, Jameson argues, is 'the threat of collective *déclassement*'. The bourgeois perspective on the lower classes is shot through with the fear of 'slipping down that painfully climbed slope of class position and business or monetary success, of falling back into the petty bourgeoisie and thence on into working class misery itself'.[115] In other words, Jameson gives a class inflexion to what David Baguley has called naturalism's 'entropic vision': the novel's paradigmatic trajectory of depletion and decline is now tied to the anxieties of a bourgeoisie that doubts its own dominance.[116] On this reading, it would seem particularly apposite that Zola reflected on his own origins as a writer mid-way through the composition of *Germinal*, in his preface to the new edition of *Les Mystères de Marseille*. To suggestions that he was ashamed of his early works and had wished to consign them to obscurity (as 'a corpse to hide'), Zola boldly objected: 'Why should I be ashamed of them? They gave me bread at one of the most desperate times of my life. Despite their irremediable mediocrity, I still feel a sense of gratitude towards them.'[117] At the very least, he concluded, the reader will better grasp the sheer willpower and labour the author had needed to raise himself up from 'this third-rate work to the literary effort of the *Rougon-Macquart*'. Reclaiming his status as a self-made man, Zola contemplates the spectre of his former mediocrity, and with it, implicitly, the alternative narrative of his own failure.[118]

If we now circle back to *Germinal*, we might venture that what Zola projects onto his hero is the same fear: of falling back into the crowd or the anonymity of poverty. 'Wouldn't the end of the strike mean the end of his role [. . .]', Zola has Étienne reflect, 'reducing his existence to the mindless routine of the mine and the repulsive life of the village?' (378; 452). For Étienne's antipathies towards the crowd are also Zola's own; and in exposing his militant leader's impulses, the writer-intellectual is, in one respect, interrogating the alienation inherent to his own position. Jameson's reading of Gissing's fiction, and of *Demos* in particular, can provide us, as I have argued, with the terms in which to think through Zola's suspicions of the working-class militant, along with the self-reflexive scrutiny that implies. The concept of *ressentiment* – Jameson calls it 'that fundamental nineteenth-century ideologeme' – is, first and foremost, a *story* about class struggle: its purpose is to prove the proletariat irredeemable; to demonstrate the impossible authenticity of the working-class leader; to write off radical impulses as envy; to uphold, finally, social distinctions as facts of nature.[119] The case Jameson makes for Gissing's fiction as a negotiation with, or working-over of, this 'ideologeme' allows us to better grasp why Zola's leader must be punished, and indeed why his strike must fail.

What, though, we might also need to ask, of the decidedly different notes on which these writers bring their respective novels of populism to a close? Gissing, as we have seen, has Mutimer die at the hands of Demos, while Zola spares the life of Lantier so that he might envisage, in the final pages, a reprisal of his socialist experiment in the novel's afterlife.[120] Not only, then, does Zola refrain from punishing the militant with the same cruelty as Gissing (instead, heaping suffering on those workers the leader incites), he allows Lantier to start over – to restate, that is, 'his absolute faith in a forthcoming revolution, the real one, that of the workers' (521; 580). The dream of a 'grassroots' revolution, to co-opt the organic metaphor Zola deploys at the novel's close, is thus revived by the militant's imagination. Of course, the narrative remains resolutely ambivalent about the prospective vision it supplies, as well as about the redeemability of its hero. But what Zola allows Étienne to do at the close is veer ominously, one last time, from disillusionment to enchantment – or more precisely, from resentment to idealism: 'he forgot that these wretches had stoned him, and he started to *dream again of changing them into heroes*, of leading the people' (515, emphasis added; 574). As Étienne walks away from the community that has become a disaster zone, he indulges what the narrative perceives, I shall now suggest, to be the most problematic quality of the socialist leader's imagination: the obstinate desire to idealise those workers he would seek to represent.

Never idealise!

The naturalist writer's mistrust, or 'resentment', of the militant socialist reproduces, in one sense, an ideological theory of revolution that is immanent in late nineteenth-century culture. But the novelist's attitude had also been a specific object of debate in the months directly preceding the publication of *Germinal*. Paul Alexis broached the issue, in fact, in the weeks following his dealings with Zola over Guesde. On 5 April 1884,

Alexis penned an article for the daily newspaper *Le Matin*, called simply 'Naturalisme', in which he discussed the movement's relationship with socialist politics. Alexis reproduced a letter he had (purportedly) received from a reader, one Lucien Pemjean, in which he returned to the question Alexis had posed to Guesde earlier that year in his column for *Le Cri du peuple*: 'Are socialism and naturalism not simply two sides of the same coin?'[121] If, as Pemjean claims, Guesde had reportedly answered in the affirmative, why do naturalist writers treat socialist activists with such disdain? In his reply to Pemjean's letter, Alexis defended his allies' suspicions of such figures as follows:

> Our purported contempt for social activists stems from the fact that they seem to us entangled in biases and resentments that prevent them from seeing the truth. They are sectarian, for the most part; they are not men of free observation. Glaring proof of this lies in the fact that *they wish to cast a veil over the failings of the people, that raw material of the ideal society they dream about.*[122]

Socialism and naturalism were compatible bedfellows, Alexis insisted. But the socialist's blinkered, or skewed, relationship to the truth was emblematised by his inclination to idealise the people, precisely by censoring their failings, and to make this (mis)representation the engine of social transformation.

Alexis was rehearsing the cautions Zola had sounded a few years earlier across his journalism on Republican politics, especially in the wake of critical reactions to *L'Assommoir*. In other words, Alexis deemed socialists guilty of the same inclinations Zola had determined in those he dismissively called romantic Republicans – those whose flawed vision for the nation rested on the idealisation, even dogmatic idolisation, of a people that 'must be worshipped on bended knee, under threat of the severest punishment'.[123] Despite its rhetoric of adoration, romanticism's populist fantasy is construed by Zola as a form of fundamental disregard for the people whose apotheotic self-image it supplies. Effectively, what Zola sought to identify, and castigate, as we saw in Chapter 1, was a style of political thinking, which was not necessarily tied to any one type of political opinion. Those politicians who engaged in 'pure speculation, [...] treating mankind and the world as though they were a simple geometry theorem' could, Zola made clear, just as well be royalist as Republican.[124]

Zola later reiterated the fundamentals of this critique when reflecting on the politics of *Germinal*. In a letter to journalist Georges Montorgueil on 8 March 1885, Zola intimated, in the same vein as Alexis, that socialism demanded a naturalist sensibility. Moreover, the naturalist writer's truth-telling was the condition of proper political engagement on behalf of the working class:

> Perhaps this time people will stop seeing me as a detractor of the people. Is not the true socialist the one who speaks of poverty, [...] who shows the misery of hunger in all its horror? Those who glorify the people are lyrical souls who should be sent back to the humanitarian daydreams of '48. If the people are so perfect, so divine, why seek to improve their fate? No, they are down low, mired in ignorance and mud, and we must try to lift them out of this state.[125]

To idolise, or idealise, the *peuple* was, in Zola's reckoning, precisely to impede the political work of reformism, to indulge in an ineffective humanitarianism that, yet again, Zola implicitly attached to Hugo. Zola thus restated here the defence of his own miserabilism, which he had first properly articulated in the wake of the outcry caused by *L'Assommoir* when Hugo himself had reportedly questioned the writer's 'right to lay bare poverty and misfortune'.[126]

We have seen how, in his open letter to Guyot, Zola took to task critics of the right-thinking Left – those who claimed he had unjustly misrepresented the people as nothing but idlers and drunkards – and this by denigrating idealism, in art as in politics. But he also pointed as part of this defence to the sheer variety of working-class characters his novel encompassed. In fact, Zola ventured, he had gone so far in *L'Assommoir* as to betray his own aesthetic principles by creating a 'model' worker in the blacksmith Goujet: 'There are noble characters among the people, I know full well, since I have depicted one in my book. Even – shall I admit it? – I fear I may have lied a little with Goujet, for I have occasionally attributed feelings to him that do not belong to his background.'[127] It is an admission – an embarrassment, almost – that is, I think, best read in conjunction with Sand's well-known defence of her own idealised labourer, the hero-carpenter Pierre Huguenin of her 1840 novel about journeymen artisans. (In fact, one critic made this connection when reviewing the stage adaptation of *L'Assommoir*, likening Goujet to 'one of Mme Sand's workers, a blacksmith from the *Compagnon du tour de France*'.)[128] Here, in her 1851 'Notice' to a new edition of the novel, Sand retaliates against accusations of implausibility:

> in some classes, this was declared impossible, an exaggeration. I was accused of flattering the people and wanting to embellish them. Well, why not? Why, supposing my type were too idealised, would I not be allowed to do for the men of the people what I had been allowed to do for other classes?[129]

Sand boldly assumes the scandal her worker-hero generated by exposing the double standards that govern the technique of embellishment: idealisation is only considered implausible, and thus impermissible, when applied to the proletariat.[130] Her portraiture is captured, then, as a deliberately provocative violation of the doctrine of *vraisemblance* that regulates mimetic fiction; it is an affront to those class-bound rules determining the novel's arbitration over what counts as exaggeration, and what should be deemed 'impossible'. In Zola's hands, the ideal worker must either be rerooted in mimesis ('there are noble characters among the people, I know full well') or else accounted for, in a manner of self-reproach, as a lie. For proletarian idealisation is, Zola implies, unavoidably a gesture of *déclassement* ('I have occasionally attributed feelings to him that do not belong to his background'). As such, it troubles his own conception of the naturalist novel, according to which the 'people' should function, to borrow Jameson's terms, as a 'classificatory concept' – that is, as a self-identical class the writer can dispassionately observe.[131]

We are now better placed to grasp the aesthetic, or representational, stakes of the *ressentiment* Zola expresses towards his militant hero. Étienne's ambitions *for* the people are not simply a means to forge his own political career; they rely on a rhetoric of idealisation that, Zola implies, betrays a fundamental antipathy towards those workers on whose behalf he would seek to advocate:

> As for the workers, whose stench of poverty now offended him, he still felt the need to cover them in glory, and he pictured them as the only heroes, the only saints, the only nobility, and the only force which could redeem humanity. He already saw himself on the rostrum leading the people to triumph, if the people didn't eat him alive before he got there. (521; 580)

Disgust and fear: these are the twin emotions that, paradoxically, feed the militant's idealist project, which is articulated here as a special kind of dogmatism. Put differently, Étienne's 'need' to heroise, or glorify, the people as a legitimate agent of history is held to derive – in a vital contradiction – from a latent sense of contempt, an inability to tolerate the worker *as he is*. At the novel's close, Étienne's prospective daydreaming thus returns the reader to fraught questions about the proper relationship between the aesthetics and politics of representation, about who has the right to speak in the name of the people, and how that speech should describe the people it intends.

Of course, it is conspicuous just how much the novel insists at its close on the political maturity Étienne feels he has gained in the aftermath of the strike. His 'Bildung' manifests itself, in fact, as an inclination to patience, to reason, and a trust in the power of the law: 'Now that he had sown his wild oats, [. . .] his ideas were maturing [*sa raison mûrissait*].' (523; 582) Whether or not Étienne's 'impossibilist' imagination has been indelibly tempered, what we are witnessing is the spurned leader's attempt to build, not least in his own mind, a new sense of legitimacy. Indeed, if the narration makes almost imperceptible the individual consciousness through which its last images of an imminent, subterranean uprising are filtered, this is, I am suggesting, all the better to perform its own hesitation, even scepticism, about the future it augurs – about how to tell an authentic narrative of revolution from a bogus one, a genuine visionary from a false prophet. (The latter surely finds its hyperbolic, theological expression in Abbé Ranvier and his vehement promise of salvation.) In this sense, a fundamental contradiction might be said to govern the novel's concluding lyrical vision of 'a black and avenging army of men, germinating slowly in its furrows, [. . .] until one day soon their ripening would burst open the earth itself' (524; 583). In the words of Irving Howe, 'the myth of [the people's] emergence contains within itself the negation of that greatness': the possibility of 'a ghastly dialectic of history, new rulers and oppressors: the Rasseneurs, the Plucharts, and even the Lantiers of tomorrow, raised to the status of leaders and bureaucrats'.[132] Thus the perennial question Zola's novel poses – who, if anyone, can be trusted to announce to the people its future? – is arguably turned back on itself with the indeterminate poetic vision on which it ends.

With this question in mind, let us now return, once more, to Lethbridge's account of the play of mirrors in *Germinal*, which allows the writer to project both aspirations and anxieties about his own vocation onto his militant hero. What we have hinted at here is just how that self-reflexive introspection might work differently still: to interrogate the ethical legitimacy of his own means of storytelling. Take, as a salient example, Étienne's internal deliberations over the rightfulness of urging his fellow strikers to persist in their struggle, in the face of dwindling resources:

> Should he still spur them on, now that there was neither money not credit left? And how would things turn out, if no help arrived, if everyone's spirits were vanquished by hunger? Suddenly, he saw a vision of disaster: children dying, mothers sobbing, while the men, thin and haggard, marched back down into the pits. (233; 319)

Effectively, what Étienne countenances is the disaster of a failed strike, the macabre, or miserabilist, dénouement of the novel seen in advance.

Indeed, can we not hear in the hesitations of our strike leader the voice of a writer, contemplating his options, his plot, his ending? Elsewhere, the emerging drama of Étienne's self-doubt is cast as the play of two rival voices: driving the crowd to greater acts of rebellion, 'he heard another voice within him, the voice of reason, asking in astonishment what the purpose of all of this could be' (354; 430). At such moments, we might submit, the ethical dilemma at stake in Étienne's idealist 'experiment' – the peddling of an impossible promise – marries with the novel's own. The strike leader's uncertainty appears to articulate the naturalist narrative's own equivocation about its catastrophic logic.

Catastrophic Idealism

Ultimately, it is left to La Maheude, the novel's archetypal victim – the one who pays the highest price – to absolve Étienne of his heavy sense of responsibility: 'You realize that in the end it's not really anyone's fault. . . No, it's really not your fault, it's everyone's fault' (518; 577). Toying with the epideictic rhetoric that befits the aftermath of tragic episodes, the miner, 'having resumed the calm demeanour of a reasonable woman', lays the blame on everybody and nobody. Already, in the wake of Maheu's death, La Maheude had borne no grudges, instead deconstructing her own idealism with the cold knowledge of hindsight:

> You get all excited, you suffer so much from what you've got that you ask for what you can't have. I was daydreaming like a beast in a field, I saw a life where everyone lived in friendship, and believe me, I was floating on air, my head in the clouds. Then *you fall down in the mud* and break your neck. . . It wasn't true. There weren't any of those things we dreamed of out there at all. (443, emphasis added; 508)

There is, of course, something painfully pathetic about La Maheude's recapitulation of the strike as a futile, or misguided, speculation, couched as it is in the idiom of self-derision. Nowhere, to recall Jameson, are those 'impulses toward the future and toward radical change' so 'systematically reified'. Here, the worker is made to swallow the object lesson of the naturalist novel: the 'law', that is, governing the structure of Zola's fiction whereby, as Schor puts it, 'what goes up must come down'.[133] Still more precisely, Zola has La Maheude reprise one of the master-metaphors of his own theory of idealism, which he had expounded in his 1879 'Lettre à la jeunesse': 'It is time to prove to the next generation that the real crooks are the rhetoricians [Zola is targeting Renan and Hugo], and that *after every leap towards the ideal, there is an inevitable collapse into the mud*.'[134]

Now we can see just how directly, how heavy-handedly, naturalist metadiscourse is calqued in La Maheude's monologue. And just in case we managed to miss it the first time, the narrator relays Étienne's perception of the victim (his victim?), 'shattered by her terrible fall from the heights of her ideal'.[135] To draw on Andrew J. Counter's analysis of repetition in Zola, we are surely witnessing here the novelist's 'didactic ramming home of a "thesis"'.[136] But what 'thesis', in this instance? In its original setting, the 'thesis' of the fall relates to the history of a nation. For France's defeat at the hands of the Prussians is, on Zola's telling, the logical result of the nation's regrettable *engouement* for an idealistic kind of patriotism, which proves to be nothing but hollow rhetoric. Naturalism is thus held up as a prophylactic against those (invariably) twinned dangers of literary and political idealism: setting the Republic on sure foundations first means cultivating a new, anti-idealist literary sensibility. In turn, naturalism's supposed *nostalgie de la boue* is reimagined as the dispassionate registration of a post-idealist state, concerned as it is with the aftermath of an idealist politics that, Zola claimed, 'will inevitably lead to all kinds of catastrophe'.[137]

What should we make, then, of Zola's transplantation of this trope into his *roman du peuple*? Zola is no doubt rehearsing analogous points: his strikers are seduced by a political rhetoric of idealism that is always, in Zola's reckoning, a literary rhetoric; and La Maheude's epiphany thus serves to prove the same thesis. But what Zola has set up, in theory, is also nothing more than a form or pattern, one that is endlessly available to be filled by different content. Indeed, it is a pattern that surely crystallises what Jameson (following Lukács) describes as the inadequacy of the naturalist novel, insofar as this has 'ceased to become the privileged instrument of the analysis of reality, and has been degraded to a mere illustration of a thesis'.[138] Unlike Balzac, 'who does not really know what he will find beforehand', Zola 'already *knows* what the basic structure of society is, and this is his weakness' (194; original emphasis). Most plainly, history in Zola's *Rougon-Macquart* cycle is, as Jameson points out, 'the object of a diagnostic already confirmed in advance': the fall of the Second Empire providing the series' closure.[139] On these terms, Zola's trope of the muddy fall might be taken as the paradigmatic image or set-piece in which the naturalist novel's self-fulfilling mode of narration, of history-telling, is condensed, fixed, or (Jameson would say) 'reified'. Certainly, we have witnessed how, to paraphrase Jameson, the strike must fail, the result of the 'experiment' set in advance. Or, in the terms we have privileged in this chapter, we have seen how naturalism is bound to cast radical idealism as an impossibilism.

Nevertheless, Zola's novel is, I hope to have shown, hardly blind to the issues with this logic. In fact, Zola self-consciously incorporates such a knowing sense of historical determinism into his strike narrative via the arch-realist, or fatalist, Bonnemort. The elderly, decrepit miner claims to have learned the all-important (Marxian) lesson that history is bound to repeat itself—only as tragedy, he might add, not as farce: 'Oh, I've seen a lot, I've seen them all! Forty years ago they threw us out of the managers' offices, and they drew their swords on us!' (215; 302). At moments such as this, the naturalist novel morbidly sends up its own pessimism, its histor-ical vision of cyclicality, as but one prophetic narrative among others. So too, of course, does the naturalist novel mercifully cast the alternative, impossibilist imagination as a special kind of madness. And yet, the narrative can never fully espouse the convictions of its own resident Possibilist, whose righteous realism always threatens to collapse into cynicism. The charge of political 'implausibility' may be salutary, but it can, as we have seen, always be co-opted by conservative interest.

Ultimately, Rasseneur and his watered-down reformism fail to offer a way out of the novel's political impasse: both he and Étienne incur, at different moments, the ingratitude of the crowd they each wish to com-mand – the novel making victims of them both, via separate scenes of lapidation. Arguably, then, our attention to the strident critique of utopianism peddled by Zola's strike novel risks obscuring the less obvious ways in which – to co-opt Jameson's possible 'definition' of realist fiction – the narrative carries out 'the very interrogation of realism and the realistic itself'. And this not so much in the modernist sense Jameson intends (though that surely can be argued too) than as a political and ideological discourse.[140] For, in one respect, the problem Zola presents us with is not dissimilar to the neoliberal condition described by Mark Fisher as 'capitalist realism', the conception that there is no viable, coherent, imaginable alternative to the current order. Of course, 'what counts as "realistic"', Fisher clarifies, 'what seems possible at any point in the social field, is defined by a series of political determinations'.[141] When Zola ventriloquises the capitalist's discourse of cautious paternalism in *Germinal*, it is also this suspicion that the author is impressing upon us.

In the end, naturalism is, I have argued, bound to conceive of itself as a possibilism, wedded to 'realism' as the only practical and ethical form of politics. And yet, it nevertheless remains drawn to those scenarios in which possibilism becomes an impossible proposition. Certainly, Zola has us recognise that the worker's attempt to think (to make) his or her condition otherwise – to reimagine the status quo – is born of an encounter *with* the impossible. Let's return, then, to La Maheude's aphoristic diagnosis of a (class) condition: 'you suffer so much from what you've got that you ask for what you can't have'. Here, the novel quietly acknowledges the base logic of the 'mass idealism' it unleashes: that the pursuit of the unrealisable becomes irresistible when the material conditions of life have been made untenable or insufferable. This, in any case, is how Judith Butler characterises the capacious category of 'uprisings': as 'an angry refusal of the condition under which dignity, held in place by the moral limits of what should be endured, is denied or destroyed'.[142] Tied together by a 'shared indignation', those who rise up – and who form a 'we' in the process – 'are making a bid for a livable life' (25–26). Such, then, are the tensions, not least of tone and emotion, that run through Zola's visceral account of populist hope – tensions that the novel arguably fails to resolve, despite the insistence with which it proves Zola's anti-idealist 'thesis'. Here, perhaps, is the rub: that the form that 'thesis' takes in the novel is so very overdetermined, so brazen as to be almost unconvincing. In this sense, we might understand the paradigm of the fall as a knowing imposition, a fixation on disaster, on calamity even, as the only way of managing the tensions and contradictions the novel's story of popular idealism has released. It is, after all, a vital irony of *Germinal* that the novel does not find its ending in the bloody failure of the strike, but in *another* catastrophe: the dynamiting of the mine, perpetrated by Souvarine. The anarchist's 'plot' (in a double sense) displaces the strike action; it intervenes, we might say, while socialists are fighting amongst themselves over the paths of reform and revolution.

With Souvarine's deed, Zola pushes the tragic conclusion of the strike into the realm of humanitarian disaster, effectively deploying one of those 'shorthand explosive devices', in Jameson's words, capable of bringing the plot 'to a timely end (in an untimely fashion)'.[143] On this reckoning, the naturalist writer's recourse to melodramatic violence as the means of narrative closure would represent yet another kind of aesthetic failure: an attempt on Zola's part to escape from what Lukács called 'the counter-artistic consequences of his own naturalism'.[144] In political terms, meanwhile, the 'explosive device' produces little more than a 'pseudoevent' that would unburden the novel of its own failed socialist plot.[145] Now it would be hard, of course, to argue away the novel's diversion from the drama of mass struggle at its core, or indeed to see in the miners' return to drudgery anything less than another pessimistic indictment of the inescapability of the capitalist order. The class conflict that the strike unleashes is, at the novel's close, folded back into the eternal (cyclical) order of the suprahistorical. In fact, it is precisely 'the strike's turn towards a mythical horizon' that, Émilien Carassus suggests, distinguishes *Germinal* from preceding strike novels.[146] And yet, there is surely more, we might surmise, to Zola's anarchist 'plot', and the disaster it wreaks, than a melodramatic 'solution' to the novel's irresolvable contradictions. Rather, what we witness towards the end of the novel is the displacement of one type of political idealism with another. For the anarchist's is a dark idealism; it too is catastrophic – not, as Zola warns his readers elsewhere, by harbouring a dangerous delusion, but rather in its very mode, means, or even, we might say, aesthetic. 'Anarchists [. . .] are poets. Theirs is the eternal *dark poetry* [. . .]. They are passionate beings with the minds of visionaries, desperate for the dream', Zola later declared in the wake of a spate of anarchist bombings in 1892.[147]

A decade earlier, Zola had written an article on the possibility of a Russian Republic, painting for his readers the dreams of nihilists (Zola is thinking, above all, of Bakunin), whose impatience with the recalcitrant masses would lead them to 'bring about a general cataclysm, from which Russia will emerge entirely renewed'.[148] The prospect of a bloodbath as the condition of national regeneration is, of course, one Zola declares horrifying. Better to adopt the experimental politics he expounds by redeploying that endlessly adaptable dictum: 'Russia will be naturalist, or it will not be.'[149] And yet, if Zola plays on these fears in *Germinal*, offering up in his Russian miner Souvarine a mindset of quasi-pathological fanaticism, we also need to wrestle with the fact that the novelist ascribes to the anarchist a singular lucidity. Souvarine is singled out as the only character capable of seeing the strike for what it is (174; 267): a rebellion that has been orchestrated by the Company in order to minimise losses during an economic depression. Eschewing the tactics of socialist struggle as 'another load of rubbish!' (142; 270), meanwhile, Souvarine's version of radical militancy – of heroism – offers an openly critical alternative to the political trajectory pursued by the likes of Étienne and Rasseneur: 'The bandit is the real hero', he insists, 'the popular avenger, the active revolutionary who despises phrases lifted from literature' (242; 328). Unlike the worker leader, who remains trapped, as Susan Harrow puts it, within 'the supply-stream of available discourses', Souvarine's spectacular act will speak for itself.[150] Clearly, he embodies a kind of radical freedom that commands terror and admiration in equal measure. Or to return to the Jamesonian terms that have guided our reading, Souvarine escapes the model of *ressentiment* in which Zola's socialist militants are otherwise caught: he appears, we might say, as an avatar of the alienated intellectual, whose ruthless detachment from his fellow workers would render him uniquely capable of authenticity.

Remarkably, of all the predictions for the future that the novel contains, it is, as Roger Ripoll points out, only Souvarine's projected future that appears unfiltered through a character's imagination, owned instead by the narrator: 'He will doubtless be to blame when the bourgeoisie in its death throes finds the cobbles starting to split upon under its feet with every step that it takes.'[151] Only the anarchist points, that is, to the otherwise inconceivable: the end of a class, a threat to 'the solidity of social reality'.[152] Souvarine's act of violence thus becomes the emblem of that apocalyptic vision with which Zola seeks to shake the master class from its complacency: 'There is perhaps still time to avoid the ultimate catastrophe. But you must be quick to act justly. Otherwise, this is the danger: the earth will open up and nations will be engulfed in one of the most appalling upheavals in history.'[153] With this statement of a reformist agenda, Zola sets out the novel's conscious purpose to militate against those disasters it takes upon itself to imagine. And yet, within the narrative, the anarchist's bloody gesture is ultimately folded back into Zola's myth of regeneration. For in the aftermath of catastrophe, the anarchist will become the third term around which class consensus can conceivably be built.

When Étienne, trapped in the collapsed mine and on the brink of death, is at last hauled out into the light, he sees before him none other than the engineer Négrel, who has coordinated the community's rescue mission with heroic determination. The ensuing embrace between worker and bourgeois is pure melodrama, its symbolism made (*almost* self-parodically) unambiguous: 'these two men who despised each other, the rebellious workman and the sceptical boss, fell on each other's necks, heaving great sobs, as they felt a common humanity well up deep within them' (511; 571). Of course, in this scene of sentimental reconciliation, we find in miniature the paradigm of universal cross-class solidarity on which, as we shall see in Chapter 5, Zola's later utopian fiction will be predicated. This is 'the kiss between brothers' that Zola makes the emblem of his future Republic in *Travail* (1901), realised at last once humanity has exhausted its appetite for catastrophic violence.[154] In a stroke of wish-fulfilment, Zola allows himself to envisage, with a straight face, the very idealism his miners had caressed: all citizens are bound together 'as a fraternal people, reconciled in a common ideal, in the kingdom of heaven at last brought down to earth'.[155] In this 'anti-*Germinal*', as Mitterand describes it, even the arch-collectivist Bonnaire and the died-in-the-wool anarchist Lange are converted to the cause of Zola's messianic leader Luc Froment, whose blend of early nineteenth-century utopian socialist thought guides him in fashion-ing a world from which class struggle can be obliterated.[156] Those internal divisions on the Left are thus finally rendered void, as all 'socialists of warring sects' are won over to Luc's inclusive vision.[157] As if to draw a direct line from *Germinal*, Zola has *Travail* open with a failed strike that has decimated the community. This time, though, the strike will not augur conflict to come; it will instead be, as Mitterand notes, 'the last of history', even, it would seem, the beginning of the end of history.[158]

*

In his turn-of-the-century utopian rewriting of *Germinal*, Zola makes socialism *work*. But in doing so, he abandons the conviction we saw him express to Montorgueil in the wake of *Germinal*'s publication: that 'real-ism' – or in Zola's polemical mode, anti-idealism – is the only effective political means available to 'the true socialist'. With this claim for realism in mind, I wish to make one final return to Jameson. For the socialist function of the naturalist novel that Zola promotes in his letter to Montorgueil arguably aligns with the senses of what Jameson has called the 'politics of realism', and specifically of 'social realism'. The type of literature, that is, that sets out to confront the reader with things and people they have never seen before, conditions they had never suspected. Such fiction operates, Jameson contends, on the assumption that this 'epistemological dimension' will provoke pity or indignation – in short, a political (re)action:

> Any theory of political realism will thus also involve a rhetoric, and will then confront the problem of the way in which the new hitherto unseen realities are staged: will the protagonists be victims, for whose suffering one feels pity; or will they be heroes of resistance, who (however they fail) inspire emulation along with hatred for their oppressors? *Or, perhaps, as with the naturalists, they will simply inspire their comfortable bourgeois readers to a certain satisfaction with their own estate*, and a thankfulness that they have not been and will never be placed in such circumstances themselves.[159]

Jameson differentiates the conservative political project of naturalist fiction here with a biting sense of irony. So much so, in fact, that we might be tempted to turn, with tongue in cheek, the terms of his critique of Gissing back onto the critic and ask: why does Jameson *resent* the naturalist writer? And of what is that resentment the symptom? After all, we can object, those possible alternative political reactions to realist literature that Jameson describes – generating pity for its victims' suffering or inspiring readers to emulate its protagonists' heroism – can be applied to Zola's *Germinal* more convincingly than to most novels; and, indeed, Jameson knows it to be the case.

Not only was pity fundamental to the rhetoric Zola deployed in capturing the intended politics of his proletarian novel, the political 'uses' of *Germinal* were extolled by socialists, moderate and radical alike.[160] Upon the novel's serialisation in *Le Cri du peuple*, its first instalment timed to coincide with Bastille Day, the journalist Séverine prefaced Zola's work with a 'Lettre à Jean Labeur', in which she entreated the worker to take the story seriously, to harness it as a political 'weapon'.[161] In the wake of Hugo's death (just weeks earlier), readers must find political inspiration, Séverine went on, in Zola's new school of modern fiction. A few days later, Guesde himself alluded to the political relevance of the novel, describing Zola's coal mine as a modern Bastille.[162] But perhaps few episodes captured more decisively the extent of *Germinal*'s political effects – or of the political idealism it could inspire – than the Decazeville miners' strike that broke out on 26 January 1886. When the deputy manager of the implicated Société de l'Aveyron, Jules Watrin, was seized by the crowd and defenestrated, several newspapers were led to conclude, variously with exhilaration and horror, that life appeared to be imitating art. According to a powerful article in *Le Cri du peuple*, what we were witnessing was 'the revenge of the Maheus'.[163] In an interview with *Le Gaulois*, published three days after the event, Zola emphatically denied any responsibility in the drama at Decazeville: 'What happened yesterday is a cruel demonstration of the ideas I have defended. It's one of those ghastly, dreadful murders committed by the reckless crowd, the idiotic masses.'[164] Was it really reasonable, Zola continued, to imagine every miner 'placed under [his] tutelage'? If anything, the novelist would be bound to sympathise with the victim, by all accounts 'an educated man, a cultured mind' – and, of all those involved, Zola added, probably the only one to have read *Germinal*. . .

No doubt Zola was wilfully downplaying the appeal his strike novel held for working-class readers. When *Le Cri du peuple* and *L'Intransigeant* set up a support fund for the Decazeville strikers in the days that followed, several signatories declared themselves to be readers of *Germinal*; their generosity was, as Marion Glaumaud-Carbonnier has shown, folded into an imaginary allegiance to Zola's miners as a sort of 'rallying cry'.[165] But what might strike us about Zola's unequivocal disavowal of responsibility for the political energies his novel was deemed to have released is just how it rehearses those very ethical quandaries the writer had already imagined.

In yet another interleaving of fiction and history, Zola was forced, like Étienne, to confront those radical fantasies that may well run athwart his intentions. In one sense, then, Zola's gesture provides further confirmation, if it were needed, of the fundamentally conservative politics of naturalism that Jameson describes. However, the episode also makes clear that such conservatism does not preclude radical engagement: this is one scenario of what happens, that is, when the alienated worker gets his or her hands on Zola's novel, rather than Jameson's notional 'comfortable bourgeois readers'. Of course, to invoke the controversial reception of *Germinal* on the Left as a measure of the novel's politics is hardly to offer an adequate way out of the oppressive vision of naturalism *as a form* that is the burden of Jameson's argument in *The Political Unconscious*. But if anything, what those powerful, working-class reactions to *Germinal* demand of us is a way of reading the novel's impossibilism as something other than naivety.

Notes

1 Friedrich Engels, letter to Margaret Harkness, April 1888; reprod. in *Karl Marx, Friedrich Engels on Literature and Art: A Selection of Writings*, ed. Lee Baxandall and Stefan Morawski (New York: International General, 1973), p. 116. On the reception of Zola in the Marxist tradition, see Aurélie Barjonet, *Zola d'ouest en est: le naturalisme en France et dans les deux Allemagnes* (Rennes: Presses Universitaires de Rennes, 2010), pp. 17–20, 59–74.
2 See, in particular, Georg Lukács, 'Narrate or Describe?' (1936), in *Writer and Critic, and Other Essays*, ed. and trans. Arthur Kahn (London: Merlin Press, 1970), pp. 110–48 (p. 142); and 'The Zola Centenary', in *Studies in European Realism: A Sociological Survey of the Writings of Balzac, Stendhal, Zola, Tolstoy, Gorki, and others*, trans. Edith Bone (London: Hillway Publishing, 1950), pp. 85–96. Zola himself identified the 'principle of contradiction' that Marxist criticism has determined in Balzac: 'Besides, there is nothing more peculiar, Zola wrote, 'than this support of absolute power, when his talent is essentially democratic and he has written the most revolutionary work that can be read'. Zola, 'Balzac', in *Les Romanciers naturalistes*, in *OC*, vol. 10, 467–68.
3 'The Zola Centenary', p. 87 (original emphasis).
4 Discussions of Lukács's judgements on Zola include: Jacques Pelletier, 'Lukács, lecteur de Zola', *Les Cahiers naturalistes*, 41 (1971), 58–74; Ian H. Birchall, 'Georg Lukács and the Novels of Émile Zola', *The Sociology of Literature: Applied Studies*, 26 (1978), 92–108; Brian Nelson, 'Zola, Lukács and the Aesthetics of Realism', *Studi Francesi*, 71 (1980), 251–55; Patrick

Brady, 'Lukács, Zola, and the Principle of Contradiction', *L'Esprit créateur,* 21:3 (1980), 60–68. An important argument that returns across these essays is that Lukács failed to distinguish Zola's theoretical positions from his practice of fiction writing.

5 Fredric Jameson, *The Political Unconscious: Narrative as a Socially Symbolic Act* (London; New York: Routledge, 1983), p. 180.

6 Michael Hardt and Antonio Negri, *Assembly* (New York: Oxford University Press, 2017), p. 241. It was shortly after the Commune that Zola noted his idea for '[a] second working-class novel. Particularly political. The worker of the the insurrection [. . .], of the Commune. A photograph of an insurgent killed in 1848. Leading to May 1871'. Paris, Bibliothèque nationale, NAF 10345, fol. 129.

7 Naomi Schor, *George Sand and Idealism* (New York: Columbia University Press, 1993), p. 84.

8 Jameson, *The Antinomies of Realism* (London: Verso, 2015), p. 2, fn 3.

9 Zola speaks of his 'socialist novel' in a letter to Jacques van Santen Kolff, 8 December 1884; *Corr*, vol. 5, 196.

10 Paul Leroy-Beaulieu, *La Question ouvrière au XIXe siècle*, 2nd edition (Paris: G. Charpentier, 1881 [1872]), p. 5. Discussing Zola's reading of the Belgian economist Émile de Lavaleye, Jean-Louis Cabanès writes: 'the analogy between socialism and religion appears [. . .], to the economist as to the writer, self-evident, even commonplace'. 'Zola, lecteur d'Émile de Lavaleye: imitation et invention', *La Fabrique des valeurs dans la littérature du XIXe siècle* (Pessac: Presses Universitaires de Bordeaux, 2017), pp. 40–53 (p. 46).

11 BN, NAF 10308, fol. 358.

12 Jacques Noiray, '*Germinal,* roman mystique', in *Le Simple et l'Intense: Vingt études sur Émile Zola* (Paris: Classiques Garnier, 2015), pp. 149–62 (p. 160). See also Sophie Guermès's discussion of socialism and (or as) religion, in *La Religion de Zola: naturalisme et déchristianisation* (Paris: Champion, 2003), pp. 273–93.

13 'À Minuit: l'auteur de *Germinal* interviewé', *Le Cri du peuple,* 10 March 1885, pp. 3–4 (p. 3).

14 On Zola's engagement with economic thought in his planning of the novel, see Christophe Reffait, 'Libéralisme et naturalisme: remarques sur la pensée économique de Zola à partir de *Germinal*', *Romanic Review,* 102:3–4 (2011), 427–48 (p. 429). See also Guermès, *La Religion de Zola*, p. 276.

15 Émile Zola, *Germinal,* trans. Peter Collier (Oxford: Oxford University Press, 1993), p. 168. For the original French, see *Germinal. Œuvres complètes,* ed. Colette Becker (Paris: Classiques Garnier, 2017), p. 260. Hereafter all references to *Germinal* are interpolated in the text and correspond to these editions: the translation first, and the original second.

16 See 'La Conférence de redoute', *Le Cri du peuple,* 10 March 1884, p. 3. On Zola's visit to Anzin, see Henri Mitterand, 'Zola à Anzin: Les mineurs de *Germinal*', *Travailler,* 7 (2002), 37–51.

17 'Premières notes sur Guesde', written by Paul Alexis on 9 March 1884. *Naturalisme pas mort: lettres inédites de Paul Alexis à Émile Zola, 1871–1900*, ed. B. H. Bakker (Toronto: University of Toronto Press, 1971), pp. 264–66 (p. 264, original emphasis). Zola subsequently met with Guesde on 2 May 1886 to discuss agricultural politics in preparation for *La Terre*, and jotted down his 'Notes Guesde'. In his correspondence with Zola, of 25 April 1886, Alexis described Guesde as 'flying high – that is, a dreamer – and now the soul of the *Cri [du peuple]*'. *Naturalisme pas mort*, p. 312. See Robert H. McCormick Jr, 'Zola, Jules Guesde et la question sociale', in *Zola sans frontières*, ed. Auguste Dezalay (Strasbourg: Presses Universitaires de Strasbourg, 1996), pp. 85–92.

18 BN, NAF 10307, fol. 497.

19 The first Congrès ouvrier took place in Paris from 2 to 10 October 1876, and it was at the Congrès ouvrier de Marseille in 1879 that the first socialist party was established. For accounts of schisms in the following decade, see Emmanuel Jousse, *Les Hommes révoltés: les origines intellectuelles du réformisme en France (1871–1917)* (Paris: Arthème Fayard, 2017); Christopher K. Ansell, *Schism and Solidarity in Social Movements: The Politics of Labor in the French Third Republic* (Cambridge: Cambridge University Press, 2007), pp. 74–98; and Leslie Derfler, *Paul Lafargue and the Founding of French Marxism, 1842–1882* (Boston, MA: Harvard University Press, 1991), pp. 177–203.

20 Guesde was editor-in-chief of *L'Égalité*, which had a stop-start existence and adopted the title *Le Socialiste* in 1885. See *La Naissance du Parti ouvrier français: correspondance inédite*, ed. Emile Bottigelli and Claude Willard (Paris: Messidor/Éditions sociales, 1981), p. 18. Zola named a newspaper *Le Prolétaire* in his manuscript, before changing it to *Le Vengeur*. See Elliott M. Grant, 'The Newspapers of *Germinal*: Their Identity and Significance', *The Modern Language Review*, 55 (1960), 87–89 (pp. 87–88).

21 'Foire aux candidats', *L'Égalité*, 15 October 1882, p. 1.

22 'Aux amis et aux ennemis', *L'Égalité*, 11 December 1881, p. 1.

23 See Benoît Malon, *Le Nouveau Parti: II. Le Parti ouvrier et sa politique*, 2nd edition (Paris: Derveaux, 1882), p. 58.

24 Joffrin, cited in Alexandre Zévaès, *Le Socialisme en France depuis 1871* (Paris: Bibliothèque-Charpentier, 1908), p. 57.

25 'Encore l'Union socialiste', *Le Prolétaire*, 19 November 1881, p. 2.

26 'Aux amis et aux ennemis'. See also Paul Lafargue's article 'Le Possibilisme', in which he accused Broussists of abandoning collectivism. *L'Égalité*, 5 February 1882, pp. 3–4.

27 No cuttings from these newspapers can be found among Zola's notes. As McCormick Jr suggests, it was via *Le Cri du peuple* – 'a newspaper Zola even seems to have subscribed to' – that he would have encountered Guesde's political thought. 'Zola et les "Notes Guesde"', *Les Cahiers naturalistes*, 69 (1995), 181–95 (p. 183).

28 Julia Nicholls, *Revolutionary Thought after the Paris Commune, 1871–85* (Cambridge: Cambridge University Press, 2019), pp. 179–206 (p. 188).

29 Brousse, 'Encore l'Union socialiste'.

30 'Encore l'Union socialiste'; emphasis added.

31 'I already see [Rasseneur] being less advanced than Étienne, merely demanding reforms; he is a possibilist. Étienne is, on the contrary, a strict collectivist. Souvorine is an anarchist.' BN, NAF 10307, fol. 497. See also BN, NAF 10308, fol. 355.

32 BN, NAF 10308, fols 85–86.

33 'Les Éléctions', *Le Figaro*, 24 August 1885, p. 2 (emphasis added).

34 According to Jousse, Broussists aimed to 'instil through reforms the seeds of revolution, which, once grown, will make the capitalist system implode'. *Les Hommes révoltés*, p. 20.

35 For a standard view, see anon., 'À travers la politique', *Gil Blas*, 23 September 1885, p. 2.

36 Baguley, '*Germinal*, une moisson de texte', *Revue d'histoire littéraire de la France*, 85:3 (1985), 389–400 (p. 397).

37 'Encore l'union socialiste'.

38 Brousse, *Dictature et Liberté* (1884), cited in David Stafford, *From Anarchism to Reformism: A Study of the Political Activities of Paul Brousse within the First International and the French Socialist Movement* (London: The London School of Economics and Political Science, 1971), p. 185.

39 Henri Galiment, 'Réalisme et romantisme', *Le Prolétaire*, 1 November 1890, p. 2.

40 The first instalment appeared in *Le Bien public* on 13 April 1876. But on 7 June, before the serialised version of *L'Assommoir* had reached its midway point, publication ceased.

41 '*L'Assommoir*. À monsieur le Directeur du *Bien public*', *Le Bien public*, 13 February 1877, p. 2 (emphasis added).

42 'La Politique expérimentale', *Le Figaro*, 28 March 1881, p. 1.

43 '*L'Assommoir*. À monsieur le Directeur du *Bien public*' (emphasis added).

44 On Zola's critique of Hugo, especially his entwined vision of literature and politics, see Roger Ripoll, 'Zola juge de Victor Hugo (1871–1877)', *Les Cahiers naturalistes*, 46 (1973), 182–204.

45 'Victor Hugo', *Le Figaro*, 2 November 1880, p. 1 (emphasis added).

46 See Michelle Perrot, *Les Ouvriers en grève, France 1871–1890* (Paris: Mouton & Co and École Pratique des Hautes Études, 1974), vol. 2, 48.

47 See Zola's letter to Francis Magnard, of 4 April 1885. *Corr*, vol. 5, 253.

48 On Brousse's view of the strike, see Stafford, *From Anarchism to Reformism*, pp. 187–88.

49 At their founding Congrès de Roanne in September 1882, Guesdists stated their commitment to fostering trade unions. On the complexities of their position, see Robert Stuart, *Marxism at Work: Ideology, Class and French Socialism during the Third Republic* (Cambridge: Cambridge University Press, 1992), pp. 180–89.

50 Guesde, 'Le Résultat', *Le Cri du peuple*, 18 April 1884, p. 1. BN, NAF 10307, fol. 399.

51 Guesde, *La République et les Grèves* (Paris: Bibliothèque socialiste, 1878), p. 30.

52 *Marxism at Work*, p. 195. Jean-Numa Ducange similarly describes Guesde's vision of the strike as 'a "school of warfare" for the organisation of labourers', *Jules Guesde: l'anti-Jaurès?* (Paris: Dunod, 2017), p. 46.

53 Anon., 'Fin de Grève', *Le Socialiste*, 15 May 1886, p. 1.

54 BN, NAF 10307, fol. 398.

55 On Guyot's novel, see Émilien Carassus, *Les Grèves imaginaires* (Paris: Éditions du CNRS, 1982), pp. 89–91.

56 Yves Guyot, *La Famille Pichot: scènes de l'enfer social* (Paris: Jules Rouff, 1882), p. 158.

57 'Notes Guyot', MS 10308, fols 195–201.

58 Guyot, 'La Grève d'Anzin', *Le Voltaire*, 23 July 1878, pp. 1–2, and 25 July 1878, p. 1.

59 Georges Grison, 'Le Mineur d'Anzin', *Le Figaro*, 26 February 1884, p. 2. BN, NAF 10307, fol. 403.

60 'Lettres économiques', *Le Sémaphore de Marseille*, 19 March 1884, p. 1; BN, NAF 10307, fol. 405.

61 Anon., 'Au pays noir', *L'Écho du Nord*, 28 February 1884; BN, NAF 10307, fol. 402.

62 The Loi Waldeck-Rousseau was passed on 21 March 1884, while the Anzin strike was ongoing. In reality, the government had tolerated union activity since the 1860s. Zola hints at this development at the close of *Germinal*: 'Yes, La Maheude was right when she said, with her usual good sense, next time it would be the real thing; they would [. . .] form trade unions, as soon as the law allowed it' (523; 582).

63 *Journal officiel de la République. Débats parlementaires. Chambre des députés: compte rendu in extensio*, 35ᵉ séance, 7 March 1884, p. 658.

64 See Laure Murat, *The Man Who Thought He Was Napoleon: Toward a Political History of Madness*, trans. Deke Dusinberre (Chicago, IL and London: The University of Chicago Press, 2014), pp. 147–97.

65 In *La Question ouvrière au XIXᵉ siècle*, Leroy-Beaulieu included a note of caution over women's 'powerful, if indirect and latent, influence'. 'The greatest misfortune of our times is that they are starting to be won over by socialism; they can be found at the forefront of strikes, public meetings, and riots', pp. 333–34. See also Zola's preparatory notes: BN, NAF 10307, fol. 207.

66 Zola, *La Débâcle*, ed. David Baguley (Paris: Classiques Garnier, 2012), p. 710. For a discussion of Zola's harnessing of 'bon sens' as a Republican quality, see David Charles, 'Zola à l'épreuve de la Commune', *COnTEXTES*: http://journals.openedition.org/contextes/9924

67 *Grand Dictionnaire universel du XIXᵉ siècle*, 17 vols (Paris: Administration du Grand Dictionnaire universel, 1866–77), vol. 8 (1872), 1520.

68 BN, NAF 10308, fol. 202; original emphasis.

69 Letter to Van Santen Kolff, 6 October 1889. *Corr*, vol. 6, 423.

70 Zola, 'Notes parisiennes: le congrès ouvrier', *Le Sémaphore de Marseille*, 5 October 1876, p. 1.

71 'Échos de Paris: La Politique', *Le Figaro*, 17 April 1884, p. 1.

72 *Les Ouvriers en grève*, vol. 1, 65. According to Perrot, between 1864 and 1914, 56% of strikes were successful. The fact that larger strikes were more likely to succeed meant that 64% of strikers prevailed in this period. Of the ten years in which failed strikes outnumbered successes, these almost all fell between 1875 and 1888, 'the trend towards depression bringing with it deeper crises' (67).

73 Guesde, 'Le Salut', *L'Égalité*, 8 January 1882, p. 1. *Germinal*, 378; 452.

74 Rosa Luxemburg, *The Mass Strike, the Political Party and the Trade Union*, trans. Patrick Lavin, reprinted in *Reform or Revolution and Other Writings*, ed. Paul Buhle (Mineola, NY: Dover Publications, 2006), pp. 101–82 (p. 143; emphasis added).

75 Naomi Schor, *Zola's Crowds* (Baltimore, MD: Johns Hopkins University Press, 1978), p. xiv.

76 Armand Dayot, *Salon de 1884* (Paris: Baschet, 1884), pp. 15–16.

77 See 'Au jour le jour: Les réunions d'hier', *Le Temps*, 8 April 1884, p. 2.

78 Grison, 'Le Mineur d'Anzin', *Le Figaro*, 26 February 1884, p. 2.

79 'Les grèves du nord', *Le Voltaire*, 7 April 1884, pp. 1–2 (p. 1); BN, NAF 10308, fol. 400.

80 F. M., 'Échos de Paris: la politique', *Le Figaro*, 17 April 1884, p. 1 (emphasis added).

81 'Mes Notes sur Anzin', BN, NAF 10308, fol. 219. Basly went on to become the socialist deputy for Pas-de-Calais in 1885.

82 BN, NAF 10307, fol. 456.

83 Henri Marel, 'Étienne Lantier et les chefs syndicalistes', *Les Cahiers naturalistes*, 50 (1976), 26–39 (p. 31).

84 Leroy-Beaulieu, *La Question ouvrière au XIXe siècle*, p. 83.

85 BN, NAF 10307, fol. 494. Zola insists in his notes on Étienne's basic education ('Doesn't have any books, one or two perhaps'; BN, NAF 10308, fol. 11).

86 *The Political Unconscious*, p. 182.

87 This section of the chapter reprises parts of my article, 'Zola et Gissing: le Demos des deux côtés de la Manche', *Les Cahiers naturalistes*, 94 (2020), 131–42.

88 *La Question ouvrière au XIXe siècle*, p. 38.

89 Chantal Jacquet, *Les Transclasses, ou la non-reproduction* (Paris: Presses Universitaires de France, 2014).

90 BN, NAF 10307, fol. 169.

91 *The Political Unconscious*, pp. 176, 178.

92 George Gissing, *Demos: A Story of English Socialism*, ed. Pierre Coustillas (Brighton: The Harvester Press, 1972), p. 453.

93 Claude Duchet, 'Le Trou des bouches noires: parole, société, révolution dans *Germinal*', *Littérature*, 24 (1976), 11–39 (37).
94 Schor, *Zola's Crowds*, pp. 50, 53; and for a discussion of lapidation across Zola's fiction, pp. 52–67.
95 *Zola's Crowds*, p. 51.
96 Naomi Schor, 'Zola and "la nouvelle critique"', *L'Esprit créateur*, 11 (1971), 11–20 (p. 15).
97 *Les Mystères de Marseille*, ed. Daniel Compère (Paris: Classiques Garnier, 2018), p. 358.
98 John C. Lapp identifies the marchers of *Les Mystères* as 'the precursors of the striking miners in *Germinal*. *Zola Before the 'Rougon Macquart'* (Toronto: University of Toronto Press, 1964), p. 80.
99 *The Political Unconscious*, pp. 187–88.
100 *The Political Unconscious*, p. 188.
101 'Hippolyte Taine et la révolution française', in Émile Zola, *Lettres de Paris, choix d'articles traduits du russe et présentés par Phillip A. Duncan et Vera Erdely* (Paris: Droz and Minard, 1963), pp. 31–42 (p. 41).
102 *Le Messager de l'Europe*, February 1876 (607–28); repr. in Zola, *OC*, vol. 7, 607–28 (625). Zola devoted a long column to each volume of Taine's *Origines de la France contemporaine*, in February 1876 and May 1878. See Sophie Guermès, *La Fable documentaire: Zola historien* (Paris: Champion, 2017), pp. 46–51.
103 Here, I am taking up Jameson's claim: 'What is most striking about the theory of *ressentiment* is its unavoidably autoreferential structure', *The Political Unconscious*, p. 189.
104 See Mitterand, '"La vision rouge de la Révolution…" De Germinal à Thermidor', *Romantisme*, 82 (1993), 3–16 (p. 10).
105 *The Political Unconscious*, p. 181.
106 'La République et la littérature', in *OC*, vol. 9, 488–507 (505; my emphasis). In Zola's article on Léon Gambetta, he also berates politicians as 'failed novelists and dramatists' and 'fourth-rate journalists', sold out to 'powerful ambition'. 'Esclaves ivres', *Le Figaro*, 29 August 1881, p. 1.
107 *The Political Unconscious*, p. 189.
108 Robert Lethbridge, 'Étienne Lantier "romancier": genèse et mise en abime', *Les Cahiers naturalistes*, 59 (1985), 43–54 (p. 54).
109 BN, NAF 10308, fol. 351.
110 'Étienne Lantier "romancier"', 47. Lethbridge explicitly takes up Schor's assertion, in *Zola's Crowds*, that 'Zola's leaders are all variants on the writer' (p. 77).
111 Jules Huret, 'Les Littérateurs et la politique: M. Émile Zola', *Le Figaro*, 4 August 1893, p. 2 (original emphasis).
112 Ph. Dubois, interview with Zola, 'Zola ne sera pas député', *L'Aurore*, 4 November 1897, pp. 1–2 (p. 2).
113 Guillaume McNeil Arteau, 'Zola politique: parlementarisme, représentation, médiation', *Romantisme*, 171 (2016), 129–44 (p. 129).

114 Zola's letter to Antony Valabrègue, 4 April 1867. *Corr*, vol. 1, 485–87 (p. 485).

115 *The Antinomies of Realism*, pp. 148–49.

116 David Baguley, *Naturalist Fiction: The Entropic Vision* (Cambridge: Cambridge University Press, 1990).

117 Zola's 1884 preface to the Charpentier edition of *Les Mystères de Paris*, pp. 473–75 (p. 474).

118 In the wake of Zola's commercial success with *L'Assommoir*, Edmond de Goncourt sniffily noted in his *Journal* that 'Zola, in his moment of triumph, has something of the parvenu about him, coming by an unexpected fortune.' 19 February 1877; *Journal: mémoires de la vie littéraire*, ed. Robert Ricatte (Paris: Robert Laffont, 1989), vol. 2, 1173.

119 *The Political Unconscious*, p. 73.

120 Only in *Le Docteur Pascal* (1893) do we learn that the strike leader would become a vigorous defender of the Commune, for which he will subsequently be deported. *R-M*, vol. 5, 1017.

121 Trublot (pseudonym), 'À Minuit', *Le Cri du peuple*, 2 January 1884, p. 3.

122 Alexis, 'Naturalisme', *Le Matin*, 5 April 1884, p. 1; emphasis added.

123 'La République et la littérature', 493.

124 Zola, 'La République en Russie', *Le Figaro*, 21 March 1881; repr. in *Une campagne*, 795–800 (795).

125 *Corr*, vol. 5, 240–41.

126 Hugo's reaction reported by Alfred Barbou, *Victor Hugo: sa vie, ses œuvres* (Paris: Librairie universelle d'Alfred Duquesne, 1880), p. 285.

127 Zola, '*L'Assommoir*', *Le Bien public*, 13 February 1877, p. 2.

128 Henry Fouquier, 'Causerie dramatique', *Le XIXe siècle*, 21 January 1879, pp. 1–2 (p. 1).

129 George Sand, *Le Compagnon du Tour de France*, ed. René Bourgeois (Grenoble: Presses Universitaires de Grenoble, 1988), p. 31.

130 This is the burden of Schor's brilliant discussion of the novel in *George Sand and Idealism*, pp. 89–92.

131 *The Political Unconscious*, p. 178.

132 Irving Howe, 'The Genius of *Germinal*', *Encounter*, 34 (1970), 53–61 (55–56).

133 *Zola's Crowds*, p. 52.

134 'Lettre à la jeunesse', in *OC*, vol. 9, 349–70 (p. 350; emphasis added).

135 443; 508. The image is first deployed to describe the Maheu family's abrupt return to reality after Étienne's bombastic prophesies of a transformed society: 'They had suddenly felt as though they were going to be rich, and now they fell back down with a crash into the mire' (170; 263).

136 Andrew J. Counter, 'Zola's Repetitions: On Repetition in Zola', *The Modern Language Review*, 116:1 (2021), 42–64 (p. 60).

137 '*L'Assommoir*. À monsieur le Directeur du *Bien public*. '

138 Jameson, 'The Case for Georg Lukács', in *Marxism and Form: Twentieth-Century Dialectical Theories of Literature* (Princeton, NJ: Princeton University Press, 1971), pp. 160–205 (p. 195).

139 *The Antinomies of Realism*, p. 74.

140 Jameson, 'Antinomies of the Realism-Modernism Debate', *Modern Language Quarterly*, 73:3 (2012), 475–85 (p. 479).

141 Mark Fisher, *Capitalist Realism: Is There No Alternative?* (Ropley: Zero Books, 2009), p. 13.

142 Judith Butler, 'Uprising', in *Uprisings*, ed. Georges Didi-Huberman (Paris: Gallimard, 2016), pp. 23–36 (p. 24).

143 *The Antinomies of Realism*, p. 154.

144 Lukács, 'The Zola Centenary', p. 93.

145 Jameson uses the term in *Marxism and Form*, p. 201.

146 Carassus, *Les Grèves imaginaires*, p. 97. The ideological stakes of this 'mythification' of social history have been well-rehearsed, most authoritatively by Mitterand, for whom Zola's insistent naturalisation of both class difference and class struggle diminishes any sense of historical change or contingency. *Le Discours du roman* (Paris: Presses Universitaires de France, 1980), pp. 140–49. See also Philip Walker, *'Germinal' and Zola's Philosophical and Religious Thought* (Amsterdam: John Benjamins, 1984), pp. 40, 62.

147 Jean Carrère, 'Entretiens sur l'anarchie: Chez M. Émile Zola', *Le Figaro*, 25 April 1892, p. 2.

148 'La République en Russie', *Une campagne*, 798.

149 'La République en Russie', *Une campagne*, 800.

150 Susan Harrow, *Zola, The Body Modern* (Oxford: Legenda, 2010), p. 200. On Souvarine, see Eduardo A. Febles, *Explosive Narratives: Terrorism and Anarchy in the Works of Émile Zola* (Amsterdam: Rodopi, 2010), pp. 33–63; and Éléonore Reverzy, 'Fonctions du révolutionnaire. Le personnage de Souvarine dans *Germinal* de Zola', in *Figures de l'émigré russe en France au XIXᵉ et XXᵉ siècle: fiction et réalité*, ed. Charlotte Krauss and Tatiana Victoroff (Leiden: Brill, 2012), pp. 163–76.

151 *Germinal*, 476; 539. Roger Ripoll, 'L'avenir dans *Germinal*: destruction et renaissance', *Les Cahiers naturalistes*, 50 (1976), 115–33 (p. 125).

152 Jameson, *The Antinomies of Realism*, p. 5.

153 Letter to David Dautresme, 11 December 1885; *Corr*, vol. 5, 347.

154 Zola, *Travail. Œuvres complètes. Les Quatre Évangiles – II*, ed. Fabian Scharf (Paris: Classiques Garnier, 2021), p. 603.

155 *Travail*, p. 583.

156 Mitterand, 'L'Évangile social de *Travail*: un anti-*Germinal*', *Mosaic*, 3 (1972), 179–87.

157 *Travail*, p. 582.

158 Mitterand, *Discours du roman*, p. 157.

159 'Antinomies of the Realism-Modernism Debate', 477–78 (emphasis added).

160 Several socialist newspapers asked Zola for permission to serialise the novel. See, for instance, Zola's generous reply to *Le Peuple de Bruxelles* on 15 November 1885. *Corr*, vol. 5, 335–36.

161 Séverine, 'Lettre à Jean Labeur', *Le Cri du peuple*, 14 July 1885, p. 4.

162 Guesde, 'Les Bastilles modernes', *Le Cri du peuple*, 17 July 1885, p. 1. The editors of *Le Socialiste* (Guesde included) would, however, be critical of Zola's negotiations with censors over the theatre adaptation of *Germinal* – especially the cutting of the scene in which soldiers fired at striking miners. See, for example, 'M. Goblet et M. Zola', *Le Socialiste*, 7 November 1885, p. 1.

163 Labruyère, 'La revanche des Maheu', *Le Cri du peuple*, 30 January 1886; cited in Marion Glaumaud-Carbonnier, 'Zola à l'étalage: l'écrivain au carrefour, effets de "kioscopie"', *Les Cahiers naturalistes*, 95 (2021), 221–36 (p. 231).

164 Louis Lambert, 'À Médan: chez l'auteur de *Germinal*', *Le Gaulois*, 29 January 1886, p. 2.

165 Glaumaud-Carbonnier, 'Zola à l'étalage', 231.

CHAPTER 3

S/Z: Le Rêve

In the wake of George Sand's death on 8 June 1876, Ivan Turgenev urged Zola to devote his monthly article in the St. Petersburg magazine *Le Messager de l'Europe* to the great writer, who had long been a dear friend of the Russian novelist. The result was a sprawling obituary-cum-literary manifesto, which, Zola acknowledged, 'shows on every line that I understand the novel in a completely opposite way to George Sand'.[1] Balancing due reverence and critical judgement had been an awkward task, and one he was glad to lay to rest. When Zola's appraisal arrived, Turgenev felt it had fallen distinctly wide of the mark: 'the article is very nice – but a little harsh', he confided to Flaubert. 'Zola cannot deliver a comprehensive judgement on Mme S[and]. There is too much distance between them.'[2] It would surely be hard to quibble with Turgenev's reproach of Zola's tactless severity. Zola may have been openly critical of the eulogy that Victor Hugo composed for Sand's funeral at Nohant, claiming it lacked 'more profound, human emotions'. Yet his own extended necrology hardly tapped into the depth of feeling that Hugo had apparently failed to supply.[3] More compelling still – and no doubt it was for Flaubert too, given his great affection for his 'chère maître' – is Turgenev's verdict on Zola as an inadequate judge, even a bad reader, of Sand. Zola penned his obituary just as he was making waves with *L'Assommoir*; in fact, the novel's serialisation in *Le Bien public* had been suspended on the day of Sand's death. It was a coincidence that no doubt fed into Zola's overdetermined vision of a changing of the guard. Rooted in his own aesthetic principles, Zola's account of Sand's life and works aired more than anything, as he was well aware, their irreconcilable differences.

Those differences, it will now be clear, lie at the heart of this book, and of its account of Zola's complex, and sometimes contradictory, negotiations with the aesthetic mode that he associated most closely with Sand: idealism. What I wish to establish more specifically in this chapter is the constitutive importance of Zola's relationship to Sand – a relationship which, to misappropriate Roland Barthes's landmark study of Balzac, I should like to think of as another 'S/Z'.[4] After all, Balzac represents, as we shall see in Zola's obituary of Sand, the third point in the naturalist author's triangle of nineteenth-century literary history: Balzac-Sand-Zola. Unlike the marginal divergences that fuelled Zola's anxious scribbling of the 'Differences between Balzac and myself' at the inception of *Les Rougon-Macquart*, Zola's emphatic, at times arch, differentiation from Sand could be, even needed to be, spoken out loud.[5] This authorial self-fashioning demanded the projection of Sand as his (and, by extension, Balzac's) specular antithesis. What it tended to occlude, as I argue throughout this book, was their inextricability, the play of alterity and sameness captured by Barthes – if we take him, once again, out of context: 'S and Z are in a relation of graphological inversion: the same letter seen from the other side of the mirror.'[6] The connection is, of course, pure felicity. But before we deem such onomastic play gratuitous, we might recall Zola's own fascination with the act of naming, and, most importantly for us, Zola's decision to call his writer alias Sandoz – S/ando/Z; Sand[oZ] – in his artist novel *L'Œuvre* (1886). In a tantalisingly brief footnote to her *George Sand and Idealism*, Naomi Schor pointed to the wider implications of this name-play. It suggests, she argued, that Zola's 'relationship to Sand was more complex and ambivalent than one might at first surmise and confirms the intimate relationship of idealism and naturalism, for Sandoz combines both Sand and a partial anagram of Zola'.[7] In *L'Œuvre*, a novel that otherwise deals so self-consciously in a Bloomian 'anxiety of influence', this incorporation of the woman writer involves a peculiar sleight of hand. Zola's tortured painter, Claude Lantier, laments his generation's indelible taste for romanticism, while Sandoz speaks of his despair at having been born 'at the confluence of Hugo and Balzac' – those two rival fathers in Zola's Oedipal drama.[8] What such fretful negotiations with one's predecessors leave unspoken is the possible third term, already inscribed in the writer-double's name: Zola *as* Sand.

My main contention in this chapter is that Zola does entertain precisely this possibility – of incorporating, if not being, Sand – two years later in *Le Rêve* (1888), a novel we might describe as the most experimental of the *Rougon-Macquart* cycle, if not in the strict sense Zola had famously given to the term. For *Le Rêve* represents, I wish to argue, a return to Sand's writing, and above all, to her brand of idealism, which Zola had evoked at such length, and with such strength of feeling, in his obituary of the writer over a decade earlier. There, as we shall see, Zola had repeatedly assimilated Sand, and her idealist aesthetic, to the figure of the dream: 'George Sand is, then, the dream', he concluded, 'a portrait of human life, not as the author has observed it, but rather as [she] wishes she had the power to create it'.[9] Zola thus claimed to find in Sand's writing an anti-mimetic impulse, an insatiable desire to refashion the world *as it is* through the power of the creative imagination, which he rooted in the particular conditions of her childhood. Zola's Sand is an incorrigible, and unequivocally caricatural, *rêveuse*, who serves as an expedient foil to the naturalist author's own sober respect for the reality principle. The case I want to make here is that Zola's portrait of Sand bears on his novel of the dream, and on the trajectory of its heroine artist-fantasist, in ways that have, curiously, gone unremarked.[10] How might we read Zola's experiment with idealism in *Le Rêve* as a sustained negotiation with Sand? And what might this negotiation tell us about the naturalist novel's desire for difference?

The point of privileging Zola's relationship to Sand in this chapter is, of course, not to deny that he was negotiating in the novel with a host of other influences. Elizabeth Emery has shown how the medievalism Zola once derided in the work of both Théophile Gautier and Victor Hugo (namely, his *Notre-Dame de Paris*, 1831) finds an ironic expression in the architecture, and the archaic atmosphere, of *Le Rêve*.[11] No doubt, as Emery also suggests, Zola's foregrounding of saints, mysticism, and artisanal artefacts spoke, in turn, to the contemporary revival of medievalist interest among Symbolist writers and artists – Jean Moréas, Maurice Maeterlinck, the Pre-Raphaelites.[12] Where naturalism had become something of a foil for Symbolist experimentation, Zola gave a nod to his purported usurpers by reappropriating the objects of their own imagination. More broadly still, the title of Zola's novel seemed to function as a deliberate provocation, and precisely because this was a term he had wielded again and again to stigmatise a whole gamut of literature that privileged feeling over reason, poetry over prose, imagination over verisimilitude.[13] As we saw in Chapter 2, Zola repeatedly pastiched Hugo's self-portraiture as a prophet, by representing him instead as a blinkered dreamer, beholden to the projections of his private imagination: 'He lived through his own times without seeing them, his eyes fixed instead on his dreams.'[14] There are, though, reasons why we might choose to place Sand in particular at the heart of Zola's negotiations with aesthetic difference in *Le Rêve*. The most obvious, it will become clear, is that Zola established Sand as precisely emblematic of an entire current of the novel that rivalled Balzac's realism: she is made to stand, in other words, for a set of tendencies and inclinations that characterised other authors, but which she alone fully encapsulated. This is in no small part because she is a woman writer. For the kind of idealism Zola lambasts in the romantic tradition is consistently gendered feminine: either as the effeminate ('castrated') aesthetic of the male writer-poet; or, in Sand's case, as a congenital predisposition.[15] Zola's systematic gendering of idealism finds yet another expression, I venture, in *Le Rêve*, which is, among other things, a novel of female artistry.

With his obituary of Sand, Zola had set up the writer as the century's arch-idealist only to better perform, as we shall see, the metaphorical interment of the idealist novel altogether. Of course, this retrospective view sits uneasily, to say the least, with the exuberant admiration a younger Zola had voiced for the writer, captivated as he was by her *romans champêtres* as well as by her political vision. In letters to his childhood friend Jean-Baptistin Baille, the twenty-year-old extolled Sand's social conscience and Republican convictions: 'a patient struggle, a daily fight, from which all men will emerge as brothers, making up a single Republic that is wealthy and strong. Sadly, it is perhaps only a dream, and yet how good it would be'.[16] We shall see in Chapter 5 how Sand's dream of a fraternal Republic resurfaces in Zola's later utopian fiction when the political expediency of an idealist aesthetic had been brought home by his involvement in the Dreyfus Affair. But in the mid-1870s, the relative dogmatism at work in Zola's account of Sand was closely hitched to his wider polemic (explored in Chapter 1) against a set of contemporary idealist writers operating in Sand's lineage: Octave Feuillet, André Theuriet, Victor Cherbuliez, *entre autres*. What matters most for our reading of *Le Rêve*, however, is that the novel coincided with something like a wider recanonisation of the woman author in the later 1880s – led, above all, by antinaturalist writers and critics, keen to proclaim an 'idealist reaction'. In the latter stages of this chapter, we shall examine some of that contemporaneous critical discourse on Sand and the naturalist novel. For Zola's detractors not only revalorised her association with the idealism that the naturalist eschewed, they also sought to repackage the Sandian 'dream' for a fin-de-siècle readership, by tapping into a set of prevailing philosophical ideas about the individual consciousness and artistic representation.

This nexus of antinaturalism and idealism lies at the heart of the present chapter, the first section of which examines Zola's negotiations with his critics as part of the planning of *Le Rêve*. Zola clearly intended to set down a strategic marker of his own versatility at a moment when the naturalist novel had become a foil for new strains of aesthetic experimentation: 'I will give a sense of the moment too', Zola declared in his *Ébauche*, 'the backlash against naturalism, people's longing for a world beyond appearances, their need for an ideal, the turmoil of belief. All of this with dreams, a thoroughly idealist strand, given over to fantasy.'[17] In incorporating, or replicating, the impulses of a type of literature that styled itself as mystical, fantastic, sentimental, psychological – and, predominantly, idealist – Zola sought to produce a novel that would be distinctly out of character: 'I should like to write a book that nobody expects me to write.'[18] First, he clarified, the novel could be read by anybody, even young women ('no violent passions, then, a simple idyll'); second, he would prove himself adept at rendering the psychological life of his characters. This not only meant directly refuting critics' objections to his brand of naturalism but also taking up many of the characteristics of the idealist novel he had systematically derided. This chapter takes up Zola's wager – the possibility he describes, that is, of *writing differently*, or indeed, of *writing against himself.*

In exploring what we might think of as Zola's experiment with idealism, the chapter returns, in one sense, to a set of familiar problems for Zola critics (then as now): what exactly are we to make of his self-conscious refashioning of the naturalist novel? Ought we to accept the novel's incongruity at face value? Where did the chaste novel belong in Zola's cycle of ravenous appetites? For Henri Mitterand, *Le Rêve* can be understood as 'a break-novel' in the series, its serenity all the more pronounced for being lodged between *La Terre* (1887) and *La Bête humaine* (1890), the latter 'a violent drama, fit to give all of Paris *nightmares*'.[19] In this, he echoes Paul Alexis's account of Zola's practice, whereby he is said to alternate 'major works' with 'supposed works of repose or amusement'.[20] Henry James, meanwhile, placed *Le Rêve* in a distinct category of Zola's fiction that also included *La Faute de l'Abbé Mouret* (1875), *Une page d'amour* (1878), and *Le Docteur Pascal* (1893) – novels with which the naturalist writer was said to pay 'his express tribute to the "ideal", to the select and the charming'. For James, there was doubtless something touching about Zola dabbling in 'idyllic' subjects. There was also, he implied, something faintly ridiculous about the naturalist novelist seeking to be what he is not:

> They are matters of conscious delicacy, and nothing [...] might interest us more, literally, and might positively affect us more, even very nearly to tears, though indeed sometimes also to smiles, than to see the constructor of *Les Rougon-Macquart* trying, 'for all he is worth', to be fine with fineness, finely tender, finely true – trying to be, as it is called, distinguished – in face of constitutional hindrance.[21]

James attributes to Zola's attempt at 'fineness' a certain sincerity, even pathos, that few of his readers allowed. Instead, a hermeneutics of suspicion has tended to prevail among critics, for whom *Le Rêve* confounds and destabilises in ways that are, as both Colette Becker and Éléonore Reverzy put it, 'irksome'.[22] Such frustration stems, Reverzy explains, from the author's coquettishness, his attempt, that is, to conceal his own agendas: Zola 'gives the reader the impression that he is hiding something, that everything is not as simple as it seems'.[23] (Zola refers, in fact, in a letter to the Dutch journalist Jacques Van Santen Kolff to the novel's 'hidden philosophy').[24] For Sophie Guermès, discerning the true intention of Zola's novel relies on the reader engaging with the author's preparatory notes, 'in order to discover in the genetic layers of the text that which the writer was not inclined to state too bluntly'.[25] The critic's task would, then, be to rescue Zola's novel from a naïve reading by recuperating the author's clandestine (anti-idealist) motivations.

In what follows, we shall seek to understand the novel's playful incoherence as the sign of naturalism's unstable relationship to an idealist aesthetic that he associated most closely with Sand, and on which his doctrinaire pronouncements tell only part of the story. For Zola's scrutiny of the conditions and emergence of the idealist imagination in *Le Rêve* is also, inevitably, an interrogation of the authorial fantasies at work in the writing of the idealist novel.

'The Two Zolas'

'It is quite true that I am going through a crisis, a midlife crisis no doubt', Zola confided in a letter to Van Santen Kolff on 6 March 1889. 'For weeks, months even, I have been in turmoil, caught up in a storm of desires and regrets.'[26] The signs of an impending crisis had begun to emerge the previous autumn, when Zola went on a diet, restricting his intake of wine and starchy foods with surprising determination. By March the following year, just before his future mistress – the twenty-one-year-old linen maid Jeanne Rozerot – entered his life, he had already lost fourteen kilos; and by late spring, Jeanne was pregnant with their daughter Denise. That the planning and composition of *Le Rêve* coincide with this period of corporeal self-restraint and emotional abandon certainly invites speculation on the circulation between personal fantasy and professional reinvention. His initial idea – to which we shall return – of casting the hero as a middle-aged man, who falls in love with a teenager, appears inextricably linked to his desire to probe his own creative drives: 'Me, work, a life eaten up by literature, upheaval, crisis, the need to be loved: all this is to be examined psychologically.'[27] Whether or not *Le Rêve* 'confessionally transposed [Zola's] frustrated wishes', namely for an escape from his ailing marriage to Alexandrine, what Robert E. Ziegler terms Zola's 'Naturalism-free diet' – alluding to the slenderness of the novel as well as to its anorexic, ultimately disembodied, heroine – allows readers to think imaginatively about the sorts of condensations Zola's own dream life might have undergone in the narrative, as well as about the writer's apparent flirtation with a new aesthetic *régime*.[28]

For contemporary critics, Zola's endeavour to break with his own image tended to be interpreted, first and foremost, as a professional strategy. Take Jean-Louis Forain's caricature 'The Two Zolas' (Figure 3.1), which appeared on the front page of *Le Courrier français*. One Zola is distinctly rotund, with his fictional prostitute Nana by his side, and a copy of *L'Assommoir* in his pocket; the other, decidedly svelte, is adorned with a halo. The caption registers the saintly Zola's indignation, as he gestures to his alter ego: 'I wrote *Le Rêve*! It's that dirty old man who wrote *Nana*!' The Académie, which looms in the background, provides the context for the writer's disavowal of his notorious novel of prostitution: Zola had put himself forward for membership for the first time earlier that year. Of course, the novelist never would become an *Immortel*; and this was the first of nineteen failed attempts.[29] From the moment he broached the possibility, however, in an interview with *La Presse* on 19 July 1888, critics seized on the idea that *Le Rêve* – then midway through its serialisation – had been designed to appeal to the tastes of the Académie.[30] A few months after the election to replace the deceased académicien Octave Feuillet on 21 May 1891, *La Vie populaire* pastiched the aesthetic of Zola's *Le Rêve*: a dreaming Zola is visited by an angel holding a chair, the scene framed as a stained-glass window belonging to the 'Église de Médan'.[31] Professional ambition thus provided one way of rationalising the novelist's act of self-reinvention, though Zola steadfastly denied any such motivations.[32]

What Zola did acknowledge was that this project – 'a fantasy, a flight of fancy, which I have been mulling over for a long time', he told Van Santen Kolff – was a response to a wider backlash against his brand of naturalism.[33] *Le Rêve* was conceived in the aftermath of what became known as the 'Manifeste des Cinq', the open letter of 18 August 1887, signed by five young writers in protest at the vulgarity of his latest novel *La Terre*, even before its serialisation was complete.[34] The 'Manifeste' sought to bind *l'homme et l'œuvre* together in crudely physiological ways, *La Terre*'s 'violent penchant for obscenity' connected to 'the illness of the writer's loins', which the authors diagnosed as the combination of a renal disorder and a sexual psychopathology. The novel's scatological excesses demonstrated that Zola's famous artistic credo needed to be refashioned as 'a "corner of nature seen through a *morbid sensorium*"'. Alongside this pseudo-medical explanation for the novelist's 'aberrations', the authors

Figure 3.1   Jean-Louis Forain, 'The Two Zolas'.
Caricature in *Le Courrier Français*, 16 November 1890 [front cover]. Courtesy of the Bibliothèque nationale de France.

cited 'the unconscious development of an insatiable appetite for sales', skilful as he had become at capitalising on the pornographic reputation his series had acquired.

Though such indictments were hardly original, framed as they were as a revolt in Zola's own ranks, they signalled, we saw in Chapter 1, the burgeoning of a broader antinaturalist reaction. Ten days later, Anatole France pronounced his own judgement on *La Terre* as 'the Georgics of Filth'.[35] France objected to the self-seeking opportunism that clearly drove the 'Manifeste'; the authors' speculations about Zola's physiological condition went, he said, beyond the limits of permissible criticism. And still, he produced a similar characterisation of the novel as tasteless, gratuitously obscene, and poorly observed. Most serious of the novel's deficiencies, for France, was its categorical denial of all that is good, charming, beautiful, noble – in short, Zola's irrepressible need to *deidealise*:

> Never had anyone tried so hard to debase mankind, to insult every image of beauty and love, to deny everything that is good and proper. Never had anyone shown such disregard for the ideal of mankind. [...] There are wondrous forms and noble thoughts on earth. There are pure souls and brave hearts. M. Zola is oblivious. (3)

Shortly after, Ferdinand Brunetière joined the chorus with his essay 'The Bankruptcy of Naturalism', in which he derided the novelist's invariable privileging of sensation over sentiment, appetite or instinct over thought, stomach (as so many commentators put it) over brain: 'Eating, drinking, and the rest – hardly anything else happens in the ninety-five instalments I have read of *La Terre*.'[36] In short, Brunetière – like France – was rehearsing longstanding critiques of the naturalist novel: that it offered blunt tools with which to probe the complexities, struggles, and dramas of the human psyche – or, in the spiritualist term of his critics, which Zola duly reprised, the soul. If naturalism could afford, at best, a superficial mode of observation, this was because of the 'contempt that he [Zola] has always declared for psychology'.[37]

It was in the light of such objections to naturalism's purportedly exclusive fascination with the physiological that Zola declared, in his *Ébauche* for *Le Rêve*, a determination to prove that he could turn his hand to the life of the mind:

> I would like to force people to admit that I am a psychologist. Some psychology, then, or what passes for it (!): a struggle of the soul, the never-ending struggle between passion and duty, or a different struggle: between maternal love and passion, or filial love and another feeling.[38]

We shall track, in due course, Zola's alternative definitions of psychology through the trajectory of his foundling heroine Angélique, and what we will call, after Freud, her 'family romance' – the search, that is, for alternative (superior) parents that guides her own imaginative development. Indeed, in this sense, the poor girl's fantasy that Zola's novel describes – of rewriting her own origins, of revolting against 'the lowliness of her birth' – can be understood precisely as a negotiation with the classism that tended to underpin, implicitly or otherwise, antinaturalist discourse.[39] For critics like Brunetière, to recall the discussion in Chapter 1, what the naturalist novel lacked was the capacity to track those subtleties of feeling, passion, and imagination that could evolve in the likes of Feuillet's aristocratic subjects, unfettered by the bonds of necessity.[40]

Certainly, as Jean-Marie Seillan suggests, Zola's novel can be read as a negotiation with, even reprisal of, precisely the kind of idealist fiction that the likes of Brunetière extolled: 'focused on its future reception, the *Ébauche* for *Le Rêve* reads somewhat like a takeover bid in its plan to recycle elements of the idealist novel as part of a more comprehensive and expansive aesthetic'.[41] The idealist novel's appeal to young women readers, its anti-mimetic impulse, its devotion to psychology, its escape of the here-and-now, its decorporealised heroine: these were the features Zola set out to adopt.[42] Indeed, one critic claimed to have been reminded by *Le Rêve* of the ethereally chaste heroine of Feuillet's *Histoire de Sibylle* (1863), before concluding with tongue-in-cheek relish: 'Well, M. Feuillet's Sybille is a veritable infidel next to M. Zola's Angélique.'[43] For some, then, the novelist was to be congratulated on writing, at long last, a suitable novel for *jeunes filles*, 'soaring into the ideal', as Charles Chincholle put it, 'after the abominations of *La Terre*': 'He has leapt into *the beyond*. Many readers will surely wish he would stay there.'[44] For most, however, Zola's new-found propriety was decidedly suspect – a cover that allowed him to reintroduce his naturalist convictions via the backdoor. Catholic critics, in particular, were reluctant to credit claims of Zola's 'conversion', however broadly conceived, noting the curious absence of prayers and confessions from this tale of childhood piety. In '*Le Rêve* de Zola jugé par un catholique', Charles Brunetière (Ferdinand's brother) cautioned the reader against 'a literal reading', instead noting the play of irony at work in the novel's portrayal of religious fervour. Better, he declared, the outright atheist, for Zola was peddling in the novel 'some kind of unholiness perfumed with rose water, a hundred times more dangerous, to my mind, than the most forthright and cynical irreligion'.[45]

What such critiques effectively warned against were the risks of the naïve reading: *Le Rêve* must be understood as an imposter-text, or indeed a 'scandal', in the etymological sense of a trap (*skandalon*). Thus, Jules Lemaître, in his indignant take on Zola's (apparently oxymoronic) 'naturalist fairytale', objected to the writer's self-reinvention as a deliberate form of duplicity: 'M. Zola must make up his mind: he cannot be at once Zola and something other than Zola. . .'[46] In spite of its self-styled propriety, *Le Rêve* exuded a latent eroticism that the skilled reader could hardly ignore:

> It should be noted that M. Zola has endeavoured to write in a chaste manner. It is no less true that, despite his efforts, there is, for those able to read, perhaps as great a fixation on matters of the flesh in *Le Rêve* as in his other novels. Their smell lingers. (535)

In an interview with *Le Figaro*, given a fortnight later, Zola ventriloquised such reactions to *Le Rêve* by declaring self-parodically: 'my withered soul couldn't possibly recover its innocence [se refaire une virginité]. There are fewer ideals in *Le Rêve* than in *La Terre*'.[47] Zola's authorial reinvention, coded as his restored chastity, was thus tied to the trajectory of his heroine, whose refusal to repeat the sexual sins of her ancestors ought to guarantee the novel's (and the novelist's) impunity.

Critics thus opened up a double reading of *Le Rêve* whereby it appeared as proof of the writer's (redemptive) capacity for innocent storytelling and as an altogether 'naturalist' satire of the fairytale genre. Should readers take Zola seriously, or had he confected nothing more than an ersatz idealist novel? In his preparatory notes, Zola had declared his intention of restraining his irony in a way which would keep both straight and satirical readings in play: 'And so, *without too much irony*, it should show life as it is not, life as it is dreamt about: everybody good, everybody decent, everybody happy. An ideal life, just as is longed for.'[48] This indeterminacy precluded readers from dismissing outright the overblown idealism in which the novel deals, just as it allowed them to supply in full what the novel itself does not: a sense of the absurd. The wider question of whether the naturalist novel could change its spots preoccupied critics, for whom the attempt was either deemed an aesthetic failure or rationalised as part of an existing tendency in Zola's cycle. In another iteration of the writerly schizophrenia pictured by Forain's caricature, France lamented the novelist's attempt to depart from his 'natural' style: 'if I were forced to choose, I would still prefer M. Zola on all fours to M. Zola with wings'.[49] Better the obscenity of *La Terre* than the confected innocence of *Le Rêve*. . .

Others questioned the logic of that authorial *dédoublement* altogether. Was Zola's 'idealist' novel to be understood as *sui generis*, or could it be traced through other kinships, or indeed to other precedents? Certainly, the critic Edmond Lepelletier was not alone in considering Zola's latest novel to be in no sense *hors série*, despite its heroine being only belated added to the family tree. ('It is a new shoot that I have grafted on', Zola explained, midway through composing the novel.)[50] *Le Rêve* was, Lepelletier argued, rooted – in the arboreal metaphor he takes up from the novelist – in the wider genealogy of the cycle:

> Those who would deem *Le Rêve* a bolt from the blue, [. . .] a sort of mystical indulgence by the solitary man from Médan, [. . .] those people have either misunderstood or misremembered. *Le Rêve* is not an isolated, extraordinary, or startingly unforeseen creation among Zola's works. *This is not a crypto-gramic plant with neither stem, nor roots, nor seeds.*[51]

Lepelletier duly evokes the romance between Sylvère and Miette in *La Fortune des Rougon* (1871), and the entirety of *Une page d'amour*, as precursors of Zola's idealist turn. Beyond the series, meanwhile, there is no doubt good reason, as Marie Scarpa has suggested, to read the novel as the deferred development of the early *Contes à Ninon* (1864), specifically the orphan tale, 'Sœur des pauvres', and the miraculous love story of the adolescent embroider, 'La Fée amoureuse'.[52] Such intertextual resonances establish a sense of imaginative continuity, which would support Zola's insistence that the novel 'responds to the general philosophy of my entire work'.[53] But if *Le Rêve* galvanised such debates in the first place, it was no doubt a marker of just how self-consciously Zola toys with those critical impulses to explain (or explain away) the novel's difference, or singularity. What kind of rupture could be introduced into a series predicated on the logic of familial reproduction? Or, put differently, how could the naturalist writer be anything but the naturalist writer? Ventriloquising critiques of *Le Rêve*, not least Lemaître's, Zola evoked the limits of his authorial identity: 'My task as writer is to render the strength and power of our beastly existence [. . .]. Beyond this, I do not exist.'[54] Zola's provocation, of course, is to challenge this principle of self-identity; and he does so, as we shall see now, by fashioning an idealist heroine who succeeds in undoing her own heredity. For Angélique, as Zola later clarified via his avatar the doctor Pascal, is a figure of 'inneity' – the legacy of her parents 'merge, without a trace of either of them apparently finding its way into the new being'.[55] To establish a break in the chain of 'family resemblance': this was the wager riding on Zola's incursion into idealist territory.

Family Romances

Le Rêve opens on Christmas day morning with the abandoned young heroine, Angélique, taking refuge from the driving snow against the Sainte-Agnès door of Beaumont cathedral. On the brink of death, her petrified form resembles the virginal sculptures that adorn the cathedral's façade. Directly above her, the scene of the thirteen-year-old saint's ascension to heaven is played out: 'At the apex of the tympanum, Agnes appears in a radiant circle of light as she is received into heaven, where Jesus, her betrothed, weds his delicate young bride with a kiss of eternal rapture' (4; 816). On the threshold of the story, the reader thus encounters in miniature the fate of the virgin martyr that Angélique will set out to imitate through the novel – artistically, in reproducing the image of Saint Agnès in one of the magnificent tapestries she embroiders; and psychologically, in her own life, and death, narrative. Angélique is rescued and ultimately adopted by Hubertine and her husband Hubert, artisan embroiderers whose childless marriage is a source of quiet sorrow, their sterility explained as a punishment, exacted by Hubertine's deceased mother, for their own disobedient love affair. Angélique's hermetic childhood in the shadow of the cathedral, suffused with her reading of Jacques de Voragine's illustrated volume of saints' lives La Légende dorée, becomes the breeding ground for her fantasies. Convinced that she will marry her prince charming, Angélique finds her suitor in the illustrious Félicien d'Hautecœur, a descendant of the surviving younger branch of the line of tenth-century noblemen. Félicien's forbidding father, the bishop of Beaumont cathedral, vehemently opposes their marriage, only offering his blessing once he has read a dying Angélique her last rites. The condition of the novel's triumphant dénouement in place, Zola's heroine is returned on her wedding day to the very spot where she was rescued; and it is through the cathedral door that she, and readers, exit the story. But as the amorous pair tie the knot with a kiss, the saintly virgin dies on the cathedral threshold, 'borne off in the moment of her dream's fulfilment' (180; 994). Zola thus grants his heroine's wish of becoming one of the 'Happy Dead', those young virginal saints of La Légende dorée, whose first taste of conjugal bliss is also their last.

True to Zola's definition of psychology in his Ébauche, the narrative rehearses two related types of struggle: an internal one and a generational, or familial, one. The burgeoning of Angélique's fantasy life – her dream, that is, of an 'impossible' marriage – leads her into conflict with her adoptive mother and future father-in-law, which ultimately turns into a drama of self-denial. But Angélique's daydreaming is also centred on a reimagining of her family origins – and this, I want now to suggest, in a way that speaks evocatively to Freud's account in 'Family Romances' (1909) of the play of fantasy in early childhood life.[56] There, Freud asserts that children, particularly the highly talented, are prone to 'peculiarly marked imaginative activity':

> A characteristic example of this [. . .] is to be seen in the familiar day-dreaming which persists far beyond puberty. If these day-dreams are carefully examined, they are found to serve as the fulfilment of wishes and as a correction of actual life. They have two principal aims, an erotic and an ambitious one – though an erotic aim is usually concealed behind the latter too.[57]

Freud's description of the child's power to redraw reality through day-dream – to enact 'a correction of actual life' – maps onto Zola's account of Angélique's mysterious musings in and around the period marked by 'the fretful agitation of puberty' (55–56; 869). Left to gestate in the credulous air of the Hubert household, the embroiderer's subliminal wishes develop in conjunction with her needlework. Indeed, this labour is freighted with an overdetermined sexual symbolism (later, the needles will draw blood from her fingers without causing pain). It is to the rhythm of this activity that Angélique comes first to articulate her fantasy, to herself and to her adoptive parents. Circling around the incantatory refrain, 'Oh, what I'd like, what I'd like. . .', she gradually pins her 'vague yearnings' (41; 853) to an imaginary object: at first, a prince whom she is to marry, and then, as the chain of association unfolds, the Messiah himself: 'But Jesus is the one I want!' (46; 858). Within the narrative, it is Angélique's adoptive mother, the 'sensible' Hubertine (44; 857), who confronts the young girl's fantasies with a reminder of the reality principle: 'you'll find out how things work later [. . .]. You'll learn about life' (43; 855). But Angélique's firm insistence on the viability of the miraculous alliance, performed and fulfilled through her reverie, bears an unassailable conviction that no reasoning can temper.

In fact, if we follow Freud's argument further, then this wish-fulfilment performs another fundamental task. For the idea that dominates the child's imagination at this juncture is, Freud claims, that 'of getting free from the parents of whom he now has a low opinion and of replacing them by others, who, as a rule, are of higher social standing'.[58] In one obvious sense, Zola's novel gives free rein to this fantasy of parental substitution, allowing it to unfold uncontested precisely

because the heroine's past is reduced to a few details in the administrative booklet with which she is found:

> On the first page, [...] appeared various printed headings. After 'Surname of
> the child' a simple dash in ink filled the blank. Her 'Christian names' were
> recorded as 'Angélique, Marie'. [...] So her father and mother were unknown,
> and she had no other papers, not even a birth certificate. She had nothing
> apart from this coldly officious little book bound in pale pink cloth. (9; 821)

It is this blank or 'dash' – the absence of a family name – that allows
Angélique to compose her own bold family narrative, to turn, in Susan
Harrow's words, 'autobiographical anonymity into autobiographical sub-
limity'.[59] For the heroine's namelessness is a stigma or wound (Angélique
first appears injured as she clutches her booklet to her side) that gives rise
to a compensatory sense of pride, an insistence on her own distinction:
'I'm better than all the rest, I am! I'm better, better, better...' (9; 821).
Angélique discloses, in snatches, her itinerant childhood with a set of
substitute parents: first, the idealised maman Nini (Françoise Hamelin);
then, the Franchomme couple; and, when they both pass away, the
dissolute Rabiers, who mistreat her. In the last brutal episode before she
escapes, they attempt to gouge out Angélique's eyes, a type of torture that
already ties her to the saints' lives she will shortly discover. Hubert
subsequently tracks down Angélique's louche birth mother Sidonie
Rougon in Paris, her fabric shop a front for sexual transactions ('under
the pretence of selling lace, she sold all sorts of things', 31; 843). In a play
on the immaculate conception, Sidonie gave birth to a child, Hubert
learns, fifteen months after her husband's death, 'without knowing exactly
where she had got it' (31; 843). Scandalised, Hubert duly takes it upon
himself to 'sever this tie' (31; 844) between daughter and (bad) mother by
declaring the latter dead, the sterile couple now free to adopt Angélique.

   To harness Marthe Robert's famous reading of Freud's essay, we might
say that Zola thus establishes his heroine as both 'foundling' and 'bastard'.
The foundling plot, Robert writes, is the first stage of the family romance:
a fantasy generated by 'the unaccountable disgrace of being un-aristocratic,
unlucky [mal loti] and unloved'.[60] At the point at which a child discovers
that his parents are not the incomparable idols he had supposed, he
attempts to free himself from his origins by casting his parents instead as
strangers, and himself as an adopted child or foundling: 'he can henceforth
think of himself as a Foundling, an adopted child, to whom his true
parents – Royal, needless to say, or at least noble or influential – will
eventually reveal themselves and restore him to his rightful status' (24).

The second stage, or bastard plot, occurs after the child has learned the facts of life: he realises, that is, that '"*pater semper incertus est*", while the mother is *"certissima"*'.[61] With maternal identity fixed beyond doubt, the child begins to project his mother into 'situations of secret infidelity and into secret love-affairs', to take her as an object of sexual curiosity, all the better to challenge the father's authority. The once-idealised mother is debased in this tale of illegitimacy, through which the child elevates his father, thereby establishing the fantasy of his own social ascension: '[the mother] is reduced to the status of a [. . .] fallen woman or even prostitute'.[62] It requires minimal exegesis, of course, to identify the literalisation of these fantasies at work in Zola's narrative: the foundling is free to pursue what Robert calls 'a biographical fantasy', liberated from her birth mother via Hubert's matricidal ruse; and where the circumstances of Angélique's birth are shrouded in mystery, the illegitimate child can fabricate a glorious family narrative, by which, to echo Robert's play on Balzac's ambitions, he 'competes with the registry office' [*il fait concurrence à l'état civil*].[63]

Intriguingly, Robert makes no comment, as Marianne Hirsch points out, on Freud's gendering of the child, nor on the implications of this 'gender asymmetry' for the development of a girl's imagination, which, Freud suggests, is likely to be weaker than a boy's, whose rivalry to the father is more intense.[64] Unlike the son, Hirsch notes, the daughter 'lacks the important opportunity to replace imaginatively the same-sex parent', since the mother's identity is certain. As a result, the mother must be eliminated, and the daughter's plots 'if they are to have any import, must, like the boy's, revolve around the males in the family who hold the keys to power and ambition'. In Zola's family romance, the poor girl's erotic wish – her dream of a rich lover – duly absorbs her fantasy of ambition (social mobility), which is, of course, nothing less than the pursuit of a new genealogy, or indeed, of a new father. To employ Jacques Lacan's famous formulation quite literally, we might say that what Angélique covets most of all in her romantic narrative is the 'name of the father' [*nom du père*] that she lacks. As part of her attempt to convince Félicien's father to consent to her union with his son, she declares, with frank naivety: 'I don't love him just for himself, I also love his noble name, and the lustre of his royal fortune [. . .]. Monseigneur, is it then so terrible to love him even more because he will gratify all my childhood wishes [. . .]?' (133; 946). Of course, Angélique's pleas fail to convince Zola's immovable patriarch, 'God the Father, awful in his absolute mastery over her fate' (131; 945); and with his repeated injunction, 'Never!' (134; 948), he imposes the other sense of Lacan's expression, the father's 'non'. According to

Hubertine, the paternal objection rides on a refusal to compromise his name ('Monseigneur was said to be jealous of his name', 119; 933) – to allow, that is, the scandal that would be wrought by his son marrying beneath him, the father having already identified a suitable partner in the noble Claire de Voincourt. But it also surely matters that the reasons for the father's refusal are never disclosed in the narrative, only ever the object of the Huberts' speculation. Indeed, if they go unsaid, it is, we are invited to surmise, precisely because they are unsayable: Monseigneur's 'no' is, like that Lacan describes, implicitly associated with the prohibition of incest. On these terms, the father, whose symbolic function Zola makes so overdetermined, would intervene in the relationship between mother and child, substituting the (Oedipal) desire for the mother with his own paternal law.

   This illicit subtext is conjured up, first and foremost, by the play of resemblances that the novel makes such an extravagant, even dizzying, feature of its descriptions. As Angélique kneels before Monseigneur in the seclusion of the cathedral chapel, he is struck by the young lover's uncanny likeness to Félicien's deceased mother: 'the little blonde curls that he had kissed so wildly long ago were there before him once more' (133; 946). Yet more than a resemblance, in fact, the mother appears to have become the foundling, through a kind of metempsychosis: 'She had come to life again: it was she who wept, and who entreated him to show clemency towards passionate love' (133; 946). The bishop's wife had been found dead next to her newborn son's cot, having expired 'in the joy of kissing him': (51; 866), she is one of the many 'Happy Dead' associated with the Hautecœur lineage, and whose fate Angélique will reproduce in the novel's closing scene as a sign of her election. From beyond the grave, Félicien's mother continues to claim 'what was rightfully owed to lovers' (162; 975), entreating her husband to be lenient. But in refusing to lift his injunction, the father precipitates the death of Angélique, Félicien's mother reincarnate, and punishes his wife once more: 'he was killing her all over again' (162; 975). It is only upon the conclusion of his visit to Angélique's deathbed that Monseigneur, as though spellbound, utters the miraculously curative Hautecœur motto, 'If God wills, I will' (169; 983), kissing Angélique on the lips in another strange prefiguration of the novel's final conjugal embrace. With Angélique as good as dead, Monseigneur grants his permission in the certainty that the *passage à l'acte* – crossing the thresholds between cathedral and marital bedchamber – will not take place. The heroine realises that she has been brought back from the dead only to die once again, at the height of her scene of wish-fulfilment.

The father thus acquiesces to their forbidden love – coded as the son's Oedipal fantasy – in the knowledge that the danger of consummation has passed. And yet, the undeniably creepy scene of Angélique's last rites, in which the child is held to seduce the father through her deathly beauty, points, of course, to another version of illicit longing, whereby paternal affection is conflated with an awakened passion: 'He had loved this child from the day she had come and wept at his feet' (169; 982). Up to this point, the father's refusal to sanction his son's desires has been closely tied to his own struggle towards self-abnegation and the fulfilment of clerical duty: 'He would crush his son's passion, just as he wished to crush the passion within himself' (127; 941). And so it is, logically, only when the father is overcome by Angélique's dying body that he relinquishes the desired object to his son, in what is as much an act of self-regulation as of pity. Here, we might say, the novel's repressed or displaced Urtext becomes legible – Zola's original intention, that is, to make *Le Rêve* an intergenerational love story:

> A forty-year-old man, a stranger to love, thus far immersed in science, who falls for a sixteen-year-old child. She loves him, or believes she loves him; the whole awakening; and then, she becomes taken with a young man, a relative of the forty-year-old, youth with youth. The suffering of the forty-year-old. In the end, he surrenders and gives the young woman to the young man.[65]

This is the kernel of a narrative Zola will retain instead for *Le Docteur Pascal*, albeit shorn of the victorious young male rival: Clotilde and her uncle Pascal's incestuous, and reciprocal, love requires no such renunciation.

If the traces of that original, intergenerational fantasy are virtually suppressed in *Le Rêve*, what remains is the patriarch's mysterious struggle with his own desires, displaced from wife to would-be future stepdaughter. Indeed, the incestuous desire that will prevail in the concluding novel of the series is, though not spelt out in Zola's initial plan for *Le Rêve*, everywhere *implied*. For Zola describes in the narrative a return – and an irresistible attraction – to symmetries and likenesses, or rather to what Michel Foucault calls 'the dull figure of the "Same"', which is the very expression, Nicholas White argues, of the regressive impulse of incest.[66] Most flagrantly, this manifests itself in the novel's curious insistence on resemblances between characters. Monseigneur and Félicien are set up as doubles: 'His son looks like him; same features, a slightly prominent nose, magnificent eyes; and still youthful', Zola notes in his *Ébauche*, adding: 'Angélique must be struck by the resemblance, when she sees them together.'[67] In a further chain of resemblance, Félicien also bears an uncanny likeness to his mother; and this is said to be the very reason his father exiled him after her death – he was 'a living portrait of the woman he mourned' (126; 940) – in an episode of rejection and adoption that duplicates Angélique's own. Such assertions of an 'air de famille' are, one might object, hardly surprising. But if, as we have already noted, Angélique *also* resembles Félicien's mother, the chain of (genealogical) resemblance turns into a hall of mirrors, in which, by extrapolation, mother, wife, son, lover, and father must all look alike. . . It is surely not for nothing that Zola has Angélique embroider heraldic coats of arms (*blasons*), the very emblem of the *mise en abyme* that the novel replicates.

Of course, Zola is no doubt pastiching the narcissistic, and self-replicating, logic of the feudal bloodline, whereby Angélique's resemblance to her deceased, would-be mother-in-law might be deemed a sign of her election. In this respect, Zola's novel entertains – like much contemporaneous idealist fiction, in fact – the aristocratic fantasy of the Revolution never having happened. Yet, more broadly, these patterns of desire encapsulate the logic of duplication, or replication, on which Angélique's hagiographical narrative hinges, born as it is of a book of saints' lives that is itself predicated on the virtues of imitation. The Zolian heroine's mimetic fantasy – to replicate, that is, the fate of the 'Happy Dead', and above all, of Saint Agnès – joins a set of saintly narratives that proliferates in serial fashion. ('They all share the same story', the narrator notes; 20; 831.) In fact, in relating many of those stories within Angélique's story, the novel casts the miraculous as, ironically, 'the common rule, the ordinary way of things' (53; 866), rather than a singular or exceptional event. In the words of Jean-Louis Cabanès, 'the miraculous appears as the endless multiplication of resemblances, of coincidences, or, still rather, a similarity-duplicating machine'.[68] We shall see in Chapter 4 on *Lourdes* just how this banalisation of the miracle becomes integral to Zola's aesthetic, as much as ideological, critique of the Catholic shrine. But what might strike us about that law of mimetic replication in *Le Rêve* is just how it extends beyond those legendary episodes the narrative relays to govern, even saturate, the world that Angélique inhabits. Alongside the likenesses that bind the cast of its family romance, the narrative has its hero and heroine resemble their saintly avatars, whose images are inscribed in the fabric of the cathedral: the statue of Saint Agnès, and the stained-glass window depicting Saint George, who is in turn likened to Christ. When Félicien commissions Angélique with crafting a mitre for his father, emblazoned with the saint's image, the heroine confirms through her own precise copy – made from

Félicien's drawing of the statue – their striking kinship: 'Oh! She looks just like you!', Félicien declares (86; 899). Zola has Angélique trapped, however blissfully, in a universe of endless reflexivity, where the coincidence of resemblance has become the rule – and this because, as Zola suggested in his notes, Angélique's 'milieu' is itself to be understood as a reflection of her imagination; and this 'milieu' acts upon her, in turn, via a kind of feedback loop ('un effet de retour').[69]

This vision of the individual consciousness has philosophical implications that Zola's critics were quick to recognise, and which we shall explore in due course. But if we return for now to the language of Freud's 'family romance', we might instead venture, with Robert, that Zola's foundling remains 'imprisoned in the pre-Oedipal universe whose only law is still the omnipotence of thought'.[70] Whence Angélique's calm and absolute conviction that her dream will be realised, and which all but suppresses a sense of suspense from her love story. The point is that the foundling establishes her own form of fatalism, whereby the world will bend to the law of her own desire. Take, as perhaps the paradigmatic example of this logic, Angélique's first glimpse of Félicien: 'He looked like St George, or a superb Jesus [...]. *She recognized him perfectly*, and had never imagined him otherwise; it was he, just as she had always expected him to be' (59; 873, emphasis added). In this scene of *coup de foudre*, anagnorisis is rivalled by what Terence Cave calls its 'platonist equivalent', anamnesis – the type of recognition that is experienced as a rediscovery, or déjà-vu.[71] Put otherwise, contingency is banished from the Zolian dream-world, its play of resemblances always written in advance. The idealist imagination, Zola implies, submits to its own form of determinism.

If then, in the final stages of the novel, Angélique suffers something like a crisis of faith, this can be understood as the first (and last) episode of doubt in the power of her own imagination. Angélique's fantasy will prevail as she goes on to marry her Jesus look-alike. But it is, we should note, she who speaks the language of Christ at her moment of supplication: 'My God, why have you forsaken me?' (144; 957), Angélique cries, as she struggles to master temptation. Indeed, it is then that she recalls the administrative necklace, akin to a 'collar placed on a domestic animal', that had certified her abandonment, and which figures as a kind of stigmata ('it remained embedded in her flesh, choking her', 143; 956). With her desperate appeal to the divine Father, the foundling's 'family romance' reaches, we might say, its most hyperbolic, and ironic, expression. Yet Zola clearly means for Angélique's heroic self-sacrifice – her renunciation of gratification – to offer others the path to redemption.[72] When Félicien begs her to elope with him and escape the yoke of parental authority, she finds herself unable to leave her all-white bedchamber: 'It's as though the door has suddenly been walled up, and I can't get out' (155; 968). The narrative of illegitimate romance is closed off, as Angélique refuses to perpetrate the same 'transgression' as her adoptive parents (120; 934). Ultimately, it is her self-abnegation that will prove to be the condition of the Huberts' absolution, the overturning of the maternal 'no', and the longed-for 'child of mercy' (176; 989) that is granted to the Huberts on the adopted daughter's wedding day.

What Angélique demonstrates by her submission to Monseigneur's authority is that her rebellious streak is fully extinguished. A cloistered upbringing, discipline, and regular work have turned this ill-tempered waif and stray into a chaste, humble, and dutiful young woman: 'she had come to her perfection, having mastered her passions, mended her errors, and changed her ways' (177; 955). With the foundling's triumphant self-mastery, Zola concludes the novel's redemptive experiment to override the forces of heredity: 'a shoot of the Rougon-Macquart that has been transplanted, cultivated, and thereby saved. The whole effect of environment'.[73] Angélique's bad blood is transformed by the formative pressures of her environment, which Zola posits as the secular equivalent to the theological concept of 'grace'.[74] Yet he also insists on those pressures as a spur to the heroine's psychological, and martyrological, drama. In the penultimate scenes of the novel devoted to Angélique's self-imposed imprisonment, she sublimates her appetites (most obviously, through her refusal of food) in a heroic effort of self-denial: 'Now, it's all finished, I have triumphed over myself. . .' (157; 970). And so it is that, even when the paternal interdiction is lifted, Zola's heroine continues, at least subliminally, to renounce the possibility of gratification. To put all this differently, what prevails is Angélique's 'ego ideal' – the image, that is, of the perfect self to which the ego aspires. In the manner of the legendary narratives Angélique devours, the naturalist novel generates its own *exemplum*, through which it proves that it is capable of breaking its prevailing law of degradation: Angélique becomes, in her final apotheosis, her own sublime masterpiece.

It is, as we have seen, Angélique's foundling status that conditions her idealist imagination, just as it allows her to become an ideal heroine. In fact, it is no doubt remarkable, as Chantal Bertrand-Jennings points out, that nearly all of Zola's ideal women are orphans: Denise Baudu, Miette, Caroline Hamelin, Henriette Levasseur, Pauline Quenu, *entre autres*. . . Disconnected from their origins, they are free to remake themselves in their own image. And yet, this experimental undertaking is also, Bertrand-Jennings argues, born of an authorial complex, 'of a dream of godlike mastery, of a desire to create, from nothing, a being who would become [. . .] an idealised reflection of the virile Self'. Clotilde is, she adds, the most perfect realisation of this Pygmalion fantasy.[75] Though such a wish had long been expressed, most explicitly in *La Confession de Claude* (1865): 'I should like my bride to come to me straight from the hands of God; I should like her pure white, dead; and *I would waken her*. She would live through me.'[76] It is a curtailed version of this impossible fantasy that Zola rehearses in *Le Rêve*, where Monseigneur performs the miracle of resuscitation, purifying the virgin bride through the ritual of the last rites, only for her to be returned to a state of death-in-life suspension. 'It is understood that I am no longer saving Angélique', Zola clarified in his preparatory notes. 'I am performing only a half-miracle, that of putting her back on her feet so that she can have her dream come true, and die.'[77] Here, in a curious act of identification, projection even, the authorial will is conflated with that of the Father-miracle worker, whose belief in the thaumaturgic power of words Zola takes over. Indeed, there is surely no more compelling image of this conflation than that of Zola in his study in Paris, seated before his writing desk in an armchair emblazoned with the Hautecœur motto, 'If God wills, I will' [*Si Dieu veut, je veux*].[78] Such an elision of writer and fictional patriarch might tell us much about the megalomania at work in the creative imagination. For all that the novel tracks the idealist heroine's unwavering conviction in the omnipotence of her reverie, it is, ultimately, the prodigious author-miracle worker who sanctions Angélique's 'happy' ending by performing his own kind of magic. And so, we might well ask, given the radical availability of Zola's title: *whose* dream is it anyway?

A Woman's Work

In his essay 'Creative Writers and Day-Dreaming', written the year before 'Family Romances', Freud identified a common motivation underlying child's play, daydreaming, and the work of the imaginative writer. 'The motive forces of phantasies are', he declared, 'unsatisfied wishes, and every single phantasy is the fulfilment of a wish, a correlation of an unsatisfying reality'.[79] To provide what Freud had called, in relation to the child's daydream, 'a correction of actual life' remained the guiding impulse of the author for whom writing continues and replaces 'what was once the play of childhood'. In fact, the infantile propensity to daydream was no doubt stronger, Freud suggested, among 'comparatively highly gifted people' (just as it was with neurotics).[80] As Schor has argued in her study of Sand, what Freud's respective accounts of the family romance and author-ship share is an emphasis on 'the power to reshape reality through that prestigious faculty, the imagination'.[81] This observation frames Schor's account of Sand's idealist tendencies, which she reads through the dynamic of parental relations at work in the writer's autobiographical *Histoire de ma vie* (1854–55). In what follows, I propose to read Zola's account of Sand's life and works – namely, the obituary he penned in the weeks after her death – as yet another story of her acculturation as an idealist. And this story of Sand's burgeoning authorial imagination can be understood in turn, I want to suggest, to inflect Zola's novel of the dream and its own intertwining of Angélique's 'family romance' and her idealist bent. For what we have left largely implied until now is that the heroine embroiderer's plot constitutes, in one important respect, a *roman d'artiste*; indeed, Zola framed this as an imperative: 'she must be an artist, and her embroideries must be masterpieces'.[82] In taking up these respective narratives of creative evolution, my hunch is, in other words, that there is something like a secret kinship between Zola's foundling-artist and the Sand of his own imagination.

It is a claim that needs to be understood in relation to the wider resurgence of interest in the woman writer that coincided with the com-position and publication of *Le Rêve*. The eminent philosopher Elme-Marie Caro began his biography of Sand, for Hachette's 'Great French Writers' series, by auguring an imminent return to her writing, if not in its entirety, then at least to 'a part of her work that has been purified over time'.[83] Caro was putting the finishing touches to this work when he died suddenly in July 1887. In his book review, Anatole France extolled the philosopher's eloquent homage to Sand as 'the muse of his youth'.[84] For France, Sand's return to favour – evidenced by the speed with which Caro's biography was selling – heralded the wider revival of idealism: 'Madame Sand was a great artisan of the ideal: that is why I like and revere her.' In this, France took over Caro's account of Sand's distinctiveness as an idealist writer, even as he called for a return to the entirety of her works, however provocative (he singles out *Lélia* and *Jacques*). Earlier that year, Jules Lemaître had taken two produc-tions of Sand's plays as a pretext for the exposition of his own aesthetic vision, musing: 'And why not start liking George Sand again?'[85] The glorious reign of those idealist writers 'infatuated with the dream' in the early decades of the century had been followed by a 'return of the real', emboldened by the national trauma of 1870. The reaction, Lemaître claimed, had been inevit-able, and 'perfectly consistent with the most definitive laws of literary history'.

Now tired of what Octave Mirbeau had called the naturalist novel's 'disenchanting' investigation into 'the reason for our dreams', readers were looking to resurrect neglected idols, Sand in particular.[86] What they had once spurned, and now sought out, was Sand's gift for the 'romanesque' – her faculty of idealisation, or embellishment, twinned with the audacity of her ideas (mystical, socialist, humanitarian), which together Lemaître conjured up as the lure of the 'dream'. Does not Sand's writing represent, he asked, 'the most complete and compelling expression of the dream of life', capable of casting 'a few rays of the ideal into our sad, vapid existence'?

Clearly, for those of an antinaturalist sensibility, Sand's art of enchantment had become a necessary antidote. But what is perhaps more remarkable about such eulogies was how self-consciously they seemed to be arguing with the grand narrative of the nineteenth-century novel that Zola had systematically established in his obituary of the writer. The vision Zola provides is of a Darwinian struggle between realism and idealism, or rather, between their greatest exponents, Balzac and Sand. From these writers, Zola intones, 'flow two rivers, the river of truth and the river of dreams. [...] For nearly half a century, reality and dreams have done battle'.[87] Both Hugo and Dumas are swiftly sidelined: the former's lyrical temperament always straining away from the novel towards poetry; the latter's legacy compromised by the legion of banal imitators who followed after. Instead, Balzac and Sand emerge as privileged 'types', whose formidable productivity is matched only by their generative reach: they represent, according to Zola's genealogical model, the twin origins to which all contemporary novelists can be traced.

In schematising the differences between them, Zola draws on the familiar paradigm of the writer-clinician. Balzac's unflinching and dispassionate observation of his patient is set against Sand's falsely comforting bedside manner, her obstinate desire, that is, to cure rather than diagnose:

> Should you wish to have a clear idea of her writerly temperament, the best comparison you can draw is with a doctor – one who, after listening to his patient's chest, refrains from elaborating on the nature of their illness so as to speak only of the cure, describing with satisfaction the good health to which he will restore this ailing body. Her whole life, George Sand has longed to be a healer [...]. She was poetic by nature, unable to keep her feet on the ground, taking flight with the slightest wind of inspiration. Hence, the strange vision of humanity she has dreamt up. She distorted ever reality she touched. (728)

Sand's idealist aesthetic combines the practice of hyperbolising – an exaggeration of reality that Zola assimilates to disfigurement – and a meliorative political vision, which he aligns with the unharnessed dream.

Unlike Balzac, whose heavy limbs tether his feet to the ground, Sand appears 'lightweight' in every sense, her inability to resist lyrical flights of fancy portrayed as a congenital condition. Balzac, the anatomist, dissects the mechanics of human life with scrupulous precision; Sand, the wishful thinker, wields her pen as a blunt tool: 'In a nutshell, it is a doctor's scalpel he holds in his hand, and not an idealist's modelling tool [ébauchoir]' (729). Zola did not, of course, have to reach far for these clichés. The scalpel-wielding realist (and naturalist) was a familiar trope of Zola's writing in the 1860s, no doubt indebted to Sainte-Beuve's celebrated review of *Madame Bovary*, and its closing master-image, 'M. Gustave Flaubert wields the pen as others wield the scalpel.'[88] Sand's obstinately therapeutic aesthetic, by contrast, signalled an unwillingness to contemplate the body in all its insanitary forms. Indeed, Zola insists with a certain delight on Sand's prudishness about the 'digestive illness' that ultimately caused her death; the writer's repugnance for 'the squalor of human nature' (734) could not withstand this last revenge of the scatological.

Zola's portrait of Sand contains in miniature (at least) three key censures of idealism, which, as we saw in Chapter 1, he reformulated across his literary criticism and journalism. First, idealism is an art of falsification and embellishment, which promotes imagination over observation, passion over precision. Second, idealism is the product of the author's pathological impulse: it appears as an excessive, insatiable, 'constant need' (740), which deprives the writer of her sense of measure and, ultimately, her sense of the ridiculous: 'she goes so far as to idealise dogs and donkeys' (743). Third, idealism promotes a delusional disconnection from the referent that is, in the end, ethically irresponsible. The lie may be beautiful, but the anti-mimetic, even escapist, charm of the idealist aesthetic poses a threat to the impressionable (read: female) reader.

We shall return to those supposedly deleterious effects of Sand's fiction on her readers in due course. But what I want to dwell on here is just how Sand provides Zola with the impetus he needs to bring full-term the feminisation of the idealist aesthetic that he had, as early as May 1866, articulated in the following blunt terms: 'Painting dreams is a game for children and women; men are tasked with painting reality.'[89] In effect, Zola is reiterating the gendered division of labour that Balzac had reportedly recommended to Sand: 'To idealise what is pretty and what is beautiful; that is a woman's job.'[90] For contained in their respective statements are the twin assumptions that Schor sees to be operative in the attribution of aesthetic value: first, that 'mimesis is man's work; the faithful representation of "nature" a sort of Adamic curse visited on male writers'; second, that women artists 'are essentially idealists', bound by their very nature to see 'la vie en rose'.[91] The latter claim is fundamental to Zola's account of Sand's literary 'temperament'. Against those who persist in seeing in her a reformer, or a revolutionary, Zola declares such proclivities to have been eclipsed by her sex. However superior, or idiosyncratic, the version of womanhood she embodied, Sand was forever shackled to those imperious laws of her physiology: 'she simply remained a woman, always and in all respects' (734). Beneath her student redingote, and her *quarante-huitard* ambitions, lay the long hair, heaving bosom and maternal heart of a writer 'tethered, fatally, to her sex' (734). Not only, then, has Sand's masculinity, or androgyny, been overstated – 'too much has been said about her virile nature' (734) – few women, Zola argues, possessed a more refined feminine sensibility. Zola's determination to reclassify Sand as a womanly woman thus goes hand in hand with his devalorisation of the idealist aesthetic. For to reimpose the clarity of gender difference is to tie the entirety of Sand's literary production to her constitutional (that is to say, flawed) way of seeing the world, to have her writing bear 'the irremediable hallmark of her sex' (736), and to consign her to the sphere of female particularity. In fact, we might venture that it is precisely with this emphatic refeminisation of Sand that Zola sets out the conditions of his schematic literary history: the triumph, that is, of Balzac's muscular poetics – and its naturalist successor, guided by 'the virility of the true' – over those strands of romanticism and idealism that are either effeminate or strictly feminine.[92]

While Zola claims, then, to give Sand her due – her place, that is, in the evolution of the novel – his obituary clearly betrays the same parricidal logic he repeatedly declared necessary to his naturalist campaign. Of his relentless polemic against romanticism, Hugo in particular, Zola remarked, 'I had to knock the enemy on the head.'[93] With Sand's passing, Zola triumphantly tolls idealism's death knell and proclaims in no uncertain terms realism, and its naturalist offshoot, to be the most powerful and enduring literary lineage – or to adapt the familial master-trope of Zola's Rougon-Macquart epic, the legitimate line: 'I believe the time has arrived for sensitive souls to grieve the passing of the pure fiction novel. [...] At this moment, in the struggle between truth and dream, truth is prevailing.[94] Zola offers proof of the idealist's demise in two forms. First, by determining in what he calls Sand's 'splendid autumn' works the distinct influence of a rising naturalist movement: in a kind of aesthetic miasma, Sand's poetic temperament was indelibly, and unconsciously, altered by 'the atmosphere of precise analysis that dominated in her old age' (745). Second, Zola insists that Sand's popularity had already declined, her later novels, all of which were pre-published in the *Revue des Deux Mondes*, enjoyed by an ever-diminishing readership. The imperative, as Seillan suggests, is to relegate Sand and her works to another age, 'to make them seem like an anachronistic relic'.[95] It is, then, hardly surprising that Zola takes the conclusion of *Indiana* to be the most emblematic episode of Sandian poetics: the heroine's failed suicide, and her new beginnings on Bernica with the brooding Sir Ralph, appear spectacular, extraordinary, implausible, and underwritten by a puerile, female fantasy. 'What an astonishing ideal!', Zola exclaims. 'In order to understand such an ending, nowadays, we would have to try to go back to 1830 and its strange kinds of imagination' (738). With this affected reader-response, Zola performs the principal gesture of his obituary: that of consigning Sand to the fate of unintelligibility.

If we return now to those mutual entailments of authorial creativity and childhood fantasy with which we began, what might strike us about Zola's vision of the nineteenth-century novel – as split into two great, clashing currents – is just how evocatively it maps onto Robert's classic account of the family romance in literature. Namely, her guiding contention that the novel can be understood as 'the battlefield where two equally fascinating myths of omnipotence fight for supremacy': the myths of the foundling and the bastard.[96] 'Strictly speaking', Robert ventures,

> there are but two ways of writing a novel: the way of the realistic Bastard who backs the world while fighting it head on; and the way of the Foundling who, lacking both the experience and the means to fight, avoids confrontation by flight of rejection. (37)

The bastard writer (Robert's archetype is Balzac) pays homage to the real, 'to things as they are', placing limits on his imagination and respecting the bounds of probability and verisimilitude, all while confronting a world that is fundamentally dissatisfying. Foundling texts (Robert singles out *Don Quixote*, *Robinson Crusoe*, various romantic novels, and all kinds of fairy-tales) are conceived by the fantasist who is 'bewitched by his visions and transformations, creating in isolation and against reality a dream world unrelated to experience'. All nineteenth-century novelistic production, Robert claims, reflects 'this latent conflict between two different psychic ages' (143): indeed, even within the corpus of a single writer, or within a single text, this struggle is played out. Robert cites Balzac's *Louis Lambert* and Flaubert's *La Tentation de Saint Antoine* as examples of the realist writer embracing 'the other side' (38), while Zola's fiction is said to contain 'a dose of the unreal' that turns the naturalist, at moments, into a visionary.

We might, of course, wish to add *Le Rêve* to Robert's model of internal alterity.[97] But clearly, Zola's own schematic account of the struggle between two (arche)types of authorial temperament seeks to collapse, rather than probe, such potential nuances. Sand's idealism is cast, to adopt Robert's typology, as a 'foundling' form; and its privileged object, Zola claims, is those 'passions' which, though hampered by obstacles and social prejudices, are ultimately victorious, 'resulting in happiness'.[98] For Anatole France too, the forces of love represented the central axis of Sand's universe, her works giving voice to 'a most audacious assertion of the rights of passion'.[99] (These are, we should recall, the exact terms Zola attributes in *Le Rêve* to Félicien's mother, whose role it is to press for those rights from beyond the grave.) Purchased at the cost of plausibility, the happy ending fulfils the protagonist's passionate wishes, just as it betrays the author's impulse to prove the omnipotence of her own imagination. To this end, Zola conjures up Sand at her writing table in the still of night, with neither plan, nor notes, nor documents, inventing stories from the resources of her mind: 'Characters emerged as she wrote, events unfurled; and so, calmly, she let her thoughts run on.'[100] Crucially, this model of creativity is rooted in Sand's childhood and what Zola describes – taking up Sand's own account in her *Histoire de ma vie* – as an early propensity to daydream: 'she would soon fall into a dream, her eyes wide open. Vision, for her, was turned inwards' (736). In fact, Caro, too, pictured Sand as a 'dreamer' from birth, her early years dominated by an incessant and (over) active imagination, which would become the font (or 'image store') of her future writing.[101] But in Zola's hands, the adult writer's ongoing attachment to her fantasy life is caricatured instead as an unreasonable childishness with which she endows her heroines in turn: 'This constant need for idealism, [. . .] this way of dreaming a life more open, more poetic, more ethereal ultimately descends into childish fantasy' (740). Sand's childhood *apprentissage* is figured, in short, as a stage of psychological immaturity that the writer ought to have outgrown.

If there is, as I am suggesting, something to be gained by reading Zola's obituary of Sand alongside *Le Rêve*, it is for the way it crystallises the stakes of Zola's novel as another *roman d'artiste*, one that rehearses those conditions in which the idealist imagination takes root – and this precisely in the phase of childhood development that we have already tracked. In his account of Sand's early years, Zola follows the author's autobiography in locating the origins of her creativity in the illustrious figure of Corambé, a semi-pagan, semi-Christian deity who first appeared to her in a dream: 'The prodigious powers of invention and idealisation were already apparent' (730). Though it was, Zola surmises, the formative period of Sand's (or Aurore's) adolescence that produced in her a life-long 'need to expend herself on work or dreaming' (731). Of the thirteen-year-old Aurore's admission to a convent in Paris, newly separated from her mother and grandmother, Zola recounts:

> Initially, she was unruly and nearly turned the convent upside down. Then, suddenly, kneeling in chapel one morning, she believed she had been touched by grace. She experienced such an attack of piety that she talked about becoming a nun. That is the story of this period of her life; Corambé was forgotten, and Jesus replaced him. (731)

Although the religious fervour to which Aurore succumbs is short-lived – she soon seeks out other passions, initially dabbling in theatre – this miniature narrative of adolescent reform and self-discipline bears more than a passing resemblance to Angélique's trajectory: her own impulsive devotion; the salutary effects of a cloistered environment; her belief in divine grace; and, of course, the libidinal conflation of Christ with an illustrious hero of her imagination (Félicien-Saint George).

The point of connecting these episodes is not to imply that Zola's extravagant waif is an undisclosed double of Aurore but rather to discern a type of psychological narrative that Zola associates with the idealist imagination in both cases. Those twin impulses of work and daydream that emerge in the adolescent Aurore similarly dominate Angélique's hermetic existence – her erotic and creative desires combined in the golden thread with which she generates her 'poor girl's dream' (44; 857). Indeed, through her exquisite artistry, Angélique undertakes a kind of dream-work akin to that which Zola envisages for Sand. Gifted though his heroine is in the fastidious craft of mimesis (she works on the mitre Félicien commissions with 'all the patience of a painter working with the aid of a magnifying glass', 81; 894), she is nevertheless prone to submit to the same impulse to 'embroider' the truth – that which Zola describes as Sand's 'need to correct and to see humanity in a beautiful light'.[102] In fact, it is this tempering of verisimilitude that, we are told, imbues her work with a kind of miraculous surplus:

> Silk and gold thread came alive in her hands, her smallest figures shone with mystical beauty. She gave herself up entirely to her work, which was continually enriched by her fertile imagination and her belief in a world beyond appearances. [...] She had a talent for drawing that was frankly

miraculous, shaped not by any teacher, but simply by the evening study she had done by lamplight; and so she was able to improve on her models [*corriger ses modèles*], or simply abandon them, trusting instead to her imagination, and bringing forth astonishing creations with the point of her needle. (35; 847)

It is no doubt a testament to Zola's ongoing fascination with this type of creative instinct that Angélique's mystical absorption, her flights of the imagination, will be reattributed in his metafictional closing novel of the series to another young female artist, and another foundling figure: Clotilde Rougon. Tasked by Pascal with creating plates to illustrate his botanical treatises on the genetics of plant life, Clotilde initially brings to her copies of her uncle's specimens a rigorous attention to detail ('a meticulousness, an exactitude of line and colour, that was extraordinary', 8; 920). But this work of precision soon yields to an art of pure invention: '[she] had just thrown down, on another sheet of paper, a whole cluster of imaginary flowers, dream flowers, extravagant and superb'. Exasperated, Pascal turns to his housekeeper, who is busy mending clothes, and exclaims, taking Clotilde's 'mutinous head' in his hands: 'While you're at it, Martine [. . .], sew up this noggin for me, as well; it's sprung a leak' (9; 921). As, in Janet Beizer's words, the 'last avatar of the ancestral "cerveau fêlé"', Clotilde represents 'the culmination of a series of Zola's creative excesses that are metaphorically incorporated by women. One easily imagines Zola, à la Flaubert, confessing his submerged projection: "Clotilde Rougon, c'est moi"'.[103]

Here, at last, we come to the proposition that has hovered over this chapter: that Zola's overdetermined account of aesthetic differences allows him to project those idealist tendencies that he cannot tolerate within himself onto women – most obviously, Sand, but also those female artists who are made to embody her congenital extravagance. In the end, it is, of course, the scientist Pascal who will 'sew up' Clotilde's leaking head; in administering 'the terrible lesson in life', he tempers, or 'corrects', her heredity, which is tantamount to her idealism ('her need for illusion and lies, for immediate happiness', 286; 1209). After Pascal's death, Clotilde looks back on her pastel drawings – divided into two types, 'the accurate ones and the fantastical ones' – and recognises in this distinction 'all the duality of her nature': her 'passion for truth' and 'her need for another world beyond appearances' (285; 1208). And so, while Angélique remains blissfully, if fatally, caught in the trap of her imagination, Clotilde comes to represent a happy compromise: 'the passion for truth broadened by equal interest in the unknown' (288; 1212). Won over to Pascal's scientific credo, she nevertheless inflects it with what the novelist called 'Clotilde's question mark'.[104] Zola gives his heroine if not the last word, then the last character.

Naturalism *in extremis*

At the end of the Rougon-Macquart cycle, Clotilde, the idealist heroine, becomes the idealised heroine, precisely because of the education Pascal provides, joined as it is to her sexual initiation. In *Le Rêve*, Angélique's unwavering attachment, in art as in life, to 'the perpetual falsehood of the dream' (120; 933) can have only one logical consequence: her willing renunciation of existence. Zola determines in the heroine's idealism a perverse, even pathological, need to perpetuate her dislocation from the world of the referent, from matter, all of which amounts to a kind of death drive. Indeed, it is in this spirit that he challenges, and overwrites, Sand's self-diagnosis, which she is reported to have uttered just before she died: 'I have imbibed too much of life.'[105] Having reflected a great deal on this statement, Zola declared himself unable to make head nor tail of it: 'Her whole existence has been one long pursuit of the ideal [. . .]. I picture her instead, at her final hour, opening her eyes to the reality of things in this world, and in discovering the truth, crying out: "I have imbibed too many dreams"' (737). This fanciful reimagining of Sand's deathbed epiphany seeks, retroactively, to stigmatise her idealism as a form of delusion: Zola has Sand, *in extremis*, see the light, as though emerging from a lifetime of reverie.

For the readers of Sand's fiction, meanwhile, the pursuit of the ideal, with its tempestuous highs and lows, could only have one issue – the close of the book, which has deprived them of an appetite for real life:

> Place George Sand's novels in the hands of a young man or woman: they will emerge from their reading all aquiver, left with the waking memory of a charming dream. Thereafter, it is likely they will be hurt by life, that they will feel disheartened, disorientated, prone to embark on all kinds of naïve and fanciful adventures. These books open up the land of make-believe, leading inevitably to a sudden fall [culbute] into reality. (746)

Zola provides here an earlier iteration of the master-metaphor that we tracked in Chapter 2 through *Germinal*: the post-idealist 'fall', the collapse into the mud, or – as he put it in his 1879 'Lettre à la jeunesse' – the tragic aftermath of the idealist's 'leaps [culbutes] towards the ideal'.[106] Of course, Zola gives full play to the erotic, or rather sordid, overtones of the disenchanting 'culbute' that awaits the reader of Sand's fiction, having applied the term liberally in *Germinal*, and again in *La Terre*, to the workers' sexual promiscuity. Despite its air of chastity, idealism is for Zola, we saw in Chapter 1, the royal road to perdition: 'it is the ideal that creates the adulteress'.[107] And in Zola's theory of the idealist novel's immoral duplicity, Sand is the chief culprit: 'George Sand has created an entire generation of insufferable dreamers [rêveuses] [...]. When a woman takes a lover, there is always an idealist novel behind it.'[108] In a brutally overdetermined sex scene of *Pot-Bouille* (1883), Zola staged precisely this, when Zola's womaniser Octave Mouret forces himself upon the naive married mother Marie Pichon, who remains under the charm of the novel he had lent to her, Sand's *André*. Functioning, in Nicholas White's words, as 'an accessory to adultery', Sand's novel leaves the heroine-reader in a perilous state of absorption that serves to obscure the impending scene of entrapment.[109] When the pair examine the damage to the binding of Sand's book, which had been shaken from the kitchen table during their encounter, Marie utters the disabusing conclusion that Zola's vision of Sand demands: 'It was always going to finish badly.'[110] This, we might say, is the archetypal scene, or privileged mood, of the naturalist novel's anti-idealist crusade: the autopsy of the daydream that it sets out to proscribe.

What, then, are we to make of Zola's refusal, at the end of *Le Rêve*, to break the spell of his heroine's daydream, fuelled as it is by the reading and images she has imbibed? The closing scene of the novel brings its heroine – in the manner of Zola's readers of Sand – to the point of awakening. As the 'miraculous wedding' (178; 992) concludes, and Angélique and Félicien make their triumphant exit towards crowds of well-wishers, the cathedral doors are flung open, 'a blade of bold daylight [piercing] through the dark wall' (179; 993). The virgin bride moves towards the light: 'she was emerging from the dream, advancing to where she would at last enter reality' (180; 993). But on the threshold of the door against which the nine-year-old Angélique had been found and brought back from the dead, the procession comes to a halt: 'Had she not experienced all the happiness there was to know? After this, surely life held no further joy? With a final effort she strained upwards and put her mouth to Félicien's. And with this kiss, she died.' Frozen in this moment of ecstasy, Angélique remains suspended on the point of the threshold, *l'entre-deux*: she disappears into the breach between the dream and the real – or, we might say, into the gap between the idealist and realist plot. For in a reversal of the realist novel's punishment of the fallen woman, Angélique dies *so as not to fall*.[111] 'Yes, death, rather than a life of sin', affirmed Hubertine as Angélique lay on her deathbed (148; 961). Zola thus denies his heroine the unambiguous felicity that he had originally envisaged. Midway through his plans for the novel, Zola noted a change of heart: 'To have Angélique victorious and alive at the end, is to repeat Denise. In both cases, a young woman prevailing on account of her virtue, coming to riches [. . .]. The idea is the same. Therefore, Angélique must either fail to triumph or die.'[112] The compromise, he concluded, was to have Angélique die in the splendour of her longed-for nuptials, thereby curtailing this version of the poor girl's fantasy while granting her wish not to wake up.

In taking Angélique's fantasy to the limit, Zola brings the novel to the brink of self-implosion. The heroine fades, 'at the pinnacle of her happiness', into nothingness, and takes the novel along with her: 'Félicien clasped just a soft and cherished wisp of a thing, the wedding gown made of lace and pearls, a handful of fine feathers left behind by a bird' (180; 994). The residual feathers appear at once as a self-referential allusion to the inky traces of the fantasy described, and as another metonymy for the airborne idealist.[113] As the narrative punctures its own illusion, the enchanted reader, as critic Gabrielle Mourey remarked, is subject to a 'painful collapse into the Real [chute dans le Réel]'.[114] If in its concluding lines, however, the novel asserts with a curious insistence its own happy ending ('it was a death without sadness', 180; 993), this is because – we are made to infer – it is impossible to mourn that which was never really there... In other words, Zola has already cast doubt on Angélique's existence, musing, in the indeterminate mode of *style indirect libre*: 'Wasn't she just a thing of appearance, which would conjure forth an illusion, and then vanish?' (55; 869). At the close of the novel, the notion of her unreality is deemed conclusive: 'It had been a thing of appearance only, generating an illusion and then fading away. All is but a dream' (180; 994). With this final flourish, Zola ventured, according to France, perhaps 'the only philosophical observation he had ever made'.[115] It was, in any case, a hypothesis with which France was inclined to agree, though he struggled to imagine 'the author of *Pot-Bouille*' dabbling in metaphysics, 'anxiously interrogating the veil of Maya, and probing the bottomless ocean of appearances'. Could the naturalist novelist *think* – and, more to the point, could he think about *thought*?

With its late theoretical swerve, the narrative seemed to collapse its take on idealist aesthetics – its conjuring with 'life as it is not' – into an experiment with a myriad tradition of philosophical thought, which Zola yoked together in his notes as 'doctrines that deny the reality of the outside world'.[116] No doubt Zola had Schopenhauer in mind, whose version of idealism the novelist would have encountered (albeit second-hand) through his preparatory reading for *La Joie de vivre* (1884).[117] Indeed, France's reference to the veil of Maya hints at the German philosopher's wider influence. Schopenhauer's axiomatic claim, 'the world is my representation', provided a vital impetus for contemporary writers and artists, who mistook it to imply – as Zola's allusion makes clear – the denial of the world's empirical reality. By the late 1880s, this very principle of subjective idealism had become the guiding light of Symbolist art, expounded by the likes of Gustave Kahn and Remy de Gourmont. 'All that I think is real', the latter declared, 'thought is the only reality'.[118] Though Zola made no reference to individual philosophers in his planning notes, he stated clearly his intention of demonstrating a broadly neo-idealist thesis:

> Such that the milieu, my supposed grace from God, would come from man; it would fit with the theory that the illusion of our senses is all there is, that we create the world, that everything <u>starts from us only to return to us</u>. The dream, in short. And so it would be a way of opening up the book at the end to show that all is but a dream, that each one of us is but an appearance that vanishes after creating an illusion.[119]

It was, of course, a theory that obviously contradicted Zola's own intellectual position. In 'Le Roman expérimental', he had lambasted those he called idealists, who luxuriated in the unknown, believing that 'the truth is inside them and not in things themselves'.[120] But such ideas about epistemological relativity and the superiority of mind over matter were very much floating in the air, part of a prevailing mood, in the months surrounding the publication of Zola's novel. In March 1888, the philosopher Alfred Fouillée published 'La métaphysique et la poésie de l'idéal' in the *Revue des Deux Mondes*, in which he sought to bring together experimental methods and speculative philosophy as ways of grasping 'how the universe is felt, thought, and willed by human consciousness'.[121]

The artistic implications of the idealist 'thesis' Zola evokes in his notes had, meanwhile, been explored by Guy de Maupassant in his essay 'Le Roman' – penned in September 1887, and subsequently appended to *Pierre et Jean* (1888). Taking over the premise that individuals were bound to generate their own representation, their own 'illusion', of the world based on their subjective experience, predispositions, sense perceptions and impressions, Maupassant declared himself sceptical about that notion of the 'real' which writers and artists claimed to capture:

> Besides, how childish to believe in reality when each of us carries our own in our thought and our organs! Our eyes, our ears, our sense of smell and taste, all of them different, create as many truths as there are men on earth.[122]

All any artist can aspire to do, Maupassant concluded, is reproduce his own version of the truth as faithfully as possible: for 'to make things realistic' [faire vrai] is, he added, inevitably a form of illusion-making. In one sense, Maupassant was reiterating the philosophical relativism Mirbeau had expressed in his censure of naturalist fiction, 'Le Rêve', three years earlier. 'There is nothing absolutely correct and nothing absolutely true', Mirbeau declared, 'or rather there exist as many human truths as there are individuals'.[123]

This kind of subjectivist posture was replayed again and again by Zola's critics in seeking to undermine naturalism's pretensions to entertain a privileged relationship to the truth. Indeed, it found perhaps its most strident expression in the article France wrote on Sand's idealism, which appeared just as Zola was starting work on *Le Rêve*. With Maupassant's essay no doubt ringing in his ears, France tapped into a set of philosophical propositions about the unknowability of the external world as a way of collapsing the aesthetic superiority the naturalist had claimed over his idealist counterpart:

> Naturalist art is no truer than idealist art. M. Zola does not see man and nature with more truth than Madame Sand saw them. [. . .] Naturalists and idealists alike are the playthings of appearances; they are *both prey to the idols of the cave.* This is the name Bacon gave to the principle of our eternal ignorance, the ignorance to which our human condition condemns us, enclosed as we are within ourselves, as though inside a rock, solitary and delirious, with the world around us. Well, seeing as all the accounts we give of nature have as little objective reality as any other, [. . .] why should we not seek out charming images, nor savour images of beauty and love over others? *Dream for dream, why should we not choose the most agreeable?*[124]

Beholden as we are to the appearances the mind imposes on us – to our 'idols', in Francis Bacon's terms – we are bound to set forth an image of the world that will fail to coincide with the real 'in itself'. Contrary to what the naturalist writer would have us believe, he cannot know how the world is, or indeed *if* it is, independently of his representations of it. France thus tapped into the terms of idealist philosophy to overturn the principle that Zola had placed at the heart of his reproach of Sandian idealism: the ethics of verisimilitude, which the naturalist makes his standard. It made no sense, France's argument went, to oppose the real and the ideal – to claim to privilege the former as the repository of truth – when the ideal was in fact 'the only reality we are permitted to grasp'. France could then shift the terms of the debate to centre instead on aesthetic taste: if naturalist and idealist writers alike produce a 'dream', the reader should surely choose that which yields the greatest pleasure, that which charms, consoles, provides uplift. When, two years later, Lemaître likewise called for a return to Sand, it was with a similar exhortation to embrace our condition as dreamers: 'The world lives by dream alone.'[125] The Sandian dream – utopian, corrective, prescriptive – is that which sustains us in a world where dreaming is all there is. Filtered in this way through the philosophical fixations of the late 1880s, Sand's idealism is harnessed by an anti-naturalist campaign that seeks to collapse the very aesthetic and ethical distinctions Zola had used her to draw. In France's cave, all writers are idealists. What readers like France encountered in the philosophical coda to Zola's *Le Rêve* was, then, an act of ventriloquism that, 'without too much irony', already provided for just such a possibility.

*

With *Le Rêve*, Zola offered up a response to those charges brought against the naturalist novel, and precisely against the naturalist author's disregard for, and abuses of, the ideal. The particular matrix of idealism, psychology, and class at work in *Le Rêve*, whereby the foundling's psychic drama is tied to her coveting of a noble lineage, can be understood, I have suggested, in Freud's terms of the 'family romance' – and in turn, as a pastiche of the elitism that characterised antinaturalist proponents of the idealist novel. It also allowed Zola to reflect on the very status of naturalist fiction, speaking at once to his own provocative self-portraiture as the reformed novelist, and to the wider question of whether the naturalist novel could itself adapt, even escape, its own apparently determining logic of self-replication. Cast by a critic like Lepelletier as 'an unfortunate, ill-conceived work [. . .] that will add nothing to Zola's great project', *Le Rêve* seemed to invite musings on genealogy, toying with its self-image as a problematic offspring, or – in Robert's vocabulary – a foundling text.[126] Certainly, *Le Rêve* inserts itself, knowingly and strategically, into an ongoing dialogue about the rights, dangers, and limits of literary fiction, one which, I have argued, we need to understand in relation to a prevailing idealist 'reaction' that harnessed Sand as its touchstone. Of course, what we are dealing with, on both sides of the polemic, is a series of misprisions of Sand and her idealism: prized by antinaturalists for her beautiful, uplifting, and 'agreeable' dreams (at the expense of her class and gender politics), and dogmatically overdetermined by Zola as a fanciful anti-realist, beholden to her feminine temperament. If though, as I have argued, Zola's engagement with idealism in *Le Rêve* involved a necessary return to Sand, and in effect to the doctrinaire declarations he made about her idealist fiction some twelve years earlier – dismissed, as it was, as a 'dead convention' – this also implies a negotiation with idealism that was both ongoing and less straightforward than he would have us believe.[127]

In one respect, Zola's obituary of Sand can be read, to borrow Slavoj Žižek's terms in his commentary on Lacan, as a sort of 'settling of accounts'. For in keeping with Lacan's distinction between the 'real (biological) death and its symbolization', Zola's Sand must (like Angélique, in fact) 'die twice', and her brand of the novel along with her.[128] If Sand's presence can still be felt in *Le Rêve*, then, it is no doubt proof of what Schor describes in *Zola's Crowds* as the writer's belief 'that the dead never really die'. In fact, Schor argues that, from the dead buried in the Aire Saint-Mittre who urge Miette and Silvère to marry, to the dead women who haunt *La Faute de l'Abbé Mouret*, *Au Bonheur des dames*, and, of course, *Le Rêve*, 'the invisible crowd of the dead is one of the most active in Zola'.[129] Angélique's love story is traversed by voices from beyond the grave: the nocturnal mutterings of indistinct souls, or 'whisperings, coming from the invisible realms' (56; 869), that seem to announce her fate, along with the powerful voices of two mothers: the one (Hubertine's) punishing the daughter's love affair, and demanding Angélique's death in turn; the other (Félicien's) claiming 'what was rightfully owed to lovers' and beseeching her husband to sanction the heroine's fairytale ending. What Zola's peculiar conclusion allows for is the heeding of both (incompatible) demands, which ultimately, of course, means the satisfaction of neither. Perhaps the least we can say about this dialogue with the dead (mother) is that it rehearses the enduring question of just what kinds of wish-fulfilment – and, indeed, what kinds of purported maternal influence – the naturalist novel could allow itself to assimilate.

If we are inclined to read *Le Rêve*, then, as a drama, or working through, of Zola's obsession with idealism, it is because it allows us to probe, rather than resolve, the contradictory drives the novel sustains; to allow for, rather than explain away, Zola's apparently wilful incoherence. In the words of Robert E. Ziegler, 'Angélique's drive-gratifying experience of reading is the opposite of Zola's own critics, whose impulse is to reconcile an anomalous text with the rest of his fictional corpus' – and, we should add, with the naturalist credo he expounds elsewhere.[130] By this reckoning, Zola would produce only a counterfeit or masquerade idealist novel, granting Angélique her wish only to stage once more its fatal consequences. And yet, in the distorting mirrors of *Le Rêve*, the heroine's fantasy is itself, as we have seen, already subject to, even owned by, the conflicting impulses, drives, prohibitions, and wishes of others.

Indeed, if we return once more to a question we have already posed in this chapter – 'whose dream is it anyway?' – we might now circle back to *Le Docteur Pascal* in order to take in one final image: that of Zola's avatar avidly reading his illustrated copy of the Old Testament. Not unlike Angélique, Pascal becomes enraptured by engravings that produce a powerful form of identification – in this case, with King David – as he wishes for the sexual satisfaction that Angélique ultimately denies herself: 'His own dream, gazing on these primitive old engravings, ended up taking on a certain reality. Abishag came into his dismal room, [. . .] opened her bare arms, her bare body, all her divine nakedness, to make him the gift of her magnificent youth' (131; 1048–49). Where Pascal consummates his relationship with his virgin niece Clotilde – his own Abishag – the novel does, of course, fulfil his erotic wish, allowing him to secure his own futurity via reproduction. Here, the idealist conviction in the power of the imagination takes full flight, in what is an oblique, even inverted, counterpart to Angélique's textually-derived fantasy of sublimation. In the play of projection that each narrative establishes, the pleasures of the dream are, it becomes clear, also the author's own.

Notes

1 Émile Zola, letter to Turgenev, 21 June 1876, *Corr*, vol. 2 (1980), 463–64 (p. 463). The obituary first appeared in *Le Messager de l'Europe* in July 1876 and Zola published an extract in *Le Bien public* on 11 June 1877. The full piece was reprinted in *Le Voltaire* under the title 'Études littéraires: George Sand', between 8 and 14 March 1879, and it was subsequently included in his collection *Documents littéraires* (1881).

2 Letter of 4 July 1876. Gustave Flaubert, Ivan Tourguéniev, *Correspondance*, ed. Alexandre Zviguilsky (Paris: Flammarion, 1989), pp. 176–77.

3 Zola, 'Obsèques de George Sand', *Le Sémaphore de Marseille*, 13 June 1876. Zola, *OC*, vol. 7, 549.

4 Discussions of the relationship between Sand and Zola include: Éléonore Reverzy, 'Sand et Zola: littérature et valeurs', in *George Sand: écritures et représentations*, ed. Eric Bordas (Paris: Eurédit, 2004), pp. 103–19; Martine Reid, 'Zola, lecteur de Sand', in *Signer Sand: l'œuvre et le nom* (Paris: Belin, 2003), pp. 199–223; Jean-Marie Seillan, 'Naturalisme *vs* idéalisme: L'infortune posthume de George Sand', in *Ce qu'idéal' veut dire: définitions et usages de l'idéalisme au XIXe siècle*, 2015 (3), available online: http://etudes-romantiques.ish-lyon.cnrs.fr/wa_files/IdealismeJeanMarieSeillan.pdf. Sections of this chapter draw directly on my article 'Naturalism *in extremis*: Zola's *Le Rêve*', *Romance Studies*, 33:3–4 (2015), 272–84, by kind permission of the editor.

5 See David Baguley, 'Balzac, Zola et la paternité du naturalisme', in *Balzac: une poétique du roman*, ed. Stéphane Vachon (Montreal and Saint-Denis: XYZ éditeur et Presses Universitaires de Vincennes, 1996), pp. 383–95.

6 Roland Barthes, *S/Z*, trans. Richard Miller (Oxford: Basil Blackwell, 1990), p. 107.

7 Naomi Schor, *George Sand and Idealism* (New York: Columbia Press, 1993), p. 227, fn 54. Other reflections on the etymology of Zola's pseudonym include Freud's in *The Interpretation of Dreams*, in which he claimed the novelist first inverted his name to 'Aloz'. 'No doubt this seemed too undisguised. He therefore replaced 'Al', which is the first syllable of 'Alexander' by 'Sand', which is the third syllable of the same name; and in this way 'Sandoz' came into being.' *The Standard Edition of the Complete Psychological Works of Sigmund Freud*, trans. and ed. J. Strachey, 24 vols (London: Vintage, 2001), vol. 4, 300. However, as Philippe Bonnefis has pointed out, Zola likely derived 'Sand' from his wife's name Alexandrine instead. *L'Innommable: essai sur l'œuvre d'Émile Zola* (Paris: SEDES, 1984), p. 40.

8 *R-M*, vol. 4, 48. On Zola's relationship to Hugo, see Reverzy, 'Hugo dans Zola: le procès', in *Hugo ou les frontières effacées*, ed. Y. Jumelais and D. Peyrache-Leborgne (Nantes: Pleins Feux, 2002), pp. 62–77.

9 Zola, 'George Sand', *Documents littéraires*, in *OC*, vol. 10, 727–48 (p. 728).

10 Reverzy notes that 'the word that always returns under Zola's pen to describe Sand is "dream"', but she does not make the connection to Zola's *Le Rêve*. 'Sand et Zola', p. 108.

11 Elizabeth Emery, '"A l'ombre d'une vieille cathédrale romane": The Medievalism of Gautier and Zola', *The French Review* 73:2 (1999), 290–310 (p. 293). Emery singles out Gautier's 1833 satire 'Elias Wildmanstadius ou l'homme moyen âge'. See also Reverzy, 'L'écriture du Moyen-Âge dans *Le Rêve* de Zola', *Cahiers de recherches médiévales et humanistes* [online] 11: 141–50. http://crm.revues.org/1803

12 Emery, '"A l'ombre d'une vieille cathédrale romane"', 296. Zola delivered a damning verdict on Hugo's indulgence in a kind of phantasmagoric *engouement* for the medieval. 'Hugo et Littré' (first published in *Le Figaro* on 13 June 1881); repr. in *Une campagne*, *OC*, vol. 11, 832–36 (p. 836). See also Emery, '*The Golden Legend* in the Fin de Siècle: Zola's *Le Rêve* and its Reception', in *Medieval Saints in Late Nineteenth-Century French Culture*, ed. Elizabeth Emery and Laurie Postlewate (Jefferson, NC: McFarland Press, 2004), pp. 83–116 (p. 93).

13 Quite unusually, Zola considered no alternative titles for the novel. In his *Ébauche*, Zola noted: '"Le Rêve" would be the title of the book, and I am very pleased with it.' Paris, Bibliothèque nationale, NAF 10323, fol. 226.

14 Zola, 'Victor Hugo', *Documents littéraires*, in *OC*, vol. 10, 655–77 (p. 668).

15 See for example Zola's 'Pluie de couronnes', in which he condemns the 'castrated literature' of the kind he took Ernest Renan, and the wider Académie, to encourage. 15 August 1881, *Le Figaro*; repr. in *Une campagne*; *OC*, vol. 11, 853–57 (p. 857).

16 Letter to Jean-Baptistin Baille, 2 May 1860, in Zola, *Corr*, 1 (1978), 153–59 (pp. 156–57).

17 BN, NAF 10323, fol. 222.

18 BN, NAF 10323, fol. 217. In this vein, Roger Ripoll argues that Zola attempts to 'shatter a system of categorisation that tends to class the naturalist novel as the opposite of the sentimental or psychological novel'. *Réalité et mythe chez Zola* (Lille: Atelier Reproduction des Thèses; Paris: Champion, 1981), vol. 2, 802–3.

19 Henri Mitterand, *Zola* (Paris: Fayard, 2001), vol. 2, 869. See Zola's *Ébauche* for *La Bête humaine*: BN, NAF 10274, fol. 338 (emphasis added).

20 Paul Alexis made this observation, which was also a prediction for works to come, in *Émile Zola: notes d'un ami* (Paris: G. Charpentier, 1882), p. 126.

21 Henry James, 'Émile Zola', in *Selected Literary Criticism*, ed. Morris Shapira (London: Heinemann, 1963), pp. 240–64 (pp. 256–57).

22 For Colette Becker, *Le Rêve* is 'a work whose meaning is always elusive', its indeterminate status in the series rendering it 'surprising, disconcerting, irksome'. 'Le Rêve d'Angélique', *Les Cahiers naturalistes*, 76 (2002), 7–23 (p. 23).

23 Reverzy, 'L'écriture du Moyen-Âge dans *Le Rêve* de Zola', para. 22.

24 Zola, *Corr*, vol. 6 (1987), 258.

25 Sophie Guermès, *La Religion de Zola: naturalisme et déchristianisation* (Paris: Champion, 2003), p. 270.

26 Zola, *Corr*, vol. 6, 376.

27 BN, NAF 10323, fols 221–22.

28 *Le Rêve* is the shortest novel of the *Rougon-Macquart* series. Robert E. Ziegler, 'Interpretation as Awakening from Zola's *Le Rêve*', *Nineteenth-Century French Studies*, 21:1–2 (1992–93), 130–41 (p. 130).

29 Zola began planning *Le Rêve* in November 1887, and it was published serially in *La Revue illustrée* between 1 April and 15 October 1888. Zola was a candidate at the election of 1 May 1890, which was to fill the chair left by Émile Augier. He put himself forward for nearly every election thereafter.

30 'Zola académicien', *La Presse*, 19 July 1888, p. 2. Zola was invited to contemplate the possibility shortly after having been made Chevalier de la Légion d'honneur. See Philippe Gille, '*Le Rêve*, par Émile Zola', *Le Figaro*, 13 October 1888, p. 1: 'People will say of this book: here is the piece Zola wrote in order to get his foot through the door of the Académie!'

31 [Anon.], 'Le Rêve. Vitrail de l'Église de Médan', *La Vie populaire*, 6 August 1891.

32 See Zola's 'La Critique du *Rêve*', *Le Figaro*, 5 November 1888, p. 1.

33 Letter of 14 November 1887; Zola, *Corr*, vol. 6, 207.

34 '*La Terre*. À Émile Zola', *Le Figaro*, 18 August 1887, p. 1.

35 Anatole France, 'La Vie littéraire: *La Terre*', *Le Temps*, 28 August 1887, pp. 2–3 (p. 3).

36 Ferdinand Brunetière, 'La Banqueroute du naturalisme', *Revue des Deux Mondes*, 83 (1 September 1887), 213–24 (pp. 219–20).

37 Brunetière, 'La Banqueroute du naturalisme', 219.

38 BN, NAF 10323, fols 217–18.

39 *The Dream*, trans. Paul Gibbard (Oxford: Oxford University Press, 2018), p. 143. For the original French, see *Le Rêve*; *R-M*, vol. 4, 956. Hereafter all references to *Le Rêve* are interpolated in the text and correspond to these editions: the translation first, and the original second.

40 See Brunetière, 'L'Idéalisme dans le roman', *Revue des Deux Mondes*, 69 (1 May 1885), 215–25.

41 Seillan, *Le Roman idéaliste dans le second XIXᵉ siècle: littérature ou 'bouillon de veau'?* (Paris: Classiques Garnier, 2011), p. 50.

42 Seillan, *Le Roman idéaliste*, p. 292.

43 Charles Bigot, 'Causerie littéraire: *Le Rêve*, par Émile Zola', *La République française*, 22 October 1888, p. 3.

44 Charles Chincholle, '*Le Rêve*', *Le Figaro*, 30 March 1888, p. 2; original emphasis. As we will see in Chapter 4, the entirety of Zola's works was placed on the Index in 1895. But in his own popular manual, written in 1904, Abbé Bethléem nuanced the Catholic Church's position, citing *Le Rêve* as an exception. *Romans à lire et romans à proscrire*, 2nd edition (Paris: Éditions de la Revue des Lecteurs, 1928), p. 22.

45 Charles Brunetière, '*Le Rêve* de Zola jugé par un catholique' (1890), in *Deux études critiques sur Émile Zola* (Angers: Lachèse, 1894), p. 13.

46 Jules Lemaître, 'Causerie littéraire', *La Revue bleue*, 27 October 1888, pp. 533–35 (p. 535).

47 Zola, 'La Critique du *Rêve*', *Le Figaro*, 5 November 1888, p. 1.

48 BN, NAF 10323, fols 226–27 (emphasis added).

49 France, 'La Vie littéraire', *Le Temps*, 21 October 1888, p. 2.

50 Letter to Van Santen Kolff, 22 January 1888, *Corr*, vol. 6, 245. Angélique does not appear on the 1878 version of the family tree.

51 Edmond Lepelletier, 'Chronique des livres: *Le Rêve*, par Émile Zola', *L'Écho de Paris*, 6 November 1888, p. 2 (emphasis added).

52 Marie Scarpa, *L'Éternelle jeune fille. Une ethnocritique du 'Rêve' de Zola* (Paris: Honoré Champion, 2009), pp. 68–69. See David Baguley on the fairytale genre in Zola's fiction in *Zola et les genres* (Glasgow: University of Glasgow French and German Publications, 1993), pp. 19–40.

53 'La Critique du *Rêve*'.

54 'La Critique du *Rêve*'.

55 Zola, *Doctor Pascal*, trans. Julie Rose (Oxford: Oxford University Press, 2020), p. 90. The original reference is found in *R-M*, vol. 5, 1007. Further references to the novel – translation and original – are interpolated in the text.

56 Jean Bellemin-Noël undertakes a psychoanalytical examination of *Le Rêve* as 'the very novel of the "family romance"'. See *Interlignes: essais de textanalyse* (Lille: Presses Universitaires de Lille, 1988), pp. 141–64 (p. 141). My own reading focuses on the resonances with Freud for Zola's exploration of Angélique's burgeoning imagination – and idealist spirit.

57 Freud, 'Family Romances', *Complete Psychological Works*, vol. 9, 235–41 (p. 238).

58 'Family Romances', p. 239.
59 Susan Harrow, *Zola, The Body Modern: The Pressures and Prospects of Representation* (Oxford: Legenda, 2010), p. 124.
60 Marthe Robert, *Origins of the Novel*, trans. Sacha Rabinovitch (Brighton: Harvester, 1980), p. 24.
61 'Family Romances', p. 239.
62 Robert, *Origins of the Novel*, p. 28.
63 Robert, *Origins of the Novel*, pp. 24, 30.
64 Marianne Hirsch, *The Mother/Daughter Plot: Narrative, Psychoanalysis, Feminism* (Bloomington: Indiana University Press, 1989), p. 56.
65 BN, NAF 10323, fols 219–20.
66 Nicholas White, 'Le Docteur Pascal: entre l'inceste et "l'innéité"', *Les Cahiers naturalistes*, 68 (1994), 77–88 (p. 82).
67 BN, NAF 10323, fol. 204.
68 Jean-Louis Cabanès, 'Rêver *La Légende dorée*', *Les Cahiers naturalistes*, 76 (2002), 25–47 (p. 26).
69 BN, NAF 10324, fols 193–94.
70 Robert, *Origins of the Novel*, p. 37.
71 Terence Cave, *Recognitions: A Study in Poetics* (Oxford: Clarendon Press, 1990), p. 144.
72 In this respect, Guermès remarks that Angélique 'feels herself entrusted with a mission: to wash away the stain of original sin'. *La Religion de Zola*, p. 263.
73 BN, NAF 10323, fol. 199.
74 'It should be noted that, here, the *milieu* plays the same role as grace, in theology' (BN, NAF 10324, fol. 189).
75 Chantal Bertrand-Jennings, *L'Éros et la femme chez Zola: de la chute au paradis retrouvé* (Paris: Éditions Klincksieck, 1977), pp. 124–25.
76 Zola, *La Confession de Claude*, in *OC*, vol. 1 (2002), 481 (emphasis added).
77 BN, NAF 10323, fol. 180.
78 See Evelyne Bloch-Dano, *Chez Zola à Médan* (Saint-Cyr-sur-Loire: Christian Pirot, 1999), p. 71.
79 'Creative Writers and Day-Dreaming', *Complete Psychological Works*, vol. 9, 141–53 (p. 146).
80 'Family Romances', p. 238.
81 *George Sand and Idealism*, p. 169.
82 BN, NAF 10323, fol. 245.
83 Elme-Marie Caro, *George Sand* (Paris: Hachette, 1887), p. 5.
84 France, 'La Vie littéraire', *Le Temps*, 6 November 1887, p. 2.
85 Lemaître, 'George Sand', *Le Figaro*, 29 April 1887, p. 1.
86 Octave Mirbeau, 'Le Rêve', *Le Gaulois*, 3 November 1884, p. 1.
87 Zola, 'George Sand', 728.
88 Sainte-Beuve, '*Madame Bovary*, par M. Gustave Flaubert', *Le Moniteur universel*, 4 May 1857, p. 3. In 'Deux définitions du roman' (1866), Zola described the modern novelist as an anatomist: 'Like the surgeon, he feels

neither shame nor repugnancy when he investigates human wounds.' *OC*, vol. 1, 503–12 (p. 510).

89 Zola, 'Les réalistes du Salon', first printed in *L'Événement* on 11 May 1866; repr. in *Mon Salon. Œuvres complètes.Critique littéraire et artistique*, vol. 1, *Écrits sur l'art*, ed. Robert Lethbridge (Paris: Classiques Garnier, 2021), pp. 156–61 (p. 156).

90 See Sand's *Histoire de ma vie*, in *Œuvres autobiographiques*, ed. Georges Lubin (Paris: Gallimard, 1971), vol. 2, 162.

91 *George Sand and Idealism*, p. 44.

92 See Zola, 'Lettre à la jeunesse', in *OC*, vol. 9, 349–70 (p. 350). Martine Reid describes Zola's 'gendered reading of literary history' in similar terms. *Signer Sand*, p. 215.

93 Zola, 'Adieux', first published in *Le Figaro* on 22 September 1881; repr. in *Une campagne*, *OC*, vol. 11, 872–77 (p. 875).

94 Zola, 'George Sand', 747.

95 Seillan, 'Naturalisme *vs* idéalisme', p. 3. As Seillan points out, Joris-Karl Huysmans shared this perspective of generational distance, labelling Sand, in 1887, 'an old spinner of second-rate ideals'.

96 Robert, *Origins of the Novel*, p. 144.

97 Robert alludes to Zola in describing the naturalist's capacity to 'instil into a "slice of life" a dose of the unreal, or some stylistic ingredient that betrays the true visionary'. *Origins of the Novel*, p. 38.

98 Zola, 'George Sand', 745.

99 France, 'La Vie littéraire', *Le Temps*, 6 November 1887.

100 Zola, 'George Sand', 737.

101 Caro, *George Sand*, pp. 13, 16.

102 Zola, 'George Sand', 740.

103 Janet Beizer, *Ventriloquized Bodies: Narratives of Hysteria in Nineteenth-Century France* (Ithaca, NY: Cornell University Press, 1994), p. 173.

104 BN, NAF 10290, fol. 191.

105 Zola, 'George Sand', 737.

106 Zola, 'Lettre à la jeunesse', in *OC*, vol. 9, 350.

107 Zola, 'Lettre à la jeunesse', 369.

108 Zola, 'De la moralité dans la littérature', *Documents littéraires*, in *OC*, vol. 10, 809–29 (p. 828).

109 White, *The Family in Crisis in Late Nineteenth-Century French Fiction* (Cambridge: Cambridge University Press, 1999), p. 33.

110 *R-M*, vol. 3, 77.

111 More broadly, Bertrand-Jennings notes the tendency of 'Zola's young women [to] die just as they stand on the threshold of life, as though to preserve, in extremis, their precarious virginity', *L'Éros et la femme chez Zola*, p. 102.

112 BN, NAF 10323, fols 302–3.

113 Ripoll similarly describes the ending of *Le Rêve* as a form of self-implosion: 'The novel [...] ultimately ends up interrogating its own existence, by

asserting its complete unreality.' *Réalité et mythe chez Zola*, vol. 2, 821. See also Michel Serres on *Le Rêve* in *Feux et signaux de brume: Zola* (Paris: Grasset, 1975), p. 237: 'Nothing is left beneath the white dress. Nothingness of the body, of the name, of desire. [. . .] Non-existence of the story.'

114 Gabrielle Mourey, 'Le Rêve', *Le Parisien*, 22 October 1888, p. 1.

115 France, 'La Vie littéraire', *Le Temps*, 21 October 1888, p. 2.

116 BN, NAF 10324, fol. 187.

117 Zola drew on Jean Bourdeau's popular anthology, *Pensées et Fragments*, first published in 1881, and Théodule Ribot's *La Philosophie de Schophenhauer* (1874). Émilie Piton-Foucault describes *Le Rêve* as 'a veritable mise en abyme of the Schopenhauerian artwork'. *Zola ou la fenêtre condamnée: la crise de la représentation dans 'Les Rougon Macquart'* (Rennes: Presses Universitaires de Rennes, 2015), p. 724.

118 Remy de Gourmont, *L'Idéalisme* (Paris: Mercure de France, 1893), p. 13. Gustave Kahn claimed that much Symbolist thought was rooted in 'this purely idealist philosophical principle that would have us reject material reality entirely and accept that the world exists only as a representation', 'Réponse des symbolistes', *L'Événement*, 28 September 1886, p. 3.

119 BN, NAF 10324, fol. 194 (original underlining).

120 Zola, 'Le Roman expérimental', in *OC*, vol. 9, 324–48 (p. 340).

121 Alfred Fouillée, 'La métaphysique et la poésie de l'idéal', *Revue des Deux Mondes*, 86 (1888), 110–40 (p. 115).

122 Guy de Maupassant, *Pierre et Jean*, ed. Marie-Claire Ropars-Wuilleumier (Paris: Livre de Poche, 1984), p. 22.

123 'Le Rêve', *Le Gaulois*, 3 November 1884, p. 1.

124 France, 'La Vie littéraire', 6 November 1887, p. 2 (emphasis added).

125 Lemaître, 'George Sand', *Le Figaro*, 29 April 1887, p. 1.

126 Lepelletier, 'Chronique des livres: *Le Rêve*, par Émile Zola'.

127 Zola, 'George Sand', 748.

128 Slavoj Žižek, *The Sublime Object of Ideology* (London: Verso, 1989), pp. 134–35.

129 Schor, *Zola's Crowds* (Baltimore, MD: Johns Hopkins University Press, 1978), p. 120.

130 Ziegler, 'Interpretation as Awakening from Zola's *Le Rêve*', 138.

CHAPTER 4

Doubting Thomas
Lourdes, Naturalism, and the Miracle

On 19 August 1892, Zola arrived in Lourdes on the Pyrénées-Express, just as the fortnight of the annual pilgrimage to the Catholic shrine was getting underway. Despite his best efforts to remain incognito, the national press quickly caught wind of his visit. Never before, remarked the Catholic newspaper *La Croix*, had journalists shown so much interest in the rituals of pilgrimage.[1] Predictably, many of those reports on Zola's stay were quick to exploit the caricatural possibilities of the naturalist writer's communion with the divine. In one illustration, Zola emerges from a dip in the water at Lourdes adorned in the robes of the Académie – his transformation into an *Immortel* witnessed by a delegation of characters from his Rougon-Macquart novels (Figure 4.1).[2] In another, 'Saint Zola' himself, adorned with a halo, accomplishes the miracle of turning Lourdes water into 'naturalist moonshine' (Figure 4.2). Effectively reigniting those conjectures about Zola's spiritual and ethical redemption that had surfaced with *Le Rêve*, commentators delighted in imagining the naturalist novelist's repentance and eventual conversion to the Catholic faith. Journalist and playwright Albert Millaud envisaged Zola's sense of contrition upon returning from Lourdes, now bent on rewriting his Rougon-Macquart novels in a wholesome style – starting with the scandalously titillating washhouse scene of *L'Assommoir*.[3] Another dramatist imagined Zola-the-pilgrim's moment of epiphany thus:

> Virgin of Lourdes, [...] when I arrived here my heart was swollen with pride; I denied the miracle, and now the miracle is happening to me. My eyes are finally opening. [...] The long Rougon-Macquart saga appears to me in its full horror. My hands have sullied everything they have touched.[4]

The idea that the Virgin Mary might see fit to bestow her grace on the sinful author, at last alive to the errors of his (naturalist) ways, loomed large in speculations about Zola's visit. If, as is the case here, sarcasm tended to

Figure 4.1   Vignola, 'The Latest Lourdes Miracle'.
Caricature in *Le Gueux*, deuxième année, no. 18, October 1892. Album / Collection Kharbine-Tapabor.

prevail, the writer's immersion in the Pyrenean shrine nevertheless held out, for some, the promise of allaying his misconceptions about the Catholic faith.

On the whole, Zola was warmly welcomed by the city and shrine's officials, who were inclined to believe in the goodwill and spirit of open-mindedness he declared. Across 242 pages of notes, the writer carefully documented his impressions, as well his numerous conversations with the clergy and medical doctors working in the sanctuary, cautiously suspending his judgement – at least so he claimed – on those scenes of faith and healing he witnessed on the ground. When interviewed before his departure by a journalist from *Le Gaulois*, Zola duly refrained from denying outright the singularity of those supposedly 'extranatural' events that were held to have taken place at the shrine. He did admit, though, to a cautious

Figure 4.2   Gilbert-Martin, 'Saint Zola'.

Caricature in *Le Don Quichotte*, 19 année, no. 949, 4 September 1892 [front cover]. Courtesy of the Bibliothèque nationale de France.

scepticism: 'I am like Saint Thomas. I want to feel the miracles, thrust my hands into the wounds, make sure they are truly healed [cicatrisées].'[5] The Catholic writer Léon Bloy subsequently seized on Zola's comment as confirming an entirely appropriate intellectual genealogy: 'Any man of intelligence will readily acknowledge that Saint Thomas is the patriarch of the positivists.'[6] Embarking on his new trilogy of novels, *Les Trois Villes* – of which *Lourdes* would be the first volume – Zola had described himself, no doubt with tongue in cheek, as an 'old, dyed-in-the-wool positivist', inscribing his naturalist aesthetic in a tradition of Enlightenment thought from which he had inherited, among other things, an attachment to the philosophical value of doubt.[7] With this particular self-portrait, of course, Zola derives from the discourse of the Bible itself the icon of scepticism with which he frames his own counter-discourse. Jesus's stigmata, or crucifixion wounds, represent the material support for faith on which Saint Thomas depends: 'Except I shall see in his hands the print of the nails, and put my finger into the print of the nails, and thrust my hand into his side, I will not believe.'[8] Though Zola's harnessing of this analogy is faintly paradoxical – for him, it is only the healed (and so disappearing) wound that provides proof of the miracle cure – what he claims to share with the apostle is a distrust of the visual. It is not enough for our Zola-Saint Thomas to see; only touching is believing.

Via his hero-double, the doubting priest Pierre Froment, Zola duly returns in *Lourdes* to the same epistemological and semiotic dilemma: 'the impossibility of proving whether there was a miracle or not'.[9] The burning question of how the miracle cure could be evidenced, which signs could be trusted and which proofs harnessed, lay at the heart, as we shall see in this chapter, of contemporary theological and medical debates; and our aim in what follows is to better understand the aesthetic and ideological stakes of Zola's divisive intervention in these matters, together with the heated polemic it provoked. Broadly speaking, such struggles over the legitimacy of the miracle rehearsed, of course, the wider ideological polarisation at the fin-de-siècle between the secular Third Republic and the Catholic Church; and much ink was spilt on both sides. In their respective histories of Lourdes, both Ruth Harris and Suzanne K. Kaufman discuss the importance to the shrine's history of Zola's visit in 1892, the media circus that accompanied it, along with the publication of the novel itself.[10] As the first fictional account devoted to the mass phenomenon of the Lourdes pilgrimage, Zola's novel 'did more', Harris writes, 'than any other publication to bring the sanctuary [. . .] and the debate over the nature of healing to the wider public'.[11] *Lourdes* certainly instigated a war of words, and a deluge of refutations and open letters in the press and in pamphlet-form – largely from the clergy, but also doctors and writers – all of which amounted to something like an 'affair'.[12] The official Catholic response to Zola's novel was unequivocal: on 19 September 1894, shortly after its publication in book form, *Lourdes* was placed on the Index; and just a few months later, on 25 January 1895, the novelist's entire works were added retrospectively.[13] Zola reacted to the decree by lamenting the sheer injust-ice of those who painted him as a 'priest-eater', when his real provocation had simply been to unveil 'all the hidden dramas of Lourdes'.[14] It is doubtless a sign of the passionate controversy the novel stoked that, at the time of Zola's death in 1902, *Lourdes* was outsold only by *La Débâcle* and *Nana*.[15]

Structured around five days of national pilgrimage, the novel recounts the frustrated love affair between Pierre Froment, who is struggling to regain his faith, and Marie de Guersaint, his childhood friend, who has travelled to Lourdes in search of a miracle, having been disabled by a riding accident. The novel's centrepiece is Marie's long-awaited cure, following a feverish night spent alone at the sacred grotto. But where Marie believes her recovery to be an act of the Virgin's beneficence, Pierre concludes – following the initial diagnosis of Marie's physician – that her illness is hysterical, and therefore that her cure is to be explained on psychological grounds, rather than as an act of divine intervention. Further cases that Pierre encounters during his visits to the shrine's Medical Bureau only compound his doubts over the legitimacy of those miracles it claims to certify; and the novel concludes with Pierre's reflections, as he returns to Paris, on the pitiful condition of mankind, and its desperate recourse to illusion as the antidote to suffering.

In tandem with its sentimental plot, Zola devotes a significant part of the novel to telling the story of the pilgrimage's origins, and of the city's extraordinary development in the wake of the visions of the fourteen-year-old girl, Bernadette Soubirous, in 1858. The Massabielle Grotto, in which Bernadette claimed to witness the Virgin Mary on eighteen separate occasions – between 11 February and 16 July – was subsequently trans-formed into a sanctuary and quickly became a nationally recognised healing shrine. The first national pilgrimage to Lourdes took place in 1873, and the movement rapidly gained momentum. According to Harris, more than one and a half million pilgrims made the trip in 1908, on the fiftieth anniversary of the apparitions.[16] The story of Lourdes in the latter decades of the century is thus one in which the most ardent expressions of faith intermingled with commercial development;

and Zola himself was fascinated, as Colette Becker has demonstrated, by Bernadette's 'beautiful dream' – and the 'beautiful story' it produced – as the prodigious origin-point of a phenomenon of mass experience and consumption.[17] As we shall see, Zola's novel tracks the expanding city as a site of such contradictions, caught between the burgeoning materialism to which mass pilgrimage gave rise and the naïve, rustic Pyrenean simplicity that the shrine's founding visionary embodied.

The fact that *Lourdes* was, in part, a fairly transparent *roman à clef* made it a lightning rod for wider debates about the authenticity of those proliferating narratives of the shrine's recent history. In transposing many of the figures Zola met, and events he witnessed, the novel's implicit claims to referentiality invited refutations in ways a purely fictional account surely would not have. This chapter engages with some of those critics: most prominently, Gustave Boissarie, director of the shrine's medical bureau at the time of Zola's visit; Henri Lasserre, Catholic author of a history of the shrine and the apparitions, *Notre-Dame de Lourdes* (1869), which was one of the bestselling books of the century; and Monseigneur Antoine Ricard, a cleric from Zola's hometown, Aix-en-Provence. For Boissarie and Lasserre, both of whom had welcomed Zola during his visit to Lourdes – and who would both be represented via fictional doubles in the resulting novel – the author's account was experienced as an act of personal betrayal. 'The future convert', comments Bertrand Marquer, 'was really a Judas'.[18] For Ricard, meanwhile, his declared disappointment rested on the realisation that the 'new course' the novelist had seemed to augur in writing *Le Rêve* had failed to materialise: with *Lourdes*, the hopes of believers like himself were dashed.[19] All three were implicated in the play of refutations and counter-refutations that followed the publication of *Lourdes*, and across which two main points of controversy returned. First was that of the authenticity of those miracles Zola was supposed to have witnessed during his stay, together with the validity of his own fictional transposition of those *miraculés* he encountered. Second was that of Zola's retelling of the history of Lourdes, in particular the story of the young Bernadette and the events that led to the shrine's foundational apparitions.

Predictably, most attempts to discredit Zola's version of events in *Lourdes* took aim at the novelist as a partial, and unfaithful, witness on the ground. Though yet more striking, as we shall see, were claims that the naturalist novelist was guilty of the same indulgences – naivety, conjecture, fantasy, even idealism – with which he charged his Catholic adversaries. Effectively, the task of delegitimising Zola's intervention also meant determining lapses and inconsistencies in the literary project he claimed to set himself. Indeed, such wranglings over both the historiography and the theological legitimacy of the shrine, I shall venture, had more to do than might first appear with the shifting, contemporary discourses on naturalist aesthetics, and its rival forms, against which Zola's novel was conceived. For, as Elizabeth Emery has argued, Zola's initial plans for *Lourdes* 'show the extent to which the project emerged in reaction to contemporary criticism' – most conspicuously, to the gathering idealist backlash we tracked in Chapter 1.[20]

On the first line of his dossier, Zola duly declared: 'In a time marked by mysticism and the revolt against science, a worthy subject: to show man's perennial need for the supernatural.'[21] This imperative meant grappling with the increasing clamour of a generation desperate for a way out of what they perceived to be the aesthetic and intellectual cul-de-sac of naturalist fiction. Such a turn had just been set out with great force in Joris-Karl Huysmans's novel of the occult *Là-bas* (1891); its opening invective, voiced by the learned Des Hermies, charges naturalism with having 'embodied materialism in literature', and in turn with extolling the democratisation of art. Bound by its dogged positivism, its blunt denotation of visible phenomena, its narrow-minded obsession with man's instinctual and sensuous existence, naturalism had '[denied] the dream', in failing to allow for the invisible, the irrational, the life of the soul and the spirit as well as the flesh.[22] In what can be read as a projection of Huysmans's internal debate, the novelist Durtal responds by calling instead for 'a spiritualist naturalism': a redeemed version of naturalist writing that would be rooted in descriptive detail and careful documentation, all while remaining open to the suprasensible, to the power of the ideal.

Of course, Zola was hardly immune to such critiques.[23] *Là-bas* appeared almost concurrently with the series of interviews that made up Jules Huret's famous *Enquête sur l'évolution littéraire* – indeed, it was serialised in the same newspaper – and together they crystallised the prevailing antinaturalist drive: above all, the spiritual revival that took the varied forms of neo-Catholicism, mysticism and occultism. As we saw in Chapter 1, Zola acknowledged in his own interview with Huret the appeals of those who wished for the novel to expand its vision of human needs and impulses, so as to better capture the 'soul' of modern society – tentatively suggesting that he might give his contemporaries what they asked for.[24] Four months later, in September 1891, Zola hit upon his subject, as he passed briefly through Lourdes for the first time.[25] Indeed, as plans for *Les Trois Villes* took shape, it quickly became clear that Zola would take up the terms and techniques of his rivals, not just as an object of analysis, but as a new form: 'I will step outside reality', he declared in an early interview about the series, 'in the last volume, *Paris*, I will advance into the world beyond; I will probe the future, in a nutshell, of socialism; I will fall into or rise up to idealism'.[26] Zola's foray into the supernatural in *Lourdes*, which he began writing on 5 October 1893, allowed him to incorporate the precisely anti-materialist reaction, and at a moment when – according to the medico-literary diagnostics of Huret's *enquête* – the ailing naturalist novel itself appeared in need of some kind of divine intervention.

No doubt, then, we will want to conceive of Zola's turn to Lourdes, this 'divine land of dreams', as a strategic move, allowing him to tackle his adversaries on their own ground.[27] Certainly, this was the rationale the novelist himself provided in an interview with Gaston Deschamps: 'If, after all, there were a moral movement, an idealist evolution, it would be nice to take the lead on it, unless it were more advantageous to stop it in its tracks.'[28] Elsewhere, though, Zola hinted at a greater ambivalence about his own aesthetic and philosophical convictions – even at a degree of self-doubt: 'I have applied positivist principles to literature. [...] I may no longer believe in these principles as fervently as I once did. Nonetheless, I am still certain that I was right at the time.'[29] Pointing to the possibility of a certain revisionism in his attitudes towards the metaphysical thus allowed Zola to rebuff those who claimed to see through his foray into the Pyrenean land of the supernatural for what it was: a pretext to advance his anti-clerical agendas, or as the journalist Henri Rochefort hoped, to pen 'a Catholic *Assommoir*'.[30] As it was, few were inclined to credit this indeterminacy as anything other than a performance. 'Oh, [Zola] is not turning over a new leaf, that old snake; and he is hardly *evolving*, I assure you!', declared Bloy. Quite simply, faced with a rising tide of pilgrims who would rather travel to Lourdes than read *Pot-Bouille*, 'there was an urgent need for a cautionary tale'.[31] The idea that Zola's novel of the shrine displayed a genuine authorial shift – a reaction to the antinaturalist reaction that was anything other than cynical – seemed, to the likes of Bloy, decidedly suspect.

To be sure, for all that Zola couched *Lourdes* as a drama of doubt, it would be hard to understate the narrative's firm, overarching ideological commitments, and secularising ambition.[32] This chapter looks to Zola's novel of the miracle, though especially to the heated polemic it provoked, in order to better understand the stakes of the author's divisive foray into matters of Catholic practice and dogma. More than a simple expression of Zola's anti-clericalism, the novel set in motion, I shall argue, debates that were aesthetic as much as ideological, as adversaries argued over issues of representation, facts, documents, faithfulness – and idealism. In part, then, this chapter takes a more distinctly archival approach to the questions about Zola's fraught relationship with idealism we have been exploring so far. It does so with a view to reconstructing the intellectual climate surrounding Lourdes, which offers a face of antinaturalist critique far less familiar, though no less revealing, than the attacks of well-known literary critics we set out in Chapter 1. In what follows, I make the case for reading closely a set of understudied (and some unstudied) material penned by Zola's Catholic detractors in response to *Lourdes*. Defending the divine status of the miracle against Zola's critiques and claims, these antagonists made, we shall see, a surprising effort to mobilise the language of literary critique, and in turn to cast Zola's naturalism as an illegitimate, unbelievable – even, *à la limite*, idealist – aesthetic mode.

Parts One and Two track Zola's various attempts to demystify and discredit the currency of the miracle on which Lourdes's spiritual and commercial capital rests. Parts Three and Four focus on Zola's controversial investigation into the originary figure of the Lourdes shrine, Bernadette, and the writer's search for a set of truths about her life and visions that would prove, once and for all, the sceptic right. At the close, we shall return to Zola's attachment to doubt and suspicion, in asking how his own novel of disenchantment comes to rely on some of the very techniques and methods he has sought to denounce in his adversaries.

Miraculés

Framed in ways that return us to the central terms of this book, the promise of the miracle, such as Zola encountered it in Lourdes, was that of the power of the mind, of the ideal, or dream, to alter the otherwise recalcitrant material world. Conjuring up the irresistible pull that the shrine exerts on hordes of hopeful pilgrims, Zola presented in his novel a paradigmatic vision of the idealist imagination that we have tracked thus far – that is, as a conviction in the possibility of the strictly impossible:

> over there, the Grotto was blazing in all its glory like a beacon of hope and illusion, like the revolt of the impossible and its victory over inexorable matter. Never had a more captivating novel been written to raise the souls of men above the harsh conditions of their existence. To dream this dream was to enjoy great, untold happiness. (112)

As a diagnostician of the human condition, Zola finds at the shrine yet another iteration of the same palliative promise he had determined, we saw in Chapter 2, in the political fantasies of *Germinal*, feeding off the desperation of those living an intolerable life – here, the sick and infirm for whom 'reality [. . .] was too abominable' (111). Certainly, in his reflections on Lourdes, Zola persisted in collapsing distinctions between the religious faithful and the radical Left – notably anarchists – casting them as dreamers, whose shared aspiration for a transformed existence, in this world or beyond, amounted to the same fundamental 'pursuit of the ideal'.[33] As it had in both *Germinal* and *Le Rêve*, moreover, the lure of the miracle emerges as a powerful form of aesthetic seduction or storytelling: here, as a 'captivating novel'; elsewhere, as 'far-fetched stories' (106) or 'adorable fairytales' (112), such narratives of wish-fulfilment stoking the feverish imagination of susceptible readers.

What Zola broached, in researching *Lourdes*, were the scientific grounds on which the claims of the miracle might be rationalised. The antinaturalist phenomenon par excellence, the miracle effectively emerged, in Zola's aesthetic manifesto *Le Roman expérimental* (1880), as the paradigmatic object of the experimental 'method' he submitted. The naturalist writer's (and scientist's) summative agenda was to determine precisely 'the natural, individual, and social phenomena for which metaphysics has hitherto given only irrational and supernatural explanations'.[34] Zola had long held fast to the conviction that science, and its cognate experimental literature, would continually diminish the domain of the 'beyond', 'the unknown', 'the unexplained' – all of which he blends into the 'ideal'.[35] For it was not, as Ernest Renan had famously declared, that the world was devoid of miracles, but rather, Zola insisted, the opposite: 'we live surrounded by miracles, swamped by peculiar happenings that go against the supposed laws of nature'.[36] Those phenomena – magnetism, hypnotism, and so on – were simply 'unknown forces of matter', provisional miracles awaiting their rational explanation. In *Lourdes*, Zola harnesses, in particular, the idea that matter could be subject to the influence of the mind, a possibility that was rooted in the most contemporary of medical and psychiatric discourses, especially those concerned with ideodynamism. The philosopher Alfred Fouillée wrote a series of important articles in the 1880s and '90s on this subject, tracking key developments in neuropsychiatric research. Fouillée conjured up a contemporary fascination, as Deborah L. Silverman writes, with the 'dynamic extension of inner vision to the outer world'.[37] As a concept, ideodynamism established the power of mental ideas over physical actions and states, particularly as was seen to prevail in the context of hypnosis and suggestion. This reorientation of the mind-body connection thus meant allowing for and exploring a different relationship of causality between states of consciousness and physical phenomena.

Most important for Zola's account of the miracle cure was the neurologist Jean-Martin Charcot's writing on suggestion, namely his 1892 article 'La Foi qui guérit' ('Faith Healing'). Following the media storm whipped up by Zola's stay in Lourdes, Charcot was asked by a British journal, the *New Review*, to comment on the novelist's new subject matter. Here, Charcot provided what would prove to be his last word on the question of healing and hysteria, for he died the following year. And in an intriguing instance of recursivity, Zola would himself rely on the ideas Charcot set out in that piece for his own presentation of the miracle cure in the subsequent novel.[38] Miraculous healing or 'faith healing' was, Charcot claimed, either the product of autosuggestion or provoked by such outside stimuli as group prayer and mass rituals, which entailed 'a sort of unconscious influence'.[39] This therapeutic capacity for suggestion was one to which the hysteric, Charcot insisted, was predisposed, allowing the mind to heal the body: 'the cure demands no other intervention than the power of the mind over the body'.[40] As Zola was aware, Charcot sent some of his patients to the shrine, where his own practices in the clinic had been ineffective, in the hope that the healing powers of suggestion would prevail.[41] Zola even inserts into *Lourdes* a double of Charcot in the form of Marie's physician, doctor Beauclair, who diagnoses her paralysis as an effect of hysteria and (rightly) predicts that a visit to Lourdes will produce a cure.

Certainly, Zola seems to subscribe to what Jan Goldstein has called Charcot's 'redefinition of the supernatural as the natural-*pathological*'.[42] In placing Marie's 'false' miracle at the heart of the novel, Zola harnesses the language of the clinic to demonstrate the power of mind over matter – a power that is magnified, he insists, by the suggestive rites of the pilgrimage. 'Could it be supposed', Pierre muses, 'that, in certain circumstances of extreme exaltation, the crowd became an agent of the governing will forcing matter to obey?' (348). Zola seizes on the pilgrims' collective chants, mass processions, and gestures of imitation as conduits of a kind of collective hysteria – and in ways that spoke to contemporaneous theories of crowd psychology. That same year, the sociologist Gabriel Tarde described the 'frisson of mystical fervour' that travels through the throngs at Lourdes.[43] In Zola's hands, the promiscuous crowd is figured as a breeding ground of credulity, subject to what his priest Pierre will describe in the subsequent novel *Rome* (1894) as 'the contagion of the miracle'.[44] Such metaphors of contamination find their literal (or Pasteurian) counterpart in the city's communal baths, rendered a cesspool of abjection by the excretions of the ailing bodies that enter them. 'It seemed as though it was a veritable breeding ground for all kinds of virulent germs' (180) – the real miracle of Lourdes, Pierre mused, was that anybody should make it out alive!

Unsurprisingly, Zola's recourse to the suggestion thesis as a means of explaining (away) those ostensibly miraculous occurrences at Lourdes gave rise to impassioned refutations. Lasserre, for instance, described the hypothesis as 'this false key that [Zola] uses to try to open the door and escape from all things Supernatural'.[45] But the problem of distinguishing what were known as 'therapeutic' miracles – of the kind Charcot described – from genuine instances of divine intervention was already a major concern of the shrine's apologetics. In 1883, new attempts had been made to control divine cures through the establishment of a Medical Bureau, the Bureau des Constatations Médicales, headed by the physician and ultramontanist Baron Dunot de Saint-Maclou. The Bureau sought to promote the collaboration of clerics and doctors, welcoming physicians – initially Catholic, but later of any religion, or indeed none – to attest to cures and distinguish between natural and supernatural causation. Upon Saint-Maclou's death in 1891, Dr Gustave Boissarie became director of the Medical Bureau until 1914 and was therefore in charge at the time of Zola's visit. Under his direction, the clinic drew on the latest medical theories and techniques in order to bring a new rigour to their work of recording and validating the miracle. Moved from its temporary quarters in the Garaison Father's residence, the new Bureau was positioned beneath the right arcades of the Basilica of the Rosary itself, becoming, as Kaufman puts it, 'quite literally part of the sanctuary's foundation'.[46]

Boissarie thus spearheaded the grotto's mission, setting out to develop a new discourse of the miracle that was akin to that of the medical clinic. His *L'Histoire médicale de Lourdes* (1891) was praised by Pope Leo XII and reached a wide secular audience. But this investment in scientific legitimacy on the part of the Church nevertheless risked turning, as Harris writes, into 'a Mephistophelean bargain with positivism'.[47] Indeed, Boissarie was forced to recognise the limits of this strategy in the mirror of Zola's fiction. Having welcomed Zola into his Bureau as an observer of his team's procedures during the latter's fortnight-long visit to Lourdes, the doctor failed to convert, or convince, his sceptic. Instead, in his notes taken *sur place*, Zola dismissed Boissarie's clinic as a largely ineffective mechanism for distinguishing the 'authentic' miracle from what Boissarie himself called 'the forgery of the miracle'.[48] 'There were lots of malingerers',

Zola observed, 'and in those cases, the Grotto doctor is little more than a kind of customs officer [le douanier des guérisons]: he prevents those cures that are too ridiculous from slipping through'.[49] The sanctuary thus acted as a 'visa office' (198), as Zola later put it in the novel – an instrument of policing the plausibility of those many claims made on the divine.

The negation of the miracle cure that we find in Zola's fiction is, then, based on a challenge to the scientific authority embodied by Boissarie – or rather by his unflattering double Doctor Bonamy, whose clumsy handling of the Bureau's supposedly rigorous procedures leaves plenty of room for doubt. Boissarie's reply to Zola's novel came in the form of a lecture he delivered at the Cercle du Luxembourg in Paris on 21 November 1894.[50] Widely reported by the Parisian press, this great media event brought together an educated audience, largely made up of medical students and doctors. Its dual aim was to invalidate a narrative that Boissarie held to be injurious and to put forward the doctor's own version of events – in the words of Marquer, 'a sort of anti-Lourdes'.[51] As well as defending the clinical processes in place, Boissarie accused Zola of ignorance, a lack of interest and attention (he is said to have made no notes during his visit to the Bureau), and an entirely unscientific parti-pris, which led him to ignore the proofs placed before his eyes. What Boissarie held to be Zola's wilful distortion of the facts in Lourdes went beyond differences of opinion or doctrine; it was an abuse of the novelist's freedoms. 'Novelists have privileges', Boissarie admitted. 'But they do not have the right to use the novel as a pretext for falsifying history and making the most sacred things the object of ridicule.'[52] The doctor thus framed his own corrective as the righteous triumph of 'history' over 'fiction'.

Central to Boissarie's delegitimation of Zola's narrative were three medical cases, which had inspired the novelist on his visit to Lourdes: those of Clémentine Trouvé (whom Zola renamed Sophie Couteau); Marie Lemarchand (represented by the character Élise Rouquet); and Marie Lebranchu (La Grivotte, in Zola's novel). In each case, Zola was accused of audaciously distorting the facts, by having his fictional heroines live out different fates altogether. In Zola's hands, Sophie, who is afflicted with peritonitis of the heel bone, receives a false diagnosis, since her wound had not been examined by the shrine's doctors prior to its cure. Élise Rouquet, whose face appears to be devoured by lupus, is in fact suffering from a hysterical ulcer, from which she recovers, although her cure is neither instantaneous nor complete (as claimed). And in the case of La Grivotte, who suffers from pulmonary tuberculosis, the author has her relapse on the departing train, following a brief period of remission.

In his lecture, Boissarie comes to the defence of these heroines, undertaking to restore the facts. Contrary to Zola's account, La Grivotte's counterpart, Marie Lebranchu, was still alive and perfectly well. Marie Lemarchand's cure, meanwhile, was in fact miraculously instantaneous and absolute; and as proof, Boissarie not only repeated several doctors' statements, he exhibited her before his audience.

It was the presentation of those pilgrims cured at Lourdes that provided the doctor with the highlight of his address. In an illustration of the scene that first appeared in *Le Pèlerin* (Figure 4.3), Boissarie stood beside his *miraculés* on stage, directly before an image of the Virgin of Lourdes, and received the applause of an excited crowd. With a simple, deictic gesture, Boissarie points towards the women's still bodies as indisputable proof of the illegitimacy of the Zolian text. In the preface added to the pamphlet form of Boissarie's lecture, one Pierre L'Ermite (the pseudonym of clergyman and popular journalist Abbé Edmond Loutil) drove Boissarie's point home. Exhibiting the cured was a way, L'Ermite claimed, for the doctor to '[add] to the authority of his speech the authority of palpable facts'; and he duly returned the reader to the account of Boissarie's spectacle provided in the *Journal des Débats*:

> There were a dozen *miraculés*, calmly casting their serene gaze over a thousand onlookers, and protesting SOLELY BY THEIR PRESENCE against the theories and explanations put forward by M. Zola in his latest novel.[53]

Carefully stage-managing a confrontation between the pilgrim's body and Zola's text, several extracts of which Boissarie read aloud, the doctor allowed his audience to contemplate not only the force of divine intervention, but also the injustice of Zola's portrait, in what was, L'Ermite declared, a 'resounding, inarguable victory for the Blessed Virgin'.[54] In particular, Marie Lemarchand (Zola's Élise Rouquet) – the woman who had been hideously disfigured by her illness – provided the doctor with the opportunity for a veritable *coup de théâtre*. Boissarie effectively placed side by side the disgusting portrait of Élise that Zola sketched in his novel and the body of the real woman, her beauty fully restored.[55] His audience could not only contemplate the force of divine intervention (the respective images offering a before/after contrast), but also appreciate the sheer 'injustice' of Zola's account:

> Behold Zola's lupus!

> There may still be tears in her eyes. Upon hearing just now this description of her that she had never read: 'Her head like the muzzle of a dog, her tongue lapping up water', an unspeakable emotion came over her; she cannot conceal her distress. (61)

CONFÉRENCE DU DOCTEUR BOISSARIE
AU CERCLE CATHOLIQUE DU LUXEMBOURG

Figure 4.3   Presentation by Dr Boissarie at the Cercle du Luxembourg.
Illustration in *Le Pèlerin*, 9 December 1894; reproduced in Gustave Boissarie, *Lourdes: Les Guérisons*,
series 2 (Paris: Bonne Presse, 1911), p. 24. Collection of the author.

Here, in a moment of melodrama, Boissarie ventriloquises the reaction of the woman-victim who remains silent, but whose emotions are writ large on her body. Upon witnessing the evidence, 'the audience was moved to tears' (72).

With the triumphant exhibition of the *miraculée* before a public audience, Boissarie effectively shifted the terms of the debate to centre on Zola's moral shortcomings. For the scepticism of this novelist-cum-villain amounted, Boissarie implied, to an utterly pitiless form of contempt. At stake in the doctor's theatrical counter-attack, then, was not only the writer's slanderous manipulation of the truth, but also the ethics of the naturalist narrative itself. While the Catholic press circulated the Bureau's sensational case studies of miracle cures to a wide audience, in the form of what Kaufman calls '*counter-faits divers*' – or even '*foi divers*' – naturalist fiction's assault on the counter-factual relied on its own form of 'bad faith'.[56] For Zola's Catholic detractors, his version of events was nothing short of a conspiracy, and one which had a long afterlife. As late as 23 December 1904 – more than two years after Zola's death – Marie Lebranchu wrote to Boissarie claiming that the novelist had offered to give her and her labourer husband a new life in the Belgian countryside, in order to save his reputation![57]

Such paratextual, or meta-discursive, debates demonstrate just how sensational those tactics of persuasion deployed on either side could be. They also stage, in spectacular fashion, a rivalry of representations, of proofs and counter-proofs that came to rest on the body of the *miraculée*, its wounds and its scars. In fact, it was above all on the question of 'visible wounds' that these arguments turned. For Zola publicly claimed that only their healing was to be accepted as miraculous since cures of internal or nervous illnesses could always be explained away by suggestion. Boissarie returned to this subject in his lecture when he arrived at the case of Clémentine Trouvé (Sophie Couteau), whose caries of the heel bone offered Zola the example he had been waiting for. For three years, the young girl's foot had been swollen and deformed: 'you know', Boissarie reminded Zola, 'that when the doctor thrust his stylet into the fistula, he penetrated to the bone'.[58] After bathing in the water at Lourdes, all that remained was a faint scar, referred to as the Virgin Mary's 'signature'.[59] But Zola's scepticism was unshaken. Instead, he suspected in Clémentine's readiness to retell the story of her own cure 'a gradual distortion of the truth' (98). What if the wound was already in the process of healing? Had it been seen beforehand? Would he have to believe in the stories of the pilgrims themselves, and in the accounts of their private physicians, since it was impossible to examine each invalid on arrival?

In an interview with *Le Temps*, on 26 August 1892, Zola explained how he had presented Boissarie with a solution to these refutations:

> 'Well', I told Doctor Boissarie, 'you have a way to convince everybody of their recovery. You should have a separate room in your hospital for those with visible wounds. When a patient suffering from one of these conditions is presented to you, they should be examined by a panel. A report of the findings should be written up. You could even take an instant photograph of the wound. With these precautions, nobody could be in any doubt, were the cure to take place'.[60]

In one sense, Zola's vision of a miracle committee – the majority of which would be made up of free-thinkers – echoed Renan's view that, as Robert D. Priest puts it, 'any bona-fide miracle would today have to take place under laboratory conditions in front of a team of accredited observers'.[61] But in Zola's proposition the sole guarantee of objectivity, and therefore of the miracle's authenticity, is the medium of photography: it is the only form that can render believable the divine semiotics of the wound and the scar (the 'before' and 'after'). Boissarie returned in his lecture to Zola's call for an external commission and a photographic exhibition, only to dismiss it as a shocking affront to the pilgrims' sense of propriety and an opportunistic form of exploitation: 'photographs of arms, legs. . . the most secret wounds revealed, exhibited in our streets and shop windows. [. . .] The newspapers went into raptures over [such a] scheme'.[62] Not long after the publication of *Lourdes*, and the immediate furore of its reception, photography did, however, become an important part of the shrine's apologetics.[63]

For Zola, only the art of mechanical reproduction could eradicate the counterfeit of the miracle. But for Boissarie, it was precisely the reproducibility of the miracle – its capacity for replication – that was more persuasive. When Boissarie rejected Zola's call for the absolute evidence that photographs of wounds might bring, he defended himself by pointing towards the veritable proliferation of proofs (however imperfect) with which he had presented his sceptics: 'In matters arising from testimony, we cannot lay claim to absolute mathematical rigour. But by multiplying examples and gathering all the evidence together, we come close to certainty.'[64] Contrary to this Boissarian logic, however, it is precisely the multiplication of miracles that becomes the object of satire for Zola. Recalling the Saints' Lives that had so fascinated Angélique in *Le Rêve*, Zola reflected at the end of his visit to Lourdes: 'In the midst of [. . .] this shower of miracles, it feels like going back in time to the age of *La Légende dorée*' ('Mon voyage à Lourdes', 644). In the world of the Catholic shrine, the ubiquitous miracle that reigns supreme in Angélique's universe is clearly cast as an effect of the collective hysteria of the pilgrimage:

> People were on the look-out for miracles, waiting for them with the certainty that they would arrive – countless and dazzling. [...] The miracle became the very state of nature, something habitual, so abundant as to become banal. [...] And yet more astounding were the stories that did the rounds, the calm assertions, the expressions of absolute certainty, when a delirious patient cried out that she was cured. Yet another one! Yet another! (346–47)

The miasmic discourse of the miracle courses through the delirious crowd, each story of divine intervention producing in another invalid a sense of renewed hope. Zola thus holds the miracle to operate, first and foremost, metonymically – that is, as part of a chain, whereby 'each new miracle was a promise of the next one' (207). By dint of being tirelessly replicated, the miracle paradoxically becomes – to appropriate the discourse of photography in which the shrine deals – cliché. And it is, as we shall see now, on this principle of reproducibility that the 'commerce' of Lourdes rests in Zola's account, both as a style of fiction-making and as a thriving economy.

Serial Idealism

The particular collusion of consumption and superstition in the Lourdes economy acted as a magnet for the anxieties and attacks of secular Republicans during the 1890s; and Zola's novel played an important role in galvanising debates, in Kaufman's terms, about the 'proper relationship between faith and commerce'.[65] Although the sale of certain kinds of religious souvenirs and objects of devotion was condoned by the Grotto fathers, the burgeoning marketplace that attached itself to the sanctuary brought with it new forms of mass consumption, which sought, so it seemed, to exploit the impulses of the city's credulous crowds. In the notes Zola took during his visit, he remarked disparagingly upon various aspects of the shrine's commercial life: the shop directly attached to the grotto is not only aesthetically unpleasing, it is a manifest sign of simony (608); the proliferation of candles for sale gives rise to Zola's suspicions that 'the fathers do a roaring trade in wax'; and the distribution office for Lourdes water reveals the vulgar mechanisms of mass production that speak little of the commodity's purported spiritual properties. But it was the legion of souvenir shops, selling a variety of sacred kitsch, that offered the most conspicuous display of the city's commercial interests.[66]

On 27 August, Zola noted: 'We went shopping [. . .], and I had a look at all the items' (620). His exhaustive stocktaking of religious merchandise would be transposed towards the close of *Lourdes* when his trio of pilgrims – Pierre, Marie, and her father, M. de Guersaint – visit a souvenir shop before their departure:

> There were the Blessed Virgins, large and small, in zinc, wood, ivory, and especially plaster, some stark white, others tinted in bright colours, *endlessly replicating the description given by Bernadette* [. . .]. And there was another flood of religious items: over a hundred varieties of scapularies, thousands of plates [les milles clichés] of sacred images: fine engravings, chromolithographs in glaring colours, submerged beneath a swarm of small pictures, which were coloured, gilded, varnished, decorated with bouquets of flowers, and bordered with lace. [. . .] Lastly, there were the goods from Paris, rising above and submerging all the rest: pencil-holders, purses, cigar-holders, paperweights, paper-knives, even snuff-boxes; and innumerable other objects on which the Basilica, Grotto, and Blessed Virgin constantly reappeared, reproduced in every way, by every process possible. Napkinrings, egg cups, and wooden pipes were all jumbled together in a case reserved for items selling at fifty centimes apiece, *all emblazoned with the beaming apparition of Our Lady of Lourdes.* (430; my emphasis)

In one sense, this sprawling inventory crystallises for the reader a reflection that has run throughout the novel – namely, on the uneasy coexistence of religious veneration and consumer capitalism, of gratuitous miracle and banal copy. The pilgrims are frequently reminded that 'the miracle cure cannot be bought; on the contrary, worldly riches are more of a hindrance, in the eyes of God' (445). What can be acquired – and at bargain-basement prices – is a reproduction of the apparition, the imitation-sublime of kitsch art. For such merchandise claims for itself something of the beatific character of the icon it counterfeits.

Here, then, Zola gave a particular inflexion to the logic of mass consumption that he had already described in his novel of the Parisian department store *Au Bonheur des dames* (1883). With his captivating surveys of the shop floor, Zola had conjured up the magic and phantasmagoria of consumer culture, the store's 'troubling air of mystery' (*R-M*, vol. 3, 402), the sense of merchandise taking on a life of its own, of mannequins acquiring 'souls'. At such moments, Zola came close to the terms of Marx's account of commodity fetishism in *Capital* (1867), namely the latter's assertion that as soon as a product of labour appears as a commodity, 'it is changed into something transcendent' and enigmatic; abstracted from its physical properties and uses, it acquires a 'mystical character'.[67] For Marx, then, it is 'the social character of men's labour' that is 'stamped upon the product of that labour', and this endows the object with a 'fantastic' quality.[68] Moreover, it renders the commodity, Marx adds, 'a very queer thing, abounding in metaphysical subtleties and theological niceties' (42). In one respect, the religious knick-knacks Zola describes offer a pastiche of this function of fetishism: stamped or engraved with the apparition of the Virgin – the material sign of the transcendental – the *bondieuserie* seeks to bring about, in its own way, the apotheosis of the mundane.

Put differently, in staging the vulgar materialism of Lourdes, Zola is drawn to what he perceives as a paradox: the city of the miracle capitalises on the idealism it propagates, just as its idealism is replicated through capital. Yet, for Zola's detractor Maurice Barrès, *Lourdes* in fact supplied an altogether different vision of the shrine – one that affirmed, albeit in spite of itself, the idealism Zola sought to deconstruct:

> It is commonly said that the world is driven by material forces alone. This is the doctrinal thesis of those socialists belonging to the German school. Karl Marx asserts that, in a given environment, all transformation occurs solely under the influence of economic conditions. He takes no notice of ideas. Well! Lourdes, in our view, must be invoked, in this standard debate between the German and French schools, as the typical example of a development brought about by causes that have nothing to do with economics.[69]

To adapt the terms of Marxist materialism that Barrès invokes, Lourdes in fact represents a negation of the determining relationship between (economic) base and (cultural and religious) superstructure. For in the setting of this Pyrenean backwater, it is nothing other than the child Bernadette's voice – the generative 'Word' – that transforms so extraordinarily the city's material fortunes. The curious beauty of Zola's novel would, then, reside, for Barrès, in an important contradiction: in wondering at the *voyante*'s prodigious act of raising a city, 'putting up hotels, attracting tourist trains', Zola necessarily affirms an idealist model of causation that runs counter to his materialist 'temperament'.

Barrès is no doubt right to insist on Zola's wonderment before the diminutive Bernadette's creative powers, hers being the master-voice that inaugurated the story of Lourdes, and, in some sense, its real miracle (382). However, what prevails in the novel, of course, is an attention to the ways in which that idealist moment – 'the dream of a suffering child' (385) – is contained and reappropriated by the very material and economic forces it unleashed. Indeed, the shrine's readiness to capitalise on its visionary is symbolised most saliently by the souvenir shop owned by Bernadette's brother, 'Frère Soubirous', and in which he trades on the cult of his sibling, as well as their shared patronymic – 'the brother selling the blessed Virgin that the sister witnessed' (427). Zola thus seizes on the gaudy souvenir as a foil to the inimitable, singular sacred relic, and in turn, as an emblem of the economy of mimesis that underwrites the shrine's fortunes. The *pêle-mêle* of devotional objects for sale is intended to convey variety. What it in fact connotes, in Zola's account, is the obsessive reproduction of the same: the statuettes of the Virgin Mary 'endlessly reproducing the description given by Bernadette'; 'the Basilica, the Grotto, the Blessed Virgin, reproduced in every way, by every process possible' (430). Zola is clearly alert here to the irony at work in the promiscuous circulation of the 'immaculate' icon itself. If, for Peter Brooks, Zola's courtesan Nana is a 'kitsch Venus' of the Second Empire, the endless reiteration, and recitation, of the Virgin Mary's image provides, we might say, a religious counterpart to the writer's vision of sex in the age of mechanical reproduction.[70]

In formulating such critiques, Zola found himself on common ground with Catholic writers such as Bloy and Huysmans, for whom the city's lurid commercialism triggered a strong sense of outrage. In the last book completed before his death, *Les Foules de Lourdes* (1906), Huysmans set out to provide a rebuttal of Zola's rationalist demystification of the miracle as well as his portrait of corruption at the shrine. Though what this refutation did ultimately reinscribe – albeit with an opposing ideological agenda – was a comparable disdain for the aesthetics of sacred kitsch:

> street after street is filled [. . .] with harshly tinted chromos of Bernadette, dressed in a red skirt and blue apron, kneeling, candle in hand, at the Virgin's feet; with Lilliputian statues and medals that look like toy money, struck out of copper scrap; and all these objects grow better and bigger and larger as you get nearer the new town; [. . .] the chromos get bolder, making the Soubirous girl look like a maid; the medals increase in size and their metal changes [. . .]. [S]tationery knick-knacks [. . .] are joined by items from Paris [*l'article de Paris*], jewellery from the Palais-Royal, consecrated by an appended cross or a medal.[71]

With visceral contempt, Huysmans renders the replication of sacred iconography as a kind of cheapening or debasement: commodities transform, alchemically, but only through tricks of perspective. In his extended reflections on the aesthetics of the mass-reproduced bibelot, Huysmans reserves his greatest derision, as Zola had, for '*l'article de Paris*', or what was commonly known as '*l'art sulpicien*' – objects manufactured in the Saint-Sulpice *quartier* and subsequently imported to Lourdes.

In Zola's narrative, a sustained critique of this outsourcing of production is first focalised by M. de Guersaint. For this 'artist manqué' (62), such bibelots are a bitter reminder of his own failed attempt to 'modernise the religious prints trade' (430), having sunk his last funds into a floundering colour-printing business. In this respect, Zola's M. de Guersaint, with his industrialist backstory, appears as another iteration of Flaubert's Jacques Arnoux, whose transformation from art dealer to peddler of devotional objects – based in Saint-Sulpice – is one of many disillusioning trajectories in *L'Éducation sentimentale* (1869). As the proprietor of *L'Art industriel*, Arnoux's trade in paintings, replicas, figurines, engravings, and curios had always operated in the name of a broader vulgarisation, and commercialisation, of art: 'He sought to bring about the emancipation of the arts, the sublime on the cheap.'[72] Ultimately, his cynical venture as a purveyor of religious objects – 'a way of securing his salvation and making his fortune' – appears as the logical end-point of an attitude to art as both democratic, or accessible, and mystical.[73] In one sense, then, Zola brings us to reflect on the aesthetic hold exerted by the very kind of sham objects Arnoux flogs. Not only, Zola's failed capitalist complains, are those *bondieuseries* on display poorly manufactured, but they also capture the degeneration of a model of artisanship in which the worker would impart to each artefact something of himself: most importantly, his religious fervour. M. de Guersaint's nostalgia is ventriloquised by Pierre in turn, for whom the dissociation of manufacture and spirituality signals the broader demise of the Catholic faith:

> he pictured ancient objects of worship – images, silverwork, saints made from wood and stone – all possessing a wonderful power and beauty of expression. The fact was that in those distant times workmen had been true believers; they had given themselves to their work body and soul, imparting their entirely naïve emotions to their craft, just as M. de Guersaint said. But nowadays, [...] religious objects, the rosaries, the medals, and the statuettes were manufactured in bulk in the crowded neighbourhoods of Paris by merrymaking workmen who did not even practise their religion. No wonder, then, there were all these knick-knacks, these tawdry trinkets, pretty enough to make you weep with their silly, nauseating sentimentality! (431)

With the rise of mass reproduction, the fetishised *objet du culte* is no longer invested with the quality of labour that had determined its spiritual, as well as economic, value. On the contrary, it is precisely in the absence of the artisan's spiritual investment in his artwork that the *ersatz* emotions of the kitsch artefact are confected and deployed. For these 'tawdry' commodities produce only a counterfeit, mawkish sentimentality, designed to pull on the subject's heartstrings, to exploit the emotionally vulnerable – that is to say, women like Marie.[74] In this respect, the Lourdes bibelot betrays what Theodor Adorno holds to be 'the one enduring characteristic' of kitsch: 'it preys on fictitious feelings, thereby neutralizing real ones. Kitsch is a parody of catharsis'.[75] On Zola's terms, the lachrymose *objet du culte* – 'pretty enough to make you weep' – elicits only the shadow of genuine feeling.

Here, too, of course, Zola was taking aim at a strain of religious sentimentalism to which many of his ideological adversaries also objected. For Bloy, 'the sacrilegious inanity of the Sulpicians' had displaced a naïve sense of piety once germane to the common people.[76] Zola has Pierre and M. de Guersaint voice a similar critique from within the faith of Lourdes's chocolate-box aesthetics, likewise rooted in a nostalgic idealisation of lost sincerity. Indeed, for all the ethical quandaries Zola's account of the shrine clearly entails, it is no doubt telling that the imputed crime on which he insists with the most alacrity is an aesthetic one: bad taste. As the novel's aesthete, it is left to M. de Guersaint to denounce 'the pitiful ugliness' of the modern city and its architecture, 'the dire excesses of the Rosary Church and Basilica' (431). In his own notes, Zola derided the garishly ostentatious ornamentation of the basilica, filled with tapestries, offerings, wreaths and chandeliers: 'There is not one artist among the Fathers. Altogether tawdry. No faith in beauty; it is eye-wateringly ugly' ('Mon voyage à Lourdes', 610). Though in what can only be a moment of self-irony, the novelist also claimed to recognise in the Basilica's interior the very image of his own home: 'The place is filled with ornaments (not old ones) and it looks very much like the walls of my billiards room at Médan.' In fact, for all his excoriating critique of the trade in pious kitsch at Lourdes, Zola was, like his pilgrims, nevertheless tempted to buy. He returned home with a string of rosary beads to accompany the host box and image of the Virgin on his desk.[77]

In the novel itself, Pierre opts for a portrait of Bernadette; M. de Guersaint is seduced by an ivory penholder containing microscopic photographs; and Marie chooses for herself a figurine of Notre-Dame de Lourdes. Zola has his (male) pilgrims articulate a critique of the shrine's mass-reproduced idealism, its reiteration of the metaphysical *en série*. But faith requires its material supports; and Zola tracks, accordingly, a slippage between two valences of '*crédit*' in the novel: the one '*credo*', or belief, the other economic outlay. In describing the materialism that underpins the shrine's existence, Zola reiterates his conviction that 'a Bernadette would no longer be possible in Lourdes' (506), however much her vision is the

source of its economic prosperity. On the contrary, the shrine's commercial model actually depends, Zola implies, on Bernadette's absence.
In other words, the economy of mimesis that reaches its apotheosis in
the setting of the souvenir shop involves an endless recitation of
Bernadette's vision – a proliferation of copies – that rests on the systematic
occlusion of the original. For Zola, as we shall see now, the shrine's
sequestering of its founding visionary was nothing short of a scandal.

In Search of Bernadette

In 1866, eight years after Bernadette's visions of the Virgin Mary at the
Massabielle Grotto, a railway line was opened that made the Pyrenean
backwater newly accessible, while building works transformed the grotto
into the domain of the sanctuary, capable of accommodating a rising tide
of pilgrims. That same year, Bernadette left Lourdes to continue her
noviciate hundreds of miles away, at the Saint-Gildard convent in
Nevers, where she remained until her death in 1879. At best, Zola
surmised, the removal of Bernadette from Lourdes was intended to shield
her from exploitation. At worst – and this thesis prevails – it was a
conspiracy, which allowed the Church Fathers to master Bernadette's
narrative and turn the sacred grotto into a lucrative shrine.[78] 'It seems as
though somebody has jealously hidden her away', he told Henri Lasserre,
during his stay. 'And even today, the room she left is used as a log store;
she is absent from Lourdes' ('Mon voyage à Lourdes', 616).

In this sense, Bernadette is to be understood as another one of those
original sacrificial victims on which, Naomi Schor argues, Zola's crowd
fictions rest.[79] For the story of the Lourdes shrine, as Zola tells it, hinges
solely on those fateful words uttered by one 'nervous little girl', whose
visions 'have made millions rain from the sky and brought people in
droves' ('Mon voyage à Lourdes.', 615). And yet, Zola returns insistently
to the visionary's curious disappearance from the city she transformed, and
to what he takes to be the Church's systematic erasure of Bernadette,
including from the sanctuary's official iconography. In the novel, such
suspicions are voiced by Pierre's old friend, and fellow sceptic, Doctor
Chassaigne: 'You can look, [...] but you won't find a single image of
Bernadette – not an official one – in Lourdes. Her portrait is on sale, but
otherwise it is nowhere to be found, not in a single sanctuary... It's a
deliberate omission' (384). As we have seen, Zola has his clerical double
Pierre choose one of those simple portraits of Bernadette as his sole
souvenir from the pilgrimage – 'the only [photograph], apparently, that

was taken from life' – in a gesture of recuperation parallel to the author's.[80] For Zola declares on the very first line of his *Ébauche* his wish to ascribe to the young visionary an omnipresence: 'First, I should like to put Bernadette everywhere, to make her stand out across the whole novel.'[81]

Bernadette's life story and posthumous fate are retold in *Lourdes* via Zola's hero-priest, and it was this version of events that became the principal object of clerical critique in the wake of the novel's publication. Not only did respondents rush to defend the clergy's treatment of Bernadette in the years that followed the apparitions, they also attacked Zola's troubling portrait of Bernadette as an *hallucinée*.[82] Key to these debates was the question of whether or not Bernadette's visions were genuine encounters with the divine, or, as Zola was inclined to believe and as he implied in the novel, the result of suggestion. The author thus found himself embroiled in a series of heated exchanges about the veracity, and reliability, of clerical accounts. On both sides, administrative documents were cited, witness testimonies were harnessed. Zola remained convinced that all the evidence was there for the historian (perhaps himself, he wondered) to write the definitive version of Bernadette's biography: 'I am increasingly convinced that a history of Bernadette, retold by a mind like mine – properly documented – would be the most interesting thing in the world. But a history, not a novel' ('Mon voyage à Lourdes', 601). Though Zola would never write Bernadette's life story – or indeed hagiography – this wish demonstrates just how he found himself implicated, as a historian rather than a novelist, in the competing claims over the authenticity of the shrine's founding narrative.

No doubt what intrigued Zola most about Bernadette's story was the possibility of determining the origins of her apparitions. Zola refused to accept that these emerged *ex nihilo*, instead casting them as a form of imitation – albeit unconscious. 'Certainly, she wasn't lying; she had had her vision and had heard voices like Joan of Arc.'[83] Much of the controversy that his account generated thus related to the various conjectures he makes in the novel about the kind of stories, language, and images to which Bernadette might have been exposed beforehand:

> Where was it, then, that Bernadette had seen this Blessed Virgin, so traditional in her simplistic style, unadorned by a single jewel, having but the primitive grace of a childlike people? Or in what picture book belonging to her foster mother's brother, the good priest, who read such attractive stories? In what statuette, in what painting, or stained-glass window of the colourful, gilded church where she had grown up? Above all, those golden roses on her bare feet, that delightfully adoring imagination, that pious

blossoming of womanly flesh—what chivalric romance did these come from, what story told during catechism by Abbé Ader? From what unconscious dream indulged under the shady foliage of Bartrès and accompanied by the obsessive repetition of the Hail Mary?[84]

Such conjectures and hypotheses return as an insistent refrain throughout the novel, as Zola attempts to establish what Sophie Ménard calls 'the psychogenesis' of Bernadette's vision.[85] This means fixing the apparition as a reproduction, and thereby proving that Bernadette had the opportunity to encounter the image of the Virgin Mary that she will subsequently describe, whether that be in official Catholic iconography, via secular literary (romantic) texts, or oral storytelling. The (naturalist) biographer's aim must be to reconstruct 'the milieu Bernadette was immersed in' ('Mon voyage à Lourdes', 618), so as to reroot her visions in the representations of a collective religious, cultural, and mystical imaginary. In this respect, Bernadette clearly rehearses the fate of Zola's Angélique in *Le Rêve*, whose cloistered environment compounds, as we saw in Chapter 3, her pathological desire to repeat in life the rites of hagiographical text and image.[86] Indeed, in an echo of that novel's provocative title, Zola has Bernadette confined in the above passage to a semi-conscious state of receptivity, her obsessive recitation of the Hail Mary – 'la Salutation *angélique*' – confirming her predisposition to repetition.

The point of such lengthy speculations on Zola's part was, as Jean-Louis Cabanès argues, to suggest that Bernadette's vision must have been 'predetermined by what she had already seen [*par du déjà-vu*]'.[87] And, we might add, by the 'déjà-entendu', for perhaps the most important aspect of Bernadette's apparitions were the precise terms in which the Virgin Mary had declared her identity: 'I am the Immaculate Conception' (in Bernadette's native patois, '*Que soy era Immaculada Councepciou*'). The very implausibility of the young, barely literate peasant speaking the language of the Papal decree – the dogma had been promulgated by Pope Pius IX only four years earlier – confirmed for many (Boissarie included) that the apparitions were a manifestation of divine grace:

> there was nothing new here except for that extraordinary declaration: 'I am the Immaculate Conception' [...]. As for the other words, it was possible that Bernadette had heard them and stored them in an unconscious corner of her memory. But where could that declaration have come from [...]?[88]

While the statement seemed to confirm the cult of the Immaculate Conception that had taken hold over the first half of the century, it also rendered Bernadette's testimony all the more persuasive, effectively distinguishing these apparitions, as Harris suggests, 'from similar occurrences across the Pyrenees in previous decades and centuries'.[89] In its very orthodoxy, the language Bernadette reported appeared precisely unorthodox, and so more credible as a divine apparition. Defenders of Lourdes thus tended to hitch their claims to authenticity both to the peasant's unwitting ventriloquism of Papal language and to the remarkable originality of the Virgin Mary's appearance. In the words of the then Bishop of Tarbes, Monseigneur Laurence: '[Bernadette] saw things she had never seen before, heard a language she had never heard before, and which she could recall without understanding its meaning.'[90] Bernadette had insisted on the apparition's remarkable youth and diminutive stature (she was, she claimed, as small as herself); and she described her wearing a blue sash, and a yellow rose on each foot. These details distinguished Bernadette's Virgin from orthodox Marian iconography – if not from the creatures of Pyrenean folklore and fairy tale.[91] As such, they served to rule out suggestions that the visions were derivative imitations. According to Monseigneur Ricard, '[i]t is quite obvious that Bernadette's mind and memory could not possibly have been presented with the image or the echo of what she saw and heard at the Grotto.'[92] But Zola, of course, remained unconvinced.

In the notes Zola took during his visit to Lourdes, he recounted an anecdote related to him by Abbé Pommyan, who was present at the meeting between Bernadette and the Lyonnais sculptor Joseph Fabisch, tasked with erecting a statue of Notre-Dame de Lourdes in the Grotto. Fabisch sought to elicit Bernadette's confirmation of various details concerning the Virgin's appearance, and Bernadette is said to have corrected aspects of Fabisch's model: the colour of her sash, the position of her veil, and so on. According to Pommyan, 'the sculptor, weeping (a believer), said: "She cannot be making this up, she must have seen; [her vision] is in keeping with *tradition* and its rules of art"' ('Mon voyage à Lourdes', 629; original emphasis). For Zola, such an acknowledgement was proof enough to the contrary that Bernadette's vision was nothing more than the reproduction of an aesthetic stereotype:

> For me, it is precisely because it is in keeping with tradition that I suspect Bernadette of having seen only the image of the Virgin that haunted her. It is the formation of this image in her that needs to be studied, and *its sources that need to be found*. ('Mon voyage à Lourdes', 629; my emphasis)

In a manoeuvre typical of Zola's documentation at Lourdes, a testimony that is intended as proof becomes grist to the sceptic's mill. What this reported anecdote fails to acknowledge, however, is the *décalage* between

Bernadette's vision and its reproduction. For Fabisch was purported to have taken certain liberties with her account, 'transform[ing] her words into the conventional idiom of nineteenth-century academic art', in particular by increasing both the Virgin's size and age.[93] Moreover, Bernadette is said to have dismissed Fabisch's statue (now the standard representation of Notre-Dame de Lourdes) as inaccurate: 'It's quite beautiful, but it is not "her."'[94]

In fact, Fabisch's apparent failure to capture the apparition's likeness is interpreted by the shrine's defenders as yet further confirmation of the authenticity of Bernadette's account – further proof, that is, that her vision did not proceed from imitation. Rather, as Boissarie claimed, it represented the extraordinary revelation of an idea that has no precedent:

> the apparitions were neither an illusion of her senses, nor the result of some mental disturbance. Putting side by side, on the one hand, the faculties of this most ignorant and simple-minded child, and on the other, *the vision of this ideal Virgin – a creation of the sort never seen before*, that the great minds of our finest artists had not foreseen and have struggled to reproduce – we will show just how much distance lies between the child's intelligence and her revelations.[95]

In his own refutation of Zola's novel, *La Vraie Bernadette de Lourdes* (1894), Monseigneur Ricard duly cited Boissarie's argument, wondering: 'How could the mind of this child have taken flight like that, soaring high to contemplate such a pure ideal, an ideal inaccessible to the most eminent and consummate of artists?'[96] By this reckoning, it is the very irreproducibility of Bernadette's vision that guarantees its authenticity; it is inimitable or *inédit*. Zola's response to this prevailing logic was, of course, to establish the apparition as a copy, to reinsert the apparition into the order of mimesis. If Zola entertained the idea of writing Bernadette's biography, it would surely read as a detective narrative. For its purpose was to locate the original 'suggestive' image that must, he believed, have determined Bernadette's ideation.

Bad Faith

As Zola pursued his enquiries about the visionary's childhood, his suspicions came to fall on the local priest in the village of Bartrès, Abbé Ader, believing him to have been Bernadette's spiritual guide. Zola was alerted to the priest's possible influence on Bernadette by Jean Barbet, a schoolteacher in Bartrès at the time of the apparitions and author of the *Guide de*

Lourdes et de la Grotte (1892). Zola met Barbet during his visit to Lourdes and gleaned important details about village life that seemed to confirm his hypotheses about Bernadette's early exposure to formative texts and images, both biblical and fantastical. But it was Barbet's *Guide de Lourdes* that signalled the potential importance of the parish vicar. In particular, Zola seized upon Barbet's admission that Abbé Ader had harboured a certain fascination with Bernadette. For she is said to have reminded him of the child visionaries of La Salette, Mélanie Calvet and Maximin Giraud, who claimed to have been visited by the Virgin while they tended livestock on the outskirts of their Alpine commune in September 1846.[97] 'I don't know what comes over me', Ader is said to have admitted, 'but every time I encounter this child, I feel as though I am seeing the little shepherds of La Salette'.[98] Barbet's account of the priest's fixation seemed to provide Zola with a way of predetermining the apparitions.[99] 'I think we need to look to Bartrès in order to find a full explanation. If a priest influenced her in some way', Zola noted, 'it is this Abbé Ader, who said: "She reminds me of the children of La Salette." Did he speak to her about those children? Did he have a significant influence over her?' ('Mon voyage à Lourdes', 627). By this logic, Bernadette's fate is sealed by the resemblance she bears to the young shepherdess Mélanie – the double with whom, Zola suspects, she is invited to identify.

Zola's visit to Bartrès on 28 August provided, however, no further leads: residents were reticent, and much of the old church had been destroyed. The three paintings that remained provided no obvious connection with the character of Bernadette's visions. Still, emboldened by Barbet's account, Zola pressed on with his hypothesis regardless, suggesting in his novel that Abbé Ader had planted the story Bernadette would go on to reproduce: 'And one day, after catechism, or even during the evening vigil, had he not told the wonderful story [. . .] of the Lady in the dazzling dress [. . .]?' (121). Such provocations were met with stringent denials – including Barbet's own. Monseigneur Ricard published a letter to this effect (dated 2 June) from the former teacher in his own refutation, *La Vraie Bernadette*. Here, Barbet denied that the priest had made known his musings on Bernadette's character, or likeness:

> I must speak out in the interests of the truth, and I hereby confirm that Abbé Ader, who was the epitome of prudence and discretion, never spoke of this matter, neither to Bernadette [. . .] nor to anybody in the community. Similarly, he never alluded to Bernadette, nor to the children of La Salette in his teachings, which I have heard in their entirety.[100]

Dismissing Barbet's denial in turn as an act of self-protection, Zola cited the teacher's references to Ader in his *Guide de Lourdes* and reiterated his conviction that a wealth of evidence awaits discovery: 'a wholly comprehensive file exists, made up of conclusive documents and private letters', with which an impartial historian might construct the definitive narrative of Bernadette's life.[101] Meanwhile, the municipal council of Bartrès wrote an open letter 'in the name of truth, which has been distorted most audaciously', in which they refuted Zola's portrait of village life, and of their church as a hotbed of phantasmagoria – 'a place where the child's pious imagination is supposed to have been excited by the sight of altars, sumptuously dressed in rich gilding, and blue-eyed virgins with scarlet lips'.[102] Zola received an altered version of this letter on 4 August, which he reproduced in full, along with his own response, in *Le Figaro* on 31 August. Here, Zola directed the focus away from the legitimacy of his own suppositions. In reality, he had distorted aspects of Barbet's account, and the notes he had taken betrayed a slippage on certain key details.[103] Instead, he dwelt on the extraordinariness of this intervention in the national press by a group of rural *fonctionnaires*, who were, he implied, in the pockets of the Pères de la Grotte. For it was clearly in the interests of the latter to deny the facts Zola had brought to light about Bernadette's childhood, and which, he insisted, cast doubt on 'the whole classic story of the visionary'.

On the matter of the local priest's role in Bernadette's visions, Zola stuck to his guns. Abbé Ader's absence from accounts of Bernadette's childhood, Lasserre's included, was for Zola both conspicuous and suggestive: 'there is certainly a gap here that allows for all kinds of assumptions'.[104] This oversight signalled a contrived censorship of the priest's mediating role, and was enough to legitimate the conjectures he had made: 'How can it be that there was an Abbé Ader in Bartrès who was Bernadette's first spiritual guide, who taught her catechism, who predicted her visions – and not a single historian of Bernadette's life has mentioned him!' In essence, what Zola sought to establish was the certainty of doubt: the conviction, that is, that an alternative narrative would soon displace the sanctioned one. Emboldened, Zola went on to mount a direct attack on Lasserre's history, *Notre-Dame de Lourdes*, which, although superior to other accounts of the shrine, was nevertheless written 'in complete disdain of the administrative archives'. Zola's accusation triggered the first of several open letters from Lasserre, published in different newspapers, in which he mounted both a defence of his own procedures and a counter-attack.[105]

On 28 September 1894, Lasserre insisted he had gone to the greatest lengths to ensure that he availed himself of all available evidence, sifting meticulously through the archives of the Lourdes town hall, and visiting in person the prefecture of Tarbes, and the Court of Appeal at Pau... Lasserre duly reproduced the declaration he had made in that very work to pursue the truth with impartiality, and to lay open his own practices and sources – a declaration that he had couched in the very language of the naturalist writer: 'As long as the witnesses are still alive, *I want to tell all*, to give their names and addresses, so that it might be possible to question them and repeat the investigation I conducted, in order to verify my own work.'[106] While Lasserre underscored his credentials as an independent and rigorous historian, he accused Zola of abusing the creative right of the novelist, and of fabricating 'a fanciful tale about Bernadette's early years' (48), based entirely on loose speculation and spurious witnesses. According to Lasserre, what Zola had produced, then, was not so much a work of creative fiction as an object of deliberate falsification:

> This is not a work of imagination, but a work of false testimony. Only the most minute proportions of truth are to be found inside—*the bare minimum needed by counterfeiters* to plate their copper or lead coins and then pass them off as money to countless gullible individuals, who are incapable of seeing through appearances [. . .]. This great volume against faith is, more to the point, without any good faith. (51; emphasis added)

All that remains in Zola's novel is a residual truth, a trace of veracity that allows the novelist-counterfeiter to transform base metal into accepted currency. In Lasserre's proto-Gidean account of mimetic fiction as counterfeit, credulity has, paradoxically, become the domain of the religious sceptic, who is unable to distinguish authentic from fake.

No doubt, Lasserre's accusations of bad faith rested on his personal testimonies. Lasserre had guided Zola through the sites of Bernadette's childhood, and apparently trusted in his goodwill.[107] The resulting novel, however, was deemed a distortion of these experiences. Describing Zola's reaction to Bernadette's birthplace, which Lasserre took him to visit, he insisted that the novelist had been moved to the point of tears – even belief: 'Two tears welled up in your eyes, normally so dry and impenetrable... [. . .] I had glimpsed the man of matter turning desperately toward the immaterial, and the leader of realism confused, faltering before reality.'[108] Though Lasserre did not manage to 'convert' the naturalist, Zola's dogged scepticism was, he insisted, in fact an act of self-deception and denial. In an interview Zola gave to *L'Écho de Paris*, partly in response to Lasserre's letter, he denied his critic's version of events, insisting that he would never have shed tears so easily![109] Zola went on to defend himself against those who sought to stir controversy by decrying his purported anti-clericalism: 'Indeed, there is no hurtful criticism in my book, no Voltairean jibe against religion; *on the contrary, I have idealised Bernadette*, who was really just a poor simpleton' (emphasis added). Predictably, however, Zola's appeal to idealisation as a line of defence only provided Lasserre with further ammunition:

> Shall I be so cruel as to point out to M. Zola that it is rather surprising to see him confess to flouting not just the universal laws of truthfulness that govern history, but also the specific rule of Realism, over which he presides as Pontiff—the rule dictating that one reject the *ideal* and paint things only as they *really* are.[110]

Zola's apparent concession to Catholic sensitivities was thus reframed as a betrayal of the very aesthetic principles he preached: what business could the arch anti-idealist have with the language and processes of his adversaries? Such inconsistencies offered proof, if any were needed, of the writer's readiness to go against his word.

Lasserre was by no means alone in harnessing the language of aesthetics – crucially, the terms of plausibility, realism, and faithfulness – to denounce Zola's intervention in matters of religious doctrine and practice. 'Although he presents himself as someone who simply records impressions of real life', wrote one Abbé Joseph Crestey in his extended response to *Lourdes*, 'he has lapsed into pure fantasy'.[111] For Monseigneur Ricard, too, Zola's disputation of the apparitions as acts of divine intervention, and his search for a natural cause that could explain them, required the embellishment of an overactive mind: 'you cloak this explanation in all the colours that your brilliant imagination can give to the notions it dreams up'.[112] So, in a direct retaliation against Zola's attempts to reroot Bernadette's visions in the conditions of her imaginative life – to redescribe her apparitions as a 'beautiful story' – Catholic detractors stigmatised the novelist's own imagination as a source of prejudicial falsification, prone to what we would now call 'confirmation bias'. In Abbé Crestey's words, 'his mental vision is formed solely through the lens of his biases, perhaps embellishing everything from his perspective, but in reality, distorting and diminishing everything'.[113]

The charge that Zola's naturalist fiction repeatedly broke its own laws of mimesis was, as we saw in Chapter 1, a commonplace trope of antinaturalist critique, from Jules Lemaître and Remy de Gourmont to Ferdinand Brunetière. Attempting to deconstruct the author's own aesthetic mode,

Zola's detractors claimed to identify in his prose precisely those anti-mimetic impulses he professed to be operating against. The striking redeployment of such manoeuvres in refutations of *Lourdes* might tell us much about the ideological continuum of antinaturalist criticism and conservative Catholicism in general.[114] Certainly, the interventions of these largely minor theological figures (Lasserre aside) crystallise the hardening of antinaturalist discourse into a set of recognisable and ready clichés that could be harnessed by a wide range of ideological adversaries. If tackling Zola as a would-be truth-teller – even whistleblower – meant turning to literary criticism, to matters of style and method, this was no doubt a sign of how the Lourdes debates rested on the confrontation of rival fictions far more than rival truths.

The Art of Suspicion

Determining the origins of the Lourdes apparitions mattered to Zola, precisely because his demolition of clerical doxa – and of the miracle narrative altogether – depended on it: to uncover the source of Bernadette's visions would be to make plausible the otherwise strictly implausible. Put differently, the mode of the naturalist narrative is etiological; it attempts to re-establish the connection between cause and effect that the miracle, as an act of divine intervention, appears to break. 'Operating in the same way as medicine, naturalist texts like Zola's', Robert Ziegler suggests, 'work to demystify the wonders of Lourdes, intending a transformation of incredible events into the nothingness of their explanation'.[115] This, then, is the therapeutics proper to the naturalist novel-as-positivist novel: its own speculative counter-narratives seek to sow doubt, to turn belief into disbelief.

In the case of Bernadette's apparitions, Zola must try to prove, as we have seen, that these were neither inimitable nor original, but rather beholden to a strict logic of mimesis. To redeploy the language of the shrine's commercial life, the apparition must always already be a 'souvenir'. So too, of course, must the novel's long-awaited miracle – Marie's cure from paralysis – ultimately emerge as a memory, insofar as it replicates Doctor Beauclair's original prediction: 'Beauclair had said all of that beforehand, using almost the very same words and images' (357). The 'event' of the miracle is thus swallowed up by its prophesy, as the doctor's words – repressed by Pierre, and yet 'stored away, as if against his will' – now impose themselves on his consciousness, reverberating in his ears, 'like a trumpet blast', in what is figured as a moment of awakening (348). And so it is, as

Jacques Noiray observes, that in a profoundly ironic twist, 'it is the miracle itself that ruins, for Pierre, any possibility of believing in the miracle'.[116] The only genuine cure the novel contains, Noiray qualifies, is the priest's own – and this, we might add, in making his mind up, once and for all, about the need for an alternative form of idealism, shorn of metaphysical trappings and allied with reason.[117] One that, as we shall see in Chapter 5, Zola would make the bedrock of his final series of utopian fiction, *Les Quatre Évangiles*.

What has emerged across this chapter is Zola's fixation on imitation as the shrine's master trope. From souvenir shop to grotto, via the compulsive litanies of the crowds, he renders, and amplifies, the mimetic operations of Catholic belief as a form of hysteria. Indeed, to co-opt the terms that Christopher Prendergast applies to Gérard de Nerval's late romantic fiction, we might venture that Zola determines in the workings of Lourdes a comparable 'madness of mimesis'.[118] In the case of Nerval's novella *Sylvie* (1853), the mimesis internal to the mind of the narrator involves 'a quest for an elusive point of reference, a lost (and unfindable) Referent' – that is, a solution to the enigma of Adrienne's identity. And yet, the text remains 'haunted by the signs of likenesses, resemblances, simulacra', unable to find a 'stable anchorage'.[119] In Zola's *Lourdes*, the principal hermeneutic quest is for the 'real' Bernadette, and with her, a solution to the mystery of the apparitions' point of origin. But just as the novel finds its own conjectures about that origin stalling as speculation, so too does Bernadette find herself inserted into a further, imagined chain of representation – triangulated, like Nerval's heroine doubles (Sylvie and Adrienne), with two other fictional characters through a curious pattern of likenesses. The first is Marie, whose cure at the shrine replicates, as Kathleen Ann Comfort points out, 'the very images Bernadette evoked in her accounts of the Marian apparitions she had witnessed'.[120] The second is Appoline, a salesgirl at the shop where Pierre, Marie, and M. de Guersaint buy their mementoes. This pretty young woman of high spirits, but notoriously loose morals, is found by Pierre to bear an uncanny physical resemblance to Bernadette: 'What a strange likeness, what an unexpected reincarnation thirty years on!' (434). When Pierre compares the *vendeuse* to the portrait of Bernadette in his hand, Appoline's proud aunt anticipates his reaction: 'Appoline is the spitting image of Bernadette.' As the overdetermined image of 'the new Lourdes' and its brazen sexual marketplace, Appoline at once literalises the (symbolic) prostitution of Bernadette's vision, and she allows Zola to replicate once more the prevailing confusion in his narrative over original and fake.

Unlike Nerval, of course, Zola leaves the reader in little doubt as to which woman is which. What he does cultivate, though, in tracking the shifting consciousness of his priest-double, is an almost perpetual slippage in and out of a dream state. Overcome by the sheer volume of miraculous stories Pierre hears on the train to Lourdes, 'he no longer knew where the real and the possible ended, unable, amidst this abundance of astonishing events, to tell them apart, to explain some and reject the others' (113). At such moments, Zola's narrative tends to espouse Pierre's cognitive equivocation – unable, as he is, to determine the dividing line between real and counterfeit, miraculous and pseudo-miraculous. Rhetorically at least, this is an epistemological drama that the novel ultimately insists on resolving; with Marie's 'cure' comes Pierre's disenchantment, as he at last acquires 'the courage of truth' (492). The lucid priest now adopts the voice of common sense, thereby bringing an end to the 'contagious whirlwind of madness' (214) that the narrative describes. In miniature, Pierre's capitulation to reason anticipates Freud's call, in *The Future of an Illusion* (1927), to renounce the 'infantilism' of faith, with its 'wishful illusions', in favour of an *'education to reality'*.[121] Certainly, Pierre evinces a trust in reason that is coded as the attainment of maturity; and this trajectory is folded into the overarching ambition for mankind that he – and the novel itself – sets out: 'to subject humanity to a brutal amputation, to deprive it of its dream, to forcibly remove the wonder that it requires, just as much as bread, for its sustenance' (493). At the close, Pierre-Zola appears as another 'master of suspicion', to co-opt Paul Ricoeur's epithet for Freud, Nietzsche, and Marx: his now declared imperative to unmask 'the illusions and lies of consciousness'.[122]

In putting a stop to Pierre's oscillation between belief and scepticism, the novel comes to articulate outright the agenda of demystification about which it has become – with a full sense of paradox – evangelical. Reiterating the fundamental principles of Zola's 'experimental' method, Pierre asserts his confidence that the unknown, the mysterious, the miraculous must ultimately be both knowable and rational – his guiding maxim: 'There is certainly a natural explanation which escapes me' (492). And yet, it arguably remains a vital contradiction of Pierre's, and therefore the novel's, categorical embrace of reason that this must itself be posited as a conjecture, even an act of faith. To be sure, this appeal to future knowledge is one to which Zola cleaves, as we have seen, in his own endeavour to destabilise the master-narrative on which the Catholic shrine rests. For in pointing to the conspicuous 'lacuna' in Lasserre's history of Lourdes, the novelist necessarily relied – as his adversaries readily objected – on speculation and counter-hypotheses in order to create a rival version of events, one which promised to be validated by the further disclosure of evidence it announced. To frame the miracle, as Zola does, as a form of conspiracy is to suppose a set of facts awaiting discovery, but which are currently concealed by a network of existing powers; and it is, in no small part, the task of the novelist to make this state of affairs known. Indeed, it is surely this suspicion of a prevailing conspiracy around the origins of Bernadette's visions that ties the Lourdes scandal most closely to Zola's subsequent intervention in the Dreyfus case, and those events that would, four years hence, have turned into the 'Affair' of the century.[123] The stakes of Zola's engagement on behalf of Dreyfus will be the subject of Chapter 5. But what *Lourdes*, and its polemical fall-out, already makes visible to us is just how the attempt to expose a cover-up would require, in Zola's case, another kind of fiction-making – an appeal to the imagination, to a strength of conviction, even sheer intuition, about where the truth lies.

Their brazen ideological bias aside, the repudiations of Zola's fiction of the shrine tell us much about the ways in which the naturalist novel finds itself caught up in those contradictions it seeks to diagnose. For if Zola's narrative boldly rehearses, via Pierre's internal trajectory, the ultimate victory of reason, and a renewed faith in science, the afterlife of the novel itself entails a seemingly interminable circulation of proofs and counter-proofs. No doubt documentary evidence remains, for Zola, an ideal, or as Guillaume McNeil Arteau puts it, a vital 'anchor for his own process of interpretation', promising to offer a definitive conclusion to the narrative's otherwise unsettled *enquête*.[124] And yet, in reaching something of an impasse, Zola is also obliged to resolve his drama of doubt by recourse – as his adversaries enjoyed pointing out – to the terms of his rivals. Just as Zola's reconstruction of Bernadette's story borrows from the genre of the *conte bleu*, so too does the novelist derive from Christology the means of articulating the secular idealism his hero intuits: 'A new religion!' (493).

Ultimately, in its encounter with the miracle, and with religious faith altogether, naturalist fiction finds itself curiously drawn to the aesthetic forms these phenomena take. Rather than seek to arrest the delirious processes of mimetic imitation that he identifies at the shrine, Zola replicates and amplifies them, in the iterative texture of his own lyrical prose, his litanies of merchandise, as well as in the further fakes he plants in his narrative. Even Zola's final corrective – the resurgence of Beauclair's original diagnosis that provokes Pierre's epiphanic loss of faith – acquires the same properties as the miracle narratives it refutes. It exhibits, as Marquer claims, 'the same unfathomable power of suggestive speech'.[125]

Certainly, such formal symmetry must seem suspect to the reader wishing to tell apart belief from scepticism, miracle from its pastiche. Idealism, Zola reminds us again and again, is necessarily a form of determinism: it cannot be anything but a self-fulfilling expression, as we saw with Angélique in Chapter 3, of the 'déjà-vu'. Less well-acknowledged was just how fundamental the power of suggestion, or foreshadowing, was to the workings of Zola's own fiction, whereby the logical trajectory of the narrative is, so often, seen in advance. In *Lourdes*, suggestion offers Zola a crucial way out of the strictures of belief, just as it also works to entrap the reader in another kind of promissory anticipation. Not the least ironic consequence of this, we might say, is that the cure comes to look something like the symptom. In the end, what Zola gives us in *Lourdes* is a 'false copy' – one which confronts the city of miracles with a *fiction truquée* to rival its own.

Notes

1 'Ce que disent les journaux', *La Croix*, 28 August 1892, p. 1.
2 Marie Lapière discusses the reaction of the press to Zola's visit to Lourdes in *Le Langage des sources dans 'Les Trois Villes' d'Émile Zola: la dialectique de la foi et de la raison* (Paris: Honoré Champion, 2018), pp. 153–55.
3 Albert Millaud, 'Les étapes d'une conversion', *Le Figaro*, 28 August 1892, p. 1.
4 Marie-François Lhomme (pseudonym F. Lefranc), *La Comédie d'aujourd'hui: le Pèlerin de Lourdes* ([Paris?]: A. Gaignault, 1894), p. 1.
5 Interview in *Le Gaulois*, 26 August 1892, pp. 1–2 (p. 2). Zola concludes by postponing judgement: 'As for the supernatural, I will speak about that later. What I can tell you right now is that I have seen things here that are *beyond nature [extra-naturelles]*' (original emphasis).
6 Léon Bloy, *Exégèse des lieux communs* (Paris: Mercure de France, 1902), p. 53.
7 See Zola's speech at the banquet of the Association générale des étudiants, 18 May 1893; *OC*, vol. 15, 649–54 (p. 652).
8 John 20: 25.
9 Zola, *Lourdes. Œuvres complètes*, ed. Bertrand Marquer (Paris: Classiques Garnier, 2015), p. 198. Subsequent references to this volume will appear in the body of the text. In *Lourdes*, the Bishop of Tarbes, Monseigneur Laurence, is likened to Saint Thomas for his initial reluctance to issue a decree accepting the miracles associated with Bernadette's visions (213).
10 Ruth Harris, *Lourdes: Body and Spirit in the Secular Age* (London: Viking, 1999), pp. 331–42; Suzanne K. Kaufman's *Consuming Visions: Mass Culture and the Lourdes Shrine* (Ithaca, NY and London: Cornell University Press, 2005), pp. 74–81, 169–82.
11 Harris, *Lourdes*, p. 331.

12 For a discussion of works that took issue with Zola's novel of the Shrine, see my article: 'The Affair Before the Affair: Zola, Dreyfus and the Lourdes Scandal', *French History*, 35:3 (2021), 375–97. I draw on arguments from that article in this chapter, with the kind permission of the editors.

13 See Silvia Disegni, '*Lourdes* à l'Index: le rapport de la censure pontificale', *Les Cahiers naturalistes*, 83 (2009), 263–87.

14 'À l'Index', *Le Matin*, 22 September 1894, p. 1.

15 See Alain Pagès, *Émile Zola, un intellectuel dans l'Affaire Dreyfus: histoire de 'J'accuse'* (Paris: Séguier, 1991), p. 289, fn 26.

16 Harris, *Lourdes*, p. 10.

17 Colette Becker, '"Ah! quel beau rêve qui a remué tout un monde"... La "belle histoire" de Bernadette', *Les Cahiers naturalistes*, 73 (1999), 247–54 (p. 248).

18 Marquer, 'Introduction', *Lourdes*, p. 22.

19 Monseigneur Ricard opens his *La Vraie Bernadette de Lourdes: lettres à M. Zola* (Paris: E. Dentu, 1894) by recalling his previous correspondence with Zola upon the publication of *Le Rêve*, in which he had detailed the novelist's liturgical imprecisions.

20 Elizabeth Emery, *Romancing the Cathedral: Gothic Architecture in Fin-de-Siècle French Culture* (New York: State University of New York Press, 2001), p. 46.

21 Bibliothèque Méjanes, Aix-en-Provence, MS 1456, fol. 208.

22 Joris-Karl Huysmans, *Là-bas* (Paris: Garnier-Flammarion, 1978), pp. 36, 33.

23 See Huysmans's letter to Arij Prins, 24 January 1892: 'I no longer see Zola, exasperated as he was by *Là-Bas*'. *Lettres inédites à Arij Prins, 1885–1907*, ed. Louis Gillet (Geneva: Droz, 1977), pp. 234–36 (p. 235).

24 Jules Huret, *Enquête sur l'évolution littéraire*. Preface by Daniel Grojnowski (Paris: José Corti, 1999), p. 193.

25 Zola had first turned his attention to the city some twenty years earlier. In 1872, he published a sequence of articles in *La Cloche*, expressing his contempt for the 'miracle show' mounted at Lourdes, which was orchestrated, he said, by right-wing politicians seeking a new alliance of altar and throne.

26 Zola, '*Lourdes-Rome-Paris*: une conversation avec M. Émile Zola', *Le Matin*, 5 October 1892, p. 1.

27 *Lourdes*, 106. This particular observation is made by Sophie Guermès in *La Religion de Zola: naturalisme et déchristianisation* (Paris: Honoré Champion, 2006), p. 366, and Jean-Louis Cabanès in 'L'enfance de Bernadette: effets de voix', *Les Cahiers naturalistes*, 72 (1998), 211–23 (p. 219).

28 Gaston Deschamps, 'La Vie littéraire: *Lourdes*, par Émile Zola', *Le Temps*, 5 August 1894, p. 2.

29 See Zola's interview with the Symbolist writer Charles Morice, 'Zola et l'inconnu', *Le Journal*, 20 August 1894, p. 2.

30 Henri Rochefort, 'Un Assommoir catholique', *L'Intransigeant*, 23 July 1892, p. 1.

31 Bloy, 'Le Crétin des Pyrénées', *Mercure de France*, vol. 12, no. 57, September 1894, 1–12 (pp. 2–3; 8), original emphasis.

32 In this respect, my own reading differs from Scott M. Powers's take on *Lourdes* as a '"staging of doubt" [that] is not solely a narrative ploy; it belies a genuine crisis in worldview'. *Confronting Evil: The Psychology of Secularization in Modern French Literature* (West Lafayette, IN: Purdue University Press, 2016), pp. 135–84 (p. 137).

33 Ubald Lazaze, 'Revue de la presse', *Gil Blas*, 2 September 1892, pp. 2–3 (p. 3). See also the description of anarchists Zola attributes to his hero, Pierre Froment, as 'terrible dreamers, though dreamers all the same, like those innocent pilgrims' (495).

34 Zola, *Le Roman expérimental*, in *OC*, vol. 9, 323–70 (p. 348).

35 For instance, in his speech at the banquet of the Association générale des étudiants, on 18 May 1893, Zola reflected: 'What else is the ideal but the unexplained, those forces of this vast world in which we are immersed, without them being known to us?' (*OC*, vol. 15, 652).

36 See Zola's preparatory notes for *Le Rêve*; Paris, Bibliothèque nationale, NAF 10324, fol. 186.

37 Deborah L. Silverman, *Art Nouveau in Fin-de-siècle France: Politics, Psychology, and Style* (Berkeley: University of California Press, 1992), pp. 90–91. See, for example, Fouillée's 'Le Physique et le Mental à propos de l'hypnotisme', *Revue des Deux Mondes*, 105 (1891), 429–61.

38 See Bertrand Marquer, *Les Romans de la Salpêtrière. Réception d'une scénographie clinique: Jean-Martin Charcot dans l'imaginaire fin-de-siècle* (Geneva: Droz, 2008), pp. 164–73; Isabelle Delamotte, 'La place de Charcot dans la documentation médicale d'Émile Zola', *Les Cahiers naturalistes*, 73 (1999), 287–99; Kaufman, *Consuming Visions*, pp. 169–71.

39 Jean-Martin Charcot, *La Foi qui guérit* (Paris: Félix Alcan, 1897), p. 13.

40 Charcot, *La Foi qui guérit*, p. 5.

41 See Zola's interview in *Le Temps*, 26 August 1892, p. 2.

42 Jan Goldstein, *Console and Classify: The French Psychiatric Profession in the Nineteenth Century* (Cambridge: Cambridge University Press, 1987), p. 371 (original emphasis).

43 Gabriel Tarde, 'Foules et sectes au point de vue criminel', *Revue des Deux Mondes*, 15 November 1893, 349–87 (pp. 368–69). On this subject, see Eduardo Cintra Torres, 'La foule religieuse de Lourdes chez Zola et Huysmans', *Mil neuf cent. Revue d'histoire intellectuelle*, 28 (2010), 35–58; and Soundouss El Kettani, '*Les Foules de Lourdes* ou le dernier dialogue', *Romantisme*, 151 (2011), 113–28.

44 *Rome*, in *OC*, vol. 16, 496.

45 Louis Colin, *Ce que pense Henri Lasserre du roman d'Émile Zola: conversations et interviews* (Paris: Librairie Bloud et Barral, 1894), p. 41.

46 Kaufman, *Consuming Visions*, p. 105.

47 Harris, *Lourdes*, p. 19. In his *Ébauche*, Zola remarked at length upon the absurdity of calling upon science as a support for faith, or a means to 'prove God's existence'. Bibliothèque Méjanes, MS 1455, fol. 49.

48 Gustave Boissarie, *Les Grandes Guérisons de Lourdes* (Paris: Douniol, 1900), p. 290.

49 'Mon voyage à Lourdes', in Zola, *Lourdes*, 575–644 (p. 644). Further references to these notes, included in Marquer's edition, will be interpolated in the body of the text. Zola did not, however, accuse Boissarie and his team of deliberate falsification: 'At Lourdes, there is no "tinkering". [Boissarie] [...] has proven to me that the Medical Bureau polices, as it were, the miracles it inspects'. See 'À l'Index' in *Le Matin*, 22 September 1894, p. 1.

50 The lecture was published as a pamphlet the following year, Boissarie, *Zola: conférence du Luxembourg* (Paris: Maison de la Bonne Presse, 1895). For discussions of Boissarie's lecture, see Harris, *Lourdes*, pp. 339–42; Kaufman, *Consuming Visions*, pp. 114–18; and Lapière, *Le Langage des sources*, pp. 173–82.

51 Marquer, 'Introduction', *Lourdes*, p. 28.

52 Boissarie, *Conférence du Luxembourg*, p. 3.

53 Pierre L'Ermite, 'Avant la conférence', *Boissarie, Zola. Conférence du Luxembourg*, p. xi; L'Ermite's capitals. L'Ermite recalled having sat next to the novelist, two years earlier, during his visit to the Medical Bureau. *La Croix*, 25–26 November 1894, pp. 1–2.

54 L'Ermite, 'Après la conférence', in Boissarie, *Conférence du Luxembourg*, p. 72.

55 Boissarie, *Conférence du Luxembourg*, p. 73.

56 Kaufman, *Consuming Visions*, p. 123, and see p. 97. Kaufman describes the ways in which 'the bureau's widely circulated case studies of miracle cures [...] became a new and influential literature of devotion in its own right', combining the medical case study with melodrama (p. 96).

57 See Harris, *Lourdes*, p. 423, n. 52. Harris points out that Marie Lebranchu 'remained the living embodiment for Catholics of [Zola's] bad faith', p. 304. Lebranchu's account is cited in Chanoine J.-M. Cassagnard, *Carrel et Zola devant le miracle à Lourdes* (Lourdes: Éditions de L'Œuvre de la Grotte, 1964), pp. 147–48.

58 *Conférence du Luxembourg*, p. 13.

59 Antoinette Guise Castelnuovo describes how many Catholics understood 'the trace of the illness' as 'the signature that the Blessed Virgin leaves behind, so that men might believe in the reality of the cure'. 'Photographier le miracle: Lourdes au tournant du XXᵉ siècle', *Archives des sciences sociales des religions*, 162 (2013), 161–82 (p. 169).

60 *Conférence du Luxembourg*, p. 10. See also Félix Lacaze's article, 'Ce que voudrait Zola à Lourdes', which appeared in *Le Figaro* on 5 September 1892. Lacaze, a doctor who met Zola during his visit to Lourdes in August 1892, described the writer's call for an independent commission largely made up of 'unbelievers and [...] free thinkers'.

61 Robert D. Priest, *The Gospel According to Renan: Reading, Writing, and Religion in Nineteenth-Century France* (Oxford: Oxford University Press, 2015), p. 78.

62 *Conférence du Luxembourg*, pp. 10–11.

63 With the introduction of 'before' and 'after' photographs of the *miraculés* in Boissarie's *Les Grandes Guérisons de Lourdes*, the author sought to prove, Guise Castelnuovo writes, 'the reality of the invisible through the duplication of the visible'. 'Photographier le miracle', pp. 162, 164.

64 Boissarie, *Conférence du Luxembourg*, p. 60.

65 Kaufman, *Consuming Visions*, p. 1.

66 On this subject, see my essay, 'Easy Reading: Zola's Kitsch', *Lucidity: Essays in Honour of Alison Finch*, ed. Ian James and Emma Wilson (Oxford: Legenda, 2016), pp. 72–85.

67 Karl Marx, *Capital: An Abridged Edition*, ed. David McLellan (Oxford: Oxford University Press, 1999), p. 42.

68 Marx, *Capital*, p. 43.

69 Maurice Barrès, 'L'Enseignement de Lourdes', *Le Figaro*, 15 September 1894, p. 1.

70 Peter Brooks, *Body Work: Objects of Desire in Modern Narrative* (Cambridge, MA: Harvard University Press, 1993), p. 125.

71 Huysmans, *Les Foules de Lourdes* (Grenoble: Jérôme Million, 2013), p. 71. For further discussion of Huysmans's novel, and its relationship to Zola's, see Jacques Noiray, 'Huysmans critique de Zola et du naturalisme (1884–1907)', in *Champ littéraire fin de siècle autour de Zola*, ed. Béatrice Laville (Pessac: Presses Universitaires de Bordeaux, 2004), pp. 121–39.

72 Gustave Flaubert, *L'Éducation sentimentale* (Paris: Flammarion, 2001), p. 98. See Juliette Frølich, 'L'homme kitsch ou le jeu des masques dans *L'Éducation sentimentale* de Flaubert', *Romantisme*, 79 (1993), 39–52 (p. 41).

73 Flaubert, *L'Éducation sentimentale*, p. 514.

74 Zola would articulate a similar critique in *Paris* (1898): 'People no longer believe; churches are [...] decorated with fine Gods and Virgins fit to make you weep'. *OC*, vol. 17, 126. On the role of religious sentimentalism in Zola's later fiction, *Lourdes* included, see Andrew J. Counter, 'Wilde, Zola, Dreyfus, Christ: Fin de Siècle Passions', *Representations*, 149 (2020), 103–33.

75 Theodor Adorno, *Aesthetic Theory*, ed. Gretel Adorno and Rolf Tiedemann, and trans. C. Lenhardt (London: Routledge, 1984), p. 340.

76 Bloy, *Méditations d'un solitaire en 1916*, 6th edition (Paris: Mercure de France, 1926), p. 151. On these critiques, see Pascaline Hamon, 'L'Apparition dans le renouveau spirituel littéraire fin de siècle. De Lourdes à la Salette', in *La Vierge Marie dans la littérature française: entre foi et littérature*, ed. Jean-Louis Benoit (Lyon: Jacques André, 2014), pp. 255–64 (p. 264).

77 Jean-Louis Bory, *Tout feu, tout flamme* (Paris: Julliard, 1960), p. 256. On Zola's home in Médan, see Emery, *Photojournalism and the Origins of the French Writer House Museum (1881–1914): Privacy, Publicity, and Personality* (Aldershot: Ashgate, 2012), pp. 101–02; and her article, 'Bricobracomania: Zola's Romantic Instincts', *Excavatio*, 12 (1999), 107–15.

78 See Zola's *Ébauche* for his speculations about the reasons behind Bernadette's departure from Lourdes. Bibliothèque Méjanes, MS 1455, fol. 30.

79 See Schor, *Zola's Crowds* (Baltimore, MD: The Johns Hopkins University Press, 1978), pp. 18–20. Schor does not, however, discuss Bernadette as one of these individual victims.

80 Zola, *Lourdes*, 432. According to Harris, '[t]he first saint to be photographed in her lifetime, [Bernadette] was presented in pious portraits or in the poses that she had supposedly held during the apparitions'. *Lourdes*, p. 145.

81 Bibliothèque Méjanes, MS 1455, fols 30–31.

82 See, for example, Monseigneur Ricard's portrait: 'She was a commoner, devout – but not overly so – *very positive*, entirely down to earth, the complete opposite of a fantasist, dreaming of the impossible.' *La Vraie Bernadette*, p. 128 (original emphasis).

83 *Lourdes*, 116. On Zola's interest in Jeanne d'Arc, see Becker, '"Ah! quel beau rêve qui a remué tout un monde"'.

84 *Lourdes*, 125–26. See also Zola's reflections in 'Mon voyage à Lourdes': 'was there a painting [in the church] where she might have seen the Virgin, and which suggested the vision to her? [. . .] It wasn't just the bible they read; they also read the story of *The Four Sons of Aymon*, and other chivalric adventures, tales, stories about wizards and fairies. It would be very interesting to look in those for the idea of the apparition, the Virgin with the blue sash and feet adorned with golden roses' (617).

85 Sophie Ménard, 'L'Enfantine dans *Lourdes* de Zola', in *Idiots. Figures et personnages liminaires dans la littérature et les arts*, ed. Véronique Cnockaert, Bertrand Gervais and Marie Scarpa (Nancy: PUN/Éditions Université de Lorraine, 2012), pp. 57–76 (p. 67).

86 Like Angélique, Bernadette is said to have spent much time on her embroidery once she had withdrawn to Nevers (640). Cabanès suggests that 'Bernadette's childhood is partly modelled on that of Joan [of Arc], partly on that of Angélique Rougon'. 'L'enfance de Bernadette', p. 216.

87 Cabanès, 'L'enfance de Bernadette', p. 215.

88 *Lourdes*, 128. Boissarie makes a similar point in *Lourdes: depuis 1858 jusqu'à nos jours* (Paris: Sanard et Derangeon, 1894), p. 14.

89 See Harris, *Lourdes*, p. 14.

90 Quoted by Boissarie, *Lourdes: depuis 1858 jusqu'à nos jours*, p. 58. The Catholic doctor Antoine Imbert-Gourbeyre advanced the same thesis: 'How could she have reproduced by means of hallucination something that did not exist in her mind and her memories? She could not have made the Apparition utter this proclamation of hallowed dogma'. *La Stigmatisation, l'extase divine et les miracles de Lourdes* (Paris: J. Vic et Amat, 1894), vol. 2, 350.

91 Harris, *Lourdes*, p. 77.

92 Ricard, *La Vraie Bernadette*, p. 83.

93 Harris, *Lourdes*, p. 72.

94 Ricard, *La Vraie Bernadette*, p. 95.

95 Boissarie, *Lourdes: depuis 1858 jusqu'à nos jours*, p. 14; my emphasis.

96 Ricard, *La Vraie Bernadette*, pp. 95–96. Ricard cites Boissarie's argument on pp. 82–83.

97 Zola gives a précis of his conversation with Barbet in his notes: 'This priest
    was very much aware of the shepherds of La Salette, whom he called by their
    names, and they came to mind each time he looked at Bernadette (see
    Barbet's account in his guide).' 'Mon voyage à Lourdes', 617. On Zola's
    reconstruction of Bernadette's childhood, see René Ternois, Zola et son
    temps: Lourdes – Rome – Paris (Paris: Société Les Belles Lettres, 1961),
    pp. 218–28.

98 Zola reproduces Barbet's transcription of Ader's words in the text of his
    novel (121), and he discusses the source in 'Lourdes', Le Figaro,
    31 August 1894, p. 1.

99 Kathleen Ann Comfort suggests that 'the decisive factor in Bernadette's case
    history is her identification with another Catholic mystic' the shepherdess
    Mélanie. 'Divine Images of Hysteria in Émile Zola's Lourdes', Nineteenth-
    Century French Studies, 30 (2002), 330–46 (p. 334).

100 Ricard, La Vraie Bernadette, p. 20.

101 Zola, 'Lourdes', Le Figaro, 31 August 1894, p. 1.

102 The original letter from the Conseil municipal was reproduced by Ricard, La
    Vraie Bernadette, pp. 22–23.

103 Zola had, for instance, confused the three painted and gilded altarpieces he
    saw in Lourdes with the three old altarpieces he saw in the church at Bartrès.
    This allowed him to emphasise the force of colour and imagery over
    Bernadette's imagination. See Ternois, Zola et son temps, p. 371.

104 Zola, 'Lourdes', Le Figaro, 31 August 1894, p. 1.

105 For a detailed discussion of Lasserre's dispute with Zola, see Lapière, Le
    Langage des sources, pp. 170–86.

106 Les Lettres de Henri Lasserre à l'occasion du roman de M. Zola: avec pièces
    justificatives, démentis et défi (Paris: E. Dentu, 1894), p. 33; my emphasis.

107 In his open letter of 28 September 1894, Lasserre repeated Zola's original
    assurance: 'I promise you, Monsieur Lasserre, that not a single word of mine
    will be liable to upset the friends of Lourdes'. Les Lettres de Henri Lasserre,
    p. 40 (original emphasis).

108 Les Lettres de Henri Lasserre, pp. 38–39.

109 See Zola's interview with Paul Souday in L'Écho de Paris, 2 October 1894, p. 2.

110 Les Lettres de Henri Lasserre, pp. 80–81 (original emphasis).

111 L'Abbé Joseph Crestey, Le Lourdes de Zola: critique d'un roman historique
    (Paris: Bonne Presse, 1894), p. 5.

112 Ricard, La Vraie Bernadette, p. 13.

113 Crestey, Le Lourdes de Zola, p. 6.

114 Note, for instance, that Brunetière's conversion to Roman Catholicism in
    1895 coincided with a further period of hostility towards Zola and a renewed
    disdain for the latter's scientism. See Antoine Compagnon, Connaissez-vous
    Brunetière? Enquête sur un antidreyfusard et ses amis (Paris: Seuil, 1997), p. 125.

115 Robert Ziegler, Satanism, Magic and Mysticism in Fin-de-siècle France
    (Basingstoke: Palgrave Macmillan, 2012), p. 191.

116 Noiray, 'Médecine et miracle dans *Lourdes*', in *Le Simple et l'Intense: vingt études sur Émile Zola* (Paris: Classiques Garnier, 2015), pp. 163–78 (p. 177).

117 At the close of the novel, Pierre repeats his conviction that 'there could be no healthy ideal outside the march toward the unknown, a march of discovery, the slow victory of reason' (492).

118 Christopher Prendergast, *The Order of Mimesis: Balzac, Stendhal, Nerval, Flaubert* (Cambridge: Cambridge University Press, 1986), pp. 148–79.

119 Prendergast, *The Order of Mimesis*, p. 150.

120 Comfort, 'Divine Images of Hysteria', p. 330.

121 *The Standard Edition of the Complete Psychological Works of Sigmund Freud*, trans. and ed. J. Strachey, 24 vols (London: Vintage, 2001), vol. 21, 49 (original emphasis). Guermès makes the connection with Freud in *La Religion de Zola*, p. 369.

122 Paul Ricoeur, *De l'Interprétation: essai sur Freud* (Paris: Seuil, 1965), p. 40.

123 For a full exploration of the relationship between these episodes, and Zola's involvement in each, see my article, 'The Affair Before the Affair'.

124 Guillaume McNeil Arteau, 'Enquête et documentation dans *Lourdes* de Zola', *Poétique*, 191 (2022), 59–74 (p. 71).

125 Marquer, 'Introduction', *Lourdes*, p. 42.

CHAPTER 5

On Being Right
Zola and Dreyfus

On 29 September 1899, Zola addressed an open letter to Mme Dreyfus in which he expressed his great relief at the prospect of her husband's return home from his imprisonment on Devil's Island, following his acceptance of a presidential pardon. The court at Rennes had just pronounced Alfred Dreyfus guilty yet again, upholding at his retrial the court martial's initial verdict of treason against the French Republic for the betrayal of military secrets to the German embassy.[1] Dreyfus's return to his family, Zola imagined, would no doubt be bitter-sweet, President Loubet's hypocritical pardon yet another indignity and injustice for the victim of this ignominious cover-up, who remained determined to clear his name. And yet, with Dreyfus's freedom granted, Zola could at last reflect on the prodigious resources that he and his fellow Dreyfusards had had to call upon in their heroic struggle to deliver the innocent martyr from the death-in-life imposed by his exile. With all their might, they had lifted the stone sealing his tomb – and this was nothing short of a miracle:

> Every force in society was leagued against us; the only force we had on our side was the force of truth itself. We would have to accomplish a miracle in order to resurrect the buried man. [...] He was still so far away, in his tomb, and although a hundred of us, then a thousand, then twenty thousand tried to raise that slab, the weight of all those iniquitous acts was so heavy that I feared our arms would be worn out by the supreme effort. [...] *Today, we have made the miracle happen. Two years of gigantic struggle have achieved the impossible. Our dream has been accomplished*: the victim has come down from his cross.[2]

In his fervour, Zola muddles religious metaphors: Dreyfus – the Jew – is at once Jesus, his crucifixion ended through the supreme effort of his disciples, and he is Lazarus of Bethany, brought back from the dead through the miracle performed by Christ for his followers. Zola's sleight of hand effectively displaces Dreyfus from his Calvary with an allegory of his own Christ-like deeds, and this in a way that was not untypical of Dreyfusard rhetoric.[3] 'By the magnitude of the Deed, by the energy of the Word, Zola has transformed himself into a modern-day Christ', declared the Dreyfusard writer Armand Charpentier.[4] The illustrator Orens Denizard, meanwhile, famously pictured a loin-clothed Zola, arms aloft in triumph, after descending from his cross: the mirror he holds up is an emblem of his heroic pursuit of the truth in penning his open letter to President Félix Faure, its title, 'J'accuse...!', hovering above his head like a crown (Figure 5.1). Zola, of course, stops short of replicating this iconography of self-sacrifice in his own account, preferring instead to conjure up Christ the miracle-worker as the model for the Dreyfusards' collective redemptive mission.

Such a curious appeal to the miraculous – and, moreover, to the precise miracle of Lazarus's resurrection – tells us much about the accommodations, tensions even, that emerged in Zola's writing on, and around, the Dreyfus Affair. In the lyric drama *Lazare* that Zola had penned at the same time as *Lourdes*, he had transposed Pierre Froment's scepticism about the virtues of bringing Lazarus back from the dead: 'He had often imagined Lazarus emerging from his tomb and crying: "Oh, Lord! Why have you awakened me to this abominable life?"'[5] Faced with Lazarus's regret at his resurrection, Zola's Jesus graciously performs the 'counter-miracle' of returning him to the sweet sleep from which he had been roused.[6] Clearly, the Dreyfusard appropriation of this biblical episode allows for no such misgivings: Zola displays a solid conviction in the righteousness of the secular miracle that he and his allies have wrought, just as he harnesses the same Christological reference without apparent irony. Only a few weeks later, in fact, journalist Lucien Victor-Meunier would deploy the same image in likening Dreyfus's defenders to the miners of *Germinal*, whose humanitarian efforts to rescue their trapped comrades from the collapsed mine had required a courage, daring, and strength of will to rival their own: 'we have laboured frantically, with all our strength and all our heart [...]; so much so that the day came when he resurfaced, like Lazarus emerging from his tomb'.[7] In the most fraternal episode of Zola's novel of commitment, the Dreyfusard mission found its sublime antecedent.

In Zola's case, the returns, and reformulations, of a thaumaturgical discourse are surely part of what Andrew J. Counter has called (speaking of both Oscar Wilde and Zola) the 'internal contradictions [...] that emerge most visibly in the "religious", which is not to say orthodox, turn of their later years'.[8] For Zola's involvement in the Dreyfus Affair had sharpened conflicting – though, as we shall see, not irreconcilable – impulses: on the one hand, to eliminate any ambiguities from his indictment of the Catholic

Figure 5.1   Orens Denizard, 'Zola accuses the Council of having Esterhazy
acquitted', 1899.
Postcard series 'Le Calvaire Dreyfus' (1904). History and Art Collection / Alamy Stock Photo.

church, the worst excesses of which he displays with hyperbolic clarity in his fiction transposing the Dreyfus scandal, *Vérité* (1903); on the other, to elaborate a secularised religious aesthetic through the final series to which that novel belongs, *Les Quatre Évangiles*.[9] Certainly, what might strike us about Zola's letter to Mme Dreyfus – and indeed about the wider series of articles on the Affair that Zola published in the press, later gathered together as *La Vérité en marche* (1901) – is the apparently unselfconscious way in which the rhetoric of idealism, of the dream, surfaces as the best expression of the writer's commitment. When Zola made his declaration to the jury at his trial for libel, in the aftermath of 'J'accuse. . .!', it was upon the force of the ideal that he called to articulate an unwavering conviction in his cause: 'All I have on my side is an idea, the ideal of truth and justice. I am confident. I shall carry the day.'[10] In the crucible of the Dreyfus Affair, Zola's attitudes toward naturalism's declared antithesis became, as we shall see, subject to their own kind of revisionism, as the writer sought to rescue from idealism a better version of itself: what he will call, in *Vérité*, 'a different ideal of reason and free humanity'.[11]

This chapter tracks some of the forms that 'other' idealism takes across both Zola's Dreyfus journalism and his fictional allegory of the Affair, which had only just begun to be serialised in the pages of *L'Aurore* at the time of his death.[12] In *Vérité*, Zola effectively submits the prospective, utopian vision of his first two 'gospels' (*Fécondité* and *Travail*) to a contemporary political drama that had, as yet, been denied its proper dénouement. My concern in what follows will be to examine the conditions on which he imagined not only the just resolution of the legal case, but, more broadly, the national crisis it galvanised. In doing so, this chapter takes up Lida Maxwell's compelling examination, in *Public Trials* (2014), of certain epochal moments of 'democratic failure' – the wrongful conviction of Dreyfus among them – when both legal proceedings and the public 'fail to assure justice'.[13] In reading Zola's writings on the Affair, Maxwell explores how such disillusionment can be instructive, and indeed be recast as the condition for 'future democratic possibilities' (5), namely by cultivating in the public 'a demand for a broader, fuller justice than was done – or could have been done – in courts of law' (113). Accordingly, Zola's rewriting of the Affair in *Vérité* not only augurs, as we shall see, the resurgence of the people as an agent of truth, it also enacts 'the pursuit of another kind of justice: *poetic* justice' (112; original emphasis), insofar as the work of fiction affords an alternative (or corrective) ending to the otherwise unresolved saga. Rhetorically at least, as Maxwell points out, Zola had already extolled this prevailing imperative of 'poetic justice' in his letter to Mme Dreyfus. If her husband had been failed by the court of law, she could still count, Zola insisted, on the tireless efforts of writers – 'we poets' – to announce the victim's immanent retribution for future generations: 'Tomorrow's verdict is being prepared now. It will be a triumphal acquittal, an overwhelming reparation; every generation will kneel and [. . .] will beg pardon for their fathers' crimes.'[14] The following month, in a letter to fellow writer and Dreyfusard Paul Brulat, Zola defended his prerogative to indulge in 'hypothesis, utopia' – those 'rights of the poet', or what we might call poetic licence.[15]

Zola's transposition of the Affair in *Vérité* certainly exploits that licence, while remaining true to many key historical elements: it replicates, for instance, several of the Affair's major actors; the public trial at Rennes (renamed Rozan); the forgeries used by the army; the anti-Semitic virulence directed at Dreyfus. However, the novel also operates an important double displacement: the army setting becomes the classroom, and Dreyfus's military treason is turned into a sexual crime. For the novel's central scandal is the rape and murder of a young schoolboy Zéphirin, and the wrongful framing of his uncle Simon, a Jewish schoolteacher. Zéphirin's body is discovered together with a writing sampler, bearing the victim's teeth marks, and rolled up inside the local newspaper. Like the famous *bordereau* of Dreyfus's case, this piece of inconclusive evidence becomes a prime object of dispute: tampered with at the crime scene by the Jesuit priest, Père Philibin, only a set of illegible initials (or '*paraphe*') remains. As the press whips up anti-Semitic sentiment in the citizens of Zola's fictional town Maillebois, however, suspicion soon falls on Simon, and despite the lack of evidence against him, the Jew is convicted and sent to a penal colony. In his absence, Simon's devoted brother David works tirelessly to prove his innocence, finding his greatest source of support in the freethinking *instituteur* – and the novel's real hero – Marc Froment. In his twin devotion to the pursuit of legal justice, on the one hand, and to the liberation of young minds from the doctrines of the Catholic Church, on the other, Marc expounds his secular cult of Truth – one which will entail its own sacrifices, not least the gradual breakdown of his marriage to Geneviève, a practising Catholic.

In the immediate aftermath of the abominable crime, Marc, along with other 'Simonists', rightly suspects Zéphirin's Jesuit teacher, Frère Gorgias – dubbed by one contemporary 'Esterhazy in a cassock'.[16] But the Church will stop at nothing, perjury and forgery included, to sustain its cover-up, peddling perfidious hypotheses about the accused in a desperate effort to link Simon to the incriminating document. Like Dreyfus,

Simon will eventually be retried, and convicted once again, before being offered a pardon, though no broad amnesty follows. Instead, the vast canvas of Zola's novel, which stretches the entire span of Marc's adult life, allows him to imagine the happy resolution of the Affair that he did not live to witness for Dreyfus. (The Jewish captain would only be fully exonerated in 1906.) Some three generations later, Simon's innocence is at last established, and Zola stages his full and triumphant rehabilitation in the town that had once persecuted him. With the Catholic Church's direct implication in both the crime and the cover-up brought to light, moreover, Marc's vision of a secular Republic wins out; in the closing pages, Zola augurs – in a way that spoke to raging contemporary debates over *laïcité* – the demise of the Church altogether. Pedagogical plot and legal plot are, then, ultimately entwined, as the victim's redemption rests on Marc reaping the fruits of his life-long labours: the justice brought by a new generation of freethinkers.

In putting the Church centre-stage in *Vérité* – and as the guilty party – Zola effectively amplified the invidious complicity of those religious and military institutions that he understood to be manipulating the Affair: the Republic lay in peril, he warned President Loubet, 'the target of a double-barrelled plot by clerical and militaristic forces, acting on behalf of all the reactionary forces of the past'.[17] Zola decried the state of a nation that, he insisted, was not yet firmly Republican enough, still fantasising about a return to monarchy, and still seduced by the nefarious tactics of the Catholic church, whose promotion of anti-Semitism he denounced as a desperately opportunistic means of bringing citizens back to the altar.[18] Shot through with echoes of Lourdes, meanwhile, *Vérité* firmly ties its narrative of frustrated justice to the superstitions and exploits of a powerful Catholic congregation, whose cult of Saint Antoine de Padoue is pinned to the same promise of the miracle, now shamelessly extended to all kinds of material and mercenary wishes.[19] Effectively, what Marc's mission makes clear is that the Catholic Church, as a wilful generator of invidious delusions, must disappear in order for the public to emerge as a self-sovereign guarantor of truth and justice.

To imagine a legitimate resolution to the Affair, for Zola, was thus to expose a second, and far-reaching, conspiracy behind the particular cover-up manufactured by the military and sustained with the complicity of the press and a corrupt government: that is, the deliberate deception of the public that the writer calls a 'crime against society'.[20] By shifting the focus, in *Vérité*, from courtroom to classroom, Zola makes this drama of national betrayal his overarching concern, and its correction the narrative's inexorable endpoint. For across Zola's novel and Dreyfus journalism, the miscarriage of justice, which the victim-scapegoat (*pharmakon*) suffers, is at once a symptom of the 'poison' (Zola's ubiquitous metaphor) that rages through the body politic, and the means of the nation's cure, or deliverance: 'Never has any fever made the skin break out more visibly with the pustules of disease. That disease must be cured.'[21] Such, in any case, were Zola's claims to be operating in the national interest – and this precisely in distinction to the anti-Dreyfusard discourse of *raison d'état*, which subordinated the rights of the individual, and indeed the ethical principle of truth, to pragmatic state (or patriotic) concerns. For Zola, establishing the truth for its own sake – as an ideal or absolute – was the only path to national regeneration. Broadly speaking, then, Zola cultivated in his journalism, as we shall see, a double address: to a credulous public misled by, even complicit in, the injustice he diagnosed; and to a virtuous public that already held within it all the necessary attributes to bring this injustice to an end – if only they could trust their own better judgement. What this meant for Zola, as we shall see, was conjuring up a transformed citizenry capable not only of seeing through their manipulation, but of reading in the right way.

Indeed, one of my main contentions in this chapter is that Zola understood the Dreyfus case, first and foremost, as an aesthetic problem: that is to say, as a matter of style, taste, imagination, plot – and, crucially, plausibility. Zola casts, I argue, the competing narratives over Dreyfus's (and, in turn, Simon's) guilt as appeals to different types of literary aesthetics, as much as, if not more than, to ideological principles. That longstanding quarrels over naturalist fiction shaped the Affair, the positions of some of its key protagonists, and its wider 'literary politics', has been persuasively argued by Roderick Cooke.[22] What I wish to trace out here, in the first part of this chapter, is just how questions of literary sensibility are implicated in Zola's journalistic and fictional versions of the Affair, whereby a miscarriage of justice is precisely enabled, and perpetuated, by a public of readers whose aesthetic predilections are inimical to the truth. Resolving the case itself will, then, in one sense, require Zola to establish the kind of naturalist Republic that he had optimistically announced at the end of the 1870s – one based on an (anti-idealist) appetite for reason and evidence:

> It is impossible to base any legislation whatsoever on the lies of the idealists. On the contrary, with the true documents that the naturalists provide, we will one day, undoubtedly, be able to establish a better society, which will function according to logic and method. Only when we are truthful do we become moral.[23]

In *Vérité*, Zola will effectively play out this dream of the naturalist novel as a form of statecraft, legislating for the future. When what is true comes to align with what is right and what is beautiful in Zola's ideal Republic, we witness the disappearance of politics altogether into an ecstatic kind of consensus. And yet, in order for the truth to win out, Zola's utopia must also, I argue, compromise the naturalist principles of rationality it extols. In the second and third parts of this chapter, we shall see how those popular, even populist, virtues to which the narrative appeals in its citizens – common sense, intuition, instinct – ultimately point to an alternative epistemology, which reaches beyond what the law itself can determine.

The Simplest Story

Across his journalism on Dreyfus, Zola supplied again and again what he held to be one very straightforward way of reading the Affair: as the scandal of how a false narrative – that of Dreyfus's guilt – could be passed off as truth. And this in spite of that narrative's very obvious implausibility. The case against Dreyfus was described by Zola as variously 'an old wives' tale', a 'legend', and 'the most conniving tangle of lies', all of which stretched the public's credulity to breaking point.[24] Against the suspension of disbelief that such stories demanded, Zola insisted on the glaring self-evidence of the facts, which rendered the case remarkable, if anything, for its sheer simplicity: 'The story could not be simpler'; this was an 'Affair, which is so clear and simple in itself'; '[the Affair] is as clear and simple as you please once you see it as it really is'...[25] The case for the prosecution could thus be easily dispelled, including what Zola described as its most nonsensical claim: the thesis, put forward by criminologist Alphonse Bertillon, that Dreyfus had forged his own handwriting on the *bordereau*. So obvious was the striking identity of Commandant Esterhazy's handwriting with that of the incriminating document, Zola declared, that any child could recognise the real author: 'Take any small child going by in the street, bring him upstairs, place both pieces of writing in front of him and he will tell you, "These two pages are written by the same gentleman."'[26] While Esterhazy's desperate attempts to deny this plainly implicating resemblance involved the elaboration of 'a whole laboriously complicated story' – namely, the equally tortuous claim that his handwriting must have been replicated from his own letters – Zola restated for his readers the equation of what is simple with what is true. If the nation had failed to see what was there in broad daylight, it was, Zola argued, because readers were being subjected to the regime of lies disseminated by an irresponsible press, who offered the seal of social sanction to the most 'idiotic' of claims.[27] Yet the problem remained that this style of complex fabrication, or fiction-making, seemed to appeal so irresistibly to the public's readerly tastes.

By this logic, disproving an outlandish version of Dreyfus's guilt meant stigmatising its aesthetic allure, as well as its diabolical authors. In his open letter to President Faure, Zola singled out Major Armand Mercier Du Paty de Clam as the mastermind behind the most fantastical and far-fetched of the Affair's conspiracy theories:

> He *is* the entire Dreyfus Affair. [...] He appears to have an unbelievably fuzzy and complicated mind, haunted by implausible plots and indulging in methods that litter cheap novels [romans-feuilletons] – stolen papers, [...] mysterious women who flit about at night to peddle damaging proof.[28]

Zola was wrong, though not alone, in attributing to Du Paty sole authorship. It was, in fact, General Mercier who coordinated the cover-up; and Lieutenant-Colonel Henry who was the forger of false evidence.[29] But the strange prominence accorded to Du Paty in Zola's account was, as Ruth Harris suggests, 'more than mere error'. The commanding officer's interest in spiritism and the occult signalled a pathological imagination that 'satisfied [Zola's] novelistic preoccupations'.[30] In his notes, Zola described a man thoroughly unhinged. Du Paty's shady sexual perversions and weak grasp on reality bespoke a fundamental duplicity, his actions and inclinations every bit as suspicious as his sprouting moustache:

> Du Paty, fanciful, has dabbled in everything – languages, music; decadent, superficial, skimming the surface, does everything poorly. Mistakes his fantasies for reality. Crimes in his family. Mentally unbalanced. High society, brilliant, superficial. Wagnerian. [...] Pederast.[31]

Du Paty shades here into Zola's future fictional paedophile Frère Gorgias, though it is the superior Frère Fulgence – 'a shadowy mind, unstable, and spoiled by pride' (253) – that Zola singles out as the Major's double in the novel. The echoes of *Vérité* aside, what might strike us most is, as Counter suggests, that Du Paty is repeatedly framed 'not as a novelistic villain but *as a novelist*'; indeed, the terms in which Zola's accusations are couched 'seem to announce a new suspicion of the literary imagination, which now emerges as a kind of psychological disturbance in itself'.[32] Both Decadent and degenerate, Du Paty encapsulates, Counter argues, Naturalism's rival aesthetic, 'noted for its particular imaginative faculties, as embodied in Huysmans and Rachilde'.[33]

But such suspicions of the literary, or 'romanesque', imagination also have a longer history – one closely bound up, as Ursula Bähler notes, with Zola's critique of the serial novel, or *roman-feuilleton*. After all, it is with this form that, as we saw above, Du Paty de Clam stands in almost metonymical relation in Zola's Dreyfus journalism.[34] Certainly, a refusal to espouse the aesthetic strategies of the serial novel had long framed Zola's defence of the naturalist mode. Having been accused of eliminating the role of the imagination in his fiction, Zola responded to his critics – in an 1879 article – with the following clarification:

> Certainly, yes, I reject imagination, if we mean by this the inventions of serial novelists – however much those novelists might excel in their genre, and even when their names are Alexandre Dumas and Eugène Sue. [...] Nothing could be easier [...] than inventing a story out of thin air, pushing it to *the furthest limits of implausibility*, captivating with *incredible twists and turns*. Instead, take true facts that you have observed around you, arrange them in a logical order, *fill in the gaps with intuition*, achieve the wonderful result of bringing human documents to life, [...] and you will have exercised your imaginative faculties on a higher plane.[35]

What Zola associates with the literary imagination, then, are the fanciful (and apparently facile) procedures of the serial novel, in which sensational, or arbitrary, contrivances and melodramatic twists or complications strain to excess the plausibility of the plot. The modern (read: naturalist) novel was, Zola maintained elsewhere, conceived precisely in reaction to such tastes: 'our contemporary novel tends towards ever greater simplicity, out of contempt for complicated and fanciful plots; and this amounts to a kind of revenge against adventure stories, the fantastic [le romanesque], and tall tales'.[36] The recipe for naturalist fiction prescribes, instead, the straightforward scrutiny and logical curation of factual evidence. Intuition – an authorial quality to which we shall return – is ostensibly the one imaginative faculty on which the naturalist writer may legitimately draw in turning facts into fiction.

Zola thus insists, here and elsewhere, on the conception of naturalist fiction as a sort of anti-*roman-feuilleton*, bent on extracting such forms of the 'romanesque' from its repertoire of devices:

> The foremost characteristic of the naturalist novel, of which *Madame Bovary* is the prime example, is the exact reproduction of life, the absence of any fanciful [romanesque] elements. [...] All extraordinary inventions are therefore banished. [...] No more furniture with secret compartments, no more papers brought to light just in time to save the innocent victim.[37]

The naturalist universe refuses precisely the type of 'intrigue' whereby justice is served and wrongs are redressed through the sensational exposure of proofs *ex machina*. Indeed, according to the naturalist novel's theoretical self-image, its task is to denounce the conspiratorial, and its attendant plot devices and vocabulary, in establishing its own laws of genre. That the precise example Zola gives here, moreover, augurs a happy ending – the melodramatic rescue of the innocently persecuted (!) – aligns his critique of the *roman-feuilleton* with a wider struggle: naturalism's militant anti-idealism. As Bähler notes, Zola determines in the serial novel, of the kind Du Paty has supposedly dreamt up, an embrace of implausibility that is germane to those conventional types of sentimentalism and idealism that are associated first and foremost in his mind with George Sand.[38] Certainly, Zola deploys the same terms to convey his suspicion of Sand's and Du Paty's dangerous (literary) imaginations. While, as we saw in Chapter 3, Sand's novels 'open up the land of make-believe' for her impressionable readers, Du Paty 'mistakes his fantasies for reality', falling prey to his own delusions.[39] Regardless of the different ends, then, to which a novelistic disregard for the reality principle might be put – nefarious, Machiavellian, plotting; or sentimental, even altruistic, justice—Zola diagnoses the recourse to the romanesque as a mendacious, and ultimately, pathological literary mode.

If anything, such associations reveal just how embedded Zola's defence of Dreyfus was in longstanding aesthetic agendas, namely his stigmatisation of a type of literary imagination that was made to represent naturalism's antimodel. In *Vérité*, this agenda is rehearsed precisely through the conflict between rival narratives of Simon's culpability and innocence, the former cast as an illegitimate aesthetic mode, but one which holds an irrepressible appeal: 'Such a melodrama, with its mysterious intricacies and extraordinary fairytale improbabilities, was, Marc felt sure, a legend that would become a reality, the definitive truth that people would refuse to let go' (59). Amplifying his own reproaches of the press's reporting on the Dreyfus case, Zola pours vitriol on his fictional town's newspapers for their role in feeding an appetite for the absurd embellishments that are required to seal Simon's conviction – first, in the court of public opinion; then at trial.[40] Both *La Croix de Beaumont* and *Le Petit Beaumontais* not only peddle the perfidious hypotheses of the Church brothers, they make themselves complicit in the deliberate fabrication of what is 'fake news' *avant la lettre*: 'Documents are falsified, texts are edited.'[41] As the affair draws on, Gorgias's protectors are bound to generate ever more convoluted versions of events as new inculpatory evidence emerges. Chief of these is the claim that Simon had faked the initials and stamp on the writing sampler found with Zéphirin's body, in order to shift suspicion onto the Catholic school. This plain transposition of Dreyfus's purported autoforgery appeals to the readers' conspiratorial imagination with such force that even the real culprit's own barely concealed admissions of involvement fail to dislodge it: '*Le Petit Beaumontais*'s readers were [...] delighted by this new invention of the forged stamp, which added yet another contrivance [invraisemblance] to the whole affair' (265). Spun out in episodic fashion, the elaborate concoctions of Zola's anti-heroes clearly belong to the newspaper page's bottom third, below the bar that demarcates fiction from reporting.

Not only, then, is the charge of implausibility immaterial to the reading public, the more far-fetched the story, the more tenacious, even seductive, it becomes. Though, for all such extravagance finds itself discredited by both Zola's narrator and hero-avatar, we are surely bound to acknowledge that this does not preclude Zola from drawing on the romanesque, or in fact melodrama, in the narrative itself, which abounds with caricature villains and sordid or sensational events – rape, murder, paedophilia, family dramas, even a natural catastrophe...[42] Still, the notional pedagogical challenge for Marc lies, as we shall see, in inculcating in Maillebois's citizens different readerly appetites – namely, an aesthetic taste for 'all that is pure, simple, clear' (105), and *therefore* true.

For now, though, I wish to shift our focus to the courtroom, and to Simon's trial, which crystallises the vulnerability of the law itself to precisely the same aesthetic problem Zola diagnoses in his public: a reluctance to credit the simplest story. In this respect, Zola returns to the impediment to justice he had determined in his crime novel *La Bête humaine* (1890) and its central judicial error: the wrongful conviction of the misfit Cabuche as Grandmorin's murderer. In his *Ébauche* for the novel, Zola had noted: 'The truth not admitted [by the judge] because it is too simple (*Irony*).'[43] Such irony – or, in fact, dramatic irony – colours in turn Zola's transposition of Dreyfus's case, where fashioning a complex or spurious narrative appears to be the very condition of the prosecution's success. What we find in *Vérité*, of course, is a heroic attempt to delegitimise, and overturn, a prevailing case against Simon that flies in the face of common sense, or 'bon sens' – a watchword of Zola's journalism on the Affair, and one to which we shall return. But in the process, Zola's champions of justice are forced to rely, I wish to suggest, on epistemological claims that sit uneasily alongside the naturalist method.

As Simon's valiant lawyer Delbos acknowledges from the get-go, more than simple logic and reasoning, what the defence requires is a compelling rival fiction:

> The moral impossibilities are blatant; no man with any good sense will believe Simon guilty. Besides, there are several material inconsistencies [invraisemblances]. But we cannot deny that this frightful tale is sufficiently believable to capture the imagination of the crowd, becoming one of those legendary fables that acquire the power of unassailable truths... And our weakness is that we do not have a story, the true story, to counter the legend that is being forged. (81)

In effect, Zola has Delbos rehearse Balzac's claim in his own novel of conspiracy, *Une ténébreuse affaire* (1841): 'Innocence owes a clear and plausible account of its actions. The duty of the Defence is to offer up a probable story to oppose the Prosecution's improbable story.'[44] Delbos and his fellow Simonists, Marc and David, must supply a persuasive, and crucially plausible, counter-narrative, rooted in conjectures to which the known facts give rise. Before uncovering the proof, in other words, that would (eventually) exculpate Simon, their defence must formulate its own accusation of their chief suspect Frère Gorgias, if only on the grounds of their own inductions. In this way, Zola transposed in fiction what we might call the promissory logic of the Dreyfusard battle, namely the need to generate, through speculation and hypothesis, a rival narrative of Esterhazy's guilt, which promised to be retrospectively validated by the further disclosure of evidence it announced.[45] Indeed, Zola's novel exaggerates precisely this suspense as a kind of de-dramatised delay, drawing out over decades the slow, yet inexorable, process by which Marc and Delbos's 'story' displaces the 'legend' invented by Gorgias's protectors, as its own presumptions are proven both right and righteous.

But in rehearsing the grounds on which the case for Gorgias's culpability is made – and so on which Simon's defence turns – Zola's novel attaches a peculiar weight to that expedient supplement of the naturalist method: intuition. For it is on precisely this that Zola's teacher-cum-detective relies as he seeks to reconstruct a likely narrative of the crime. Having quickly dismissed as implausible his own initial suggestion that the attack might have been the work of a vagabond, Marc comes to suspect – in a moment of 'fleeting intuition' – that the perpetrator was already known to Zéphirin, coaxing and reassuring him, before 'suddenly, abominable temptation' took over (30). Doubts and contradictions plague the hero's supposition along the way. But Marc's inevitable path from supposition to conviction is, we should recall, already announced at the outset of the novel – and precisely in the form of a preconscious feeling – as the narrator describes the latent legibility of the crime scene: '[Marc] himself was shuddering at the details he witnessed, [...] and which betrayed a shameful, sly sadism, the very signature of the defiler and murderer. Suddenly, he was struck by a feeling of certainty, which he would later remember' (26). As Counter suggests, 'such a confident appeal to the unproblematic legibility of *any* signature – let alone a metaphorical one – is either cunningly ironic or weirdly unguarded', given the ensuing miscarriage of justice will itself rest on the failure to read the semi-effaced monogram on the writing sample found in the victim's mouth.[46] Zola is rehearsing, of course, the disputes over the legitimacy of the *bordereau* as proof of Dreyfus's guilt, where determining the 'hand' was deemed fundamental to uncovering the military's traitor. But in *Vérité*, this conflation of two types of authorship is overtaken by the novel's insistence on a superior kind of metaphorical script. For Zéphirin's murder is, in every sense, a 'signature crime': it exhibits certain idiosyncrasies or hallmarks that, according to the anti-clerical logic of Simon's defenders, mean that the perpetrator could only be a man of the cloth.

By the time Marc has joined forces with Simon's lawyer, his initial hunch is firmly legitimised as the narrative reprises the same logic of intelligibility – rendered this time in the complicit mode of free indirect discourse: 'Ultimately, it was as if the rape and murder had a signature, a cruel, sly sadism, a mix of ignominy and religiosity that pointed to the habit' (82). The task of identifying an individual is then relatively straightforward, as Gorgias appears so plainly as a caricature villain: his protruding beak-like nose and wolf's teeth are the unmistakable signs of a predator in our midst. When the monk is called to the bar as a witness at Simon's trial, he displays a perverse pleasure that betrays a barely concealed sense of malice: his mouth is fixed 'in a kind of involuntary rictus, violent and mocking' (89). In this respect, Marc's deductions operate along the lines of what Carlo Ginzburg has called the 'conjectural paradigm': he attends to the details of the crime scene with a healthy scepticism, while he interprets, almost instinctively, those 'inadvertent little gestures' that are held to be symptomatic of Gorgias's violent sexual appetite.[47] It is, to recall Ginzburg, 'a whiff, a glance, an intuition' (28) that leads to the Simonists' suspicion of the monk's guilt – their consensus that 'Frère Gorgias has a bad smell about him' (83). And yet, unlike Ginzburg's paradigmatic detective, Sherlock Holmes, who discovers the perpetrator of the crime by skilfully deciphering 'clues unnoticed by others' (8),

Zola's teacher has little need for shrewdness. If *Vérité* might be best understood as a kind of anti-detective novel, it is because its only mode of suspense lies in the gradual recognition of certain obvious truths, which its unenlightened protagonists would rather repress. At Simon's trial, Gorgias's guilt is the proverbial elephant in the (court)room; his sinister, unkempt appearance produces 'out of nowhere' a collective 'shiver in the audience' (89) – a purely *intuitive*, if dis-originated, form of condemnation.

The difficulty for Simon's defenders, of course, will lie in acquiring the evidence – 'known facts, solid and proven' (85) – that will undergird these initial hypotheses and deductions. But the 'truth' that is the guiding ideal of this novel is, as we have seen, established in the immediate aftermath of the crime, and in the only form it really matters: as a conviction. That this conviction rests, however, on the foundations of an uncompromising anticlericalism leads, as Jeffrey Mehlman has remarked, to a problematic double standard in the novel: 'Marc, one feels, initially identifies the culprit in the rape case as a churchman on grounds no more probative than those of the *equally intuitive* anti-Semites who have, they feel, ample grounds for suspecting the Jew Simon.'[48] What Dorian Bell has called 'Zola's anti-anti-Semitism' is certainly at work in his parodic account of the fantasies of bloodlust that Maillebois's marauding crowds attribute to their scapegoat: Simon is branded 'the accursed Jew, the slayer of little children, who needed their virgin blood, still pure from communion, for his evil deeds'.[49] And yet, surely, equally pernicious is the anticlerical ideology that underpins Marc's conviction about the crime's real author, and in which Zola's hero enjoys, moreover, the narrator's complicity. In this regard, Zola gives full rein in the novel to the Dreyfusard fabrication of a Jesuit conspiracy, which feared that an alliance with the military would allow the Jesuits to dominate the Republic with their insidious philistinism.[50] Marc first divines the obscure machinations of Jesuit priests, Pères Philibin and Crabot, as a 'feeling that some hidden work was taking place in the shadows' (59), the malevolent plotting of 'skilful, invisible hands' (82), bent on covering Gorgias's tracks. If these convictions make their first appearance in the novel as a hunch, it is precisely because this mode of intuition is integral to Zola's sleight of hand, whereby the ideologically inevitable is given an air of contingency.

Whether ultimately proven right or wrong, then, the case for Simon's prosecution rests on the same logic as that of the case for the defence: the conviction that the perpetrator must have reverted to type. This, incidentally, was a rationale that Zola had already scrutinised in *La Bête humaine*, where the miscarriage of justice is shown to be enabled by prevailing assumptions about criminal typology. When Cabuche is brought to court on the charge of murdering Séverine Roubaud, he appears 'just as people imagined him, [. . .] the very type of the murderer, with enormous fists, carnivorous jaws'.[51] Susan Harrow is surely right in reading the innocent Cabuche's fate at the hands of the law as 'an ironic fictional anticipation' of Dreyfus's scapegoating, insofar as the establishment designates 'embodied otherness as *a priori* guilt'.[52] Though we would also have to admit that in his transposition of the Affair, Zola harnesses, and with no apparent irony, precisely this assumption of deviancy to the ends of the victim's defence. Indeed, the plausibility of either criminal narrative in *Vérité* rests on its conformity to what Nancy K. Miller has called 'a grammar of motives', in her gloss on Gérard Genette's influential narrative theory.[53] For understanding the motivations of a character means, as Genette has argued, interpreting these according to a set of general principles for behaviour, axiomatic truths, or maxims – in Miller's words, 'the *doxa* of socialities' (26; original emphasis) – that constitute public opinion:

> What remains, and what defines the *vraisemblable*, is the formal principle of respect for the norm, in other words the existence of a relation of implication between the particular behavior attributed to a given character and a given, general maxim. [. . .] [T]o understand a character's behaviour is to be able to refer to it as a received maxim, and this reference is taken as a movement from effect to cause.[54]

Our deciphering of a character's behaviour thus turns on a perpetual slippage between the codes of *vraisemblance* and *bienséance* – that is, a respective understanding of what is likely or *probable*, and what conforms to a set of *normative* (ethical) expectations or presuppositions.

Now, the attempt to establish probable cause in the Simon affair involves, as we have seen, just such a conflation of predictive and prescriptive modes: Gorgias is likely to be the perpetrator because the nature of the crime fits what we know (as a 'received maxim') to be the general conduct and perverse inclinations of Jesuit priests; and, of course, a comparable logic applies to the Jew. What Simon's defenders will do more effectively is propose a rival narrative, a 'probable story' of Gorgias's guilt that replaces one suspect ideological vision with another. Indeed, in turning the Dreyfus Affair into a sexual scandal, Zola re-centres the question of motive, at least, on that of the (proper) regulation of desire – and precisely in ways that were already, if more subtly, at stake in the original case. Take the line of argument presented by Dreyfus's lawyer, Edgar Demange, at the Rennes trial:

> I have shown you Esterhazy and Dreyfus face to face.
>
> With the former, all kinds of motives have come to light. In the latter, we have a happy man, a father, with young children, his great pride and his love; his wife, the brave and admirable spouse you know her to be; honour, wealth, everything is his, and he is going to, what: sacrifice everything! Why, I ask you?[55]

As a loving husband and devoted father, Dreyfus's exemplary domestic life is harnessed as his principal alibi, implicitly absolving him of those motives – bribery, scandal, cover-ups – that would stem from a deviant lifestyle. In turn, Simon's heterosexual normativity is, in Marc's eyes, the fundamental fact that renders those accusations of his guilt illogical, unthinkable. Or to borrow the term Miller uses to describe the unreadability of women's fiction, it generates the most fundamental of the affair's 'ungrammaticalities':

> How could you countenance for a single second the idea that this man succumbed to a sudden fit of wretched madness before returning to his bed, beside his children's cradle, and to the beloved wife waiting for him? [. . .] Simon was *naturally beyond suspicion* because of his nature, his situation, his circumstances.[56]

What Zola establishes, from the off, is the incompatibility of the accused's healthy sexual appetites (he is 'without physiological flaws') with the perverted nature of the crime. By this logic, the prosecution's narrative of Simon's guilt is undermined by certain 'moral impossibilities' (81), which place it outside the bounds of what the novel insistently terms 'good sense'. Put otherwise, the novel conveniently elides the codes of (sexual) conduct onto those of probability, in a way that appeals to a set of tacit moral beliefs.

In shifting the Affair so emphatically into the realm of the erotic in *Vérité*, Zola can be seen to amplify the discourse of personal morality that had underwritten his own interventions in Dreyfus's case. In fact, we might wish to apply to Zola's fiction the terms of Richard Sennett's corrosive deconstruction of 'J'accuse. . .!', insofar as the writer stages in his novel a similar 'trial by character', whereby 'Right and Wrong [. . .] is to be read only in terms of personality'.[57] Questions of legal proof and evidence, Sennett argues, are entirely subordinate to the ends of the author's portrait of his protagonists as 'absolutes of self', their every action read as indicators of certain flaws or excesses of character. For all that Zola invokes, in other words, the conjoined discourses of rationality and right-eousness, the 'real content' of his open letter is 'what kind of person would defend the Jewish captain, what kind of person would attack him' (249). The effect was to interpellate his readership into polarised positions on the basis of collective affinities, rather than to submit to the force of logic.

Such forms of 'character assassination' are, of course, more readily associated with the anti-Semitic Right, and Sennett identifies just such a 'disturbing parallel' with Édouard Drumont's scabrous 'L'Âme de Dreyfus', which also closes with an image of its defiant and courageous author, yielding to the noble impulse to speak out in the service of the nation.[58] To be sure, Zola replicates, crystallises even, in *Vérité* this conflation of private character and political legitimacy by placing centre-stage the cult of personality that his charismatic hero – another 'absolute of self', in Sennett's terms – inspires. Marc's exemplary and uncompromising life of devotion to the task of preparing a just future involves creating disciples ready to live by his enlightened principles. For this is, Naomi Schor writes, 'the ultimate conversion novel'.[59] If, at the outset, then, Zola attributes to Marc an obstinately atavistic trace of anti-Semitic feeling, it is only the better to demonstrate how this latent and invidious suspicion of his fellow countrymen cedes to the force of reason. In this vein, the novel dismantles some, if not all, of the specious extrapolations on which Simon's wrongful conviction rests – extrapolations of the kind emblematised in the Dreyfus Affair by Maurice Barrès's malignant declaration: 'I don't need to be told why Dreyfus betrayed. Psychologically speaking, it is enough for me to know that he betrayed. [...] That Dreyfus is capable of betrayal, I conclude from his race.'[60]

However nauseating Barrès's particular brand of racist determinism, it betrays a prejudicial logic that Dreyfus's defenders were also capable of deploying. Well before clear proof of Dreyfus's innocence could be acquired, Dreyfusards such as the historian Joseph Reinach had already made up their minds, persuaded by their suspicion that the Jewish captain's conviction was the next step in a Jesuit take-over: 'from the very first day, I had a hunch [l'intuition] that the accused was innocent. The first clue had been the seemingly deliberate fury of church newspapers, which had been indifferent to other acts of betrayal'.[61] Such assumptions, tied to pre-existing emotion and longstanding animosities, give the lie, as Ruth Harris has argued, to the prevailing 'belief in Dreyfusard "rationality"': Dreyfus's defenders were 'just as preoccupied with the interplay of reason and unreason, and intellect and instinct, as their enemies'.[62] Zola was no exception. Indeed, it is hard not to read *Vérité* as an attempt to offer a retrospective seal of sanction to precisely the kind of speculation that guides Reinach's conviction, peddling as it does its own version of the clerical conspiracy.[63] For all that the novel seeks, moreover, to unpick the causal deductions of anti-Semitic discourse that implicate its victim, it remains a crucial irony of the Simon affair that his defenders can only do so by reintroducing through the backdoor the logic of naturalisation that the narrative decries elsewhere.

If Zola recasts in fiction, then, the curious epistemological grounds on which the truth of the victim's innocence is founded, the effect, of course, is to set those conditions of knowledge beyond scrutiny. Intuition – which, we have just seen, rears its head in Reinach's account of his initial Dreyfusard conviction too – emerges as the expedient conduit for the ideological manoeuvres at work in the case; and in this, Zola was reprising the very faculty that seemed to guide his own engagement. In a letter addressed to Zola on the evening of his condemnation at trial for libel, in the wake of 'J'accuse. . . !', Stéphane Mallarmé extolled the novelist's bravery in the following terms: 'The spectacle has been given, definitively, of the limpid intuition a genius opposes to the powers that be.'[64] Zola's heroic act, as Mallarmé saw it, was to have the courage of his intuition; and on this, critics and historians have tended to follow suit. Henri Mitterand recasts Mallarmé's terms by arguing that 'The truth would win out, because this signature genius could – through intuition – bestow upon it the power of fiction.'[65] For Jean-Denis Bredin, meanwhile, Zola's clarity of perception made a virtue of necessity, at a moment when proofs remained out of reach: 'But what is surprising is the luminous power of intuition [. . .] with which Zola recognised and called out the key elements.'[66] Given the importance of reason to the Dreyfusards' self-image, such admiration for Zola's instinctive grasp of the truth seems strangely unselfconscious. It certainly tells us much about the need to rescue Zola's great act from the arbitrariness – the vagaries of the hunch – that otherwise threatens its legitimacy: intuition must become, in retrospect, the unwavering force of the righteous. And yet, as I shall argue now, Zola made no bones about the role of intuition and feeling in the shaping of his own convictions. The emboldened Republic that the writer saw emerging from the wreckage of the Affair required precisely that: a democratic, and universal, *instinct* for the truth.

Object Lesson

In his open letter to President Émile Loubet, published in *L'Aurore* on 22 December 1900, Zola registered his despondency at the decision to offer Dreyfus a pardon, signed by Loubet ten days after the verdict of the second court martial was announced. Suppressing the truth that Zola, like other Dreyfusards, had sought to establish in the pursuit of legal justice, this intervention had made it impossible to draw from events what he called 'the admirable practical lesson [*leçon de choses*] provided by the Dreyfus Affair'.[67] Never had there been such a decisive opportunity to denounce the reactionary forces at work in this most atrocious of crimes and, in turn, to rouse the conscience of the people. Loubet had effectively denied the Affair what Zola called, upon the outcome of Dreyfus's retrial, its 'fifth act': the moment of revelation, or *anagnôrisis*, fundamental to classical tragedy, and which was, Zola urged, the condition of the nation's regeneration, 'delivering us, making us young and vigorous once again'.[68] The master trope of Zola's letter to Loubet – and presumably, the denied fifth act – was a vision of the great national fanfare accompanying the innocent victim's return home: 'the enlightened people arising as one, acclaiming Dreyfus upon his return to France, the country recovering its conscience, building an altar to justice, celebrating the reconquest of glorious, sovereign law'.[69] In *Vérité*, Zola replicates this suspension of the drama, and of its resolution, by having Simon too found guilty on retrial at Rozen (Zola's Rennes), and subsequently offered a pardon in 'the most inexplicable of contradictions' (282). Initially disconsolate, Marc speaks his regret, in precisely the same terms as the novelist, at not having been able to extract from this prodigious affair 'the exemplary object lesson [leçon de choses] that the people would have been taught, in a flash of lightning' (302). Marc, like Zola, must reconcile himself to a different narrative time, recasting the victory of truth as a slow yet inexorable struggle to the light. Instead, Zola has his hero tap the rich vein of vegetal metaphors on which *Germinal* had drawn to a close: this initial 'sowing of truth and justice' will surely yield its harvest, 'even if the good seed would take many long winters to germinate in the furrow'.

To be sure, Marc's (and Zola's) self-correction tells us a great deal about the checks that the writer feels the need to place on the idealist imagination. To expect the triumph of justice to be accomplished by 'magnificent leaps' and 'dramatic turns of events' (302) is clearly construed as unreasonable. Indeed, Zola seemingly renders with such passion the 'fine dream' of national reconciliation in his letter to Loubet – and in turn has Marc do the same – all the better to admonish, ironise, and disown, what we are invited to conceive of as a *bad idealism*.[70] That is, the miraculous in different stripes, which Zola places 'outside the logical grounds of work and good sense' (108). If Zola does eventually realise in *Vérité*, as we shall see, the vision of a 'festival of reparation' (362) that was his wish for Dreyfus, it is because the narrative expands in such a way that allows for the slow-burning internalisation of that object lesson he, via his teacher-hero, wishes to impart. The novel gives full rein, in other words, to the generational, or patrilinear, logic that Zola outlined in his journalism, whereby 'each step forward is achieved at the cost of suffering: only the sons can observe the achievements of their fathers'.[71] Fittingly, the Froment brothers of Zola's final series are nothing if not creatures of (almost implausible) longevity; and in *Vérité* – one of Zola's longest novels – patience is, for heroes and readers alike, a necessary virtue.

What we can determine between journalism and allegorical fiction, then, is something of a conceptual shift, whereby the victim's exoneration is no longer strictly figured as the precondition of national regeneration, but rather as its logical endpoint. For it is, Zola makes abundantly clear, on the success of Marc's work in the classroom – rather than the procedures of the courtroom —that the novel's (and the Affair's) happy resolution really depends. Certainly, in twinning the detective, or legal, story with the pedagogical plot, Zola offers up a dual solution to what he diagnoses as a crisis of popular epistemology – and this, I want to suggest, in a way that maps onto the logic of populist politics that Sophia Rosenfeld describes in *Democracy and Truth* (2019). For, according to Rosenfeld, 'populism, as a way of thinking about and narrating the fate of truth and power, demands two basic corrective actions: revelation – or exposing the conspiracy – and restoration of a better, more just status quo.'[72] At stake in Zola's *Vérité* is, of course, precisely this dual corrective. The former hinges on the identification of the real culprit, but is, in fact, concerned with positing and revealing a yet more serious crime: the betrayal of the people's trust as a result of 'the complicity of all the powerful' (302) – priest, soldier, magistrate, minister. For the relative deprivation and naivety of Zola's 'intoxicated' *peuple* have made them, in the novel's free indirect style, 'easy prey for fraudsters and liars, for those feeding off the public's gullibility' (105). The latter demands the redemption of those same people from the dangerous deceptions of unscrupulous opportunists by providing a kind of prophylactic. Crucially, the new citizens of Zola's Republic, formed in Marc's image, will be armed with the critical tools for distinguishing fact from fiction, legitimate truths from phony ones. Though tellingly, this is cast, in keeping with Rosenfeld's criteria, as a matter of 'restoration' rather than innovation. To repurpose the language of Trumpian populism, Zola calls upon the younger generation to make France great *again*: 'France, I beg you, come to your senses, be yourself again, be that great country, France.'[73]

In good part, Zola's paean to the enlightenment of the masses is overwhelmingly familiar, its imbrication of citizenship and schooling firmly rooted in the Third Republic credo that, as Mona Ozouf puts it, 'good readers will make good voters'.[74] Yet there is more to Zola's Republican vision than the straightforward democratisation of knowledge. The road to justice, Zola insists, must pass through the truth: 'There is no justice without truth, there is no happiness without justice' (392) is the last of countless such gnomic axioms in the novel. But for all of Zola's abstractions, it also becomes clear that justice depends on a particular kind of truth; and indeed, that this truth has privileged conduits. In his 'Lettre à la jeunesse', published on 14 December 1897, Zola had pinned his hopes for Dreyfus's exoneration to the natural candour of youth. In distinction to the power of public law – 'the justice prescribed by our Codes' – Zola determined in the younger generation the capacity to become a superior arbiter, beholden to an ideal principle that can compensate for the fallibility of decision-makers: 'If you do not stand up to an entire nation, in the name of ideal justice, then who will?'[75] This is because, Zola intimates, their own sure sense of what is right and just is yet to be compromised by worldly intrigue:

> But I ask you: where will we ever find a *clear intuition of things*, an *instinctive feel* for what is true and just, if not in these fresh new souls, in these young people [. . .] whose good and upright reasoning should not yet be obscured by anything?[76]

Such invocations of the instinctual, and of intuition, appear consistent with the anti-intellectualism that runs through Zola's fictional projects. David Baguley describes Zola's suspicion of cerebral processes as 'unstable secondary phenomena', to which the wise prefer a surer, embodied instrument of perception, 'a shrewd instinct that apprehends life in its very immanence'.[77]

This mistrust of abstract thinking must go some way to explaining why Zola is at such pains in *Vérité* to distinguish his hero from the figure of the academic or expert. In his preparatory notes, Zola insisted that Marc be 'intellectually, a reasonable mind, logical and clear. Not a great scholar [un grand savant]. But knowing well what he knows and gifted with the ability to teach it effectively to others'.[78] In fact, Zola reminds us on several occasions that Marc's most impressive pedagogical skill is his ability to simplify for his pupils that which appears complex: 'his quiet conviction made its mark, obscure notions became clearer, seeming easy and simple' (39). What matters, in turn, to the pursuit of justice in the novel is not the cultivation of specialist knowledge, but rather, as we have already seen, Marc's twin faculties of

clear-sightedness and intuition. For both of the narrative's prevailing truths –
that of Simon's innocence, and that of the clerical conspiracy – are first
experienced as a *feeling*, or 'sensation' (59). In its earliest incarnations, truth
touches Zola's hero as a frisson (26), and then as a 'force' (253).

That Baguley does not trace this anti-intellectual bent through Zola's
journalism on the Affair might tell us much about the inconvenient contradictions it entails for our understanding of Zola as the champion of Dreyfusard
intellectuals; and we shall return to the troubling symmetries between anti-
Dreyfusard anti-intellectualism and Zola's own suspicions below.[79] Certainly,
in *Vérité*, Zola champions through his *instituteur* those fundamentally anti-
intellectual faculties – namely, intuition and plain common sense – that are
classically associated with ordinary folk, rather than experts, and which effectively constitute what Rosenfeld calls the people's 'imagined authority'.[80]
Indeed, populism's 'standard claim', writes Rosenfeld, 'is that "the people",
when not being misled by false authorities, are in possession of a kind of
infallible, instinctive sense of what is right and true, born of or nurtured by
day-to-day experience in the world'.[81] Zola produces, across his Dreyfus
journalism and fiction, just such a double discourse on what he tends to call
the 'the ordinary people' [le petit peuple], whereby they are at once the most
vulnerable to manipulation, the easiest to entrap in a dark web of intolerance,
dogmatism, even fanaticism; and they are a 'goodhearted, commonsensical
people', the repository of a special kind of cognition that makes them superior
truth-tellers.[82] In one respect, then, Zola is rehearsing his longstanding valor-
isation of 'popular' knowledge over and above an excessively cerebral
intelligence. In giving Marc, like all the Froment brothers, a manual trade –
in his case, lithography – Zola connects his teacher-hero to the collective
experience of the people whose practical knowledge of the world is at the root
of its candour and authenticity.[83] In turn, Marc makes it his mission to restore
to the people its own best faculties, rousing 'the intelligence of the masses'
from its 'heavy slumber' (105), first and foremost through the cultivation of
young minds.

Marc's pedagogical project is grounded in the language and ambitions of
naturalist theory: its primary task is the promotion of a searching, experimental method that would ultimately serve to reveal the falsity of received
ideas or dogma. The Catholic catechism is the much-maligned foil to
Marc's epistemological conviction that 'all so-called revealed truths are lies;
experimental truth alone is correct – the single, whole, eternal truth' (124).
In seeking to rival such forms of Catholic indoctrination, Zola's pedagogical vision reproduced many of the assumptions that had underpinned

Jules Ferry's ambitions for primary education. The *instituteur* should seek, Ferry declared, to arouse the child's natural curiosity, liberating them from the rote learning of ready-made rules and principles 'that only end up filling their young minds with vague, dense ideas, and creating a kind of intellectual gloom'.[84] These notions lay at the heart of the Third Republic's philosophy on schooling, which was steered by one Ferdinand Buisson, appointed by Ferry as director of primary education in 1879.[85] Zola would no doubt have been familiar with Buisson's militant advocacy of secular education. On 28 March 1901, Buisson delivered a speech on 'The idea of justice in teaching', to an event held by the Ligue des Droits de l'Homme de Paris, over which Zola was invited to preside; and the inextricable link between truth and justice that Buisson expounded clearly chimed with his own thinking.[86] Buisson's concern had long been to make the case for a secular morality to rival a religious education, and, in turn, for the *instituteur*'s pivotal role in developing a child's conscience. This, he had insisted, was first and foremost a matter of fostering in pupils the most natural and spontaneous faculty of human intelligence: intuition. What Buisson calls 'moral intuition' refers to man's capacity, 'innate in every heart, ingrained in every conscience', to grasp instinctively the beautiful and the good.[87] Studious reflection and the pursuit of science are a vital part of a child's further education, but what matters most, Buisson argues, is the cultivation of a kind of knowledge that is, at the earliest stage of learning, universally accessible: 'the instincts that nature gives to every man, the light of good sense'.[88]

In privileging instincts, feelings, ordinary experience, and intuitions, Buisson's pedagogy bears at least some of the hallmarks of what Rosenfeld has called a 'populist epistemology'.[89] Such assumptions certainly guide Marc's own educational experiment, which involves harnessing the child's natural, or instinctual, dispositions: principally 'this innate need for truth and justice' (125). In other words, what Marc requires of his pupils is a moral, as well as epistemic, commitment to the truth: they must be able to tell the truth, in both senses, as an act of civic virtue, and as the articulation of knowledge – acts which Zola had long considered to be one and the same. Indeed, the resolution of the affair is made to hinge on the ability of Marc's pupils to internalise – first and foremost, as a feeling, or compulsion – the moral duty of truth-telling, which the novel establishes as a kind of categorical imperative. Zola stages this connection via a minorly farcical classroom incident, in which the most stubbornly obtuse pupil of Marc's cohort, Fernand Bongard, falsely accuses his neighbour of having broken his cap. In front of Fernand's peers, Marc takes the opportunity to 'denounce the lie' (134), and with such force that Fernand immediately repents. Witness to this spectacle is the sweet, intelligent Sébastien Milhomme, who promptly confesses that he had concealed from Marc, at the time of his investigation, his knowledge of a vital piece of evidence: the writing sampler that could have exculpated Simon. Under Marc's exemplary tutelage, Sébastien has since developed an irrepressible need to tell the truth. With his belated revelation, Sébastien fulfils Marc's tentative prophesy upon their first encounter: 'would the truth emerge at long last from the mouth of this child?' (57). The narrative thus transfigures its originary crime – the strangling of Zéphirin, his mouth stuffed with a paper gag – into a proverb: out of the mouths of babes. . .

This characteristically overdetermined episode constitutes one of many such object lessons in the novel, all of which serve to demonstrate the legitimacy of Marc's inexhaustible investment in the figure of the child as the harbinger of an ideal future: 'it was the child who would overcome the final obstacles on the path to the future City of perfect solidarity!'[90] Marc's soaring vision of perfectibility across the generations drives his struggle to liberate the youth of Maillebois from the perverse stranglehold of a Catholic education, to rival, that is, the mission he ascribes to the Church: 'the conquest of the future by the child' (112). Though it is his biological daughter Louise who offers the finest example of this triumph over dogmatism, her own physiognomy displaying the dissolution of her Catholic mother's influence: 'her mother's fine features seemed to dissolve into an expression of quiet good sense that she took from her father' (205). Vitally, the paternal line dominates in the ideal daughter, whose level-headed pragmatism signals a rupture with the matrilineal legacy, an indulgence in obscurantism and superstitions traced back to Louise's maternal grandmother, the fanatical Mme Duparque. Correcting this inheritance is, clearly, the principal task of Marc's (and Zola's) wider paternalist project – one in which, we might observe, women appear as the primary beneficiaries.[91] For not only are they figured as the most susceptible to Catholic indoctrination, their role as mothers and educators makes their conversion to Marc's secular ethos all the more imperative; they too must become freethinking citizens, capable of seeing through their own exploitation and deception.

In the final stages of the novel, with Simon's innocence at last established, the culmination of this pedagogical endeavour is articulated as a clean rupture between generations. The tale of the Simon affair, as retold by his contemporaries, is simply anathema to those citizens formed in the crucible of Marc's classroom:

> People spoke only of the extraordinary story emerging from a dark and distant past, this condemnation of an innocent man, which seemed both abhorrent and inexplicable in the eyes of the new generations. [. . .] Now that the truth had been revealed in broad daylight, ascertained with an invincible certainty, children and grandchildren were unable to understand how fathers and grandfathers could have been so blindly stupid, so nastily selfish, as to fail to fathom such a simple affair. (363)

Here, Zola describes the very clear-sightedness to which he had appealed in his journalism. Caught in the novel's rear-view mirror, the story of Simon's injustice has at last become that which it already was: so strangely unbelievable. The success of Marc's mission is sealed in those scenes of intergenerational reckoning, where sons judge their fathers, and fathers duly admonish themselves.

Beyond Simon's rehabilitation in the eyes of the law, then, there is a pressing need to expiate the sins of generations past. As a form of reparation, the citizens of Maillebois build a new home for their returning victim – the inscription above his doorway signed 'The Grandchildren of his Persecutors' (353). Of course, such an instance of memorialisation is destined to serve as much as a reminder of the community's mistake, as a permanent warning against future injustices. And yet, for all that these gestures signpost, so overtly, the happy conclusion of the narrative – and this precisely as an ending to end all such narratives – the novel reserves for the reader one last test of its own thesis in the final chapter, by staging another version of its central crime. In an episode we might dub the 'Rose affair', Marc's great-granddaughter is the victim of an attempted abduction, close to the very spot on which Zéphirin had been raped and strangled. On his way home late at night, Marc is stopped in his tracks by a faint commotion and discovers lurking in the darkness the young Marsoullier (nephew of the former mayor of Maillebois), holding in his hand a white handkerchief. On the ground, a lifeless Rose lies unconscious, her body bearing the traces of a violent struggle, her dress in tatters, clumps of hair affixed to the lace of her white dress. Marsoullier claims to have been passing by when he heard a child cry out, arriving just in time to witness a man fleeing the scene. Initially, Marc suspects Marsoullier of the crime, but as Rose regains consciousness, she claims – to her mother and Marc's astonishment – to have recognised the aggressor, by his hat and beard, as her own father François, who had recently abandoned the marital home to join his mistress. Two vital, if flimsy, pieces of evidence link François to the crime: Rose's eye-witness account; and the handkerchief collected by Marsoullier, mechanically embroidered with a capital 'F' (the initial of its owner), and identical to those of François's other handkerchiefs that his wife Thérèse finds lying in his drawer at home. The available facts thus point straightforwardly towards François's guilt, but Marc's first instinct is to protest his son's innocence: 'No, no! Despite Rose's statements, and despite the handkerchief, François could not be guilty; certain moral impossibilities ruled it out, and there were arguments that outweighed the evidence' (382).

In precisely the same terms that Delbos had used to contest Simon's guilt ('the moral impossibilities are blatant'), Marc's reasoning rests on these twin convictions: that François had no motive to abduct his own daughter, since – despite having recently left his wife – he could still see her as he wished; and, in a gesture of paternal empathy, that 'a loving father [. . .] was incapable of mistreating his own daughter'.[92] At first, Marc fears another miscarriage of justice with the community falling prey to the rumour-mongering of those last-remaining Catholic *fidèles*, keen to exploit the scandal by placing François in a conspiratorial web of freemasons. But such far-fetched aspersions, or 'improbabilities', find little currency among Maillebois's new generations, schooled in the art of critical reading: 'Nowadays, people knew too much, and would hardly accept a story of this kind without using their common sense [sans raisonner]' (383). A community-wide investigation ensues; and as more clues emerge as to the culprit's identity, suspicion falls instead on Faustin Roudille, a former custodian of the monks' domain, and the sister of François's lover, Colette. When Marc confronts Marsoullier, the latter cedes to the truth-telling impulse cultivated by his schoolteacher: 'However much you want to lie, your whole being rises up to object' (386). His conscience pricked, Marsoullier freely confesses: it was Faustin he had interrupted *en flagrant délit*, disguised in a hat and fake beard(!). With this the evidence against François is promptly discarded: the incriminating handkerchief is attributed to the real culprit; and upon François's return to the family home, Rose realises she was mistaken in having recognised her father as the aggressor.

Such are the aesthetic liberties that the *roman à thèse* allows itself: this *mise en abyme* – the allegory of the novel's overarching allegory – curates for the reader an (absurdly implausible) replica of the central crime in order to demonstrate, as unambiguously as possible, the extent to which its own lessons in hermeneutics have been internalised.[93] Put differently, Zola duplicates the details of the first crime in the second so as to better insist on the asymmetry of their aftermaths. In each case, the monstrous transgression betrays the paedophilic appetites of an aberrant single man, tied to the clergy; the revelation of the culprit's true identity averts the possible crime of incest; and the potentially incriminating pieces of evidence – the writing sampler and handkerchief, both bearing initials – are at first misattributed. Indeed, the Rose affair allows Marc to justify, all over again, his privileging of intuitive knowledge over proofs – 'arguments that outweighed the evidence' – in ways which involve precisely the same elision of moral beliefs and plausibility. For the path to justice relies on an unwillingness to believe either father capable of the crime of which he stands accused. If anything, then, the second affair promotes an even greater suspicion of 'the signs, marks or tokens' that are, as Terence Cave has shown in his masterful study of *anagnôrisis*, 'a distinguishing feature of recognition plots'.[94] Insofar as both episodes demand the correction of a specious reading, or misrecognition, they rely on Marc's (and later, on others') scepticism about those clues that turn out to be fake, partial, duplicitous, a red herring – clues whose legitimacy, moreover, depends on their correspondence with a set of ideological truths. Zola's doubling of the original crime thus serves, most transparently, as the vindication of his hero's interpretative methods, and as the evidence that these are now shared by his fellow citizens.

In this respect, such internal duplication plainly bespeaks the thesis novel's endeavour to prove its own assumptions right. And yet, the very fact that justice must be served not once but twice points, just as surely, I am suggesting, towards a trouble in the narrative – one Cave identifies in the recognition plot as, echoing Ginzburg, a 'cynegetic' endeavour:

> The recognition scene shows that the beast can be caught – or at least that *a* beast can be caught; but the magic has to be constantly repeated, to exorcize the fear of all the times it hasn't worked and *we haven't noticed*: the hanging of the innocent man, the survival of the imposter, the adultery or incest that continues concealed and unchecked, the bastard brought up as rightful heir.[95]

For all that Zola's narrative is about the irrepressible outing of truth as 'a shining light' (384), as certain justice, it remains haunted by the possibility of *getting it wrong*. In other words, Zola's constant metaphorisation, or naturalisation, of the recognition plot is part of the narrative's obsessive masking of the fragile grounds on which recognition is constructed in the first place; it betrays the drive, in Cave's terms, to 'conjure away the threat of contingency'.[96] Hence, Zola's repetition of the magic serves as the proof that Simon's false condemnation was indeed the mistake to end all mistakes. If the potential for fresh tragedy, then, hangs over this final twist of the novel, it is there precisely in order to be averted, this uncanny scenario doubling the original crime in structure, albeit not in tone. Indeed, Zola's curious slip into farce – signalled by the fake beard and botched job – bears such a degree of contrivance that the episode no longer demands to be taken seriously. In the post-Affair world of the Zolian imaginary, the threat of misrecognition could only survive as melodrama.

'Queer Idealism'

In August 1903, just before the anniversary of Zola's death, Henry James published a vast retrospective essay in *The Atlantic Monthly* on the career of his French contemporary. Predictably, James reserved his strongest admiration for *L'Assommoir*, *Germinal*, and *La Débâcle*, while reiterating his esteem for the writer's 'courage in the Dreyfus connection'.[97] Penning 'J'accuse…!' was, James had declared at the time, 'one of the most courageous things ever done'.[98] But of the novel that transposed that Affair James was categorically dismissive, describing *Vérité* as a curious act of self-sabotage in which Zola set 'to wreck, poetically, his so massive identity' (252). As what was in effect Zola's last word, this strange, climactic phenomenon came up short in everything – except, regrettably, its length. Tasteless, heavy-handed, lacking in 'the finer vision of human experience' (255), James castigated Zola's later style. For it betrayed many of those qualities that presumably make for heroic acts, but which also seal the fate of bad novels: high-minded conviction, dogged patience, and the author's 'inability, once his direction taken, to entertain so much as the shadow of [a doubt]' (245). Built on Zola's unwavering self-belief, the 'fatal' deficiency of this final novel rests – like much that he wrote in the last decade of his life – on what James termed its 'queer idealism' (255), which he glossed as an egregious (and incidentally, Sandian) art of 'simplification'. Zola imposed in his last works an air of finality, chalking up his 'lesson, with loud taps and a still louder commentary […] on the blackboard'.[99]

Effectively, what James conjures up here are so many traits of the thesis novel: in Susan Rubin Suleiman's terms, its 'repressive righteousness', its appeal 'to the need for certainty, stability, and unity', and its tendency to '[infantalize] the reader' in the process.[100] That *Vérité*, especially, emblematises something of an unpalatable turn in Zola's writing has been amply asserted by critics; and we shall turn to these questions of taste, as well as the awkward conjunction of civic heroism and ideological fiction, in the book's Conclusion.[101] But in the final part of this chapter, I want to dwell on the particular ambitions driving this evolution in Zola's late style, together with the compromises it imposed, and of which the author was, in a sense, well aware. Already, in his 1896 letter 'À la jeunesse', Zola had reflected on both the prolixity and the *redondance* of his prose as betraying a certain anxiety of legibility: 'If my books are so long, and if I repeat myself so much, it is because I am always afraid of not being understood.'[102] Though what also emerges, both in that declaration and across his utopian fiction, is an insistence on the pursuit of clarity, transparency, simplicity precisely as an aesthetic ideal – and one firmly tied to his democratic vision. This was the imperative of being, as he put it in his preparatory notes for *Travail*, '<u>understood by everybody</u>'.[103]

Certainly, what Zola appears to seek to perform through his prose style in *Vérité* are those very virtues he deems necessary to the emergence of his ideal Republic. Chief among these, I would venture, is a type of sound, reasonable judgement that the narrative, as we have seen, insistently calls 'bon sens'. For common sense is, to borrow the terms of anthropologist Clifford Geertz, first and foremost a style of thought, a tone, or attitude. Beyond any identifiable content, 'what simple wisdom has everywhere in common is the maddening air of simple wisdom with which it is uttered' – it casts over the matters it describes 'an air of "of-courseness"'.[104] Zola's *Vérité* is awash in just such an 'air', its moralising glosses on the plot cultivating at least the ring of truth. When, for instance, the Zolian narrator describes Geneviève's growing instinct to return to her husband's bed, foregoing the sterile rituals of her Catholic faith, it is all the better to demonstrate 'that unique and eternal truth that makes healthy, happy couples of men and women' (290). Such a plain 'truth' is spoken in the manner of a 'truism': inarguable, consensual, natural, beyond any political or ideological partisanship – and, above all, simple. What, in fact, it reinscribes is the compulsive – and compulsory – heteronormativity on which Zola's utopia depends, its exacting sexual politics a function of its corrective idealism. The discourse of common sense thus converts ideological assumptions into a type of knowledge that is ostensibly intuitive, and universally accessible. At least rhetorically, it performs, in other words, the wider purpose Zola ascribes to his novel: 'Establish the truth, <u>one</u> truth'.[105]

More broadly, we have seen over the course of this chapter how Zola valorises simplicity as a vital counter-discourse in the Dreyfus Affair, and, in turn, how such simplicity is cast as the preserve of the young on whose sound judgement justice depends. In *Vérité* as in Zola's Dreyfus journalism, envisaging the Affair's resolution meant imagining a people no longer in thrall to two kinds of specious epistemological authorities: the

Catholic Church, and its peddling of an anti-Semitic conspiracy; and the establishment of experts and judicial powers upon whose (mis)judgement Dreyfus's erroneous conviction depends. And yet, in auguring the emergence of a self-sovereign, truth-telling people, Zola veered, as I have suggested, closer than we might otherwise imagine to the anti-intellectualism that was by and large the domain of the right. For instance, in response to the petition of support for Dreyfus in *L'Aurore* that followed Zola's 'J'accuse...!', and which was signed by a host of writers, scientists, and artists, Barrès famously railed against 'demi-intellectuals', or 'aristo-crats of thought', and their efforts to distinguish themselves from 'simple' Frenchmen.[106] Brunetière, too, reportedly decried this transformation of a cerebral elite into 'a sort of noble cast', preferring instead those relatively superior qualities that were available to the common man: 'strength of will and character, sound judgement, practical experience'.[107] Such was the contempt for a subset of self-fashioned intellectuals (with Zola at the helm) that, Dreyfus's adversaries argued, sought to deny the better judgement of the majority. Yet we also need to recall that not long before Zola had voiced his own suspicions of 'professional intellects' as a detached class, 'perhaps suited only to thinking and creating in the abstract'.[108] Against Ernest Renan's oligarchic vision of elites – savants, poets, great minds – leading the people, Zola augured 'a broader distribution of common knowledge', a narrowing gap between the masses and its intellectual guardians that would befit a rising democracy.[109] In *Vérité*, Zola effectively realised this vision of democratised education as a sure means to bring about the end of class (struggle) once and for all: 'there could be no more *déclassés*, since there were no longer any classes, nor any rebels' (375).

Like his anti-Dreyfusard antagonists, then, Zola was inclined to appeal to popular judgement, to prize the wisdom of a *demos*. The fundamental difference was that Zola insisted on drawing a distinction between, on the one hand, an irrational, impulsive, baying 'mob gone mad', whipped into hysteria by corrupt opinion-makers; and, on the other, the authentic people, as prospective harbingers of truth, that he sought to conjure into being.[110] It is, in fact, on precisely this gesture – the 'exaltation of the *real* people' – that, Rosenfeld argues, the standard populist narrative relies. 'It concludes', she adds, 'with a fairytale-like denouement and a new, mythic social role for its adherents'.[111] The masses only need to overcome their reliance on a set of elites and institutions by whom their trust has been betrayed, in order to usher in a new regime of consensus that would resolve political conflict altogether.

In essence, this is the story Zola tells in *Vérité*, the happy culmination of which is the 'festival of reparation' planned for Simon's homecoming.

Conceived as 'a moment of general reconciliation, when the whole of Maillebois would embrace once more in brotherly harmony' (360), the celebration is not only a scene of absolution, or of the expiation of collective sins, but a moment of sentimental unanimity. In fact, where each of Zola's finished *Évangiles* includes just such a scene – in *Fécondité* and *Travail*, this takes the form of a communal banquet – the celebratory assembly is, in some sense, the archetypal figure of the Zolian utopia. Certainly, the consensus these moments perform is, as Laville suggests, the ultimate 'horizon' of Zola's utopian fiction, whereby the total identification of citizens with their community is at once an ideal and a 'condition of belonging'.[112] On this reading, Zola might be understood to exploit that other iteration of 'common sense' as 'common feeling': Kant's *sensus communis* as that which, Hannah Arendt glosses, 'fits us into a community'.[113] When the citizens of Maillebois gather for the unveiling of the inscription on Simon's home, we reach the logical endpoint of Marc's redemptive mission – the scene of an autonomous, united people from which any trace of discordance or dissensus has been eliminated: 'there arose one final, mighty round of applause, which rolled on like thunder, bringing all the people together at last; not a single protest dared to undermine the celebration of truth and justice, victorious' (372). What Zola's crowning moment of 'poetic justice' demands – and this is no doubt part of James's frustration – is the censure of any tone other than harmony.[114]

For all that Zola envisions, here, the populist 'fairytale' Rosenfeld describes, it is surely an important contradiction of his novel that the final act in Marc's campaign – the obliteration of the Catholic Church – will be accomplished not by the people it redeems, but by a kind of (authorial) providence. For in the final stages of *Vérité*, the novelist becomes something of an Old Testament deity, curating an apocalyptic scene of destruction, which sees Maillebois hit by a terrible storm that engulfs the Désirade chapel. When lightning strikes, Church elder Père Théodose is burnt alive at the altar ('set ablaze like a torch', 373), while Père Crabot is crushed – in the most brazen instance of irony – by the falling statue of Saint Antoine. With the entire structure in ruins, the town will eventually establish on the former chapel's luxuriant grounds a municipal 'Palace of the people', designed for the leisure and pleasure of all citizens. Effectively, then, Zola fulfils here the wish he had expressed in his 'Lettre au Sénat': 'we, as mere citizens, would like to purify the atmosphere immediately, burn what is rotten [...], so that the body as a whole can recover its health and its strength'.[115] Catastrophe, as we saw in Chapter 2, had long been cast by Zola as the necessary condition of regeneration. In this particular fantasy of cosmic retribution, disaster is harnessed to the ends of a supralegal form of 'justice', whereby those who refuse to embrace Marc's secular new world are, in the end, smited.[116]

*

Truth, in the master-rhetoric of Zola's Dreyfus journalism has a life, and self-perpetuating force, of its own; to conceal or bury it is only to intensify its eventual explosion. It is a conviction that Zola attributes, in turn, to Marc in his *Ébauche*: '[truth] is on the march [. . .]; try as they might to contain it, it blows everything apart. <u>And in the end, he is right</u>. It is my victory.'[117] In a quasi-confessional slippage between hero and author, Zola envisages here nothing less than the pleasure of *being right*. An ageing Marc will witness the closure to the affair, the fantasy of vindication that Zola could only project into the future; he will experience 'the greatest happiness of seeing his dream come true, more and more each day' (382). In the words of contemporary author Albert Le Roy, writing just after the publication of *Vérité* in book form: 'It is a battle that Émile Zola fought twice. In real life, he was only half victorious. In the book, with Marc, he is completely triumphant.'[118] It hardly takes the most acute powers of perception, of course, to determine in Zola's rendering of his *instituteur*-hero the operation of just such a kind of projection.[119] And yet, I want to suggest upon closing, there is also something of an asymmetry at work in the dream of equivalence to which Zola admits. As Suleiman notes, 'One thing Zola leaves out [of *Vérité*], interestingly, is his own "J'Accuse" and its consequences.'[120] What, we might wonder at the last, were the compromises Zola deemed it necessary to make in order for his (hero's) vision to prevail?

If, as contemporary critics readily insisted, Zola is at his most Hugolian in *Vérité*, it is no doubt because he unfolds a latent myth of the author as truth-bearer. For Gaston Deschamps, Zola's 'hymn to the primary school teacher' could only resemble Hugo's magisterial 'Fonction du poète', in which he cast the poet as a prophet, whose noble mission it is to guide the people towards the light: 'Listen to the sacred dreamer!'[121] After all, it seemed as though Zola had effectively succumbed to precisely the very messianism, the romantic sentimentalism, he consistently associated with Hugo, and in direct opposition to which he had pitched his ethical and political vision of naturalist literature. Was *Vérité* not guilty of peddling just such a puerile dream of a transformed Republic, 'a mawkish humanitarianism steeped in a dream of universal love', for which Zola had castigated Hugo?[122] In the aftermath of Zola's death at least, few critics would wish to point to double standards. What seemed evident, though, was that Zola had been emboldened by his involvement in the Dreyfus Affair to stake his longstanding ambitions for the engaged role of the writer as a unifying figure of nations, even an international peace broker, his powerful voice – as he put it nearly a decade earlier – 'turning all suffering humanity into a single family'.[123]

Clearly, Zola indulges in *Vérité* the privileges of a poetic licence that he had long associated with the romantic writer. And yet, he nevertheless remains at pains – at least in his identification with Marc – to resist the kind of deification to which he had long objected in his contemporaries' (excessive) veneration of Hugo, whereby they rendered him, Zola lamented, 'a religion in literature'.[124] Tellingly, the more Marc's vision imposes itself, the more he is bound to exert his scrupulous sense of modesty: 'My children, my children, you mustn't make a god of me. You know very well that the churches are closing... I am simply a hardworking labourer, who has done his day's work' (392). In a Zolian utopia that has sought to eliminate false idols, there can be no place for *amour-propre*. Put otherwise, Zola can only imagine the triumph of his hero-visionary on the condition of the latter's willing self-effacement. In the hall of mirrors that is Zola's allegorical novel, the utopian leader, it seems, cannot be a professional writer, just as he cannot be a career politician nor, as we have seen, an intellectual. The narrative strains, in fact, to resolve its own uneasiness about Marc's status as both a visionary and a man of action. In another of the laborious circumlocutions it supplies, he is 'the heroic labourer of truth and justice' (64).

If *Germinal* and *Vérité* might be taken as fitting bookends for this study of idealism, it is then, in no small part, because Zola undertakes to imagine in his utopian fiction a solution to the problem of leadership – and indeed, of *ressentiment* – he had diagnosed in that earlier novel of (political) commitment. Where Étienne had served to demonstrate the impossible authenticity of the working-class militant, his aspirations for the masses tied to his own private fantasies of envy and ambition, Marc is indisputably a paragon of 'good faith'. In other words, the utopian leader has the good grace to envisage, in keeping with the novel's populist logic, his own superfluity. Ultimately, this, it seems, is one of the conditions on which idealism – or what we have called, in relation to *Germinal*, 'impossibilism' – could eventually be recast in *Vérité* as righteous optimism: 'Things that had once seemed impossible could be accomplished with ease, now that the people were better, freed from delusion and falsehood, endowed with knowledge and strength of will' (325). The legitimate political vision Zola has his hero realise is necessarily one of popular self-governance, even as the novel grapples with its own dependency on a hero. Perhaps this goes some way to explaining Zola's curious reluctance to transpose in *Vérité* the great act of engagement to which his name has since been irrevocably tied. It is surely one of the most telling ironies of Zola's destiny as a writer that, two years prior to 'J'accuse…!', and twelve before his interment in the Pantheon, he made this his rallying cry: '*pas de grands hommes!*'[125]

Notes

1 Dreyfus's initial sentence of penal servitude for life was commuted to ten years due to the court's ruling of extenuating circumstances.

2 Émile Zola, 'Letter to Madame Alfred Dreyfus', *The Dreyfus Affair: 'J'accuse' and Other Writings*, ed. Alain Pagès, trans. Eleanor Levieux (New Haven, CT: Yale University Press, 1996), pp. 143–50 (p. 144; emphasis added).

3 The raising of Lazarus is recounted in John 2:1–44. On the religious imagery associated with Dreyfus and his defenders, see Christopher E. Forth, *The Dreyfus Affair and the Crisis of French Manhood* (Baltimore, MD: The Johns Hopkins University Press, 2004), pp. 90–94; Andrew J. Counter, 'Wilde, Zola, Dreyfus, Christ: Fin de Siècle Passions', *Representations*, 149 (2020), 103–33; and John J. Cerullo, 'Religion and the Psychology of Dreyfusard Intellectualism', *Historical Reflections*, 24 (1998), 93–114.

4 Armand Charpentier, 'M. Émile Zola et l'opinion', *La Critique*, 71 (5 February 1898), 26.

5 Zola, *Lourdes*, ed. Bertrand Marquer (Paris: Classiques Garnier, 2015), p. 202. Zola dated *Lazare* 1 January 1894; *OC*, vol. 15, 583–92.

6 The term '*contre-miracle*' is used by Jean Zumstein, '"La mort est la grande douceur": Le Lazare d'Émile Zola', *Hermeneutische Blätter*, 1/2 (2009), 59–67 (p. 66).

7 Lucien Victor-Meunier, '*Fécondité*', *Le Rappel*, 16 October 1899, p. 1.

8 'Wilde, Zola, Dreyfus, Christ', 106.

9 On Zola's secularised religion, see Michèle Sacquin, 'Entre positivisme et laïcité: Zola et la "non-religion" de l'avenir, 1881–1902', in *Zola et les historiens*, ed. Michèle Sacquin (Paris: Bibliothèque nationale de France, 2004), pp. 65–75.

10 'Statement to the Jury', *Dreyfus Affair*, pp. 55–61 (p. 61).

11 Zola, *Vérité*, in *OC*, vol. 20, 254; hereafter, references are interpolated in the text.

12 *Vérité* appeared between 10 September 1902 and 15 February 1903; Zola died, in suspicious circumstances, just nineteen days after the serialisation began.

13 Lida Maxwell, *Public Trials: Burke, Zola, Arendt, and the Politics of Lost Causes* (Oxford: Oxford University Press, 2014), p. 3.

14 'Letter to Madame Alfred Dreyfus', p. 147; see Maxwell, *Public Trials*, p. 112.

15 Zola, letter to Paul Brulat, 15 October 1899; *Corr*, vol. 10, 74–75 (p. 75).

16 *Les Annales de la Jeunesse laïque*, March 1903; cited in Mona Ozouf, *L'École, l'Église et la République (1871–1914)* (Paris: Éditions Cana/Jean Offredo, 1982), p. 171.

17 'Letter to M. Émile Loubet', *Dreyfus Affair*, pp. 164–75 (p. 168). In 'J'accuse…!', Zola insisted on the clerical persuasions on certain military officers he held culpable: General de Boisdeffre was complicit 'out of intense clerical conviction', while Du Paty's forging of Dreyfus's guilt is linked with the 'clericalism that prevails in the military circles in which he moves'. 'Letter to M. Félix Faure', *Dreyfus Affair*, pp. 43–53 (pp. 52, 47).

18 'Letter to France', *Dreyfus Affair*, pp. 35–43 (p. 39).

19 The resemblances to the Pyrenean shrine are barely disguised: 'The saint had pride of place on a golden altar, always adorned with flowers and ablaze with candles, […] and a sales office was permanently installed by the vestry' (42).

20 'Letter to M. Félix Faure', p. 46.

21 'Letter to the Senate', *Dreyfus Affair*, pp. 154–64 (p. 162).

22 Roderick Cooke, *The Dreyfus Affair's Literary Politics* (Liverpool: Liverpool University Press, 2023).

23 'Lettre à la jeunesse', in *Le Roman expérimental*; *OC*, vol. 9, 349–70 (p. 361).

24 See, for instance, Zola, *Dreyfus Affair*, pp. 58, 57, 139.

25 Zola, *Dreyfus Affair*, pp. 30, 10, 13.

26 'Letter to France', p. 37.

27 'Letter to France', p. 41.

28 'Letter to M. Félix Faure', p. 44 (original emphasis).

29 At this time, the confusion over Du Paty and Henry's roles in the Affair was, as Alain Pagès points out, 'a "common mistake"'. *Émile Zola, un intellectuel dans l'affaire Dreyfus: histoire de 'J'accuse'* (Paris: Librairie Séguier, 1991), p. 114.

30 Ruth Harris, *Dreyfus: Politics, Emotion, and the Scandal of the Century* (New York: Picador, 2011), pp. 117, 118.

31 Zola, 'Notes sur l'Affaire Dreyfus', *OC*, vol. 18 (2008), 558.

32 Counter, 'A Sentimental Affair: *Vérité*', *Romanic Review*, 102 (2011), 391–409 (p. 405; original emphasis).

33 'A Sentimental Affair', 405.

34 Ursula Bähler, 'Sur les traces naturalistes de *La Vérité en marche*', *Les Cahiers naturalistes*, 82 (2008), 83–108 (p. 88). In his open letter to Félix Faure, Zola described the cover-up as the product of Du Paty de Clam's 'fertile imagination', and the challenge to his narrative of Dreyfus's guilt as 'the far-fetched, tragic work of cheap fiction [*roman-feuilleton*]'. *Dreyfus Affair*, p. 48. Pagès notes how 'the entire factual sequence of the Dreyfus Affair is indeed that of a serial novel'. *Émile Zola, un intellectuel dans l'affaire Dreyfus*, pp. 74–75. See also Pagès, 'L'Affaire Dreyfus comme roman-feuilleton', in *Il Terzo Zola: Émile Zola dopo i 'Rougon Macquart'* (Naples: Istituto Universitario Orientale, 1990), pp. 447–55. On the other side of the dispute, Maurice

Barrès drew a similar comparison in the summer of 1899: 'The judicial problem, the whole Dreyfus saga has only the crude interest of a serial novel.' *Mes Cahiers, 1896–1923* (Paris: Plon, 1994), p. 124.

35 'Les Documents humains', in *Le Roman expérimental, OC*, vol. 9, 437–41 (p. 439; my emphasis).

36 'Joris-Karl Huysmans', in *Le Roman expérimental, OC*, vol. 9, 431–34 (p. 431).

37 'Gustave Flaubert', *Les Romanciers naturalistes, OC*, vol. 10, 502–47 (pp. 502–03); see also Bähler, 'Sur les traces naturalistes', 91.

38 'Sur les traces naturalistes', 90.

39 Zola, 'George Sand', *Documents littéraires*, in *OC*, vol. 10, 727–48 (p. 746); Zola, 'Notes sur l'Affaire Dreyfus', *OC*, vol. 18, 558.

40 For instance, in his 'Letter to the Young People', Zola decried the readiness of journalists to accept the most brazen lies and refuse the most blinding truths, pp. 29–35 (p. 30).

41 *Vérité*, 259. La Croix de Beaumont is a transparent calque of the Assumptionist newspaper, *La Croix*, founded in 1880, which led the charge against Dreyfus and stirred up anti-Semitic sentiment.

42 On the romanesque in Zola's late fiction, see Béatrice Laville, *Une poétique des fictions autoritaires: les voies de Zola, Barrès, Bourget* (Bordeaux: Presses Universitaires de Bordeaux, 2020), pp. 207–17.

43 BN, MS 10274, fol 358 (original emphasis). See Philippe Hamon, 'Le juge Denizet dans *La Bête humaine*', in *Mimesis et Semiosis*, ed. Philippe Hamon and Jean-Pierre Leduc-Adine (Paris: Nathan, 1992), pp. 137–44.

44 Honoré de Balzac, *Une ténébreuse affaire*, ed. René Guise (Paris: Gallimard, 1973), p. 656. On the strategies of the prosecution in Balzac's novel, see Rebecca Sugden, 'Terre(ur): Reading the Landscape of Conspiracy in Balzac's *Une ténébreuse affaire*', *Nineteenth-Century French Studies*, 47:1–2 (2018–19), 48–65.

45 Susan Rubin Suleiman draws attention to this paradox: 'the many historians who have written detailed accounts of the Affair [. . .] have themselves indulged in a great deal of speculation, and what might be called, fiction-making, regarding the principal actors'. 'The Literary Significance of the Dreyfus Affair', in *The Dreyfus Affair: Art, Truth and Justice*, ed. Norman L. Kleeblatt (Berkeley: University of California Press, 1987), pp. 117–39 (p. 124).

46 'A Sentimental Affair', 403.

47 See Carlo Ginzburg, 'Morelli, Freud, and Sherlock Holmes: Clues and Scientific Method', trans. Anna Davin, *History Workshop*, 9 (1980), 5–36 (p. 9). Here, Ginzburg cites the art historian Edgar Wind.

48 Jeffrey Mehlman, 'Zola's Novel of the Dreyfus Affair: Between Mystique and Politique', in *Studies in Contemporary Jewry*, vol. 21, *Jews, Catholics, and the Burden of History*, ed. Eli Lederhendler (New York: Oxford University Press, 2005), 234–51 (p. 246; my emphasis).

49 Dorian Bell, 'Beyond the Bourse: Zola, Empire, and the Jews', *Romanic Review*, 102 (2011), 485–501 (p. 494). *Vérité*, 61.

50 See Geoffrey Cubitt, *The Jesuit Myth: Conspiracy Theory and Politics in Nineteenth-Century France* (Oxford: Clarendon Press, 1993), pp. 175–78. Joseph Reinach's monumental *Histoire de l'Affaire Dreyfus*, the first volume of which was published in 1901, represented the most important and substantial version of this anti-Jesuit narrative.

51 *R-M*, vol. 5, 1320. With Cesare Lombroso's anthropological theory of crime in mind, Zola noted in his *dossier préparatoire*: 'The physical type of the born criminal should be kept and embellished' (Paris, Bibliothèque nationale, NAF 10274, fols 540–41). See David F. Bell's discussion of this scene in 'Zola's Fin-de-Siècle Pessimism: Knowledge in Crisis', *L'Esprit créateur*, 32 (1992), 21–29 (pp. 25–26).

52 Susan Harrow, *Zola, The Body Modern: Pressures and Prospects of Representation* (Oxford: Legenda, 2010), p. 184.

53 Nancy K. Miller, *Subject to Change: Reading Feminist Writing* (New York: Columbia University Press, 1988), p. 26.

54 Gérard Genette, '*Vraisemblance* and Motivation', trans. David Gorman, *Narrative*, 9:3 (2001 [1968]), 239–58 (p. 241).

55 *Le Procès Dreyfus devant le conseil de guerre de Rennes (7 août – 9 septembre 1899)* (Paris: P. V. Stock, 1900), vol. 3, 742.

56 Miller, *Subject to Change*, p. 27. *Vérité*, 45; my emphasis.

57 Richard Sennett, *The Fall of Public Man* (London: Penguin, 1976), p. 246. See Alan B. Spitzer's reflections on Sennett's reading of 'J'accuse…!., in *Historical Truth and Lies about the Past: Reflections on Dewey, Dreyfus, de Man, and Reagan* (Chapel Hill: University of North Carolina Press, 2000), p. 42.

58 Drumont closes his defamation of Dreyfus as follows: 'A higher Authority told me: "Speak!" I have spoken…' 'L'Âme de Dreyfus', *La Libre Parole*, 26 December 1894, p. 1. Sennett, *The Fall of Public Man*, p. 247.

59 Naomi Schor, *Zola's Crowds* (Baltimore, MD: The Johns Hopkins University Press, 1978), p. 42.

60 *À Rennes*, in *Scènes et doctrines du nationalisme* (Paris: Félix Juven, 1902), p. 152. For an important discussion of the contradictions at play in Zola's writing about Jews, see Maurice Samuels, *The Right to Difference: French Universalism and the Jews* (Chicago, IL: The University of Chicago Press, 2016), pp. 95–116.

61 Reinach, *Histoire de l'Affaire Dreyfus* (Paris: Éditions de la Revue Blanche, 1901), vol. 1, 335.

62 Harris, *Dreyfus*, p. 9.

63 Zola sets out his own vision of the Jesuit conspiracy in his 'Letter to the Senate', p. 157.

64 Letter of 23 February 1898; cited in *Zola: mémoire de la critique*, ed. Sylvie Thorel-Cailleteau (Paris: Presses de l'Université Paris-Sorbonne, 1998), p. 50.

65 Henri Mitterand, *Zola: l'histoire et la fiction* (Paris: Presses Universitaires de France, 1990), p. 249.

66 Jean-Denis Bredin, *L'Affaire* (Paris: Juillard, 1983), p. 234.

67 'Letter to M. É Loubet', p. 170.
68 'The Fifth Act' appeared in *L'Aurore* on 12 September 1899. *Dreyfus Affair*, pp. 136–43 (p. 140).
69 'Letter to M. É Loubet', p. 170.
70 'Letter to M. É Loubet', p. 170.
71 'Letter to M. É Loubet', p. 170.
72 Sophia Rosenfeld, *Democracy and Truth: A Short History* (Philadelphia: University of Pennsylvania Press, 2019), p. 101.
73 'Letter to France', p. 41.
74 Ozouf, *L'École, l'Église et la République*, p. 104. Schor suggests that 'Zola was never closer to Hugo than in this hymn to secular education, to the enlightenment of the benighted masses.' *Zola's Crowds*, p. 43.
75 'Letter to the Young People', pp. 34–35.
76 'Letter to the Young People', p. 30 (emphasis added).
77 David Baguley, 'L'Anti-intellectualisme de Zola', *Les Cahiers naturalistes*, 42 (1971), 119–29 (p. 126).
78 BN, NAF 10344, fol. 28.
79 Sarah Al-Matary alludes to this problem in *La Haine des clercs: l'anti-intellectualisme en France* (Paris: Seuil, 2019): 'Who remembers that Zola, the archetypal Dreyfusard intellectual, had long proclaimed his anti-intellectualism?' (p. 75).
80 Rosenfeld, *Common Sense: A Political History* (Cambridge, MA: Harvard University Press, 2011), p. 9.
81 *Common Sense*, p. 6.
82 'Letter to France', p. 35.
83 According to Baguley, what distinguishes the 'intellectuals' of the last series is that they have 'respect for work and reverence for women' – the latter contrasting with the sexual inhibition that characterises the likes of Florent Quenu (*Le Ventre de Paris*). 'L'Anti-intellectualisme de Zola', 128. Victor Brombert describes the hero of *Vérité*, meanwhile, as 'an intellectual with a non-intellectual temperament'. *The Intellectual Hero: Studies in the French Novel, 1880–1955* (London: Faber and Faber, 1961), p. 74.
84 Ferry delivered this speech on 2 April 1880 to the Congrès pédagogique des inspecteurs primaires. Cited in Evlyn Gould, *Dreyfus and the Literature of the Third Republic: Secularism and Tolerance in Zola, Barrès, Lazare and Proust* (Jefferson, NC and London: McFarland & Company, 2012), p. 59.
85 Ferdinand Buisson held the post until 1896, before taking up the Chair of the Department of Education at the Sorbonne. Mitterand also notes that the school inspector, Le Barazer, is modelled on Buisson. *Zola* (Paris: Fayard, 2002), vol. 3, 731.
86 In his letter to the organisers, Zola reflected: 'Certainly, yes, justice in education; but above all, truth in education. Therein lies tomorrow's triumph. We need the people to be educated, convinced by the experimental truths of science, in order for them to become capable of justice.' Press cutting, 'Une lettre de M. Zola', attached to the *dossier préparatoire*. BN, NAF 10344, fols

273–34. On Zola's model of secular education, and his engagement with pedagogues, Buisson, Pauline Kergomard, and Émile Durkheim, see Gina K. Zupsich, 'The Gospel According to Zola: National Identity and Naturalist Utopia in Fin-de-Siècle France' (unpublished doctoral thesis, University of California, Berkeley, 2010), pp. 104–30.

87 Buisson, 'L'Intuition morale', lecture pronounced on 31 August 1878; in *La Foi laïque: extraits de discours et d'écrits (1878–1911)* (Paris: Hachette, 1912), pp. 1–10 (p. 5).

88 *La Foi laïque*, p. 9.

89 *Democracy and Truth*, p. 113.

90 *Vérité*, 332. On 'the child-focused, redemptive conclusions' to Zola's *Quatre Évangiles*, see Andrew J. Counter, 'Zola's Fin-de-Siècle Reproductive Politics', *French Studies*, 68 (2014), 193–208 (p. 201).

91 In his *Ébauche* for the series, Zola stated: 'Above all, I must captivate women.' BN, NAF 10333, fol. 381.

92 *Vérité*, 383. Gilbert D. Chaitin reads Zola's repetition of the crime as an attempt to 'exclude at all costs what [Marc] dreads the most, the possibility of the father's complicity in the crime against the child'. *The Enemy Within: Culture Wars and Political Identity in the Novels of the French Third Republic* (Columbus: Ohio State University Press, 2009), p. 221.

93 In this respect, Hannah Thompson is surely right to read this repetition as 'a rewriting, in which the traumatic experience is transformed into a happy ending made possible by the revelation of knowledge and the suppression of secrecy and silence'. 'The Truth Will Out: National and Personal Trauma in Zola's *Vérité*', in *Taboo: Corporeal Secrets in Nineteenth-Century France* (Oxford: Legenda, 2013), pp. 125–39 (p. 199).

94 Terence Cave, *Recognitions: A Study in Poetics* (Oxford: Clarendon Press, 1990), p. 250.

95 *Recognitions*, p. 254 (original emphasis).

96 *Recognitions*, p. 253.

97 Henry James, 'Émile Zola', in *Selected Literary Criticism*, ed. Morris Shapira (London: Heinemann, 1963), pp. 240–64 (p. 262).

98 See Leon Edel, *Henry James: A Life* (London: Flamingo, 1996), p. 484.

99 James, 'Émile Zola', p. 255. Figures like Marc Froment, James adds, 'show us the reasonable and the good [...] in the white light of the old George Sand novel and its improved moralities' (p. 263).

100 Suleiman, *Authoritarian Fictions: The Ideological Novel as a Literary Genre* (Princeton, NJ: Princeton University Press, 1993), p. 10. Laville takes up Suleiman's analysis, in relation to earlier novels – Zola's final series included – in *Une poétique des fictions autoritaires*.

101 Samuels remarks upon its 'unrelenting didacticism' in *The Right to Difference*, p. 107; Mehlman laments Zola's fictionalisation of the Dreyfus affair as 'a cloyingly saccharine hell', despite being 'paved with the very best intentions', in 'Zola's Novel of the Dreyfus Affair', p. 243; and Nelly Wilson evokes a novel that is paradoxically 'unreadable for being too readable', in 'La

mise en fiction de l'affaire Dreyfus: quelques réflexions sur *Vérité*, in *Il terzo Zola: Emile Zola dopo i 'Rougon-Macquart'*, ed. Gian Carlo Menichelli (Naples: Istituto Universitario Orientale, 1990), pp. 487–503 (p. 487).

102 'À la jeunesse', first printed in *Le Figaro*, 7 February 1895, then in *Nouvelle campagne*; *OC*, vol. 17, 388–91 (p. 389).

103 See BN, NAF 10333, fol. 273 (original underlining). See also Counter's discussion of Zola's repetitions, which lie 'at the very heart of the novelist's vision of a truly democratic art'. 'Zola's Repetitions: On Repetition in Zola', *The Modern Language Review*, 116:1 (2021), 42–64 (p. 44).

104 Clifford Geertz, 'Common Sense as a Cultural System', *The Antioch Review*, 33:1 (1975), 5–26 (p. 18).

105 BN, NAF 10344, fol. 563 (original underlining).

106 Barrès, 'La Protestation des intellectuels!', *Le Journal*, 1 February 1898, p. 1.

107 Reported in Maurice Paléologue, *Journal de l'affaire Dreyfus, 1894–1899* (Paris: Plon, 1955), p. 84; cited in Michel Winock, *Le Siècle des intellectuels* (Paris: Seuil, 1997), p. 26.

108 'L'Élite et la politique', first printed in *Le Figaro*, 9 May 1896, then in *Nouvelle campagne*; *OC*, vol. 17, 423–27 (425). For an earlier iteration of Zola's scepticism about academic hierarchies, see 'Notre École Normale' (1881), in *Une campagne*, *OC*, vol. 11, 805–09.

109 'L'Élite et la politique', 426.

110 Zola, 'The Minutes', *Dreyfus Affair*, pp. 22–26 (p. 22).

111 *Democracy and Truth*, p. 99 (original emphasis).

112 Laville, *Une poétique des fictions autoritaires*, pp. 157, 167.

113 Hannah Arendt, *Lectures on Kant's Political Philosophy*, ed. Ronald Beiner (Chicago, IL: The University of Chicago Press, 1992), p. 70.

114 Here, I am recalling Maxwell's term, in *Public Trials*, p. 112.

115 'Letter to the Senate', p. 157.

116 A far more subtle form of coercion characterises Zola's vision for the Jewish population. As both Bell and Samuels have argued, Zola promotes an assimilationist republican agenda, which results in the encompassing process of racial homogenisation (through intermarriage), and, ultimately, 'the complete dissipation or eradication of Jewish difference'. See Samuels, *The Right to Difference*, p. 105; and Bell, *Globalizing Race: Antisemitism and Empire in French and European Culture* (Evanston, IL: Northwestern University Press, 2018), p. 240.

117 Dossier préparatoire. BN, NAF 10344, fol. 566 (original underlining).

118 Albert Le Roy, 'Les Lettres et les mœurs', *Le Siècle*, 5 March 1903, p. 2.

119 Baguley describes 'a sort of thinly-veiled, mythicised egotism' in 'Du récit polémique au discours utopique: l'Évangile républicain de Zola', *Les Cahiers naturalistes*, 54 (1980), 106–21 (p. 118).

120 'The Literary Significance of the Dreyfus Affair', p. 130.

121 Gaston Deschamps, 'La Vie littéraire: un livre posthume d'Émile Zola', *Le Temps*, 22 February 1903, p. 2. Victor Hugo, 'Fonction du poète',

Les Rayons et les Ombres (1840); *Œuvres poétiques de Victor Hugo*, vol. 1, ed. Pierre Ablouy (Paris: Gallimard, 1974), 1023–31 (p. 1030).

122 Zola, 'Hugo et Littré', 13 June 1881, *Le Figaro*; subsequently included in *Une campagne*; *OC*, vol. 11, 832–36 (p. 833). Note also Zola's critique of Hugo's vision of the 'universal Republic': 'In aesthetic terms, nothing is more generous; it is a magnificent dream. But practically, it is somewhat childish.' 'Victor Hugo', *Documents littéraires*, *OC*, vol. 10, 655–77 (p. 658).

123 See Zola's speech 'Au banquet des marins russes', delivered 26 October 1893, in which he spoke on behalf of the Société des gens de lettres; *OC*, vol. 15, 663–64 (p. 664).

124 'Hugo et Littré', 833. In such ways, I am suggesting, Zola attenuates what Brian Nelson calls the 'messianism' of *Les Quatre Évangiles*. 'Zola and the Ideology of Messianism', *Orbis Litterarum*, 37 (1982), 70–82 (pp. 71–72).

125 'L'Élite et la politique', 426.

Epilogue
Idealism after the Act

On 5 October 1902, some fifty thousand mourners lined the streets as Zola's casket was borne from the home he shared with his wife Alexandrine on the Rue de Bruxelles to Montmartre cemetery. Among those leading the procession were Zola's Dreyfusard allies – Jean Jaurès, Octave Mirbeau, Bernard Lazare, Gabriel Monod – and, in spite of security concerns, Alfred Dreyfus himself. Alexandrine had asked Anatole France, the only *académicien* to take up Dreyfus's cause, to deliver a eulogy on behalf of Zola's friends. This was to follow the tributes paid by the Ministère de l'Instruction publique, Joseph Chaumié, and the President of the Société des gens de lettres, Abel Hermant, both of whom extolled the writer as an indefatigable champion of truth and justice. Predictably, it was France's stirring oration that resonated most powerfully with those gathered around the *tribune* and that dominated press reports of the funeral. Where Chaumié and Hermant had glanced Zola's fight for Dreyfus obliquely, France made Zola's 'great act' incandescent, the *point culminant* in the life of a man who was, France concluded – in terms emblazoned on the collective cultural memory, and indeed reprised by President Jacques Chirac on the centenary of 'J'accuse...!' – 'a moment in the history of human conscience'.[1] What struck Zola's detractors, however, and even some of his most quiescent admirers, were the pains taken by his eulogists to recast the writer's literary career in the gilded light of his sacrifice. In an extraordinary feat of revisionism, France collapsed the differences on which so much of his own polemic had once rested: 'This sincere realist', he declared, 'was an ardent idealist'.[2] At last, the writer's act accomplished, it became possible to see what had been there all along: Zola's idealism.

The following day, the anti-Dreyfusard and anti-Semitic newspaper *La Libre parole* printed an abridged version of France's eulogy directly alongside the damning indictment of Zola that France had set out some fifteen years earlier in response to *La Terre*.[3] Across these two extracts of France's writing – the first headed 'Before the Affair', the second 'After the Affair' – the reader is guided towards a set of assertions that directly contradict one another. How, the format implied, were readers supposed to reconcile the terms of France's fresh exultation of Zola with his former admonishment of the naturalist writer as a defiler of mankind, and indeed, a peerless anti-idealist? What had happened to France's excoriating verdict that (and here, his terms are highlighted in bold) 'never had anyone shown such disregard for the ideal of mankind'? Such textual juxtapositions were, of course, part of a facile strategy to send up the apparent absurdity of France's volte-face; at the very least, the writer should be made to eat his words... But anti-Dreyfusard objections to this kind of whitewashing of the naturalist novelist – France's seeming the most audacious – also resonated more widely, playing into those energetic debates to follow over whether Zola's ashes should be transferred to the Pantheon.[4]

In December 1906, the bill for the writer's state consecration was passed. But when discussions were reopened in parliament on 19 March 1908, just prior to the event, Maurice Barrès stated his vigorous opposition to defraying the costs of the official ceremony by, once again, resurrecting France's earlier charges against the Zola of *La Terre*. Before those of his fellow statesmen who would readily 'canonise' Zola – a term that provoked much hilarity on the right – Barrès was determined to prove that this hero's great deed, his penning of 'J'Accuse...!', was but a stroke of opportunism by a writer out of ideas and at the end of his career.[5] Instead of enveloping the article in 'a sort of mystical cloud', Barrès called upon his compatriots to deidealise Zola's gesture, to see it – in the spirit of naturalist discourse – 'as it really is'.[6] In retaliation, Barrès's adversaries read out extracts of France's funeral eulogy; and a month later, France himself entered the fray, stating his objections to the nationalist right's pernicious exploitation of his own former literary criticism. 'I have acknowledged the mistakes of my youth', France declared. Albeit it was first and foremost, he clarified, the great courage Zola had shown as a citizen, rather than his exploits as a novelist, that made him worthy of a place among those 'Grands Hommes' to whom the *Patrie* owed its gratitude.[7]

If I have chosen to begin the end of this book by turning to the wrangling over Zola's posthumous fortune, it is because this episode provides so arresting an example of what I have attempted to argue throughout: that differences over literary aesthetics were integral to the early Third Republic's most acute ideological conflicts; and moreover, that those differences were frequently rooted in contested visions of Zola's relationship to idealism. What France's summative judgement of Zola reveals, of course, is just how definitively the grounds of this aesthetic debate could shift in the wake of his engagement on behalf of Dreyfus, when it seemed to many that Zola the idealist need no longer be a contradiction in terms. Indeed, to come at last to a question this book has largely avoided until now, we might observe that the positing of Zola as an idealist goes hand in hand with his emergence as an exemplary *object* of idealisation – in the words of Susan Rubin Suleiman, as an archetype, 'a constructed, idealised, "sublimated" character'.[8] For while the whole Affair became steeped in a complex rhetoric of religiosity, it was Zola, writes Christopher E. Forth, who received 'the full Jesus treatment'.[9]

Of course, what we find in Barrès's campaign against the writer's Pantheonisation – his declared endeavour, that is, to combat 'Zola's apotheosis' – is precisely a reaction against this (misplaced) martyrisation and (cultish) reverence, dismissively dubbed 'izolatrie' by the nationalist right.[10] (It was a neologism coined by the pseudonymous journalist and writer Gyp in her reports on Zola's libel trial for *La Libre Parole*, and in which she cast the Dreyfusard's partisans as 'Les Izolâtres' [The Izolators].)[11] Two days after Zola's remains were transferred to the Pantheon, the popular satirical weekly, *Le Rire*, played on this perception of Zola as a false idol, devoting its back cover to Auguste Roubille's anti-Semitic caricature of the 'Izolatry or the secular beatification of Saint Zola' [Izolatrie ou béatification laïque de Saint Zola]. Roubille has Zola perched semi-naked in clouds of incense, his porcine feet aloft; two figures – including a corpulent Marianne – gaze up from below, censers in hand (Figure E.1). Clearly, the state's sanctification of its heroic truth-teller reinvigorated a largely anti-Dreyfusard counter-discourse that insistently sent up, desublimated, even obsessively degraded the writer, whose body – as well as the bodies he imagined in his novels – impinge on the scene of his immortalisation. One contemporary postcard pictured Zola's scatological characters Coupeau, Jésus-Christ, Nana, and La Mouquette (associated in the image with drink, flatulence and fornication, respectively) ascending the steps to the Pantheon, and holding aloft a chamber pot-cum-inkwell for the writer's quill (Figure E.2). Caricatures of this kind figured Zola's most audacious fictional inventions as an affront – a La Mouquette-esque moon – to the sanctity of the temple. When the nationalist right objected to the Republic's 'izolatrous' act, it was also wondering at how shifting political allegiances could attenuate, even override, certain longstanding aesthetic judgements. The great ideological schism opened up by the Affair, and by Zola's polarising intervention in it, had, they objected, somehow allowed literary history to be rewritten.

Figure E.1   A. Roubille, 'Izolatry or the secular beatification of Saint Zola'.
Caricature in *Le Rire*, 6 June 1908 [back cover]. Courtesy of the Bibliothèque nationale de France.

Figure E.2 'Transfer of his Remains to the Pantheon' [1908].
Postcard. Collection of the author.

Yet even those with opposing ideological sympathies often found themselves straining to reconcile, or at least rationalise, Zola's deed and fiction. Symbolists like Laurent Tailhade and Pierre Quillard were among those who undertook to set aside former opinions and revalorise Zola's fiction on account of his intervention. Broadly speaking, however, Dreyfusards adopted, as Christophe Reffait has argued, one of two positions: the first involved defending the idea of a consistency, or continuity, between Zola's works and his action; the second required that the intervention be abstracted from Zola's works, especially from his *Rougon-Macquart* series – though, as we shall see, less so his final novels. The latter constituted 'a sort of dualism', whereby commentators insisted on 'the moral transcendence that took place in Zola during his defence of Dreyfus'.[12] Few articulated the first, synthetic vision more eloquently than Jean Jaurès, who successfully countered Barrès's diatribe in the Chamber. (Ultimately, the vote was heavily in favour of funding the ceremony for Zola's Pantheonisation.) 'Messieurs', Jaurès objected, 'we do not accept, nay cannot accept, such an attempt to separate in Émile Zola the great man of letters from the great citizen'.[13] For what united Zola's works and his life, inextricably, was 'this passionate love of the truth'; and if the citizen's involvement in the Affair had, in some sense, repaid the writer, it was in retrospectively illuminating for many 'the profound meaning' of his fiction. For the socialist politician, 'the man of *Germinal*' – as he had put it in his testimony at Zola's trial for libel – had long been driven by an unwavering commitment to tell the truth. 'From the first of his works to the last, he has never stopped accusing', wrote the Left-wing journalist Victor Méric in his 1909 portrait of Zola.[14]

The second 'dualist' position was encapsulated, Reffait suggests, in the likes of socialist Charles Péguy. Though Péguy determined in Zola's works a profound sincerity that also guided his political engagement, he could only conceive of Zola's great civic act in terms of a 'renewal', even as a spiritual, or mystical, self-surpassing.[15] In fact, regardless of their opinions on Zola's writing, many Dreyfusard partisans shared the conviction that the Affair had unmistakeably changed Zola the man. When Mirbeau visited Zola at home on a morning of his libel trial, he reported finding the writer physically and spiritually altered: 'less nervous, less feverish than usual; he is more in control of himself – body, mind, and soul.'[16] Gabriel Trarieux noted a similar transformation in an article that he wrote for Péguy's journal, *Cahiers de la Quinzaine*, shortly after Zola's death. If there was, Trarieux acknowledged, a logical evolution from Zola's fiction to his action, the latter nevertheless involved a definitive transfiguration: 'let it not be said that this man hasn't surpassed himself, that he is still, after this act, "the same man as he was before"'.[17] Trarieux went on to recall an encounter with Zola, two years earlier – the only time they had met one-on-one. Sat at his desk, a white kerchief around his neck, Zola wore a tormented, intense expression; his face, so it seemed to Trarieux looking back, emerged from the shadows as in one of Eugène Carrière's portraits. Just before leaving, Trarieux dared to broach the question of politics. 'He gave a two-word reply, fell silent, then resumed in his biting tone: "This affair has made me a better person."'[18] Nothing more could be added, Trarieux concluded, to this sublime summation.

Now if Zola's reported admission to Trarieux strikes him, and perhaps us too, as remarkable, it is surely because autoidealisation is rarely undertaken by Zola so directly; it is, almost invariably, either couched in metaphor, paradoxically admitted through modest denial, or otherwise articulated through projection. In his last years, the writer's ego ideal would manifest itself most conspicuously via the benevolent patriarchs of his final novels; or, outside of fiction, in an emboldened identification with his own idolised and long-deceased father, François, who became one of the collateral victims of his son's involvement in the Dreyfus Affair.[19] When, in May 1898, Zola was forced to defend his father, an engineer, against slanderous accusations of embezzlement fabricated by the anti-Dreyfusard journalist Ernest Judet, he bound himself, unmistakably, to the paternal figure he set out to rescue, 'this hero of energy and work'.[20] In fact, penning his filial defence from exile in England, Zola's declared belief in his father's imminent absolution reads just as compellingly as a dialogue with himself: 'And rest assured, you will emerge radiant from this pile of mud that would sully your name.'[21] The public resurgence of Zola's father at this juncture is, of course, a matter of historical circumstance. But what might intrigue us about the discourse of glorification that Zola heaps on his biological father is just how it coincides with the predominance in his writing of what Naomi Schor calls 'paternal idealism'. As part of the taxonomy of idealisation Schor determines in George Sand, this mode draws its 'affective impetus from the idealization of her dead father'.[22] But in the wider application Schor gives, it also involves the writer becoming an ideal:

> This is, not surprisingly, the most prestigious and the most enabling form of idealism, the one identified with the highest forms of human achievement. [. . .] The paternal idealist seeks not to lose himself in the idealized Other but rather to introject his (or her) qualities. Paternal idealism gratifies narcissism but does so in a way that enhances the narcissist instead of diminishing him. [. . .] Paternal idealism is the idealism of those that set themselves up as models for others (autobiographers), of writers who also view themselves as leaders (poet-magi, writers *engagés*).[23]

On this last point, Schor doubtless has Zola in mind, as well as Hugo – or better still, we might venture, Zola *as* Hugo. The Zola, that is, of *Vérité*, with its 'reincarnation', as Schor had put it in *Zola's Crowds*, 'of the Poet-Magus as a primary-school teacher'.[24]

If, at times, this book has taken up the trope of the 'family romance' in tracking Zola's relationship to idealism, most obviously his relationship to Sand, it is in no small part because Zola's own various reflections on the formation of the writerly ego invite it. But for all that we can determine in Zola's last works of fiction an ongoing negotiation with Sand's idealist aesthetics, it is arguably Zola's indebtedness to Hugo that takes on a new prominence in the aftermath of 'J'accuse..!'. When Zola claimed his 'right as a poet' in fashioning his lyrical, utopian fiction, he no doubt had a Hugolian licence in mind.[25] Indeed, despite Zola's repeated animus towards the kind of personality cult Hugo embodied, the identification between them could not but seem overdetermined. 'In retrospect', writes Jeffrey Mehlman, 'Zola during the Affair – even to the detail of his exile – appears to have been the last man of the nineteenth century (or the first of the twentieth) to have taken himself for Victor Hugo.'[26] Certainly, admiring commentators of Zola's post-'J'accuse...!' fiction privileged comparisons with the deceased national hero, whose crypt in the Pantheon Zola would ultimately share, alongside Alexandre Dumas.[27] And when Barrès, Jaurès, and others debated the conditions of Zola's Pantheonisation in March 1908, Hugo predictably emerged as a principal point of reference – cast by Barrès as a 'grandiose expression of French idealism', who had, for all his flaws, warned several generations off 'abject literature'.[28] For Zola's enemies, the eternal cohabitation of Hugo and Zola was a matter of sheer impropriety (Barrès's word is 'inconvenance'). For many of Zola's Dreyfusard champions, the writer's intervention in public life had only sealed the naturalist novel's virtuous – Hugolian – mission: 'this is the supreme rule of moral order, even more so than the literary kind, that Hugo had exercised at the end of his life', declared the Symbolist poet and theoretician Gustave Kahn, in his review of *Fécondité*. 'Like Hugo, he has been the voice of the weak: and he occupies the place where the great poet once was.'[29] For the journalist Lucien Victor-Meunier too, the first of Zola's *Quatre Évangiles* conjured up Hugo's imperative to dream the world better: 'Dreaming a daydream is good, dreaming a utopia is better. So, you need to dream, do you? Well, dream man better. You want a fantasy? Here's one: the ideal...'[30] What, it seemed, Zola had accomplished, in the wake of 'J'accuse...!', was to submit the lyrical imagination to the ends of a social conscience – to become, in Kahn's words, a 'writer of the practical dream', or, precisely, to become Hugo.[31]

Wherever we might stand on the much-debated question of Zola's evolution as a writer, we are bound to acknowledge the irresistible pull of biographical destiny as something of an ultimate horizon for our reading of his fiction. Certainly, to account for idealism in Zola is inevitably, or perhaps especially, to grapple with this question of teleology that the Dreyfus Affair imposes. With the inauguration of the Maison Zola-Musée Dreyfus at Médan in 2021, those legacies of work and act, fiction and life, find themselves, for the very best reasons, figuratively as well as architecturally adjoined.[32] Where the Dreyfus Affair is still regarded, in Shlomo Sand's words, 'as the ideal type of intellectual mobilization', Zola continues to be enshrined as a cultural and intellectual icon, whose legend has been bankrolled, in part, by the Republic.[33] On the centenary of Zola's death, in a speech given at Médan, President Jacques Chirac called upon fellow citizens to honour the memory of a man who was:

> one of the most admirable symbols of the fight for the founding principles and ideals of our nation. For, in fact, to speak of Émile Zola is quite simply to speak of France. [. . .] Of this France which – more than simply a territory – is a language, an idea, an ideal of justice and freedom. This is the France from which Zola descends.[34]

Where much of this book has been devoted to reconstructing the specific functions of idealism in aesthetic, philosophical, and political discourses around the end of the nineteenth century, it must also, ultimately, contend with this diffusion, or dissolution, of idealism into a rhetoric of virtuous patriotism, even nostalgia. In the rear-view mirror of centenary celebrations, Zola becomes the vanishing point of the French Republic's own idealised self-image. For Chirac makes Zola consubstantial with a nation – or rather, with the *idea* of a nation, one unfettered by parochialism, and whose ideals are, in fact, its best export. No doubt one of the political intentions behind this manoeuvre is to refute those chauvinistic versions of nationalism expounded by the likes of Barrès, who insisted that the foreign, or 'anti-French', elements of Zola's writing were there in plain sight.[35] By distinction, Zola is held to epitomise an idealism that is, specifically, French, but only in the sense that France itself would stand for a set of civilised values that can be shared well beyond its borders. In short, the particular idealism Chirac, like many others, identifies with Zola is a universalism.

In this respect, Chirac cleaves to the vision of France's global-historical destiny that Zola sets out most explicitly around the Dreyfus Affair: in his journalism, in his last cycle of fiction, and in the embryonic project he imagined in his final year, *La France en marche* – a theatrical counterpart to *Les Quatre Évangiles*, which envisaged the future of a nation elected to forge the just world of tomorrow.[36] When Zola delivered his declaration to the jury at his trial for libel, he relativised the current crisis by placing it on 'the global-imperial scale', as Dorian Bell puts it, 'of France's messianic redemption and reshaping of the world'.[37] For what was really at stake in this particular miscarriage of justice, Zola insisted, was the altogether more fundamental question of whether the nation could remain an ideal, a quintessential model of Republicanism, worthy of emulation:

> There is no Dreyfus Affair any longer. There is only one issue: is France still the France of the Revolution and the Declaration of the Rights of Man? the France which gave the world liberty, and was supposed to give it justice? Are we still the noblest, most fraternal, most generous of peoples?[38]

If, in one sense, this book can be understood to rehearse something of a conversation between Naomi Schor's *Zola's Crowds* and her *George Sand and Idealism*, it has also, at the last, circled back to the topic that Schor was working on at the time of her death in 2001, the fundamentals of which she had set out in an article published that year, 'The Crisis of French Universalism'.[39] No doubt there would be much to say about this particular (it is by no means the only) line of evolution in Schor's thought. But what strikes me about this last project now, as I bring my own to a close, is just how insistently Schor conceptualises universalism as an idealism – one whose noblest principles and most clearly ideological excesses, we might then wish to add, can be found in Zola. For though Zola does not figure directly in Schor's project, one of its ambitions is nevertheless to scrutinise the legacy of the kind of claims for the nation that Zola makes above: the guiding idea, that is, that 'France's national particularity is precisely to embody the universal.'[40] Indeed, it is to none other than Chirac – and his vision of *la francophonie* – that Schor turns for a paradigmatic exposition of 'France's role as leader among the nations'.[41]

The ideological implications of this vision are spelt out by Schor; and not least among these is the framing of French colonialism as a *mission civilisatrice*, 'as an act of generosity rather than of oppression, conferring upon its objects the privilege of participating in France's defining universalism'.[42] In such a spirit, one of the most important currents of Zola scholarship in recent years has been devoted precisely to debunking the ambitions of the writer's republican universalism, namely by interrogating the imperialist, and assimilationist, drives at work most conspicuously in his later fiction.[43] The imperious vision, that is, of 'France as saviour, redeemer, deliverer. Sovereign', as Zola described it in his plans for his final, unfinished novel, *Justice*.[44] Just how we might ultimately square this critique with our continued regard for Zola's virtuous stand against anti-Dreyfusard 'particularism' is yet to be seen. In one sense, the problem remains that where Zola is at his most idealistic, he is, by and large, at his at his most nakedly ideological, and in effect his least palatable. In *Le Plaisir du texte*, Barthes singled out Zola's *Fécondité* as a work in which 'the ideology is flagrant, especially sticky: naturism, family-ism, colonialism'.[45] Only the most obdurate of critics could make a case for reading Zola's last works of fiction on the grounds of pleasure alone. For these are, in Henri Mitterand's words, 'massive, voluminous, dense works, laden with lectures and theses, and which have not aged well'. Albeit, Mitterand added, 'they remain essential reading for anybody interested in ideas, social attitudes, [...] in the fantasies France harboured at the turn of the twentieth century'.[46] If, so the logic goes, we can overcome our own distaste for Zola's laborious prose and 'sticky' (*poisseuse*) ideology, the pay-off is great: not only can we read for ideas, we can privilege Zola as a window onto a cultural moment, even, as Nicholas White suggests, as a 'cultural historian *avant la lettre*'.[47] At this juncture, we might wish to recall Schor's own admission of a deep aversion to some of Sand's writing, including to 'one of her lesser late fictions'. 'The least pleasurable text by Sand that I read in the course of working on her', Schor reflected, 'was not so much boring as it was almost literally nauseating'.[48] If idealism as an aesthetics – as opposed to as a politics, an ethics, or psychic process – is, for Schor, at the very least 'an acquired taste', it follows that the gratification she derives from Sand is, first and foremost, 'cognitive' rather than 'affective': 'there is real pleasure', she declares, 'in *thinking about the ideal*' (216; original emphasis).

Now, I do not wish to supplement Schor's reflections with my own (no doubt unoriginal) reader response to Zola's late fiction. But if Schor's admission is, I think, such a powerful one, it is because it captures precisely the kind of sublimation the literary critic regularly performs, and, indeed, often sees it as her duty to perform. For Zola scholars, in particular, I would venture, this suppression of 'affective' response brings with it another important form of gratification: *the pleasure of critique*. It is certainly a revealing paradox that where Zola arguably harnesses, in his final works, the affective or sentimental clout of literary fiction most strenuously, the critic rarely finds it more necessary to call upon her impervious detachment or vigilance. But even putting aside this later work, surely few writers in the French tradition have proven more amenable to critique than Zola – and this in many of the senses of the term adumbrated by Rita Felski: as a sceptical mode, an ironic mood, a form of suspicion. 'Seizing the upper hand', Felski explains, 'critics *read against the grain* and between the lines; their self-appointed task is to draw out what a text fails – or wilfully refuses – to see'.[49] Of course, one of the aims of this book has been to show how such a gesture of critique was already dominant at the end of the nineteenth century, not least among those of Zola's readers who claimed to determine in the naturalist writer an idealist *sans le savoir*, or *malgré lui*. More recently, the task of reading Zola against himself – or 'à rebours', as I put in Chapter 1 – has been recast as a worthier mandate, even a rescue mission. To recall the imperative set out by Mitterand: 'we must defend Émile Zola against himself as much as his critics'.[50] More often than not, this means registering the tensions and contradictions between (naturalist) theory and fiction, between principle and praxis. Or, to return to Andrew J. Counter's reflections on a prevailing 'symptomatic' reading of Zola that we broached in the Introduction, it means mining the aesthetic and ideological slippages, incoherences, and ambiguities of his literary writing, 'those elements that the text does not master', even (or especially) at its most ostensibly monologic or dogmatic.[51] In the spirit Counter and Felski describe, Zola critics (myself included) often endeavour to scrutinise the 'limits' of the naturalist project, to identify where texts fail, equivocate, or are less coherent than they might appear. At their most generous, such critiques read (or redeem) those lapses as signs of a self-aware, modernist sensibility, even ideological subversion; at their most grudging, they see through a naïve mimeticism, an unavowed, or unwitting, ideological complicity. If, by and large, the former reading predominates, it is (we might imagine Felski arguing) because what the literary critic values most in Zola is precisely a version of the critique she undertakes: debunking, ironic, suspicious – and what, we might then add, Zola-*qua*-naturalist debunks, ironises, and suspects most strenuously of all is idealism.

It is not my intention to quibble with the many virtues of critique as such, but rather to reflect on what other moods Zola's writing – especially his handling of idealism – might demand. At the very least, we might observe that the dominance of critique as a paradigm, register or rhetoric in Zola studies clearly sits uneasily, or dissonantly, with the tone we often deploy to conjure with the writer's biographical destiny. Put differently, the 'dualism' Reffait identified in many Dreyfusard (re)readings of Zola's work is still, to some extent, operational. In fact, it is arguably at its most overdetermined in the line of Marxist criticism that runs from Georg Lukács to Fredric Jameson, and which has cleaved, as we saw at the outset of Chapter 2, to a vision of the naturalist writer as a passive, if critical, spectator of public life. To claim, as Lukács does, that the champion of Dreyfus was in fact cut off 'from the struggles of his time', might well – Jameson acknowledges – 'seem wilful and perverse'.[52] Yet this is the crux of Lukács's master comparison between Balzac and Zola (which Jameson largely adopts), whereby naturalist description and its push towards average types convey only a sense of powerlessness in the face of historical contingency. The Dreyfus Affair, Lukács declared, 'came too late and was too much a mere episode in Zola's life to effect any radical change in his creative method'.[53] Framed as an epilogue, or belated addendum, Zola's heroic public engagement did not allow him to cast off the sense of resignation and detachment that Lukács saw precluding the naturalist novel's ability to imagine agency. This is, notably, a judgement on Zola's career that both Marxist critics take over from 'so unpolitical a writer' as Henry James – namely, as we saw in Chapter 5, that which he set out in his retrospective essay, published shortly after Zola's death.[54] While James was unequivocal about Zola's courageous defence of Dreyfus, he could only lament that when life did eventually 'swoop down' on the author, in the most extraordinary fashion, it was 'too late in the day' to renew a creative imagination that 'was already fatigued and spent'.[55] Effectively, James resists the kind of retrospection that would have Zola's earlier writing conform with his civic act, and instead wonders how so strange, so odd, a 'climax' obliges us to look awry at what had gone before – '[casting] back over' the most accomplished works of his 'middle years the queerest grey light of eclipse' (252).

It is easy to see why James's idiosyncratic version of Zola's life and letters might appeal to the likes of Lukács and Jameson. Indeed, precisely because of his role in the Affair, Zola provides a hyperbolic expression of Marxist critique's counterintuitive (or to recall Jameson's terms, 'perverse') divorce of political content, or authorial intention for that matter, and the ideological operations of form. Of course, we might wish to argue that such injunctions against affording the writer's political commitment the power to redeem, or determine a new course for, the naturalist novel, ultimately do little to help us grapple with the distinctive project of Zola's final novels (of which, incidentally, neither Lukàcs nor Jameson make explicit mention). But we would also no doubt wish to remain wary of allowing Zola's political sincerity to dictate the terms of our reading. Looking back at a certain strand of Dreyfusard literary criticism in the immediate aftermath of Zola's intervention, we witness just how powerfully admiration can disarm, even displace, critique altogether. Take by way of example the kind of exuberant veneration with which Mirbeau concluded his response to the novel Zola started from exile:

> Reading *Fécondité*, and each of its ardent, passionate pages, I also felt something of an *indescribable affection* for Zola as kind of miracle-worker, who destroys only the better to rebuild, and who is greater, more sincere, more optimistic than ever, amidst the insults and ignorance he endures, pursuing through quagmire and calvary, [. . .] for the glory of the world, his human and divine vocation.[56]

For Zola's most ardent supporters, it was (politically) impossible not to be *moved* by the writer's sheer resolve, to hold apart, that is, the life and the page. When *Vérité* appeared in book form, five months after Zola's death – black borders framing the novel in a sign of mourning – critics duly handled the book with hushed reverence, skimming over its obvious aesthetic flaws. 'Just as we tend to wilfully ignore the faults of those no longer with us, it seems fitting to overlook in this work the lack of taste, the unwieldiness, the repetitions, and the dross that its author makes his standard.'[57] Instead, reviewers dwelt, by and large, on those virtues that echoed his great intervention: optimism, sincerity, eloquence.

No doubt today's Zola scholar is far more likely to agree with the principle, if not the spirit, of Rachilde's well-known objection to (the reaction to) *Fécondité*: 'I see no need to admire a bad novel just because it follows a fine deed.'[58] And yet, in Rachilde's case, this claim to the autonomy of aesthetic judgement, we must recall, carries its own pernicious ideological agenda: anti-Semitism.[59] Indeed, for all that we might baulk at the critical quiescence that characterised some of Zola's Dreyfusard readers, we must also contend with the uncomfortable fact that resistance to the idealism of Zola's post-'J'accuse. . .!' fiction tended to be voiced most ardently by his (ideological) adversaries. Plainly, for Zola's champions, to frame Zola as an idealist writer was to deploy a counter-discourse, to redeem him from the kind of stereotypical debasement perpetuated by the anti-Dreyfusard right. Thus, extolling the virtues of Zola's high-minded late fiction, Hermant could defiantly declare in his funeral eulogy: 'This man with a passion for greatness, who has been accused of baseness and banality, reached the land of dream [la chimère] and utopia.'[60] All this is to say, of course, that the Zola scholar remains caught in something of a bind: the very commitment, and clarity of conviction, we venerate – even, let's say, idealise – in Zola's citizenship

tends to appear as offputtingly righteous or doctrinaire transposed into
fiction. And yet, it remains to be seen whether redoubling our own
inscrutable critical detachment before Zola's most earnest literary writing,
or even deidealising Zola's heroic, civic gesture, can offer an adequate
solution. Where, instead, I think we might start is by asking what Zola's
idealism can tell us about our own.

Notes

1 *Discours prononcés aux obsèques d'Émile Zola le 5 octobre 1902* (Paris: Fasquelle,
   1902), p. 36. See President Chirac's open letter, of 8 January 1998, to the
   families of Dreyfus and Zola: www.vie-publique.fr/discours/127551-lettre-de-
   m-jacques-chirac-president-de-la-republique-adressee-la-f. Stellio Lorenzi's
   telefilm, *Émile Zola ou la conscience humaine*, aired on French television
   in 1978.
2 *Discours prononcés aux obsèques d'Émile Zola*, p. 3. As discussed in the
   Introduction, France had already determined 'the most ardent idealism' in
   Zola's writing a decade earlier, though this was conceived purely as a betrayal
   of his aesthetic principles as a naturalist writer. 'La Vie littéraire: un roman et
   un ordre du jour – *Le Cavalier Miserey*', *Le Temps*, 6 March 1887, p. 2.
3 'Deux pages d'Anatole France', *La Libre parole*, 6 October 1902, p.1. The
   excerpted literary criticism was France's 'La Vie littéraire: *La Terre*', *Le Temps*,
   28 August 1887, pp. 2–3.
4 For full discussions of debates surrounding Zola's Pantheonisation, see Michel
   Drouin, *Zola au Panthéon: le quatrième affaire Dreyfus* (Paris: Perrin, 2008);
   Antoine Compagnon, 'Les Ennemis de Zola', in *Zola au Panthéon: l'épilogue
   de l'affaire Dreyfus*, ed. Alain Pagès (Paris: Presses Sorbonne Nouvelle, 2010),
   pp. 17–31; and Alain Pagès, *Émile Zola: de 'J'accuse' au Panthéon* (Saint-Paul:
   Éditions Lucien Souny, 2008).
5 The 19 March 1908 debate of the Chambre des députés is reproduced in *Zola
   au Panthéon, 1908–2008*, preface by Alain Pagès (Paris: Éditions du patrimoine, 2008), pp. 19–59 (pp. 21, 31). Barrès had already set out these
   arguments in 'Émile Zola comme Littérateur', *L'Écho de Paris*,
   10 March 1908, p. 1.
6 *Zola au Panthéon, 1908–2008*, p. 32.
7 France's article appeared in the Viennese *Neue Freie Presse* on 16 April 1908;
   cited in Vincent Duclert, 'La République et l'héroïsme démocratique au
   tournant du siècle', in *Zola au Panthéon: l'épilogue de l'affaire Dreyfus*,
   pp. 73–96 (p. 84). In 2008, on the centenary of Zola's transfer to the
   Pantheon, the President of the Assemblée Nationale, Bernard Accoyer,
   recalled that 'Deputies wanted to commemorate Zola as a writer, but still
   more as the author of "J'accuse."' See Accoyer's preface to *Zola au Panthéon,
   1908–2008*, pp. 7–11 (p. 9).

8 Susan Rubin Suleiman, 'L'engagement sublime: Zola comme archétype d'un mythe culturel', *Les Cahiers naturalistes*, 67 (1993), 11–24 (p. 13).

9 Christopher E. Forth, *The Dreyfus Affair and the Crisis of French Manhood* (Baltimore, MD: The Johns Hopkins University Press, 2004), p. 92. Octave Mirbeau was one of the most arduous exponents of this discourse, lauding in a letter to Zola 'his lofty, impassioned sense of moderation that borders on saintliness' (23 December 1898); cited in Pierre-Jean Dufief, 'Mirbeau face à Zola', in *Champ littéraire fin de siècle autour de Zola*, ed. Béatrice Laville (Pessac: Presses Universitaires de Bordeaux, 2004), pp. 153–63 (p. 160).

10 *Zola au Panthéon, 1908–2008*, p. 32.

11 See Gyp's article covering the trial, 'Les Izolâtres', *La Libre Parole*, 3 March 1898, p. 1. She also published a dialogue novel, *Les Izolâtres*, the following year. Willa Z. Silverman broaches this dimension of Gyp's writing in 'Gyp and Flammarion: A Marriage of Love or Convenience?', *The French Review*, 73 (2000), 910–20 (p. 910).

12 Christophe Reffait, 'Les réticences des dreyfusards envers l'œuvre de Zola', in *Zola au Panthéon: l'épilogue de l'affaire Dreyfus*, pp. 123–37 (p. 125).

13 *Zola au Panthéon, 1908–2008*, p. 50.

14 Victor Méric, *Portraits d'Hier. Émile Zola* (Paris: Fabre, [15 March] 1909), p. 29.

15 Reffait, 'Les réticences des dreyfusards', p. 132.

16 Octave Mirbeau, 'Un matin, chez Émile Zola' (dated 19 July 1898); in *Livre d'hommage des lettres françaises à Émile Zola* (Paris: Société libre d'Édition des Gens de Lettres, 1898), pp. 72–75 (p. 73).

17 Gabriel Trarieux, 'Émile Zola, homme d'action', appeared in a special number of *Cahiers de la Quinzaine* devoted to Zola, published 4 December 1902; fifth *cahier* of the fourth series, pp. 22–28 (p. 27). On Trarieux's article, see Reffait, 'Les réticences des dreyfusards', pp. 132–34.

18 'Émile Zola, homme d'action', p. 28.

19 See Henri Mitterand, *Zola: la mort du père* (Paris: Imago, 2021).

20 See Ernest Judet, 'Zola père et fils', *Le Petit Journal*, 23 May 1898. Zola mounted his initial defence in 'Mon père', which appeared in *L'Aurore*, 28 May 1898; see *Zola: l'Affaire Dreyfus*, ed. Jean-Denis Bredin (Paris: Imprimerie nationale, 1992), pp. 213–23 (p. 221).

21 'Mon père', *Zola: l'Affaire Dreyfus*, p. 223.

22 Naomi Schor, *George Sand and Idealism* (New York: Columbia University Press, 1993), p. 165.

23 Schor, *George Sand and Idealism*, p. 195.

24 Schor, *Zola's Crowds* (Baltimore, MD: The Johns Hopkins University Press, 1978), p. 43.

25 See Zola's letter to M. B. Mendes de Costa, 16 November 1899: '*Les Quatre Évangiles* will run from the year 1900 to the year 2000. That is my right as a poet.' *Corr*, vol. 10, 95.

26 Jeffrey Mehlman, 'The Dreyfus Affair', in *A New History of French Literature*, ed. Denis Hollier (Cambridge, MA: Harvard University Press, 1994), pp. 824–30 (p. 829).

27 Take, for example, Lucien-Victor Meunier, '*Fécondité*', *Le Rappel*, 16 October 1899, p. 1; and Gaston Deschamps, 'La Vie littéraire. Un livre posthume d'Émile Zola', *Le Temps*, 22 February 1903, p. 2

28 *Zola au Panthéon, 1908–2008*, p. 34.

29 Gustave Kahn, '*Fécondité*', *La Revue blanche*, 20 (1899), 284–93.

30 '*Fécondité*', *Le Rappel*, 16 October 1899, p. 1.

31 '*Fécondité*', *La Revue blanche*, 292.

32 The official website of the Maison Zola-Musée Dreyfus sets out this twinning thus: 'Connected in their lifetime by an uncompromising struggle for truth and justice, Zola and Dreyfus are now celebrated together, in this place that symbolises the way in which their fates collided and the values they fought so hard to defend.' www.maisonzola-museedreyfus.com/.

33 Shlomo Sand, *The End of the French Intellectual: From Zola to Houellebecq*, trans. David Fernbach (London: Verso, 2018), p. 40.

34 6 October 2002; www.elysee.fr/jacques-chirac/2002/10/06/declaration-de-m-jacques-chirac-president-de-la-republique-sur-loeuvre-et-les-combats-demile-zola-medan-le-6-octobre-2002.

35 'Astute minds have always sensed that there is something foreign, even anti-French, about Zola's talent.' Barrès, *Scènes et doctrines du nationalisme* (Paris: Félix Juven, 1902), p. 41.

36 On this project, see Mitterand, *Zola* (Paris: Fayard, 2002), vol. 3, 751–53.

37 Dorian Bell, *Globalizing Race: Antisemitism and Empire in French and European Culture* (Evanston, IL: Northwestern University Press, 2018), p. 240.

38 'Statement to the Jury', pp. 55–61 (p. 60).

39 Schor, 'The Crisis of French Universalism', *Yale French Studies*, 100 (2001), 43–64.

40 Schor, 'French Feminism is a Universalism', *Bad Objects: Essays Popular and Unpopular* (Durham, NC: Duke University Press, 1995), pp. 3–27 (p. 5).

41 'The Crisis of French Universalism', 45, fn. 4.

42 'French Feminism is a Universalism', p. 6.

43 See, for example, Maurice Samuels, *The Right to Difference: French Universalism and the Jews* (Chicago, IL: The University of Chicago Press, 2016), pp. 95–116; Bell, *Globalizing Race*, pp. 228–47; Carmen K. Mayer-Robin, 'The "African Pages" of Zola's *Fécondité*: Testimony to Colonial Politics and Attitudes about Race during the French Third Republic', *Romance Notes*, 47 (2006), 5–14; Corinne Saminadayar-Perrin, 'D'impossibles nouveaux mondes: Zola, *L'Argent/Fécondité*', *Les Cahiers naturalistes*, 88 (2014), 27–44; Jean-Marie Seillan, 'Zola et le fait colonial: les raisons d'un rendez-vous manqué', *Les Cahiers naturalistes*, 88 (2014), 13–26.

44 Zola, 'Pour *Justice*'; *OC*, vol. 20, 397–400 (p. 398).

45 Barthes added, '*nonetheless* I continue reading the book'. *The Pleasure of the Text*, trans. Richard Miller (New York: Farrar, Straus and Giroux, 1975), p. 32 (original emphasis).

46 Mitterand, 'La vérité et l'utopie: *Les Quatre Évangiles*', *Le Roman à l'œuvre: genèse et valeurs* (Paris: Presses Universitaires de France, 1998), pp. 214–31 (p. 216).

47 See Nicholas White, 'Introduction: Zola, Cultural Historian *avant la lettre?*', *Romanic Review*, 102.3–4 (2011), 295–303.

48 *George Sand and Idealism*, p. 214.

49 Rita Felski, *The Limits of Critique* (Chicago, IL: The University of Chicago Press, 2015), p. 1 (emphasis added).

50 Mitterand, *Le Regard et le signe: poétique du roman réaliste et naturaliste* (Paris: Presses Universitaires de France, 1987), p. 55.

51 Andrew J. Counter, 'Le Symptôme de Zola: fragment d'autoanalyse critique', *Les Cahiers naturalistes*, 91 (2017), 61–71 (p. 62).

52 Fredric Jameson, *Marxism and Form: Twentieth-Century Dialectical Theories of Literature* (Princeton, NJ: Princeton University Press, 1971), p. 202.

53 Georg Lukács, 'The Zola Centenary', in *Studies in European Realism: A Sociological Survey of the Writings of Balzac, Stendhal, Zola, Tolstoy, Gorki, and others*, trans. Edith Bone (London: Hillway Publishing, 1950), pp. 85–96 (p. 90). Lukács describes how Zola '[gave] himself up to Utopian reveries, to a watered-down revival of Utopian socialism' late in life. *The Historical Novel*, trans. Hannah and Stanley Mitchell (London: Merlin Press, 1962), p. 265.

54 Jameson, *Marxism and Form*, p. 202.

55 Henry James, 'Émile Zola', in *Selected Literary Criticism*, ed. Morris Shapira (London: Heinemann, 1963), pp. 240–64 (p. 262).

56 Mirbeau, '*Fécondité*', *L'Aurore*, 29 November 1899, p. 1 (emphasis added).

57 Marcel Ballot, '*Vérité* par Émile Zola', *Le Figaro*, 26 February 1903, pp. 4–5 (p. 4).

58 Rachilde, 'Les Romans. Émile Zola, *Fécondité*', *Mercure de France*, 119 (November 1899), 485–93 (p. 487).

59 As Reffait notes, this 'dualist' line of argumentation was 'prone to lapse into an anti-Dreyfusard monism'. 'Les réticences des dreyfusards', p. 136. Rachilde opens her review with a characteristically anti-Semitic address: 'Pay up, gentlemen Israelites; this is written especially for you and your patriarchal families, families of patriarchs, societies within society, states within the State' (485).

60 *Discours prononcés aux obsèques d'Émile Zola le 5 octobre 1902*, p. 18.

Bibliography

The place of publication is Paris for works in French, and London for works in English, unless otherwise stated.

Primary Material: Literature

Balzac, Honoré de, *Une ténébreuse affaire*, ed. René Guise (Gallimard, 1973).
Flaubert, Gustave, *L'Éducation sentimentale* (Flammarion, 2001).
Gissing, George, *Demos: A Story of English Socialism*, ed. Pierre Coustillas (Brighton: The Harvester Press, 1972).
Guyot, Yves, *La Famille Pichot: scènes de l'enfer social* (Jules Rouff, 1882).
Hugo, Victor, *Œuvres poétiques de Victor Hugo*, ed. Pierre Ablouy, 3 vols (Gallimard, 1974).
Huysmans, Joris-Karl, *À rebours*, ed. Marc Fumaroli (Gallimard, 1977).
    Là-bas, ed. Pierre Cogny (Garnier-Flammarion, 1978).
    Les Foules de Lourdes (Grenoble: Jérôme Million, 2013).
    Nouvelles, ed. Daniel Grojnowski (GF Flammarion, 2007).
Maupassant, Guy de, *Pierre et Jean*, ed. Marie-Claire Ropars-Wuilleumier (Livre de Poche, 1984).
Sand, George, *Le Compagnon du Tour de France*, ed. René Bourgeois (Grenoble: Presses Universitaires de Grenoble, 1988).
    Œuvres autobiographiques, ed. Georges Lubin, 2 vols (Gallimard, 1971).
Zola, Émile, *La Débâcle. Œuvres complètes*, ed. David Baguley (Classiques Garnier, 2012).
    Doctor Pascal, trans. Julie Rose (Oxford: Oxford University Press, 2020).
    The Dream, trans. Paul Gibbard (Oxford: Oxford University Press, 2018).
    Germinal, trans. Peter Collier (Oxford: Oxford University Press, 1993).
    Germinal. Œuvres complètes, ed. Colette Becker (Classiques Garnier, 2017).
    Lourdes. Œuvres complètes, ed. Bertrand Marquer (Classiques Garnier, 2015).
    Les Mystères de Marseille. Œuvres complètes, ed. Daniel Compère (Classiques Garnier, 2018).
    Œuvres complètes, ed. Henri Mitterand et al., 21 vols (Nouveau Monde, 2002–09).

Les Rougon-Macquart: histoire naturelle et sociale d'une famille sous le Second Empire, ed. Henri Mitterand, 5 vols (Gallimard, Bibliothèque de la Pléiade, 1960–67).

Travail. Œuvres complètes, ed. Fabian Scharf (Classiques Garnier, 2021).

Selected Primary Material: Other Pre-1920 Sources

Alexis, Paul, *Émile Zola: notes d'un ami* (G. Charpentier, 1882).

    Naturalisme pas mort: lettres inédites de Paul Alexis à Émile Zola, 1871–1900, ed. B. H. Bakker (Toronto: University of Toronto Press, 1971).

Barbou, Alfred, *Victor Hugo: sa vie, ses œuvres* (Librairie universelle d'Alfred Duquesne, 1880).

Barrès, Maurice, *Mes Cahiers, 1896–1923* (Plon, 1994).

    Scènes et doctrines du nationalisme (Félix Juven, 1902).

Bloy, Léon, *Exégèse des lieux communs* (Mercure de France, 1902).

    Les Funérailles du naturalisme, ed. Pierre Glaudes (Grenoble: Publications de l'Université Stendhal-Grenoble, 1990).

    Je m'accuse (Édition de 'La Maison de l'Art', 1900).

    Méditations d'un solitaire en 1916, 6th edition (Mercure de France, 1926).

Boissarie, Gustave, *Conférence du Luxembourg* (Maison de la Bonne Presse, 1895).

    Les Grandes Guérisons de Lourdes (Douniol, 1900).

    Lourdes: depuis 1858 jusqu'à nos jours (Sanard et Derangeon, 1894).

Brunetière, Ferdinand, 'Après une visite au Vatican', *Revue des Deux Mondes*, 127 (January 1895), 97–118.

    'La Banqueroute du naturalisme', *Revue des Deux Mondes*, 83 (September 1887), 213–24.

    'Une définition de mots', *Revue des Deux Mondes*, 92 (March 1889), 215–26.

    'L'Idéalisme dans le roman', *Revue des Deux Mondes*, 69 (May 1885), 215–25.

    'Octave Feuillet', *Revue des Deux Mondes*, 103 (February 1891), 664–94.

    'Le *Paris* de E. Zola', *Revue des Deux Mondes*, 146 (April 1898), 922–34.

    'Le Pessimisme dans le roman', *Revue des Deux Mondes*, 70 (July 1885), 214–26.

    La Renaissance de l'idéalisme (Firmin-Didot et Cie, 1896).

    'Le Roman de l'avenir', *Revue des Deux Mondes*, 105 (June 1891), 685–98.

    'Le Roman expérimental', *Revue des Deux Mondes*, 37 (1880), 935–47.

    Le Roman naturaliste (Calmann Lévy, 1883).

Buisson, Ferdinand, *La Foi laïque: extraits de discours et d'écrits (1878–1911)* (Hachette, 1912).

Caro, Elme-Marie, *George Sand* (Hachette, 1887).

Colin, Louis, *Ce que pense Henri Lasserre du roman d'Émile Zola: conversations et interviews* (Librairie Bloud et Barral, 1894).

Crestey, L'Abbé Joseph, *Le Lourdes de Zola: critique d'un roman historique* (Bonne Presse, 1894).

Dayot, Armand, *Salon de 1884* (Baschet, 1884).

Discours prononcés aux obsèques d'Émile Zola le 5 octobre 1902 (Fasquelle, 1902).

Ferry, Jules, *Discours et opinions de Jules Ferry publiés avec commentaires et notes par Paul Robiquet*, 7 vols (Armand Colin et Cie, 1893–98).

Flaubert, Gustave, and Ivan Tourguéniev, *Correspondance*, ed. Alexandre Zviguilsky (Flammarion, 1989).

Correspondance, ed. Jean Bruneau and Yvan Leclerc, 5 vols (Gallimard, Bibliothèque de la Pléiade, 1973–2007).

Fly [pseud. Charles-Armand Dieudé-Defly]. *Enquête sur le roman romanesque ('Le Gaulois', 1891)*. Introduced by Jean-Marie Seillan (Amiens: Centre d'Études du Roman et du Romanesque de l'Université de Picardie, 2005).

Fouillée, Alfred, 'La Métaphysique et la poésie de l'idéal', *Revue des Deux Mondes*, 86 (1888), 110–40.

'Le Mouvement idéaliste en France', *Revue des Deux Mondes*, 134 (1896), 276–304.

France, Anatole, 'Octave Feuillet', in *La Vie littéraire* (Calmann-Lévy, 1891), troisième série, pp. 368–78.

Goncourt, Edmond, and Jules de, *Journal: mémoires de la vie littéraire*, ed. Robert Ricatte, 3 vols (Robert Laffont, 1989).

Gourmont, Remy de, *L'Idéalisme* (Mercure de France, 1893).

'Les racines de l'idéalisme', *Mercure de France*, October 1904, 5–24.

Grand Dictionnaire universel du XIXe siècle, 17 vols (Administration du Grand Dictionnaire universel, 1866–77).

Guesde, Jules, *La République et les Grèves* (Bibliothèque socialiste, 1878).

Guyau, Jean-Marie, *L'Art au point de vue sociologique* (Félix Alcan, 1889).

Huret, Jules, *Enquête sur l'évolution littéraire*. Preface by Daniel Grojnowski (José Corti, 1999).

Huysmans, J. K., *Lettres inédites à Arij Prins, 1885–1907*, ed. Louis Gillet (Geneva: Droz, 1977).

Imbert-Gourbeyre, Antoine, *La Stigmatisation, l'extase divine et les miracles de Lourdes* (J. Vic et Amat, 1894).

James, Henry, *Selected Literary Criticism*, ed. Morris Shapira (Heinemann, 1963).

Lasserre, Henri, *Les Lettres de Henri Lasserre à l'occasion du roman de M. Zola: avec pièces justificatives, démentis et défi* (E. Dentu, 1894).

Laveleye, Émile de, *Le Socialisme contemporain* (Brussels: Librairie Européenne C. Muquardt, 1881).

Lemaître, Jules, *Les Contemporains: études et portraits littéraires*, 7 series (H. Lecène et H. Oudin, 1886–99).

Leroy-Beaulieu, Paul, *La Question ouvrière au XIXe siècle*, 2nd edition (G. Charpentier, 1881 [1872]).

Livre d'hommage des lettres françaises à Émile Zola (Société libre d'Édition des Gens de Lettres, 1898).

Malon, Benoît, *Le Nouveau Parti: II. Le Parti ouvrier et sa politique*, 2nd edition (Derveaux, 1882).

Marx, Karl, *Capital: an abridged edition*, ed. David McLellan (Oxford: Oxford University Press, 1999).

Marx, Karl and Friedrich Engels, *Karl Marx, Friedrich Engels on Literature and Art: A Selection of Writings*, ed. Lee Baxandall and Stefan Morawski (New York: International General, 1973).

Maupassant, Guy de, *M. Émile Zola* (Quantin, 1883).

La Naissance du Parti ouvrier français: correspondance inédite de Paul Laforgue et al., ed. Emile Bottigelli and Claude Willard (Messidor/Éditions sociales, 1981).

Pellissier, Georges, *Le Mouvement littéraire au XIXe siècle*, 6th edition (Librairie Hachette et Cie, 1900).

Portraits d'Hier. Émile Zola (Fabre, [15 March] 1909).

Le Procès Dreyfus devant le conseil de guerre de Rennes (7 août – 9 septembre 1899) (P. V. Stock, 1900).

Reinach, Joseph, *Histoire de l'Affaire Dreyfus*, 7 vols (Éditions de la Revue Blanche [vol. 1]; E. Fasquelle [vols 2–7], 1901–11).

Renan, Ernest, *Discours de réception à l'Académie française prononcé le 3 avril 1879*, Bibliothèque nationale, Paris, NAF 16384.

Ricard, Monseigneur Antoine, *La Vraie Bernadette de Lourdes: lettres à M. Zola* (E. Dentu, 1894).

Rod, Édouard, *Nouvelles Études sur le XIXe siècle* (Lausanne: F. Payot, 1899).

Sautour, Auguste, *Idéal et naturalisme, à propos du roman 'L'Amour de Jacques' de Charles Fuster* (Fischbacher, 1891).

Symons, Arthur, *The Symbolist Movement in Literature*, ed. Matthew Creasy (Manchester: Carcanet Press, 2014).

Taine, Hippolyte, *De l'Idéal dans l'art: leçons professées à l'École des Beaux-Arts* (Germer Baillière, 1867).

Les Philosophes français du XIXe siècle, 2nd edition (Librairie de L. Hachette et Cie, 1860).

Philosophie de l'art (Fayard, 1985).

Tarde, Gabriel, 'Foules et sectes au point de vue criminel', *Revue des Deux Mondes*, 15 November 1893, 349–87.

Zévaès, Alexandre, *Le Socialisme en France depuis 1871* (Bibliothèque-Charpentier, 1908).

Zola, Émile, *Correspondance*, ed. Bard H. Bakker, 11 vols (Montreal; Paris: Presses de l'Université de Montréal and CNRS, 1978–2010).

The Dreyfus Affair: 'J'accuse' and Other Writings, ed. Alain Pagès, trans. Eleanor Levieux (New Haven, CT: Yale University Press, 1996).

Face aux romantiques, preface by Henri Mitterand (Brussels: Éditions complexes, 1989).

Lettres de Paris, choix d'articles traduits du russe et présentés par Phillip A. Duncan et Vera Erdely (Droz and Minard, 1963).

Œuvres complètes. Critique littéraire et artistique, vol. 1, *Écrits sur l'art*, ed. Robert Lethbridge (Classiques Garnier, 2021).

Zola au Panthéon, 1908–2008, preface by Alain Pagès (Éditions du patrimoine, 2008).

Zola: l'Affaire Dreyfus, ed. Jean-Denis Bredin (Imprimerie nationale, 1992).

Zola: mémoire de la critique, ed. Sylvie Thorel-Cailleteau (Presses de l'Université Paris-Sorbonne, 1998).

Secondary Material

Adorno, Theodor, *Aesthetic Theory*, ed. Gretel Adorno and Rolf Tiedemann, and trans. C. Lenhardt (Routledge, 1984).

Al-Matary, Sarah, *La Haine des clercs: l'anti-intellectualisme en France* (Seuil, 2019).

Al-Matary, Sarah and Stéphane Zékian, 'Antiromantismes', *Romantisme*, 182 (2018), 5–14.

Ansell, Christopher K., *Schism and Solidarity in Social Movements: The Politics of Labor in the French Third Republic* (Cambridge: Cambridge University Press, 2007).

Apter, Emily, *Continental Drift: From National Characters to Virtual Subjects* (Chicago, IL: University of Chicago Press, 1999).

Arendt, Hannah, *Lectures on Kant's Political Philosophy*, ed. Ronald Beiner (Chicago, IL: The University of Chicago Press, 1992).

Baguley, David, 'L'Anti-intellectualisme de Zola', *Les Cahiers naturalistes*, 42 (1971), 119–29.

'Balzac, Zola et la paternité du naturalisme', in *Balzac: une poétique du roman*, ed. Stéphane Vachon (Montreal and Saint-Denis: XYZ éditeur et Presses Universitaires de Vincennes, 1996), pp. 383–95.

'Du récit polémique au discours utopique: l'Évangile républicain de Zola', *Les Cahiers naturalistes*, 54 (1980), 106–21.

'The Function of Zola's Souvarine', *The Modern Language Review*, 66:4 (1971), 786–97.

'*Germinal*, une moisson de texte', *Revue d'histoire littéraire de la France*, 85:3 (1985), 389–400.

Naturalist Fiction: The Entropic Vision (Cambridge: Cambridge University Press, 1990).

Zola et les genres (Glasgow: University of Glasgow French and German Publications, 1993).

Bähler, Ursula, 'Sur les traces naturalistes de *La Vérité en marche*', *Les Cahiers naturalistes*, 82 (2008), 83–108.

Barjonet, Aurélie, *Zola d'Ouest en Est: le naturalisme en France et dans les deux Allemagnes* (Rennes: Presses Universitaires de Rennes, 2010).

Barthes, Roland, *S/Z*, trans. Richard Miller (Oxford: Basil Blackwell, 1990).

The Pleasure of the Text, trans. Richard Miller (New York: Farrar, Straus and Giroux, 1975).

Becker, Colette, '"Ah! quel beau rêve qui a remué tout un monde"... La "belle histoire" de Bernadette', *Les Cahiers naturalistes*, 73 (1999), 247–54.

'Le Rêve d'Angélique', *Les Cahiers naturalistes*, 76 (2002), 7–23.

Zola: le saut dans les étoiles (Presses de la Sorbonne Nouvelle, 2002).

Beillacou, Florence, 'Tuer l'idéal: l'anti-romantisme de Zola et les naturalistes' (unpublished doctoral thesis, Paris, Université Sorbonne Paris Cité, 2018).

Beizer, Janet, *Ventriloquized Bodies: Narratives of Hysteria in Nineteenth-Century France* (Ithaca, NY: Cornell University Press, 1994).

Bell, David F., 'Zola's Fin-de-Siècle Pessimism: Knowledge in Crisis', *L'Esprit créateur*, 32 (1992), 21–29.

Bell, Dorian, 'Beyond the Bourse: Zola, Empire, and the Jews', *Romanic Review*, 102 (2011), 485–501.

Globalizing Race: Antisemitism and Empire in French and European Culture (Evanston, IL: Northwestern University Press, 2018).

Bellemin-Noël, Jean, *Interlignes: essais de textanalyse* (Lille: Presses Universitaires de Lille, 1988).

Bertrand-Jennings, Chantal, *L'Éros et la femme chez Zola: de la chute au paradis retrouvé* (Éditions Klincksieck, 1977).

Bethléem, Abbé, *Romans à lire et romans à proscrire*, 2nd edition (Éditions de la Revue des Lecteurs, 1928).

Birchall, Ian H., 'Georg Lukács and the Novels of Émile Zola', *The Sociology of Literature: Applied Studies*, 26 (1978), 92–108.

Bloch-Dano, Evelyne, *Chez Zola à Médan* (Saint-Cyr-sur-Loire: Christian Pirot, 1999).

Bonnefis, Philippe, *L'Innommable: essai sur l'œuvre d'Émile Zola* (SEDES, 1984).

Bory, Jean-Louis, *Tout feu, tout flamme* (Julliard, 1960).

Bourdieu, Pierre, *Les Règles de l'art. Genèse et structure du champ littéraire* (Seuil, 1992).

Brady, Patrick, 'Lukács, Zola, and the Principle of Contradiction', *L'Esprit créateur*, 21: 3 (1980), 60–68.

Bray, Patrick M., *The Novel Map: Space and Subjectivity in Nineteenth-Century Fiction* (Evanston, IL: Northwestern University Press, 2013).

Bredin, Jean-Denis, *L'Affaire* (Juillard, 1983).

Brombert, Victor, *The Intellectual Hero: Studies in the French Novel, 1880–1955* (Faber and Faber, 1961).

Brooks, Peter, *Body Work: Objects of Desire in Modern Narrative* (Cambridge, MA: Harvard University Press, 1993).

Butler, Judith, 'Uprising', in *Uprisings*, ed. Georges Didi-Huberman (Gallimard, 2016), pp. 23–36.

Cabanès, Jean-Louis, 'L'enfance de Bernadette: effets de voix', *Les Cahiers naturalistes*, 72 (1998), 211–23.

'Rêver *La Légende dorée*', *Les Cahiers naturalistes*, 76 (2002), 25–47.

'Zola, lecteur d'Émile de Laveleye: imitation et invention', *La Fabrique des valeurs dans la littérature du XIXᵉ siècle* (Pessac: Presses Universitaires de Bordeaux, 2017), pp. 40–53.

Carassus, Émilien, *Les Grèves imaginaires* (Éditions du CNRS, 1982).

Cassagnard, Chanoine J.-M., *Carrel et Zola devant le miracle à Lourdes* (Lourdes: Éditions de L'Œuvre de la Grotte, 1964).

Cave, Terence, *Recognitions: A Study in Poetics* (Oxford: Clarendon Press, 1990).

Cerullo, John J., 'Religion and the Psychology of Dreyfusard Intellectualism', *Historical Reflections*, 24 (1998), 93–114.

Chaitin, Gilbert D., *The Enemy Within: Culture Wars and Political Identity in the Novels of the French Third Republic* (Columbus: Ohio State University Press, 2009).

Charle, Christophe, *Paris fin de siècle: culture et politique* (Seuil, 1998).

Charles, David, 'Zola à l'épreuve de la Commune', *COnTEXTES*: http://journals .openedition.org/contextes/9924.

Cintra Torres, Eduardo, 'La foule religieuse de Lourdes chez Zola et Huysmans', *Mil neuf cent. Revue d'histoire intellectuelle*, 28 (2010), 35–58.

Clark, Christopher and Wolfram Kaiser (eds), *Culture Wars: Secular-Catholic Conflict in Nineteenth-Century Europe* (Cambridge: Cambridge University Press, 2003).

Cohen, Margaret, *The Sentimental Education of the Novel* (Princeton, NJ: Princeton University Press, 1999).

Colin, René-Pierre, *Zola, renégats et alliés: la Répubique naturaliste* (Lyon: Presses Universitaires de Lyon, 1988).

Comfort, Kathleen Ann, 'Divine Images of Hysteria in Émile Zola's *Lourdes*', *Nineteenth-Century French Studies*, 30 (2002), 330–46.

Compagnon, Antoine, *Connaissez-vous Brunetière? Enquête sur un antidreyfusard et ses amis* (Seuil, 1997).

'Les Ennemis de Zola', in *Zola au Panthéon: l'épilogue de l'affaire Dreyfus*, ed. Alain Pagès (Presses Sorbonne Nouvelle, 2010), pp. 17–31.

Cooke, Roderick, *The Dreyfus Affair's Literary Politics* (Liverpool: Liverpool University Press, 2023).

Counter, Andrew J., 'One of Them: Homosexuality and Anarchism in Wilde and Zola', *Comparative Literature*, 63: 4 (2011), 345–65.

'A Sentimental Affair: *Vérité*', *Romanic Review*, 102 (2011), 391–409.

'Le Symptôme de Zola: fragment d'autoanalyse critique', *Les Cahiers naturalistes*, 91 (2017), 61–71.

'Wilde, Zola, Dreyfus, Christ: Fin de Siècle Passions', *Representations*, 149 (2020), 103–33.

'Zola's Fin-de-Siècle Reproductive Politics', *French Studies*, 68 (2014), 193–208.

'Zola's Repetitions: On Repetition in Zola', *The Modern Language Review*, 116:1 (2021), 42–64.

Cubitt, Geoffrey, *The Jesuit Myth: Conspiracy Theory and Politics in Nineteenth-Century France* (Oxford: Clarendon Press, 1993).

Delamotte, Isabelle, 'La place de Charcot dans la documentation médicale d'Émile Zola', *Les Cahiers naturalistes*, 73 (1999), 287–99.

Derfler, Leslie, *Paul Lafargue and the Founding of French Marxism, 1842–1882* (Boston, MA: Harvard University Press, 1991).

Disegni, Silvia, '*Lourdes* à l'Index: le rapport de la censure pontificale', *Les Cahiers naturalistes*, 83 (2009), 263–87.

Dousteyssier-Khoze, Catherine, *Zola et la littérature naturaliste en parodies* (Eurédit, 2004).

Drouin, Michel, *Zola au Panthéon: le quatrième affaire Dreyfus* (Perrin, 2008).

Ducange, Jean-Numa, *Jules Guesde: l'anti-Jaurès?* (Dunod, 2017).

Duchet, Claude, 'Le Trou des bouches noires: parole, société, révolution dans *Germinal*', *Littérature*, 24 (1976), 11–39.

Duclert, Vincent, 'La République et l'héroïsme démocratique au tournant du siècle', in *Zola au Panthéon: l'épilogue de l'affaire Dreyfus*, ed. Alain Pagès (Presses Sorbonne Nouvelle, 2010), pp. 73–96.

Dufief, Pierre-Jean, 'Mirbeau face à Zola', in *Champ littéraire fin de siècle autour de Zola*, ed. Béatrice Laville (Pessac: Presses Universitaires de Bordeaux, 2004), pp. 153–63.

Edel, Leon, *Henry James: A Life* (Flamingo, 1996).

El Kettani, Soundouss, '*Les Foules de Lourdes* ou le dernier dialogue', *Romantisme*, 151 (2011), 113–28.

Emery, Elizabeth, '"A l'ombre d'une vieille cathédrale romane": The Medievalism of Gautier and Zola', *The French Review* 73:2 (1999), 290–310.

'Bricobracomania: Zola's Romantic Instincts', *Excavatio*, 12 (1999), 107–15.

'*The Golden Legend* in the Fin de Siècle: Zola's *Le Rêve* and its Reception', in *Medieval Saints in Late Nineteenth-Century French Culture*, ed. Elizabeth Emery and Laurie Postlewate (Jefferson, NC: McFarland Press, 2004), 83–116.

Photojournalism and the Origins of the French Writer House Museum (1881–1914): Privacy, Publicity, and Personality (Aldershot: Ashgate, 2012).

Romancing the Cathedral: Gothic Architecture in Fin-de-Siècle French Culture (Albany: State University of New York Press, 2001).

Febles, Eduardo A., *Explosive Narratives: Terrorism and Anarchy in the Works of Émile Zola* (Amsterdam: Rodopi, 2010).

Felski, Rita, *The Gender of Modernity* (Harvard, MA: Harvard University Press, 1995).

The Limits of Critique (Chicago, IL: The University of Chicago Press, 2015).

Fisher, Mark, *Capitalist Realism: Is There No Alternative?* (Ropley: Zero Books, 2009).

Forth, Christopher E., *The Dreyfus Affair and the Crisis of French Manhood* (Baltimore, MD: The Johns Hopkins University Press, 2004).

The Standard Edition of the Complete Psychological Works of Sigmund Freud, trans. and ed. J. Strachey, 24 vols (Vintage, 2001).

Frølich, Juliette, 'L'homme kitsch ou le jeu des masques dans *L'Éducation sentimentale* de Flaubert', *Romantisme*, 79 (1993), 39–52.

Geertz, Clifford, 'Common Sense as a Cultural System', *The Antioch Review*, 33:1 (1975), 5–26.

Genette, Gérard, '*Vraisemblance* and Motivation', trans. David Gorman, *Narrative*, 9:3 (2001 [1968]), 239–58.

Ginzburg, Carlo, 'Morelli, Freud, and Sherlock Holmes: Clues and Scientific Method', trans. Anna Davin, *History Workshop*, 9 (1980), 5–36.

Girard, René, *Mensonge romantique et vérité romanesque* (Grasset, 1961).

Glaumaud-Carbonnier, Marion, 'Zola à l'étalage: l'écrivain au carrefour, effets de "kioscopie"', *Les Cahiers naturalistes*, 95 (2021), 221–36.

Goldstein, Jan, *Console and Classify: The French Psychiatric Profession in the Nineteenth Century* (Cambridge: Cambridge University Press, 1987).

Gould, Evlyn, *Dreyfus and the Literature of the Third Republic: Secularism and Tolerance in Zola, Barrès, Lazare and Proust* (Jefferson, NC and London: McFarland & Company, 2012).

Grant, Elliott M., 'The Newspapers of *Germinal*: Their Identity and Significance', *The Modern Language Review*, 55 (1960), 87–89.

Guermès, Sophie, *La Fable documentaire: Zola historien* (Champion, 2017).

La Religion de Zola: naturalisme et déchristianisation (Honoré Champion, 2006).

Guise Castelnuovo, Antoinette, 'Photographier le miracle: Lourdes au tournant du XXe siècle', *Archives des sciences sociales des religions*, 162 (2013), 161–82.

Hamon, Pascaline, 'Les Antinaturalismes fin-de-siècle de Barbey à Barrès (1877–1908): exploration d'un labyrinthe critique, sociologique, philosophique, esthétique et moral' (unpublished dotoral thesis, Paris, Université Sorbonne Paris Cité, 2018).

'L'Apparition dans le renouveau spirituel littéraire fin de siècle. De Lourdes à la Salette', in *La Vierge Marie dans la littérature française: entre foi et littérature*, ed. Jean-Louis Benoit (Lyon: Jacques André, 2014), pp. 255–64.

'Constructions de la notion d'idéalisme dans la critique de la fin du XIXème siècle chez F. Brunetière et R. de Gourmont' (2013), available online: www.crp19.org/filebank/568d3d82-43e7-1031-8016-8b7ac158774a/SJCPascalineHamon.pdf.

'L'idéal dans la critique littéraire fin de siècle: un étendard antinaturaliste?' (2018), available online: https://serd.hypotheses.org/files/2018/08/IdealismePascalineHamon.pdf.

Hamon, Philippe, 'Le juge Denizet dans *La Bête humaine*', in *Mimesis et Semiosis*, ed. Philippe Hamon and Jean-Pierre Leduc-Adine (Nathan, 1992), pp. 137–44.

Hardt, Michael and Antonio Negri, *Assembly* (New York: Oxford University Press, 2017).

Harris, Ruth, *Dreyfus: Politics, Emotion, and the Scandal of the Century* (New York: Picador, 2011).

Lourdes: Body and Spirit in the Secular Age (Viking, 1999).

Harrow, Susan, *Zola, The Body Modern: Pressures and Prospects of Representation* (Oxford: Legenda, 2010).

Hirsch, Marianne, *The Mother/Daughter Plot: Narrative, Psychoanalysis, Feminism* (Bloomington: Indiana University Press, 1989).

Howe, Irving, 'The Genius of *Germinal*', *Encounter*, 34 (1970), 53–61.

Jacquet, Chantal, *Les Transclasses, ou la non-reproduction* (Presses Universitaires de France, 2014).

Jameson, Fredric, *The Antinomies of Realism* (Verso, 2015).

'Antinomies of the Realism-Modernism Debate', *Modern Language Quarterly*, 73:3 (2012), 475–85.

Marxism and Form: Twentieth-Century Dialectical Theories of Literature (Princeton, NJ: Princeton University Press, 1971).

The Political Unconscious: Narrative as a Socially Symbolic Act (Routledge, 1981).

Jousse, Emmanuel, *Les Hommes révoltés: les origines intellectuelles du réformisme en France (1871–1917)* (Arthème Fayard, 2017).

Joyce, Simon, *Modernism and Naturalism in British and Irish Fiction, 1880–1930* (Cambridge: Cambridge University Press, 2015).

Kaufman, Suzanne K., *Consuming Visions: Mass Culture and the Lourdes Shrine* (Ithaca, NY and London: Cornell University Press, 2005).

Lapière, Marie, *Le Langage des sources dans 'Les Trois Villes' d'Émile Zola: la dialectique de la foi et de la raison* (Honoré Champion, 2018).

Lapp, John C., *Zola Before the 'Rougon-Macquart'* (Toronto: Toronto University Press, 1964).

Laville, Béatrice, 'L'écriture de l'utopie', in *Zola à l'œuvre. Hommage à Auguste Dezalay*, ed. Gisèle Séginger (Strasbourg: Presses Universitaires de Strasbourg, 2003), pp. 233–44.

Une poétique des fictions autoritaires: les voies de Zola, Barrès, Bourget (Bordeaux: Presses Universitaires de Bordeaux, 2020).

Lethbridge, Robert, 'Étienne Lantier "romancier": genèse et mise en abime', *Les Cahiers naturalistes*, 59 (1985), 43–54.

Lukács, Georg, *The Historical Novel*, trans. Hannah and Stanley Mitchell (Merlin Press, 1962).

Studies in European Realism: A Sociological Survey of the Writings of Balzac, Stendhal, Zola, Tolstoy, Gorki, and others, trans. Edith Bone (Hillway Publishing, 1950).

Writer and Critic, and Other Essays, ed. and trans. Arthur Kahn (Merlin Press, 1970).

Lumbroso, Olivier, *Zola Autodidacte: genèse des œuvres et apprentissages de l'écrivain en régime naturaliste* (Geneva: Droz, 2013).

Luxemburg, Rosa, *The Mass Strike, the Political Party and the Trade Union*, trans. Patrick Lavin, reprinted in *Reform or Revolution and Other Writings*, ed. Paul Buhle (Mineola, NY: Dover Publications, 2006).

Marel, Henri, 'Étienne Lantier et les chefs syndicalistes', *Les Cahiers naturalistes*, 50 (1976), 26–39.

Marquer, Betrand, *Les Romans de la Salpêtrière. Réception d'une scénographie clinique: Jean-Martin Charcot dans l'imaginaire fin-de-siècle* (Geneva: Droz, 2008).

Matthews, J. H., *Les Deux Zola: science et personnalité dans l'expression* (Geneva: Librairie E. Droz, 1957).

Maxwell, Lida, *Public Trials: Burke, Zola, Arendt, and the Politics of Lost Causes* (Oxford: Oxford University Press, 2014).

Mayer-Robin, Carmen K., 'The "African Pages" of Zola's *Fécondité*: Testimony to Colonial Politics and Attitudes about Race during the French Third Republic', *Romance Notes*, 47 (2006), 5–14.

McCormick, Robert H., 'Zola, Jules Guesde et la question sociale', in *Zola sans frontières*, ed. Auguste Dezalay (Strasbourg: Presses Universitaires de Strasbourg, 1996), pp. 85–92.

'Zola et les "Notes Guesde"', *Les Cahiers naturalistes*, 69 (1995), 181–95.

McNeil Arteau, Guillaume, 'Zola politique: parlementarisme, représentation, médiation', *Romantisme*, 171 (2016), 129–44.

'Enquête et documentation dans *Lourdes* de Zola', *Poétique*, 191 (2022), 59–74.

Mehlman, Jeffrey, 'The Dreyfus Affair', in *A New History of French Literature*, ed. Denis Hollier (Cambridge, MA: Harvard University Press, 1994), pp. 824–30.

'Zola's Novel of the Dreyfus Affair: Between Mystique and Politique', in *Jews, Catholics, and the Burden of History: Studies in Contemporary Jewry*, vol. 21, ed. Eli Lederhendler (New York: Oxford University Press, 2005), pp. 234–51.

Ménard, Sophie 'L'Enfantine dans *Lourdes* de Zola', in *Idiots. Figures et personnages liminaires dans la littérature et les arts*, ed. Véronique Cnockaert, Bertrand Gervais and Marie Scarpa (Nancy: PUN/Éditions Université de Lorraine, 2012), pp. 57–76.

Miller, Nancy K., *Subject to Change: Reading Feminist Writing* (New York: Columbia University Press, 1988).

Mitterand, Henri, *Le Discours du roman* (Presses Universitaires de France, 1980).

'L'Évangile social de *Travail*: un anti-*Germinal*', *Mosaic*, 3 (1972), 179–87.

'Le Quatrième Zola', *Œuvres et critiques*, 16 (1991), 85–98.

Le Regard et le signe: poétique du roman réaliste et naturaliste (Presses Universitaires de France, 1987).

'La vérité et l'utopie: *Les Quatre Évangiles*', in *Le Roman à l'œuvre: genèse et valeurs* (Presses Universitaires de France, 1998), pp. 214–31.

'"La vision rouge de la Révolution. . ." De Germinal à Thermidor', *Romantisme*, 82 (1993), 3–16.

Zola, 3 vols (Fayard, 1999–2002).

'Zola à Anzin: les mineurs de *Germinal*', *Travailler*, 7 (2002), 37–51.

Zola et le naturalisme, 4th edition (Presses Universitaires de France, 2002).

Zola: la mort du père (Imago, 2021).

Zola, tel qu'en lui-même (Presses Universitaires de France, 2009).

Moi, Toril, 'Idealism', *The Oxford Handbook of Philosophy and Literature*, ed. Richard Eldridge (Oxford: Oxford University Press, 2009), pp. 271–97.

Mourad, François-Marie, *Zola critique littéraire* (Honoré Champion, 2003).

Murat, Laure, *The Man Who Thought He Was Napoleon: Toward a Political History of Madness*, trans. Deke Dusinberre (Chicago, IL and London: The University of Chicago Press, 2014).

Nelson, Brian, *Zola and the Bourgeoisie: A Study of Themes and Techniques in 'Les Rougon-Macquart'* (The Macmillan Press, 1983).

'Zola and the Ideology of Messianism', *Orbis Litterarum*, 37 (1982), 70–82.

'Zola, Lukács and the Aesthetics of Realism', *Studi Francesi*, 71 (1980), 251–55.

Nicholls, Julia, *Revolutionary Thought after the Paris Commune, 1871–1885* (Cambridge: Cambridge University Press, 2019).

Noiray, Jacques, 'Huysmans critique de Zola et du naturalisme (1884–1907)', in *Champ littéraire fin de siècle autour de Zola*, ed. Béatrice Laville (Pessac: Presses Universitaires de Bordeaux, 2004), 121–39.

'J'en suis et j'en enrage': Zola romantique?' *Revue d'histoire littéraire de la France*, 116 (2016), 137–50.

Le Simple et l'Intense: vingt études sur Émile Zola (Classiques Garnier, 2015).

Ozouf, Mona, *L'École, l'Église et la République (1871–1914)* (Éditions Cana/Jean Offredo, 1982).

Pagès, Alain, 'L'Affaire Dreyfus comme roman-feuilleton', in *Il Terzo Zola: Émile Zola dopo i 'Rougon Macquart'* (Naples: Istituto Universitario Orientale, 1990), pp. 447–55.

La Bataille littéraire: essai sur la réception du naturalisme à l'époque de 'Germinal' (Librairie Séguier, 1989).

Émile Zola: de 'J'accuse' au Panthéon (Saint-Paul: Éditions Lucien Souny, 2008).

Émile Zola, un intellectuel dans l'affaire Dreyfus. Histoire de 'J'accuse' (Librairie Séguier, 1991).

Perrot, Michelle, *Les Ouvriers en grève, France 1871–1890*, 2 vols (Mouton & Co and École Pratique des Hautes Études, 1974).

Pierre-Gnassounou, Chantal, 'Fictions, imaginaires, imaginations dans "Les Rougon-Macquart" d'Émile Zola' (PhD thesis, Université de la Sorbonne Nouvelle, 1996).

Zola: les fortunes de la fiction (Nathan, 1999).

Piton-Foucault, Émilie, *Zola ou la fenêtre condamnée: la crise de la représentation dans 'Les Rougon Macquart'* (Rennes: Presses Universitaires de Rennes, 2015).

Powers, Scott M., *Confronting Evil: The Psychology of Secularization in Modern French Literature* (West Lafayette, IN: Purdue University Press, 2016).

Prendergast, Christopher, 'Evolution and Literary History: A Response to Franco Moretti', *New Left Review*, 34 (July–August 2005), 40–62.

The Order of Mimesis: Balzac, Stendhal, Nerval, Flaubert (Cambridge: Cambridge University, 1986).

Priest, Robert D., *The Gospel According to Renan: Reading, Writing, and Religion in Nineteenth-Century France* (Oxford: Oxford University Press, 2015).

Pryzbos, Julia, 'Zola's Utopias', in *The Cambridge Companion to Zola*, ed. Brian Nelson (Cambridge: Cambridge University Press, 2007), pp. 169–87.

Raimond, Michel, *La Crise du roman: des lendemains du Naturalisme aux années vingt* (José Corti, 1966).

Rancière, Jacques, *The Politics of Aesthetics: The Distribution of the Sensible*, ed. and trans. Gabriel Rockhill (Bloomsbury, 2004).

'The Politics of Literature', *SubStance*, 33:1 (2004), 10–24.

Reffait, Christophe, 'Libéralisme et naturalisme: remarques sur la pensée économique de Zola à partir de *Germinal*', *Romanic Review*, 102:3–4 (2011), 427–48.

'Les réticences des dreyfusards envers l'œuvre de Zola', in *Zola au Panthéon: l'épilogue de l'affaire Dreyfus*, ed. Alain Pagès (Presses Sorbonne Nouvelle, 2010), pp. 123–37.

Reid, Martine, 'Post-scriptum: Naomi Schor trente ans après', in *George Sand et l'idéal: une recherche en écriture*, ed. Damien Zanone (Honoré Champion, 2017), pp. 449–57.

Signer Sand: l'œuvre et le nom (Belin, 2003).

Reverzy, Éléonore, 'L'écriture du Moyen-Âge dans *Le Rêve* de Zola', *Cahiers de recherches médiévales et humanistes* [online] 11: 141–50 http://crm.revues .org/1803.

'Fonctions du révolutionnaire. Le personnage de Souvarine dans *Germinal* de Zola', in *Figures de l'émigré russe en France au XIXe et XXe siècle: fiction et réalité*, ed. Charlotte Krauss and Tatiana Victoroff (Leiden: Brill, 2012), pp. 163–76.

'Hugo dans Zola: le procès', in *Hugo ou les frontières effacées*, ed. Y. Jumelais and D. Peyrache-Leborgne (Nantes: Pleins Feux, 2002), pp. 62–77.

'Sand et Zola: littérature et valeurs', in *George Sand: écritures et représentations*, ed. Eric Bordas (Eurédit, 2004), pp. 103–19.

Ricoeur, Paul, *De l'Interprétation: essai sur Freud* (Seuil, 1965).

Ripoll, Roger, 'L'avenir dans *Germinal*: destruction et renaissance', *Les Cahiers naturalistes*, 50 (1976), 115–33.

Réalité et mythe chez Zola, 2 vols (Lille: Atelier Reproduction des thèses, Université de Lille III, 1981).

'Zola et le modèle positiviste', *Romantisme*, 21–22 (1978), 125–35.

'Zola juge de Victor Hugo (1871–1877)', *Les Cahiers naturalistes*, 46 (1973), 182–204.

Robert, Marthe, *Origins of the Novel*, trans. Sacha Rabinovitch (Brighton: Harvester, 1980).

Rosenfeld, Sophia, *Common Sense: A Political History* (Cambridge, MA: Harvard University Press, 2011).

Democracy and Truth: A Short History (Philadelphia: University of Pennsylvania Press, 2019).

Sacquin, Michèle, 'Entre positivisme et laïcité: Zola et la "non-religion" de l'avenir, 1881–1902', in *Zola et les historiens*, ed. Michèle Sacquin (Bibliothèque nationale de France, 2004), pp. 65–75.

Saminadayar-Perrin, Corinne, 'D'impossibles nouveaux mondes: Zola, *L'Argent/ Fécondité*', *Les Cahiers naturalistes*, 88 (2014), 27–44.

Samuels, Maurice, *The Right to Difference: French Universalism and the Jews* (Chicago, IL: The University of Chicago Press, 2016).

Sand, Shlomo, *The End of the French Intellectual: From Zola to Houellebecq*, trans. David Fernbach (Verso, 2018).

Scarpa, Marie, *L'Éternelle jeune fille. Une ethnocritique du 'Rêve' de Zola* (Honoré Champion, 2009).

Scharf, Fabian, *Émile Zola: de l'utopisme à l'utopie* (Champion, 2011).

Schiano-Bennis, Sandrine, *La Renaissance de l'idéalisme à la fin du XIXe siècle* (Champion, 1999).

Schor, Naomi, *Bad Objects: Essays Popular and Unpopular* (Durham, NC: Duke University Press, 1995).

'The Crisis of French Universalism', *Yale French Studies*, 100 (2001), 43–64.

George Sand and Idealism (New York: Columbia University Press, 1993).

'Zola and "la nouvelle critique"', *L'Esprit créateur*, 11 (1971), 11–20.

Zola's Crowds (Baltimore, MD: Johns Hopkins University Press, 1978).

Scott, Malcolm, *The Struggle for the Soul of the French Novel: French Catholic and Realist Novelists, 1850–1970* (Macmillan, 1989).

Seillan, Jean-Marie, *Le Roman idéaliste dans le second XIXᵉ siècle: littérature ou 'bouillon de veau'?* (Classiques Garnier, 2011).

'Naturalisme *vs* idéalisme: L'infortune posthume de George Sand', in *Ce qu''idéal' veut dire: définitions et usages de l'idéalisme au XIXᵉ siècle*, 2015 (3), available online: http://etudes-romantiques.ish-lyon.cnrs.fr/wa_files/IdealismeJeanMarieSeillan.pdf.

'Zola et le fait colonial: les raisons d'un rendez-vous manqué', *Les Cahiers naturalistes*, 88 (2014), 13–26.

'Stéréotypie et roman mondain: l'œuvre d'Octave Feuillet', *Loxias*, 17 (2007), available online: http://revel.unice.fr/loxias/index.html?id=1684.

Sennett, Richard, *The Fall of Public Man* (Penguin, 1976).

Serres, Michel, *Feux et signaux de brume: Zola* (Grasset, 1975).

Silverman, Deborah L., *Art Nouveau in Fin-de-siècle France: Politics, Psychology, and Style* (Berkeley: University of California Press, 1992).

Silverman, Willa Z., 'Gyp and Flammarion: A Marriage of Love or Convenience?', *The French Review*, 73 (2000), 910–20.

Spitzer, Alan B., *Historical Truth and Lies about the Past: Reflections on Dewey, Dreyfus, de Man, and Reagan* (Chapel Hill: University of North Carolina Press, 2000).

Stafford, David, *From Anarchism to Reformism: A Study of the Political Activities of Paul Brousse within the First International and the French Socialist Movement* (The London School of Economics and Political Science, 1971).

Stuart, Robert, *Marxism at Work. Ideology, Class and French Socialism during the Third Republic* (Cambridge: Cambridge University Press, 1992).

Sugden, Rebecca, 'Terre(ur): Reading the Landscape of Conspiracy in Balzac's *Une ténébreuse affaire*', *Nineteenth-Century French Studies*, 47:1–2 (2018–19), 48–65.

Suleiman, Susan Rubin, *Authoritarian Fictions: The Ideological novel as a Literary Genre* (Princeton, NJ: Princeton University Press, 1993).

'L'engagement sublime: Zola comme archétype d'un mythe culturel', *Les Cahiers naturalistes*, 67 (1993), 11–24.

'The Literary Significance of the Dreyfus Affair', in *The Dreyfus Affair: Art, Truth and Justice*, ed. Norman Kleeblatt (Berkeley: University of California Press, 1987), pp. 117–39.

Ternois, René, *Zola et son temps: Lourdes – Rome – Paris* (Société Les Belles Lettres, 1961).

Thérenty, Marie-Ève, 'Sacre de l'événement/sacrifice de l'écrivain. Les enquêtes littéraires dans le quotidien avant l'affaire Dreyfus', in *L'Interview d'écrivain: figures bibliques d'autorité*, ed. Sylvie Traire, Marie Blaise and Marie-Ève

Thérenty (Montpellier: Presses Universitaires de la Méditerranée, 2004), available online: http://books.openedition.org/pulm/320.

Thompson, Hannah, *Taboo: Corporeal Secrets in Nineteenth-Century France* (Oxford: Legenda, 2013).

Thomson, Richard, *Art of the Actual: Naturalism and Style in Early Third Republic France, 1880–1900* (New Haven, CT: Yale University Press, 2013).

Walker, Philip, *'Germinal' and Zola's Philosophical and Religious Thought* (Amsterdam: John Benjamins, 1984).

White, Claire, 'The Affair Before the Affair: Zola, Dreyfus and the Lourdes Scandal', *French History*, 35:3 (2021), 375–97.

'Easy Reading: Zola's Kitsch', in *Lucidity: Essays in Honour of Alison Finch*, ed. Ian James and Emma Wilson (Oxford: Legenda, 2016), pp. 72–85.

'Naturalism *in extremis*: Zola's *Le Rêve*', *Romance Studies*, 33:3–4 (2015), 272–84.

'Zola à rebours', *Les Cahiers naturalistes*, 91 (2017), 123–34.

'Zola et Gissing: le Demos des deux côtés de la Manche', *Les Cahiers naturalistes*, 94 (2020), 131–42.

White, Nicholas, '*Le Docteur Pascal*: entre l'inceste et "l'innéité"', *Les Cahiers naturalistes*, 68 (1994), 77–88.

The Family in Crisis in Late Nineteenth-Century French Fiction (Cambridge: Cambridge University Press, 1999).

'Introduction: Zola, Cultural Historian *avant la lettre?*', *Romanic Review*, 102.3–4 (2011), 295–303.

Wilson, Nelly, 'La mise en fiction de l'affaire Dreyfus: quelques réflexions sur *Vérité*', in *Il terzo Zola: Emile Zola dopo i 'Rougon-Macquart'*, ed. Gian Carlo Menichelli (Naples: Istituto Universitario Orientale, 1990), pp. 487–503.

Winock, Michel, *Le Siècle des intellectuels* (Seuil, 1997).

Ziegler, Robert E., 'Interpretation as Awakening from Zola's *Le Rêve*', *Nineteenth-Century French Studies*, 21:1–2 (1992–93), 130–41.

Satanism, Magic and Mysticism in Fin-de-siècle France (Basingstoke: Palgrave Macmillan, 2012).

Žižek, Slavoj, *The Sublime Object of Ideology* (Verso, 1989).

Zumstein, Jean, '"La mort est la grande douceur": Le Lazare d'Émile Zola', *Hermeneutische Blätter*, 1/2 (2009), 59–67.

Zupsich, Gina K., 'The Gospel According to Zola: National Identity and Naturalist Utopia in Fin-de-Siècle France' (unpublished doctoral thesis, University of California, Berkeley, 2010).

Index

Note: 'n' after a page number indicates the number of a note on that page. Page numbers in *italic* refer to figures.

For EU product safety concerns, contact us at Calle de José Abascal, 56–1°,
28003 Madrid, Spain or eugpsr@cambridge.org.